John McDowell:
Experience, Norm, and Nature

Blackwell
Publishing

John McDowell:
Experience, Norm, and Nature

Blackwell
Publishing

John McDowell: *Experience, Norm, and Nature*

Edited by **Jakob Lindgaard**

EUROPEAN JOURNAL OF PHILOSOPHY BOOK SERIES

Series editor: Robert Stern

Books in this series have originated from articles previously published in the *European Journal of Philosophy,* with the addition of further material. They reflect the focus and quality of the *EJP,* while broadening the range of work that it can publish.

For further information about the journal please visit:
http://www.blackwellpublishing.com/ejop

All the papers in this book, except for the Introduction and Responses, were first published in earlier issues of *European Journal of Philosophy* (chapters 2–9 in volume 14, issue 2 and chapter 10 in volume 15, issue 2).

BLACKWELL PUBLISHING
350 Main Street, Malden, MA 02148-5020, USA
9600 Garsington Road, Oxford OX4 2DQ, UK
550 Swanston Street, Carlton, Victoria 3053, Australia

First published 2008 by Blackwell Publishing Ltd.
ISBN 978 1 4051 5988 3 (paperback)

Library of Congress Cataloging-in-Publication Data

John McDowell: experience, norm, and nature/edited by Jakob Lindgaard.
    p. cm. -- (European journal of philosophy)
  Includes index.
  ISBN 978-1-4951-5877-3
  1. McDowell, John Henry. I. Lindgaard, Jakob.

  B1647.M144J64 2008
  192--dc22

                   2008000973

Typeset by Macmillan, India
Printed and bound in Singapore
by Fabulous Printers

The publisher's policy is to use permanent paper from mills that operate a sustainable forestry policy, and which has been manufactured from pulp processed using acid-free and elementary chlorine-free practices. Furthermore, the publisher ensures that the text paper and cover board used have met acceptable environmental accreditation standards.

For further information on Blackwell Publishing, visit our website:
http://www.blackwellpublishing.com

Contents

Contents

Contributors

Bill Brewer is Professor of Philosophy at the University of Warwick. He is the author of *Perception and Reason* (1999). Forthcoming book: *Perception and its Objects*.

Willem A deVries is Professor of Philosophy at the University of New Hampshire. His books include *Hegel's Theory of Mental Activity* (1988), (with Timm Triplett) *Knowledge, Mind, and the Given: Reading Wilfrid Sellars's "Empiricism and the Philosophy of Mind"* (2000), and *Wilfrid Sellars* (2005).

Hans Fink is Senior Associate Professor of Philosophy at the University of Aarhus. His books include *The Analysis of Goodness* (1973).

Christoph Halbig is Professor of Philosophy at the University of Jena. He is the Author of *Objektives Denken, Erkenntnistheorie und Philosophy of Mind in Hegels System* (2002), and *Praktische Gründe und die Realität der Moral* (2004).

Stephen Houlgate is Professor of Philosophy at the University of Warwick. His books include *An Introduction to Hegel. Freedom, Truth and History*, 2nd ed. (2005) and *The Opening of Hegel's Logic. From Being to Infinity* (2006).

Jakob Lindgaard has received his PhD in Philosophy from the University of Warwick.

Sabina Lovibond is Fellow and Tutor in Philosophy at Worcester College, Oxford University. Her books include *Realism and Imagination in Ethics* (1983) and *Ethical Formation* (2002).

John McDowell is University Professor of Philosophy at the University of Pittsburgh. His books include *Mind and World* (1994), and the collections *Mind, Value, and Reality*, and *Meaning, Knowledge, and Reality* (both 1998).

Charles Travis is Professor of Philosophy at King's College London. His books include: *The Uses of Sense: Wittgenstein's Philosophy of Language* (1989) and *Unshadowed Thought: Representation in Thought and Language* (2000).

Kenneth R. Westphal is Professor of Philosophy at the University of Kent. His books include *Hegel's Epistemological Realism* (1989), and *Kant's Transcendental Proof of Realism* (2004). Forthcoming book: *Hegel's Critique of Cognitive Judgment*.

Michael Williams is (Krieger-Eisenhower) Professor of Philosophy at Johns Hopkins University. His books include *Unnatural Doubts* (1992), *Groundless Belief*, 2nd ed., (1999), and *Problems of knowledge* (2001). Forthcoming book: *Curious Researches: Reflections on Skepticism Ancient and Modern*.

Introduction

Jakob Lindgaard

1. John McDowell is a rare philosopher. He has a remarkable ability to engage critically with historical figures such as Aristotle, Kant, Hegel, Wittgenstein, and Sellars whilst retaining analytical acuity in his contributions to debates in contemporary philosophy. And he has the courage and intellectual integrity to challenge assumptions that guide both contemporary debates and orthodox approaches to those historical figures. The papers and responses collected in this volume bear witness to this fact.

They are the result of a week-long conference held at the University of Warwick, England, and University of Aarhus, Denmark in May 2005. This setting made possible extended and recurrent discussions of central themes in McDowell's work. The result is philosophy come alive. Genuinely original ideas have been introduced and old renounced. This is also rare.

2. All of the papers and responses collected here address at least one of three major themes in McDowell:

    (i)   Perceptual experience
    (ii) Normativity or rationality
    (iii) Nature

One group of papers is directly concerned with the cogency of McDowell's readings of especially Kant, Hegel, and Sellars in relation to these themes. The other group addresses the themes directly.

3. Before turning to the papers, let us have a brief look at the overall framework of McDowell's work. I think there are four key traits to this framework. The first key trait is the idea that the phenomena with which McDowell is concerned—e.g. ethical, epistemological, semantic, and mental phenomena—can be made properly intelligible only within the framework for which Sellars has coined the phrase 'space of reasons' [SOR]. When we place something in the SOR, we are not giving an empirical description of the phenomenon. We are not subsuming it under the so-called 'realm of law' [ROL] or giving a causal explanation of it in strict nomological terms. Rather, we are making it intelligible in terms of its rational credentials, its justification, its warrant, etc. Save by reference to normative or rational relations, there is no understanding of these phenomena. So McDowell believes.

Understanding the relation between the SOR and the ROL is not always straightforward. What exactly are the *relations* and *relata* of this distinction? I think there are four available answers to this question in the literature. First, the distinction can represent a way to construe the *mind-body* or *mind-brain* relation. Our SOR normative conceptual capacities, for example, are construed to be *sui generis* in relation to our ROL sentient and dispositional abilities. Secondly, it can represent a distinction in the ways we can construe the relation between *mind* and *world*. Arguably, the ways we can be rationally or normatively constrained by the mind-independent world are very different from the ways the nerve-endings of our sensory apparatus can stand in nomological causal relations to the world. Thinking about the sun is different from being blinded by it. The third candidate version of this relation is the more general distinction between SOR-facts, -properties, or -relations and ROL-facts, -properties, or -relations. Normative SOR-facts about concepts, for instance, are of a different sort than ROL-facts such as marks on paper. The fourth version of the distinction is to acknowledge that there is one world, but two very different ways of talking about it, the SOR-way and the ROL-way. We do not talk about *different* things; rather we talk *differently* about (the same?) things. They are different ways of taking or treating something or someone, different types of 'scorekeeping', different orders of intelligibility or understanding, Dennett-style 'stances', Fregean 'modes of presentation', Brandomian 'proprieties' (not properties), Sellarsian 'placings', and the like. On this fourth and last version we make a semantic ascent and operate at one remove from a commitment to how things are.

4. There is pressure, McDowell argues, towards an 'interiorization' of the SOR. 'This happens when we suppose we ought to be able to achieve flawless standings in the space of reasons by our own unaided resources, without needing the world to do us any favours'.[1]

The most immediate source of this pressure is the 'Myth of the Given'. Like the SOR, this is also a Sellarsian notion. The Myth is 'a mistake of a piece with the so-called "naturalistic fallacy" in ethics'.[2] It is 'a mongrel resulting from a crossbreeding of two ideas':[3] (1) The idea that there are certain inner episodes of sensed particulars 'which can occur to human beings (and brutes) without any prior process of learning or concept formation'[4] and (2): '[t]he idea that there are certain inner episodes which are non-inferential knowings'[5] of a kind that presuppose learning and concept formation. Or, in McDowell's words from his opening paper to this volume 'Avoiding the Myth of the Given', it is 'the idea that sensibility by itself could make things available for the sort of cognition that draws on the subject's rational powers'.[6] In terms of the SOR and ROL distinction introduced here, it is the idea that ROL-processes by themselves can have a rational bearing on, e.g., empirical beliefs at home in the SOR.

According to McDowell, there is a tendency to recoil from the Myth into a coherentist, idealist, or anti-realist conception of the mind as a 'self-contained game' and language as 'spinning frictionless in a void'.[7] Thought is detached from the world, the SOR from the ROL. External constraint on thought goes missing. It simply becomes mysterious how SOR phenomena such as language and mind can stand in any relation to mind-independent physical objects at home in the ROL. McDowell wants to resist the interiorization that leads to this mystery. This is the second key trait of the overall framework of McDowell's work.

The remedy is to argue that SOR conceptual capacities come in two very different modes, the paradigmatic free exercise thereof in making up our minds about what to believe or judge about the world, and as actualized passively when conceptual contents are 'evoked' or 'wrung' from us by the object perceived.[8] McDowell thinks that the capacity to be saddled with conceptual contents in perceptual experience is asymmetrically dependent on the capacity to exercise conceptual capacities freely in judgement. Someone can enjoy a conceptually contentful perceptual experience only if that someone can already apply concepts freely in beliefs and judgements, not vice versa. But still, the idea that we can have our conceptual capacities 'evoked' or 'wrung' from us in perception serves to remove the felt need to appeal to ROL-items such as mere sensations below some imagined 'line' in order, e.g., to explain the for McDowell all important normative dimension to intentionality. This normative dimension stems from the idea of being able to be normatively answerable to the mind-independent world through perception.

There are more strands to McDowell's conception of perceptual experience than this.[9] The overall aim, however, is to make available the idea that we can be normatively answerable to the mind-independent world through perceptual experience. Only thus can we resist the tendency to interiorize the SOR, the second key trait of McDowell's overall framework.

5. There is a further obstacle to the acquiescence in this normative conception of perceptual experience, however. This obstacle also finds a pertinent expression in Sellars:

> [I]n the dimension of describing and explaining the world, science is the measure of all things, of what is that it is, and of what is not that it is not.[10]

This is known as Sellars's *scientia mensura* dictum. There is a massive intuitive appeal to its metaphysical tidiness; and to the absence of philosophical pretension. There is a methodological lesson to be found here: when we want to understand 'what there is', our methods and explanatory resources must be those of the natural sciences. And there is an ontological lesson: we must reject an *a priori* metaphysics that invokes unmoved movers, first principles, forms, or a substance inaccessible to scientific investigation. The natural world is whatever way the natural sciences take it to be.

Disregarding the detail of the dialectical setting, this is the obstacle McDowell refers to as 'bald' or 'constricted' naturalism. The idea is that if we want to avoid arguments from queerness, commitments to fantastically inflated 'off the scale' metaphysics, anti-realism, non-factualism, or outright scepticism about, e.g., the content of mental states or episodes, the aboutness or normative dimension to mental content must be able to be reconstructed in (or eliminated in favour of) terms that reflect this ontology. Perceptual experience, in particular, is construed in strictly nomological causal terms. It is at home in the ROL, not in the SOR.

To dismantle this further obstacle, McDowell says we need to rethink not only 'our conception of nature', but also 'what it takes for a position to deserve to be called "naturalism"'.[11] This is the third key trait of McDowell's overall framework. This rethinking does not involve the introduction of Cartesian mind-stuff or para-matter into our conception of the natural world. Metaphysical over-indulgence does not follow. What does follow is a call for a more 'relaxed' or 'liberal' conception of the natural, a conception that includes human 'second nature'. 'Second nature' is a label for acquired capacities, not for innate abilities, or abilities developed through mere biological maturation. In particular, it is the label for the sorts of conceptual capacities we (rational animals) acquire from being 'initiated' or 'inculcated' into the SOR in our upbringing. These SOR capacities are not merely super-imposed on top of the ROL abilities with which we have been naturally endowed, e.g. our sensory abilities. Rather, they come to 'permeate actualizations of our animal nature'.[12] We have what non-rational animals have. But we have it in a different form. Human second nature, according to McDowell, is a card carrying member of nature. But it is a member of nature on 'a conception of nature that includes the capacity to resonate to the space of reasons'.[13]

Thus rethought, nature is no longer an obstacle to the conception of perceptual experience as a conceptually contentful relation of normative answerability to the mind-independent world. *Pace* the mythical appeals to raw atomistic bits of ROL Givens in sensation, perceptual experience can be a genuine tribunal over the rational credentials of our empirical beliefs. The pressure towards the interiorization of the SOR goes away.

6. McDowell's methodological convictions constitute the fourth key trait of his overall framework. They are often taken to be the defining trait of his thinking. There are two sides to his methodology, his 'modesty'-induced denial that the relation between mind and world or language and world can be explained, as it were, from 'sideways-on',[14] and his Wittgenstein-inspired general conception of philosophy as a diagnostic deconstruction of illusions of genuine philosophical problems.[15]

The basic positive side to his appeal to modesty is the idea that an account of, e.g., conceptual content must be given 'from within' the conceptual framework itself. This can seem a truism. Certainly McDowell thinks it is. But the negative bite of his appeal to modesty is that it has proven difficult to put into practice. There is a standing tendency to assume an 'as from outside perspective' e.g. on the relation between language and (i) the psychological processes lying behind, (ii) the manifested behaviour lying outside, or (iii) the antics of the physical world lying below language. This tendency should be resisted, according to McDowell, because there simply is no such perspective to be exploited.

A typical objection to McDowell is that he needs to 'say more' about this or that phenomenon for his account to be fully satisfactory. In response, McDowell repeatedly says that it is not his aim to construct comprehensive theories or to address genuine philosophical problems in a systematic fashion. This attitude is often referred to as McDowell's 'quietism'. This label is misleading, however. The idea is not that we should simply be quiet when confronted with purportedly genuine philosophical problems or challenges. McDowell wants to reveal these problems and challenges to be but illusions, present a diagnosis of the assumptions that get us entangled in these illusions, and point towards a cure. This can take hard work. And it can require that we invoke the vocabulary of those of us caught up in the illusions. But the purpose is to unmask the purported problems or challenges as what they are, mere illusions, and to show us a way to discard them.

This sums up what I take to be the four most prominent traits that constitute a unifying framework for McDowell's otherwise diverse contributions. They are four traits that constitute the framework within which the three themes addressed in this volume—(i) perceptual experience, (ii) normativity or rationality, and (iii) nature—are central junctures. Let us now have a brief look at the papers and responses.

7. McDowell's opening paper 'Avoiding the Myth of the Given' is published here for the first time. It is the outcome of a prolonged discussion with especially Charles Travis about perceptual experience. In the opening sections, McDowell claims that the Myth of the Given can be avoided only if we are willing to countenance the fact that rational conceptual capacities are operative already in perceptual experience, and not just in subsequent empirical beliefs or judgements. This is orthodox McDowell. But he goes on to renounce two of his prior assumptions: the idea that this requires that we need to credit experiences with *propositional* content, and the idea that experience would need to include *everything* the experience enables its subject to know non-inferentially.

In relation to the second assumption, he is now willing to countenance the idea, for example, that my experience can make a bird visually present to me, but that it takes my *recognitional capacity* to enable me to know non-inferentially that what I see is a cardinal. This brings McDowell to the first assumption. He now thinks that the conceptual content related to proper and common sensibles is not *propositional*, but *intuitional* in the Kantian sense of 'having in view' (*Anschauung*). Intuitional content is not, and often cannot be discursively articulated. It is *given*, not the result of the subject's actively putting significances together. But for all that, it is conceptual; it is 'suitable to be the content associated with a discursive capacity'.[16]

McDowell finishes his paper, first with a rehearsal of the claim, *pace* Bill Brewer's and Travis's contributions to this volume, that conceptual (not *propositional*) capacities must be in play already in perceptual experience in order to avoid subscribing to a form of the Myth of the Given, and secondly with a renewed argument against Davidson—in light of McDowell's renunciation of the first assumption, the idea that perceptual experience has propositional content—that empirical beliefs can acquire their rational credentials non-inferentially through perceptual experience, and not only, as Davidson has it, through inferential structures.

8. In his 'Perception and Content', Brewer puts in question what he labels the 'content view' [CV] of perceptual experience. CV is the idea that perceptual experience is to be characterized, at least in part, by its *representational content*. The basic model of representational content is the idea that *a* is *F*. But McDowell's idea that singular components of genuine perceptual contents are object-dependent demonstrative senses also represents a CV. And so does Brewer's own prior idea from his 1999 *Perception and Reason* that such perceptual contents are instantiation-dependent predicational demonstrative senses.[17]

According to Brewer, the trouble with CV, no matter how refined, is that it retains two fatal features, the idea that perceptual contents allow for mistakes, and the idea that such contents allow for a kind of generality. Brewer lays out what he takes to be the objectionable consequences of these two features and contrasts them with his own purportedly Berkeleyan alternative. This alternative is the idea that perceptual experience gives us direct (non-conceptual) access to mind-independent objects. Errors and illusions, on this account, are the products of the subject's active responses to experience, not something we can be passively saddled with in experience.

In response, McDowell agrees that perceptual experiences as opposed to merely seeming perceptual experiences should present us directly with mind-independent objects. But he urges that the so-called 'good disjunct' on his disjunctive conception of perception—the idea that an experience is an episode in which someone, e.g., *sees* something to be the case, and not a mere seeming to see—eliminates the possibility of falsity. It does not just reduce its scope. He also maintains that access to objects of the sort that can enable knowledge of them requires that this access is contentful. The alternative is a form of the Myth of the Given.

9. Willem deVries also addresses a side to McDowell's conception of experience. But he does this by way of challenging McDowell's reading and discussion of the role Sellars assigns to the concept of sense impressions in giving a purportedly Kantian account of intentionality. More specifically, in his paper 'McDowell, Sellars, and Sense Impressions' deVries disputes five theses that he takes McDowell to foist on Sellars about the role sense impressions play in giving such an account. All five theses, deVries argues, are incompatible with Sellars's philosophy.

Simplified somewhat, the question is what role if any the 'below the line' ROL impressions can play in giving an account of the objectivity of 'above the line' SOR thoughts. Are the impressions needed in a transcendental justification of the objectivity of thought? Are they causally dispensable? Are they phenomen-ologically idle? And does invocation of them involve, *per impossible*, a sideways-on perspective on the relation between the conceptual and the non-conceptual?

In response, McDowell claims that it is not Sellars's conception of sensations or sense impressions that stand in the way of fully appreciating the Kantian idea of intentionality McDowell endorses. Rather, it is Sellars's scientism that stands in the way. This said he turns to each of the five queries raised by deVries about his reading of Sellars.

10. In his paper 'Three Sorts of Naturalism', Hans Fink presents an analysis of the concept of nature in relation to McDowell's discussions of ethical naturalism. Fink and McDowell agree that we should resist the constrictions that the concept of nature is likely to undergo in contemporary thinking. And they agree that alternative non-naturalist accounts of ethical norms should be resisted. But Fink thinks that the second sort of naturalism McDowell introduces in his 'Two Sorts of Naturalism'[18] must be found wanting.

Following an instructive typology, first of modern ordinary uses of the term 'nature' and then of the conceptions of nature (or '*physis*') we find in Aristotle and the old Plato, Fink formulates three alternative conceptions of nature, two constricted sorts—a materialist and an idealist—and a third completely unrest-ricted and all-inclusive sort. He endorses the third sort and finds support for it in Heraclitus, in Spinoza, in Wittgenstein, in Adorno, and in Dewey. It is an anti-dualist, anti-reductionist sort of naturalism. It is an absolute naturalism that allows for no absolute discontinuities; 'nothing could be non-natural, unnatural, supernatural or extra-natural'.[19] Nature is everything that is the case, everything that happens. There is nothing over and above this. *Pace* McDowell, Fink does not operate with a sharp distinction between first and second nature. And he finishes with a challenge to McDowell to say exactly where and why he insists we draw a line between nature and something else.

McDowell begins his response with a minor remark about his reading of Philippa Foot's ethical naturalism in the mentioned paper 'Two Sorts of Naturalism'. He then goes on to resist Fink's pressure to come out and say more by way of developing what McDowell takes to be a 'positive doctrine' about the concepts of nature and naturalism. The dialectical context of McDowell's appeals to 'Greek' or 'relaxed' naturalism is supposedly much more limited. It was merely meant to exercise what McDowell takes to be a bit of common sense, the idea that our responsiveness to reasons, whilst *extra*-natural by the scientistic naturalist's lights, is no more mysterious than walking or eating. And no less real.

11. The main claim in Christoph Halbig's 'Varieties of Nature in Hegel and McDowell' is that McDowell's take on the idea of 'second nature' reveals the presence of an uneasy position between what Halbig refers to as 'Wittgensteinian quietism' and the constructive philosophy of a 'Hegelian hyperbolic system'.[20] Halbig poses two questions in relation to McDowell's distinction between 'first'

and 'second' nature. First, he suggests that they are categorically distinct in such a way that it becomes mysterious how they can be related. And secondly, he urges McDowell to clarify whether the distinction is a methodological distinction between two orders of intelligibility or an ontological distinction between two different levels of reality. Halbig thus suggests that there are lingering residual tensions in McDowell's proposed 'relaxed naturalism'.

He then goes on to argue that Hegel comes in helpful here. Nothing is gained, however, from merely looking up Hegel's remarks on 'zweite Natur', 'second nature'. According to Halbig, the role this notion plays in Hegel is very different from the role it plays in McDowell. Hegel's discussion of the relation between Nature and Spirit (especially in the *Encyclopedia* §381) is more to the point. But the result of this discussion is the erection of an elaborate theory, directly at odds with McDowell's Wittgensteinian methodology. But Halbig argues that the Hegelian approach is required in order to lay to rest the tensions that remain in McDowell's approach.

McDowell's response to Halbig is twofold. As in his response to Fink, McDowell thinks Halbig misconstrues the context of McDowell's play with 'second nature' and thereby makes it seem more contentious and theoretical than it was meant to be. His answers to Halbig's two questions on the relation between 'first' and 'second' nature reflect this response. Secondly, McDowell wants to resist Halbig's reading of Hegel. McDowell claims that Hegel's 'zweite Natur' is closer to his own conception of 'second nature' than Halbig has us think. This is also the case with respect to Hegel's conception of the relation between Nature and Spirit. According to McDowell, there is plenty of scope to take Hegel's project 'to make clear a way of thinking composed of elements that are [. . .] innocuous, like Wittgenstein's reminders'.[21]

12. Stephen Houlgate pursues the strand in Halbig's paper that aims to establish significant differences between McDowell and Hegel. In his paper 'Thought and Experience in Hegel and McDowell', Houlgate is, however, silent on the relative persuasiveness of the two.

This is the most prominent difference: According to Houlgate's Hegel, it is wrong to think that empirical concepts are grounded in perceptual experience. They are the conditions of perceptual experience, and they are acquired through language. They enable us to understand that what is given in sensation is a world of objective, re-identifiable, spatio-temporal things. If we want to know what the world requires us to think, we should turn instead to the *a priori* categories and concepts of thought. These categories and concepts reflect the fact that *being* constrains our thought internally and immanently. This does not mean that we can deduce from pure thought the fact that there is a cardinal in front of us. What it does mean is that thought knows the categorical, ontological structure of being *a priori*. Thought is 'beings own understanding of itself'.[22]

Also, according to Houlgate's Hegel, we never passively *take in* facts or conceptual contents. We take in sensory contents. To experience something is actively to judge or understand things to be thus and so. Houlgate concludes that for Hegel 'the world exercises authority over perceptual experience through thought'.[23]

In his response to Houlgate, McDowell hesitatingly suggests that Houlgate's reading of Hegel is questionable on a number of points, points that appear to McDowell to exaggerate the difference between himself and Hegel. For example, McDowell takes the idea that we have raw, unconceptualized sensations though we are not aware of them to be unHegelian. Also, McDowell agrees that perceptual experience is inseparable from the active making of judgements. But that is because the ability to enjoy a perceptual experience is inseparable from the *ability* to make a judgement, not because perceptual experience is itself an active judgement. And he takes Hegel to concur. Finally, McDowell thinks Houlgate's reading of the role of 'positing' in Hegel implies a subjective idealism about the phenomenal world, something McDowell also finds to be incompatible with his reading of Hegel. The net result is a picture of Hegel that appears less incompatible with the line on perceptual experience that McDowell urges.

13. In her 'Practical Reason and its Animal Precursors', Sabina Lovibond takes her point of departure in her conviction that there is a lack of clarity on what exactly separates human ethical life from the life of non-human animals. She works with Alasdair MacIntyre's claim that for those like Heidegger, Gadamer, and McDowell who operate with a strong distinction between animal and human cognitive life, it becomes mysterious how the distinctive aspects of human ethical agency could ever have emerged; let alone how they can ever emerge in the course of individual human development. MacIntyre takes issue with the entrenched philosophical habit of contrasting our own species with an undifferentiated category of 'other' animals, rather than paying attention to the massive differences that exist. As an example of sophisticated animal capacities, Lovibond mentions N'kisi, an African grey parrot, which supposedly has a vocabulary of 950 words, an ability to use words in context, with the proper tenses, and often in an inventive way.[24] Hardly something you would expect of an earthworm.

MacIntyre argues that these and other sophisticated animals enjoy perceptual experiences with the all-important 'as-structure', that they recognize other individuals, notice their absence, greet their returns, and that they act for reasons. This is taken to suggest that there is a 'scale or spectrum' rather than a single line of division between 'them' and 'us'. MacIntyre still recognizes that human beings are the uniquely ethical species, however, and that there is a *sui generis* character to human practical rationality. The challenge, according to Lovibond's discussion of McDowell, is to find out what exactly this difference is. She points to a number of features. But most important, here, is the McDowellian idea that mature human life is characterized by displaying the ability to a 'free distanced orientation', an ability to 'step back' from our inclinations and evaluate them critically. In ethical life this enables us to reflect and make choices in relation to the over-arching aim of 'living well all things considered'; especially, Lovibond adds, in light of the human awareness of death.

In response, McDowell commends what he takes to be Lovibond's clarity on the purpose-relativity of insisting on discontinuities vis-à-vis continuities between human rational animals and others. McDowell's reason for insisting on a distinction is that non-rational animals can be trained to respond to signposts in particular ways. But such responses reflect nothing but their 'habituation-induced' propensities towards a particular sort of behaviour; they do not act on an understanding. On McDowell's account, only rational animals can display understanding. And only those who can display understanding can understand the idea of 'living well in general'. Thus, only rational animals could be ethical animals. Also, McDowell acknowledges that non-human animals can respond to food *'as* food', but that this does not imply that they have the concept 'food'. This requires more than mere animal intelligence.

14. In his 'Contemporary Epistemology: Kant, Hegel, McDowell', Kenneth R. Westphal takes McDowell to agree that we require a 'socio-historically grounded epistemological realism',[25] and that Kant and Hegel are important aids in delivering on this requirement. He then argues that even taking into consideration McDowell's recent and more detailed approaches to Kant and Hegel, (i) McDowell still must be found wanting in his account of a number of key points in their views of human knowledge, (ii) that this shortcoming is due to McDowell's therapeutic methodology, and (iii) that this mars McDowell's own 'transcendental' project.

Westphal points to four issues in McDowell's alleged misappropriation of Kant and Hegel: (1) the relation between understanding and sensibility, (2) Kant's and Hegel's *tout court* rejection of givenness by reference to the character and preconditions of singular thought, (3) the role of Kant's transcendental deduction in relation to an account of objective purport, and (4) the question whether mental content externalism can be proven transcendentally.

On the first issue, Westphal takes McDowell to overstate the role free rational judgements play in Kant's account of empirical intuitions. More precisely, Westphal thinks this is due to McDowell's unwarranted conflation of 'spontaneity' and 'freedom' in his reading of Kant. On the second issue, Westphal argues that sensation and conception are coextensive throughout the entire scope of our perceptual experience of surrounding objects and events.[26] Thirdly, Westphal argues that McDowell has Kant wrong on the relation between the famous *B160* footnote and the second half of the *B* Deduction from the first *Critique*. Finally, Westphal agrees with McDowell that Kant's transcendental idealism does stand in the way of proving mental content externalism, but goes on to suggest that McDowell is mistaken as to the nature of Hegel's advance over Kant in this respect.

McDowell takes Westphal's reading of him to be a travesty. First, McDowell says that Westphal displays no understanding of the purpose of his 'therapeutic' methodology. Then he explains his reading of especially Kant, but also of Hegel on the points raised by Westphal. These points include McDowell's reading of the *B160* footnote in relation to the two-part structure of the *B*-deduction; the relation between those two parts; the relation between the 'understanding' and 'the transcendental power of imagination' in Kant; McDowell's objection to Kant's conception of intuitions as generated by spontaneous (not free) intellectual activity; and McDowell's rejection of Westphal's attempt to enrol Sellars as a protagonist of the externalist approach, Westphal wants to read into Kant.[27]

15. In his 'Science and Sensibility: McDowell and Sellars on Perceptual Experience', Michael Williams poses three questions on the relation between McDowell and Sellars on perceptual experience, and gives a negative answer to all of them: (1) McDowell and Sellars are not all that close, (2) McDowell does not get Sellars entirely right, and (3) McDowell's criticisms of Sellars are not well-aimed.

Williams opens his paper with an instructive summary of what he takes to be the three main components of McDowell's *Mind and World*—a problem, its solution, and an explanation why this solution is so difficult to see or accept—and goes on to show how it can seem easy to find direct counterparts in Sellars. But appearances are deceiving. There are significant differences between the two, both 'above-the-line' in the 'space of reasons', and 'below-the-line' in the 'realm of law'. For one, Williams does not find McDowell's above-the-line distinction between experiences and judgements in Sellars. Experiences are not 'passive' in McDowell's sense; they are perceptual 'takings'. There is still a difference (between mental acts and mental actions, or between 'ought to be' and 'ought to do'). But this is a different difference. On Williams's reading, Sellars also thinks that 'mere causal connections' to objects can be 'epistemically significant'.[28] This causal relation is part of the source of authority that perceptual takings exhibit. Williams concludes that Sellars neither recognizes nor needs to recognize McDowellian experiences.

Pace McDowell, Williams contends that Sellars also thinks that the 'above-the-line' strictly conceptual aspect to experience is incomplete on its own. For scientific reasons (in Sellars's *Empiricism and the Philosophy of Mind* [*EPM*]) or transcendental reasons (in Sellars's *Science and Metaphysics* [*SM*]) a complete account will have to include invocation of raw 'below-the-line' 'sensations' or 'impressions' as well. This is needed in order to be able to say what ostensible seeings and veridical seeings have in common. Williams denies that they play any epistemic-foundational role anywhere in Sellars—not even in the transcendental role McDowell has them playing in *SM*—but that they, also *pace* McDowell, must play an indispensable explanatory role in order to avoid lingering idealism-charges. They do this by securing the causal connectedness to our surroundings. This issue bears on a further important distinction in Sellars, to which Williams turns in the final section of his paper, the distinction between the 'Manifest' image of man as a thinking and feeling being versus the 'Scientific' image of man as a complex physical system. There Williams tries to set straight what he thinks is a conflation in McDowell of his approach to the 'transcendental question' with the clash of the two images of man, with a view to the role of philosophy vis-à-vis science.

The main thrust of McDowell's response is straightforward. McDowell thinks that he is more Sellarsian about experience than Williams thinks. But he has 'no sympathy with Sellars's scientism'.[29] First, McDowell draws our attention to the metaphorical character of Sellars's claim that experiences, 'so to speak', contain claims evoked or wrung from us by the object perceived. Experience, in Sellars, does not have the assertional character Williams thinks it has. According to McDowell, Sellars's metaphor suggests that it is experiences that make claims, not the subjects of experience. Secondly, McDowell denies that the Myth pivots on a conflation of the 'ought to be' and 'ought to do' sorts of normativity. The Myth, according to McDowell is 'the idea that merely being impinged on by causal force originating in an object can constitute a cognitive status',[30] the idea that mere causes can justify. Thirdly, McDowell argues that Sellars *does* expand his class of experiences so as to include 'ostensible seeings', but that Sellars does not quite get the details of this idea under control. Fourthly, McDowell argues, again *pace* Williams, that Sellars does make room for the nuanced non-Mythical idea that knowledge does have foundations; non-inferential knowledge acquired through the actualizations of conceptual capacities in experience. Fifthly, McDowell defends his critique of Sellars's claim that experiencings involve not only conceptual goings-on, but also non-conceptual sensations. Finally, McDowell says why he thinks Sellars's proposed 'synoptic vision' vision of the 'Manifest' and 'Scientific' images of man is misconceived, why Sellars's scientism leads him astray, and why there was never any conflation in McDowell's own thinking on the relation between the 'transcendental question' and the relation between those images.

16. According to Charles Travis, McDowell introduces a 'Condition' on perceptual experience that renders impossible the basic intuition that perceptual experience 'makes our surroundings bear on what we are to think.[31] The Condition is the idea that perceptual experience is a phenomenon characterized by standing in rational relations, by being a standing in the space of reasons. The problem is that most objects of the natural world are characterized by standing in relations of a very different kind, viz. strictly causal relations. This includes the relation between the physical object and the sensory system of the perceiver. Thus, it becomes difficult to see how such objects and relations can have any bearing, through perceptual experience, on what to think. Also, this difficulty is exacerbated by the fact that for McDowell the space of reasons is co-extensional with the space of concepts. This renders mysterious the relation of non-conceptual objects and non-conceptual relations to conceptual contents and relations.

The purpose of Travis's 'Reason's Reach' is to repudiate the Condition. The main point of his paper is that reason does not stop short of non-conceptual objects and relations. This, supposedly, makes available the idea that perception is of our surroundings, of what is in them, and of how, what is in them, is like. Or, to use Travis's example, it makes available the idea that seeing a red piece of meat on a white rug (something non-conceptual), the piece of meat, the white rug, and their relation bear rationally on what I should think about the scene.

In response, McDowell does insist on *a* condition (if not Travis's Condition): 'reason's reach extends no further than conceptual capacities can take it'.[32] But this condition does not exclude pieces of meat from standing in rational relations to our empirical beliefs. The conceptual is unbounded. And so is reason. The piece of meat is a constraint on empirical thought from outside *thinking*, but not from outside of the *thinkable*.[33] Harking back to the point made in his opening paper 'Avoiding the Myth of the Given', McDowell no longer thinks perceptual experiences have propositional content; but they are still actualizations of conceptual capacities, and thus have conceptual content. This is required, according to McDowell, to avoid subscribing to the Myth. Travis thinks that conceptual capacities come into play only in our responses to things we experience anyway, without recourse to conceptual capacities. To McDowell, this is a version of the Myth. And, harking back to his response to Brewer, Myth-avoidance is the main motivation for McDowell's condition.[34]

Jakob Lindgaard
Department of Philosophy
University of Warwick
Coventry CV4 7AL
UK

NOTES

[1] McDowell 1995: 395–396.

[2] Sellars 1956: §5.

[3] Ibid: §7.

[4] Ibid.

[5] Ibid.

[6] McDowell 2008a: 2.

[7] McDowell 1994: 5, 11.

[8] For the 'evoked' and 'wrung' imagery, see Sellars 1956: §16(b).

[9] One further strand is McDowell's disjunctivist denial that there is an inference from the subjective indistinguishability between a genuine seeing and an illusion to the so-called 'highest common factor' account of experience when confronted with arguments from illusion. Another further strand adds to the dimension introduced here—that in order to have perceptual experience, one must already have concepts—the inverse idea that anyone who does not have perceptual experience, does not have concepts either. McDowell thinks of this as two reciprocally dependent transcendental or logical orders. Arguably, this dimension is at odds with the asymmetry-thesis from above, but this is not the place for such discussion.

[10] Sellars 1956: §41.

[11] McDowell 1994: 77.

[12] Ibid: 109.

[13] Ibid.

[14] See especially McDowell 1987 & 1997.

[15] See especially McDowell 1992.

[16] McDowell 2008a: 7.

[17] Brewer's paper thus represents a genuine *Kehre*, a hairpin bend in his account of perception.

[18] McDowell 1996.

[19] Fink 2008: 68.

[20] Halbig 2008: 73.

[21] McDowell 2008b: 223.

[22] See Houlgate 2008: 100 for this use of Hegel's wording. See also footnote 61 for Houlgate's take on Halbig's proposed interpretation of Hegel.

[23] Houlgate 2008: 104.

[24] See Lovibond 2008: 122, note 29.

[25] Westphal 2008: 124.

[26] See Westphal 2008: 132 for this way of phrasing his objection.

[27] On this last point, see McDowell 2008b: 244.

[28] Williams 2008: 164.

[29] See McDowell 2008b: 248.

[30] Ibid: 251.

[31] Travis 2008: 176.

[32] McDowell 2008b: 259.

[33] See also McDowell 1994: 28, for the introduction of this distinction.

[34] I should like to thank the Department of Philosophy, University of Warwick and Michael Luntley for hosting the first stint of the conference from where the papers in this volume originate. Also, thanks to the Department of Philosophy, University of Aarhus and Hans Fink for hosting the second stint. Without the *European Journal of Philosophy* and Robert Stern, this volume would never have seen the light of day. Thanks to Stern and the *EJOP* for both financial and editorial support. Finally, thanks to Stern and Julie Zahle for their comments on the penultimate draft of this Introduction.

REFERENCES

Fink, H. (2008), 'Three Sorts of Naturalism', in J. Lindgaard (ed.), *John McDowell: Experience, Norm, and Nature*. Oxford: Blackwell, 52–71.

Halbig, C. (2008), 'Varieties of Nature in Hegel and McDowell', in J. Lindgaard (ed.), *John McDowell: Experience, Norm, and Nature*. Oxford: Blackwell, 72–91.

Houlgate, S. (2008), 'Thought and Experience in Hegel and McDowell', in J. Lindgaard (ed.), *John McDowell: Experience, Norm, and Nature*. Oxford: Blackwell, 92–111.

Lovibond, S. (2008), 'Practical Reason and Its Animal Precursors', in J. Lindgaard (ed.), *John McDowell: Experience, Norm, and Nature*. Oxford: Blackwell, 112–123.

McDowell, J. (1987), 'In Defence of Modesty', in B. Taylor (ed.), *Michael Dummett: Contributions to Philosophy*. Dordrecht: Martinus Nijhoff.

—— (1992), 'Meaning and Intentionality in Wittgenstein's Later Philosophy', in P. A. French, T. E. Uehling and H. K. Wettstein (eds.), *Midwest Studies in Philosophy: The Wittgenstein Legacy*. Notre Dame: University of Notre Dame Press.

—— (1994), *Mind and World*. Cambridge Mass: Harvard University Press.

—— (1995), 'Knowledge and the Internal', *Philosophy and Phenomenological Research*, 55: 877–893.

—— (1996), 'Two Sorts of Naturalism', in *Mind, Value, and Reality*. Cambridge, Mass: Harvard University Press, 167–197.

—— (1997), 'Another Plea for Modesty', in R. G. J. Heck (ed.), *Language, Thought, and Logic: Essays in Honour of Michael Dummett*. Oxford: Oxford University Press.

—— (2008a), 'Avoiding the Myth of the Given', in J. Lindgaard (ed.), *John McDowell: Experience, Norm, and Nature*. Oxford: Blackwell, 1–14.

—— (2008b), 'Responses', in J. Lindgaard (ed.), *John McDowell: Experience, Norm, and Nature*. Oxford: Blackwell, 200–267.

Sellars, W. (1956), 'Empiricism and the Philosophy of Mind', in *Science, Perception, and Reality*. Atascadero, California: Ridgeview Publishing Company, 1963. (As indicated, the original year of publication is 1956. It was reprinted for the first time with added footnotes in this 1963 collection of Sellars's papers.)

Travis, C. (2008), 'Reason's Reach', in J. Lindgaard (ed.), *John McDowell: Experience, Norm, and Nature*. Oxford: Blackwell, 176–199.

Westphal, K. R. (2008), 'Contemporary Epistemology: Kant, Hegel, McDowell', in J. Lindgaard (ed.), *John McDowell: Experience, Norm, and Nature*. Oxford: Blackwell, 124–151.

Williams, M. (2008), 'Science and Sensibility: McDowell and Sellars on Perceptual Experience', in J. Lindgaard (ed.), *John McDowell: Experience, Norm, and Nature*. Oxford: Blackwell, 152–175.

1

Avoiding the Myth of the Given

John McDowell

1. What is the Myth of the Given?

Wilfrid Sellars, who is responsible for the label, notoriously neglects to explain in general terms what he means by it. As he remarks, the idea of givenness for knowledge, givenness to a knowing subject, can be innocuous.[1] So how does it become pernicious? Here is a suggestion: Givenness in the sense of the Myth would be an availability for cognition to subjects whose getting what is supposedly Given to them does not draw on capacities required for the sort of cognition in question.

If that is what Givenness would be, it is straightforward that it must be mythical. Having something Given to one would be being given something for knowledge without needing to have capacities that would be necessary for one to be able to get to know it. And that is incoherent.

So how can the Myth be a pitfall? Well, one could fall into it if one did not realize that knowledge of some kind requires certain capacities. And we can see how that might be a real risk, in the context in which Sellars mostly discusses the Myth, by considering a Sellarsian dictum about knowledge.

Sellars says attributions of knowledge place episodes or states 'in the logical space of reasons'.[2] He identifies the logical space of reasons as the space 'of justifying and being able to justify what one says'. Sellars means to exclude an externalistic view of epistemic satisfactoriness, a view according to which one can be entitled to a belief without being in a position to know what entitles one to it. Knowing things, as Sellars means his dictum, must draw on capacities that belong to reason, conceived as a faculty whose exercises include vindicating one's entitlement to say things. Such a faculty acquires its first actuality, its elevation above mere potentiality, when one learns to talk. There must be a potential for self-consciousness in its operations.

Now consider how this applies to perceptual knowledge. Perceptual knowledge involves sensibility: that is, a capacity for differential responsiveness to features of the environment, made possible by properly functioning sensory systems. But sensibility does not belong to reason. We share it with non-rational animals. According to Sellars's dictum, the rational faculty that distinguishes us from non-rational animals must also be operative in our being perceptually given things to know.

This brings into view a way to fall into the Myth of the Given. Sellars's dictum implies that it is a form of the Myth to think sensibility by itself, without any involvement of capacities that belong to our rationality, can make things available for our cognition. That coincides with a basic doctrine of Kant.

Note that I say 'for *our* cognition'. It can be tempting to object to Sellars's dictum on the ground that it denies knowledge to non-rational animals. It is perfectly natural—the objection goes—to talk of knowledge when we say how the sensibility of non-rational animals enables them to deal competently with their environments. But there is no need to read Sellars, or Kant, as denying that. We can accept it but still take Sellars's dictum, and the associated rejection of the Myth, to express an insight. Sellars's dictum characterizes knowledge of a distinctive sort, attributable only to rational animals. The Myth, in the version I have introduced, is the idea that sensibility by itself could make things available for the sort of cognition that draws on the subject's rational powers.

2. A knowledgeable perceptual judgment has its rational intelligibility, amounting in this case to epistemic entitlement, in the light of the subject's experience. She judges that things are thus and so because her experience reveals to her that things are thus and so: for instance, she sees that things are thus and so. The intelligibility displayed by such an explanation belongs to a kind that is also exemplified when a subject judges that things are thus and so because her experience merely seems to reveal to her that things are thus and so. These uses of 'because' introduce explanations that show rationality in operation. In the kind of case I began with, rationality enables knowledgeable judgments. In the other kind of case, reason leads its possessor astray, or at best enables her to make a judgment that merely happens to be true.

In Kant, the higher faculty that distinguishes us from non-rational animals figures in experience in the guise of the understanding, the faculty of concepts. So to follow Kant's way of avoiding the Myth of the Given in this context, we must suppose capacities that belong to that faculty—conceptual capacities—are in play in the way experience makes knowledge available to us.

For the moment, we can take this introduction of the idea of conceptual capacities quite abstractly. All we need to know so far is that they must be capacities that belong to a faculty of reason. I shall try to be more specific later.

I have invoked the idea of judgments that are rationally intelligible in the light of experience, in the best case to the extent of being revealed as knowledgeable. There is an interpretation of this idea that I need to reject.

The idea is not just that experience yields items—experiences—to which judgments are rational responses. That would be consistent with supposing that rational capacities are operative only in responses to experiences, not in experiences themselves. On this view the involvement of rational capacities would be entirely downstream from experiences.

But that would not do justice to the role of experience in our acquisition of knowledge. As I noted, even for Sellars there is nothing wrong with saying things are given to us for knowledge. The idea of givenness becomes mythical—becomes the idea of Givenness—only if we fail to impose the necessary requirements on getting what is given. And it is in experiencing itself that we have things perceptually given to us for knowledge. Avoiding the Myth requires capacities that belong to reason to be operative in experiencing itself, not just in judgments in which we respond to experience.

3. How should we elaborate this picture? I used to assume that to conceive experiences as actualizations of conceptual capacities, we would need to credit experiences with *propositional* content, the sort of content judgments have. And I used to assume that the content of an experience would need to include *everything* the experience enables its subject to know noninferentially. But both these assumptions now strike me as wrong.

4. Let me start with the second. We can question it even if, for the moment, we go on assuming experiences have propositional content.

Suppose I have a bird in plain view, and that puts me in a position to know noninferentially that it is a cardinal. It is not that I infer that what I see is a cardinal from the way it looks, as when I identify a bird's species by comparing what I see with a photograph in a field guide. I can immediately recognize cardinals if the viewing conditions are good enough.

Charles Travis has forced me to think about such cases, and in abandoning my old assumption I am partly coming around to a view he has urged on me.[3]

On my old assumption, since my experience puts me in a position to know noninferentially that what I see is a cardinal, its content would have to include a proposition in which the concept of a cardinal figures: perhaps one expressible, on the occasion, by saying 'That's a cardinal'. But what seems right is this: my experience makes the bird visually present to me, and my recognitional capacity enables me to know noninferentially that what I see is a cardinal. Even if we go on assuming my experience has content, there is no need to suppose that the concept under which my recognitional capacity enables me to bring what I see figures in that content.

Consider an experience had, in matching circumstances, by someone who cannot immediately identify what she sees as a cardinal. Perhaps she does not even have the concept of a cardinal. Her experience might be just like mine in how it makes the bird visually present to her. It is true that in an obvious sense things look different to me and to her. To me what I see looks like (looks to be) a cardinal, and to her it does not. But that is just to say that my experience inclines me, and her similar experience does not incline her, to say it is a cardinal. There is no ground here for insisting that the concept of a cardinal must figure in the content of my experience itself.

It would be right to say I am unlike this other person in that I see that the bird is a cardinal; my experience reveals to me that it is a cardinal. But that is no problem for what I am proposing. Such locutions—'I see that . . .', 'My experience reveals to me that . . . ' —accept, in their 'that . . . ' clauses, specifications of things one's experience puts one in a position to know noninferentially.[4] That can include knowledge that experience makes available by bringing something into view for someone who has a suitable recognitional capacity. And as I have urged, content whose figuring in such knowledge is owed to the recognitional capacity need not be part of the content of the experience itself.

5. Should we conclude that conceptual capacities are not operative in having objects visually present to one, but only in what one makes of what one anyway sees? Should we drop the very idea that perceptual experiences had by rational animals have conceptual content?

That would be too drastic. Nothing in what I have said about recognitional capacities dislodges the argument that on pain of the Myth of the Given, capacities that belong to the higher cognitive faculty must be operative in experience. In giving one things to know, experience must draw on conceptual capacities. Some concepts that figure in knowledge afforded by an experience can be excluded from the content of the experience itself, in the way I have illustrated with the concept of a cardinal, but not all can.

A natural stopping point, for visual experiences, would be proper sensibles of sight and common sensibles accessible to sight. We should conceive experience as drawing on conceptual capacities associated with concepts of proper and common sensibles.

So should we suppose my experience when I see a cardinal has propositional content involving proper and common sensibles? That would preserve the other of those two assumptions I used to make. But I think this assumption is wrong too. What we need is an idea of content that is not propositional but intuitional, in what I take to be a Kantian sense.

'Intuition' is the standard English translation of Kant's '*Anschauung*'. The etymology of 'intuition' fits Kant's notion, and Kant uses a cognate expression when he writes in Latin. But we need to forget much of the philosophical resonance of the English word. An *Anschauung* is a having in view. (As is usual in philosophy, Kant treats visual experiences as exemplary.)

Kant says: 'The same function which gives unity to the various representations *in a judgment* also gives unity to the mere synthesis of various representations *in an intuition*; and this unity, in its most general expression, we entitle the pure concept of the understanding'.[5] The capacity whose exercise in judging accounts for the unity of the content of judgments—propositional unity— also accounts for a corresponding unity in the content of intuitions. Sellars gives a helpful illustration: the propositional unity in a judgment expressible by 'This is a cube' corresponds to an intuitional unity expressible by 'this cube'.[6] The demonstrative phrase might partly capture the content of an intuition in which one is visually presented with a cube. (I shall return to this.)

Propositional unity comes in various forms. Kant takes a classification of forms of judgment, and thus of forms of propositional unity, from the logic of his day, and works to describe a corresponding form of intuitional unity for each. But the idea that forms of intuitional unity correspond to forms of propositional unity can be separated from the details of how Kant elaborates it. It is not obvious why Kant thinks the idea requires that to every form of propositional unity there must correspond a form of intuitional unity. And anyway we need not follow Kant in his inventory of forms of propositional unity.

Michael Thompson has identified a distinctive form of propositional unity for thought and talk about the living as such.[7] Thompson's primary point is about a form exemplified in saying what living things of certain kinds *do*, as in 'Wolves hunt in packs' or 'The lesser celandine blooms in spring'. But Thompson's thought naturally extends to a form or forms exemplified in talk about what individual living things *are doing*, as in 'Those wolves are hunting' or 'This lesser celandine is coming into bloom'.[8] And it would be in the spirit of Kant's conception to identify a corresponding form or corresponding forms of intuitional unity, one of which we might find in my visual experience of a cardinal. The concept of a bird, like the concept of a cardinal, need not be part of the content of the experience; the same considerations would apply. But perhaps we can say it is given to me in such an experience, not something I know by bringing a conceptual capacity to bear on what I anyway see, that what I see is an animal—not because 'animal' expresses part of the content unified in the experience in accordance with a certain form of intuitional unity, but because 'animal' captures the intuition's categorial form, the distinctive kind of unity it has.

The common sensibles accessible to sight are modes of space occupancy: shape, size, position, movement or its absence. In an intuition unified by a form capturable by 'animal', we might recognize content, under the head of modes of space occupancy, that could not figure in intuitions of inanimate objects. We might think of common sensibles accessible to sight as including, for instance, postures such as perching and modes of locomotion such as hopping or flying.

We can avoid such issues by concentrating, as Sellars often does, on visual presentness of things like coloured cubes. But even with this restricted focus, there is still a complication. If there can be visual intuitions whose content is partly specifiable by, say, 'that cube', intuitions in which something's being cubic is visually given to one, then the higher cognitive faculty needs to be in our picture not just to account for the unity with which certain content figures in such an intuition, but also, in the guise of the productive imagination, to provide for part of the content itself—supplying, as it were, the rest of the cube, behind the facing surfaces. Sellars often uses the example of a pink ice cube, and one reason is presumably that it allows him not to bother with this complication, because he envisages his ice cube as translucent, so that its back can be actually in view.[9]

6. So far, conceptual capacities are on the scene only as the kind of capacities that must be in play in experience if we are to avoid the Myth: capacities that belong to rationality in a demanding sense. But I undertook to try to be more specific.

If the idea of the conceptual singles out a kind of content, it seems right to focus on the content of judgments, since judging is the paradigmatic exercise of theoretical rationality.

We can think of judgments as inner analogues to assertions. That makes it natural to count judging as a *discursive* activity, even though the idea of discourse has its primary application to overt performances.[10] In an assertion one makes something discursively explicit. And the idea of making things explicit extends without strain to judging. We can say that one makes what one judges explicit to oneself.

I said we should centre our idea of the conceptual on the content of judgments. But now that I have introduced the idea of the discursive, I can put the point like this: we should centre our idea of the conceptual on the content of discursive activity.

Now intuiting is not discursive, even in the extended sense in which judging is. Discursive content is articulated. Intuitional content is not.

Part of the point is that there are typically aspects of the content of an intuition that the subject has no means of making discursively explicit. Visual intuitions typically present one with visible characteristics of objects that one is not equipped to attribute to the objects by making appropriate predications in claims or judgments. To make such an aspect of the content of an intuition into the content associated with a capacity that is discursive in the primary sense, one would need to carve it out, as it were, from the categorially unified but as yet unarticulated content of the intuition by determining it to be the meaning of a linguistic expression, which one thereby sets up as a means for making that content explicit. (This might be a matter of coining an adjective. Or the expression might be one like 'having that shade of colour'.) Perhaps one can bypass language and directly equip oneself with a counterpart capacity that is discursive in the sense in which judging is discursive. There would be the same need to isolate an aspect of the content of the intuition, by determining it to be the content associated with a capacity to make predications in judgments.

And articulating goes beyond intuiting even if we restrict ourselves to aspects of intuitional content that are associated with discursive capacities one already has.

In discursive dealings with content, one puts significances together. This is particularly clear with with discursive performances in the primary sense, whose content is the significance of a combination of meaningful expressions. But even though judging need not be conceived as an act spread out in time, like making a claim, its being discursive involves a counterpart to the way one puts significances together in meaningful speech.

I mean this to be consistent with rejecting, as we should, the idea that the contents one puts together in discursive activity are self-standing building-blocks, separately thinkable elements in the contents of claims or judgments. One can think the significance of, say, a predicative expression only in the context of a thought in which that content occurs predicatively. But we can acknowledge that and still say that in discursive activity one puts contents together in a way (not sure) that can be modelled on stringing meaningful expressions together in discourse literally so called.

That is not how it is with intuitional content. The unity of intuitional content is *given*, not a result of our putting significances together. Even if discursive exploitation of some content given in an intuition does not require one to acquire a new discursive capacity, one needs to carve out that content from the intuition's unarticulated content before one can put it together with other bits of content in discursive activity. Intuiting does not do this carving out for one.

If intuitional content is not discursive, why go on insisting it is conceptual? Because every aspect of the content of an intuition is present in a form in which it is already suitable to be the content associated with a discursive capacity, if it is not—at least not yet—actually so associated. That is part of the force of saying, with Kant, that what gives unity to intuitions is the same function that gives unity to judgments. If a subject does not already have a discursive capacity associated with some aspect of the content of an intuition of hers, all she needs to do, to acquire such a discursive capacity, is to isolate that aspect by equipping herself with a means to make that content—that very content—explicit in speech or judgment. The content of an intuition is such that its subject can analyse it into significances for discursive capacities, whether or not this requires introducing new discursive capacities to be associated with those significances. Whether by way of introducing new discursive capacities or not, the subject of an intuition is in a position to put aspects of its content, the very content that is already there in the intuition, together in discursive performances.

I said that the unity of intuitional content is *given*. Kant sometimes implies a different picture. He says, for instance, that 'all combination, be we conscious of it or not, ... is an act of the understanding (*Verstandeshandlung*)' (B130). In its context, this remark implies that we actively put content together in intuitions no less than in judgments (though with intuitions the activity has to be unconscious). And that goes badly with my claim that intuitional content is not discursive. But Kant does not need to hold that the unity of intuitional content is not given. What he really wants to insist is that it is not Given: that it is not provided by sensibility alone. In intuiting, capacities that belong to the higher cognitive faculty are in play. The unity of intuitional content reflects an operation of the same unifying function that is operative in the unity of judgments, in that case actively exercised. That is why it is right to say the content unified in intuitions is of the same kind as the content unified in judgments: that is, conceptual content. We could not have intuitions, with their specific forms of unity, if we could not make judgments, with their corresponding forms of unity. We can even say that the unity-providing function is essentially a faculty for discursive activity, a power to judge. But its operation in providing for the unity of intuitions is not itself a case of discursive activity.

Not that it is a case of prediscursive activity, at least if that means that intuiting is a more primitive forerunner of judging. The two kinds of unity that Kant says are provided by the same function, the unity of intuitions and the unity of judgments, are on a level with one another.

7. In a visual intuition, an object is visually present to a subject with those of its features that are visible to the subject from her vantage point. It is through the presence of those features that the object is present. How else could an object be visually present to one?

The concept of an object here is formal. In Kant's terms, a category, a pure concept of the understanding, is a concept of an object in general. A formal concept of, as we can naturally say, a kind of object is explained by specifying a form of categorial unity, a form of the kind of unity that characterizes intuitions. Perhaps, as I suggested, following Thompson, 'animal' can be understood as expressing such a concept.

On the account I have been giving, having an object present to one in an intuition is an actualization of capacities that are conceptual, in a sense that belongs with Kant's thesis that what accounts for the unity with which the associated content figures in the intuition is the same function that provides for the unity of judgments. I have urged that even though the unity-providing function is a faculty for discursive activity, it is not in discursive activity that these capacities are operative in intuitions. With much of the content of an ordinary visual intuition, the capacities that are in play in one's having it as part of the content of one's intuition are not even susceptible of discursive exercise. One can make use of content's being given in an intuition to acquire a new discursive capacity, but with much of the content of an ordinary intuition, one never does that. (Think of the finely discriminable shapes and shades of colour that visual experience presents to one.) Nevertheless an intuition's content is all conceptual, in this sense: it is in the intuition in a form in which one *could* make it, that very content, figure in discursive activity. That would be to exploit a potential for discursive activity that is already there in the capacities actualized in having an intuition with that content.[11]

In an intuition, an object is present to one whether or not one exploits this potential for discursive activity. Kant says the 'I think' of apperception must be able to accompany all *Vorstellungen* that are mine, in a sense that is related to the idea of operations of the function that gives unity both to judgments and to intuitions (B131). An object is present to a subject in an intuition whether or not the 'I think' accompanies any of the intuition's content. But any of the content of an intuition must be able to be accompanied by the 'I think'. And for the 'I think' to accompany some of the content of an intuition, say a visual intuition, of mine is for me to *judge* that I am visually confronted by an object with such-and-such features. Since the intuition makes the object visually present to me through those features, such a judgment would be knowledgeable.

We now have in view two ways in which intuitions enable knowledgeable judgments.

One is the way I have just described. A potential for discursive activity is already there in an intuition's having its content. And one can exploit some of that potential in a knowledgeable judgment that redeploys some of the content of the intuition. In the kind of case that first opens up this possibility, one adds a reference to the first person. When the 'I think' accompanies some content provided in an intuition, that yields a knowledgeable judgment that I am confronted by an object with such-and-such features. But being in a position to make such a judgment is being in a position to judge that there is an object with such-and-such features at such-and-such a location. One need not explicitly refer to oneself in a judgment whose status as knowledgeable depends on its being a discursive exploitation of some of the content of an intuition.

The other way intuitions make knowledge possible is the way I illustrated with my knowledge that a bird I see is a cardinal. Here a knowledgeable judgment enabled by an intuition has content that goes beyond the content of the intuition. The intuition makes something perceptually present to the subject, and the subject recognizes that thing as an instance of a kind. Or as an individual; it seems reasonable to find a corresponding structure in a case in which an experience enables one to know noninferentially who it is that one is perceptually presented with.

8. Travis urges that experiences do not represent things as so.[12] If experiences are intuitions, he is strictly correct. Anything that represents things as so has propositional content, and I have been spelling out a conception of intuitions on which they do not have propositional content. But though Travis is right about the letter of the thesis that experiences represent things as so, he is wrong about the spirit, as we can see by considering the first of those two ways in which intuitions enable judgments that are knowledgeable. Though they are not discursive, intuitions have content of a sort that embodies an immediate potential for exploiting that same content in knowledgeable judgments. Intuitions immediately reveal things to be the way they would be judged to be in those judgments.

When Sellars introduces the conceptual character he attributes to experiences, he describes experiences as 'so to speak, making' claims or 'containing' claims.[13] If experiences are intuitions, that is similarly wrong in the letter but right in spirit. Intuitions do not have the sort of content claims have. But intuitions immediately reveal things to be as they would be claimed to be in claims that would be no more than a discursive exploitation of some of the content of the intuitions.

When Travis says experiences do not represent things as so, he does not mean that experiences are intuitions in the sense I have been explaining. He says experience is not a case of intentionality, and I think it is fair to understand him as denying that conceptual capacities are in play in experience at all. Visual experiences bring our surroundings into view; that should be common ground. Travis's idea is that the way experience makes knowledge available can be understood, across the board, on the model of how an experience might enable me to know that what I see is a cardinal. In Travis's picture conceptual capacities are in play only in our making what we can of what visual experiences anyway bring into view for us, independently of any operation of our conceptual capacities.[14] In Travis's picture, having things in view does not draw on conceptual capacities. And if it does not draw on conceptual capacities, having things in view must be provided for by sensibility alone.

The trouble with this is that it is a form of the Myth of the Given. We do not fall into the Myth just by supposing that features of our surroundings are given to us in visual experience. But in Travis's picture that givenness becomes a case of Givenness.

Travis thinks the idea that experiences have content conflicts with the idea that experience directly brings our surroundings into view. He is not alone in this.[15] Wanting, as is reasonable, to keep the idea that experience directly brings our surroundings into view, he is led to deny that experiences have content. But there is no conflict. Intuitions as I have explained them directly bring objects into view through bringing their perceptible properties into view. Intuitions do that precisely by having the kind of content they have.

If intuitions make knowledge available to us, merely seeming intuitions merely seem to make knowledge available to us. It is often thought that when people urge that experiences have content, they are responding to a felt need to accommodate the fact that experience can mislead us.[16] But the proper ground for crediting experiences with content is that we must avoid the Myth of the Given. Making room for misleading experiences is a routine by-product.

9. Donald Davidson claims that 'nothing can count as a reason for holding a belief except another belief'.[17] His point is to deny that beliefs can be displayed as rational in the light of episodes or states in sensory consciousness—unless that means they can be displayed as rational in the light of *beliefs about* episodes or states in sensory consciousness. That would put the potential rational relevance to beliefs of episodes or states in sensory consciousness on a level with the potential rational relevance to beliefs of anything at all that one might have beliefs about.

In previous work, I took it that Davidson's slogan reflects an insight: that conceptual capacities must be in play not only in rationally forming beliefs or making judgments, but also in having the rational entitlements one exploits in doing that. But I urged that the insight, so understood, permits judgments to be displayed as rational in the light of experiences themselves, not just in the light of beliefs about experiences, since we can understand experiences as actualizations of conceptual capacities.[18]

Trying to spell out this possibility, which I found missing from Davidson's picture, I made one of the assumptions I have here renounced: that if experiences are actualizations of conceptual capacities, they must have propositional content. That gave Davidson an opening for a telling response. Davidson argued that if by 'experience' we mean something with propositional content, it can only be a case of taking things to be so, distinctive in being caused by the impact of the environment on our sensory apparatus. But of course his picture includes such things. So I was wrong, he claimed, to suppose there is anything missing from his picture.[19]

I want to insist, against Davidson, that experiencing is not taking things to be so. As Travis urges, our visual experiences bring our surroundings into view. Some of what we are thereby entitled to take to be so, in judgments that would be rational given what is visually present to us, we do take to be so. But even when we detach belief-acquisition from explicitly judging things to be so, as we should, we exaggerate the extent of the doxastic activity experience prompts in us if we suppose we acquire all the beliefs we would be entitled to by what we have in view.

So I agree with Travis that visual experiences just bring our surroundings into view, thereby entitling us to take certain things to be so, but leaving it a further question what, if anything, we do take to be so. But as I have argued, Travis's version of that thought falls into the Myth of the Given. And if we avoid the Myth by conceiving experiences as actualizations of conceptual capacities, while retaining the assumption that that requires crediting experiences with propositional content, Davidson's point seems well taken. If experiences have propositional content, it is hard to deny that experiencing is taking things to be so, rather than what I want: a different kind of thing that entitles us to take things to be so.

If experience comprises intuitions, there is a way between these positions. Intuitions bring our surroundings into view, but not in an operation of mere sensibility, so we avoid Travis's form of the Myth of the Given. But the conceptual content that allows us to avoid the Myth is intuitional, not propositional, so experiencing is not taking things to be so. In bringing our surroundings into view, experiences entitle us to take things to be so; whether we do is a further question.

As I said, there are two ways in which experience, conceived as comprising intuitions, entitles us to moves with discursive content. It entitles us to judgments that would exploit some of the content of an intuition, and it figures in our entitlement to judgments that would go beyond that content in ways that reflect capacities to recognize things made present to one in an intuition. But as I have insisted, in intuiting itself we do not deal discursively with content.

I mentioned Sellars's proposal that the content of an intuition might be captured, in part, by a form of words like 'this red cube'. Content so expressed would be fragmentary discursive content. It might be part of the content of a judgment warranted in the second of those two ways, where what one judges includes, over and above content contained in the intuition itself, concepts whose figuring in the judgment reflects recognitional capacities brought to bear on something the intuition makes present to one. Thus, a bit of discourse that begins 'This red cube . . . ' might go on ' . . . is the one I saw yesterday'.

I think this indicates that Sellars's proposal is useful only up to a point. It might seem to imply that intuitional content is essentially fragmentary discursive content. But intuitional content is not discursive content at all. Having something in view, say a red cube, can be complete in itself. Having something in view can enable a demonstrative expression, or an analogue in judgment, that one might use in making explicit something one takes to be so, but the potential need not be actualized.

10. Davidson's slogan as it stands restricts the way beliefs can be displayed as rational to exploitations of *inferential* structures. It implies that giving a reason for holding a belief is depicting the content of the belief as the conclusion of an inference with the content of another belief as a premise.

I proposed to modify Davidson's slogan by saying that not only beliefs but also experiences can be reasons for belief. And according to my old assumption experiences have the same kind of content as beliefs. So it was understandable that I should be taken to be recommending an inferential, or at least quasi-inferential, conception of the way experience entitles us to perceptual beliefs.[20]

That was not what I intended. I did not mean to imply that experience yields premises for inferences whose conclusions are the contents of perceptual beliefs. On the contrary, I think experience directly reveals things to be as they are believed to be in perceptual beliefs, or at least seems to do that. But it is hard to make that cohere with supposing experiences have the same kind of content as beliefs. That is just a way of registering how persuasive Davidson's 'Nothing is missing' response is, so long as we do not question the assumption that conceptual content for experiences would have to be propositional.

Taking experience to comprise intuitions, in the sense I have explained, removes this problem. It should not even seem that the way intuitions entitle us to beliefs involves an inferential structure. If an object is present to one through the presence to one of some of its properties, in an intuition in which concepts of those properties exemplify a unity that constitutes the content of a formal concept of an object, one is thereby entitled to judge that one is confronted by an object with those properties. The entitlement derives from the presence to one of the object itself, not from a premise for an inference, at one's disposal by being the content of one's experience.

On the interpretation I offered at the beginning, Sellars's view of the Given as a pitfall to be avoided, in thinking about experience, is an application of his thought that knowledge, as enjoyed by rational animals, draws on our distinctively rational capacities. I have just explained how that does not imply that the warrant for a perceptual judgment is quasi-inferential.[21]

Finding such an implication is of a piece with thinking Sellars's Kantian understanding of what knowledge is for rational animals over-intellectualizes our epistemic life.[22] This needs discussion, but I shall end by briefly arguing that it is the very reverse of the truth.

An intellectualistic conception of the human intellect regards it as something distinct from our animal nature. The best antidote is to see capacities of reason as operative even in our unreflective perceptual awareness.

It is utterly wrong to think Sellars's conception implies that all of our epistemic life is actively led by us, in the bright light of reason. That rational capacities are pervasively in play in human epistemic life is reflected in the fact that any of it *can* be accompanied by the 'I think' of explicit self-consciousness. But even though all of our epistemic life is able to be accompanied by the 'I think', in much of it we unreflectively go with the flow.

I said that all of our epistemic life can be accompanied by the 'I think'. Sub-personal occurrences in our cognitive machinery are not a counter-example to this claim. They are not, in the relevant sense, part of our epistemic life. No doubt knowledge of how our cognitive machinery works is essential for a full understanding of how it can be that our epistemic capacities are as they are. But having a standing in the space of reasons—for instance, being in a position to see that things are thus and so—is not a sub-personal matter. It is true that the sub-personal machinery that enables us to have such standings operates outside the reach of our apperception. And there are, unsurprisingly, similarities between our sub-personal cognitive machinery and the cognitive machinery of non-rational animals. But that does not threaten the idea that rational animals are special in having epistemic standings to which it is essential that they are available to apperception.

What makes Sellars's internalistic conception appropriate for our perceptual knowledge is not that in perception we engage in rational activity on the lines of reasoning—something that might be regarded as separate from our animal nature, specifically, for present purposes, our sentient nature. That *would* be over-intellectualizing our perceptual knowledge. But the reason why internalism is correct about our perceptual knowledge is that rational capacities, and hence availability to apperception, permeate our experience itself, including the experience we act on unreflectively in our ordinary coping with our surroundings. Such is the form that animal engagement with the perceptible environment takes in the case of rational animals.

John McDowell
Department of Philosophy
University of Pittsburgh
Pittsburgh, PA 15260
USA
jmcdowel@pitt.edu

NOTES

[1] Sellars 1963: §1.

[2] Sellars 1963: §36.

[3] Thanks to Travis for much helpful discussion.

[4] These locutions can even be understood in such a way that inferential credentials are not ruled out for the knowledge in question. Consider, for instance, 'I see that the mailman has not yet come today'.

[5] Kant 1929: A79/B104-5.

[6] Sellars 1967: 5.

[7] See Thompson 1995.

[8] A form or forms: perhaps we should distinguish an animal version from a non-animal version. A special case of the animal version would be a form for talk of intentional action, which is the topic of Anscombe 1957.

[9] See DeVries 2005: 305, n. 18.

[10] Perhaps it is already metaphorical even in that application. See Engstrom 2006 for some remarks on how the discursive understanding can be conceived as running about, which is what the etymology of the term indicates that it should mean.

[11] Intuitional content that is not brought to discursive activity is easily forgotten. This does not tell at all against saying it is conceptual content, in the sense I have tried to explain. See Kelly 2001.

[12] See Travis 2004.

[13] Sellars 1963: §16.

[14] 'In making out, or trying to, what it is that we confront'—Travis 2004: 65.

[15] See, e.g., Brewer 2008.

[16] See Brewer 2008.

[17] Davidson 2001: 141.

[18] See, e.g., McDowell 1994.

[19] For a particularly clear expression, see Davidson 1999. Berkeley colleagues of Davidson's have weighed in in a similar vein. See Stroud 2002 and Ginsborg 2006. For an independent expression of a similar view, see Glüer 2004.

[20] See Wright 2002.

[21] For the idea that Sellars's rejection of the Given amounts to the thesis that the warrant for perceptual judgments is inferential or quasi-inferential, see Bonevac 2002.

[22] See Burge 2003.

REFERENCES

Anscombe, G. E. M. *Intention*. Oxford: Blackwell.

Bonevac, D. (2002), 'Sellars vs. the Given', *Philosophy and Phenomenological Research*, 64: 1–30.

Brewer, B. (2008), 'Perception and Content', in J. Lindgaard ed., *John McDowell: Experience, Norm, and Nature*. Oxford: Blackwell, 15–31.

Burge, T. (2003), 'Perceptual Entitlement', *Philosophy and Phenomenological Research*, 67: 503–48.

Davidson, D. (1999), 'Reply to John McDowell', in L. E. Hahn ed., *The Philosophy of Donald Davidson*. Chicago and LaSalle: Open Court.

—— (2001), 'A Coherence Theory of Truth and Knowledge', in D. Davidson, *Subjective, Intersubjective, Objective*. Oxford: Clarendon Press.

DeVries, W. A. (2005), *Wilfrid Sellars*. Chesham: Acumen.

Engstrom, S. (2006), 'Sensibility and Understanding', *Inquiry*, 49: 2–25.

Ginsborg, H. (2006), 'Reasons for Belief', in *Philosophy and Phenomenological Research*, 72: 286–318.

Glüer, K. (2004), 'On Perceiving That', *Theoria*, 70: 197–212.

Kant, I. (1929), *Critique of Pure Reason*, trans. N. Kemp Smith. London: Macmillan.

Kelly, Sean Dorrance (2001), 'Demonstrative Concepts and Experience', *Philosophical Review*, 110: 397–420.

McDowell, J. (1994), '*Mind and World*. Cambridge, Mass.: Harvard University Press.

Sellars, W. (1963), 'Empiricism and the Philosophy of Mind', in W. Sellars, *Science, Perception and Reality*. London: Routledge and Kegan Paul.

—— (1967), *Science and Metaphysics*. London: Routledge and Kegan Paul.

Stroud, B. (2002), 'Sense-Experience and the Grounding of Thought', in Nicholas H. Smith ed., *Reading McDowell: On Mind and World*. London: Routledge.

Thompson, M. (1995), 'The Representation of Life', in R. Hursthouse, G. Lawrence and W. Quinn eds., *Virtues and Reasons: Philippa Foot and Moral Theory*. Oxford: Clarendon Press.

Travis, C. (2004), 'The Silence of the Senses', *Mind*, 113: 57–94.

Wright, C. (2002), 'Human Nature?', in Nicholas H. Smith ed., *Reading McDowell: On Mind and World*. London: Routledge.

2

Perception and Content

Bill Brewer

It is close to current orthodoxy that perceptual experience is to be characterized, at least in part, by its *representational content*, roughly, by the way it *represents* things as being in the world around the perceiver. Call this basic idea the *content view* (CV). There is debate within (CV) concerning the extent to which such content captures the *subjective nature* of experience; and, indeed, this issue poses something of a dilemma for (CV). For, consider the content of any particular perceptual experience. Is this very content also the content of a possible non-experiential thought or belief by the subject? If so, then what is added to it, in perception, to produce the characteristically conscious, subjective nature of the experience? If not, then how are we to explain its status as an *essentially experiential* representational content—a genuine content, which nevertheless cannot be the content of anything other than perceptual *experience*? This dilemma is in my view ultimately fatal, although I do not pursue it directly here. My aim is rather to bring out as clearly as I can what I regard as the core errors of (CV) which lie behind the dilemma.

The obvious model of representational content, for expounding (CV), is that of a person's *thought* about the world around him, as this is expressed in his linguistic communication with others, and registered by their everyday attitude ascriptions to him. Let us begin, then, with S's thought that *a* is *F*: a thought about a particular object in his environment, *a*, to the effect that it is *F*. Call this the initial model for content, (IM).

Motivated in part by the need to achieve a satisfactory relation between the content and the consciousness of perception, in the context of (CV), McDowell insists at this point upon a crucially qualified application of (IM) to the case of perceptual experience, by stressing that the singular components of genuinely perceptual contents are *object-dependent demonstrative senses* (see esp. McDowell 1998a, 1998b, Lect. III, and 1998c). We therefore move from S's thought that *a* is *F* to his thought that that (man, say) is *F*. He adds a further qualification, that a person has no real control over which such contents come to him in perception: given the way things are in the world around him, and the various interests and concerns which he has in attending to it as he does, he is simply 'saddled' with determinate such contents (see esp. McDowell 1994). Thought, on the other hand, is an operation of his spontaneity: he is in a certain sense free in his active formulation of the content '*a* is *F*' in thought.[1]

I endorse both of these qualifications in *Perception and Reason* (1999). Not wishing to do any injustice to the properties which we perceive the things around us to have, though, in comparison with the objects themselves which we perceive to have them, I add a third. The general components of genuinely perceptual contents are *instantiation-dependent predicational demonstrative senses* (Brewer 1999 ch. 6, esp. 186 ff.). So we arrive at a specific version of (CV), on which perceptual experience is supposed to be, or at least involve, the passive entertaining, or coming to mind, of doubly world-dependent demonstrative contents such as that that (man) is thus (in height, facial expression, or whatever).[2]

I now think that all of this is too little too late, as it were: the whole framework of (CV) has to be rejected. Even its most modified version, above—on which perceptual experience is assimilated to being saddled with doubly world-dependent demonstrative contents—retains two fundamental features of (IM), which are in my view objectionable in any account of perceptual experience. The first is that contents admit the possibility of falsity, and that genuine perception is therefore to be construed as a *success*, in which the way things experientially seem to the subject to be is determined as *true* by the way things actually are in the world around him. It might just as well have been false instead. The second is that contents involve a certain kind of *generality*, representing some object, or objects, as being a determinate *way*, that a range of qualitatively distinct such things in general may be. These two objectionable features of (CV) turn out to be intimately related. Pinpointing them in the variously modified versions of (CV) is far from straightforward, and almost nothing in this area is uncontroversial; but my project for what remains of this paper is to work out their objectionable consequences in detail.[3]

1. The Possibility of Falsity

According to (CV), perceptual experience is (partially) to be characterized by its *representational content*: the way it represents things as being in the world around the perceiver. Such contents are determined as true or false by the way things actually are out there. On the highly plausible assumption that perceptual contents are not normally necessary truths, they admit the possibility of falsity. Genuine perception therefore involves a *successful match* between mind and world, between content and fact, which might instead have been otherwise, in correspondingly unsuccessful cases.

As I read McDowell, his version of (CV) exhibits this feature straightforwardly. Perception has object-dependent demonstrative content, 'that (man) is F', for example. This has a particular man in the world as a constituent, upon whose existence, and appropriate relation with the subject, the experience essentially depends. The content is true if that man is indeed *F*, and false if he is not. I understand McDowell's view to be that the latter is a genuine possibility, which obtains in certain cases of illusion; or, if not in illusion itself, then in cases in which a person maintains endorsement of the content of his perception whilst that very object ceases to be *F*, out of view, say.

The possibility of falsity is less straightforward on the version of (CV) which I defend in *Perception and Reason*. For I insist also upon the involvement in

genuine perceptual contents of instantiation-dependent predicational demonstrative senses. Experiences therefore depend, amongst other things, upon, both
the existence of a particular object in the world, and its instantiation of a specific
property, which jointly suffice for the truth of their contents of the form 'that
(man) is thus (in height, facial expression, or whatever)'. The possibility of the
falsity of the contents which characterize such experiences still exists, though,
and is arguably actual in a case like the following. *S* sees a man with a certain
facial expression; her experience has the content 'that (man) is thus (in facial
expression)'; the man turns away and simultaneously changes his facial
expression, but *S* retains the belief which she acquired by simply endorsing
the content of her perception: the content is false. It might be replied that the
perceptual content, strictly speaking, is identified after the turning away by
the sentence 'that (man) was thus (in facial expression)', which is true. Given
that the time intervals involved may be arbitrarily short, and that the endorsement of any content takes time, this reply is likely to create general difficulties
for the (CV)-theorist. In any case, less controversial possibilities suffice to make
the point. The initial perceptual content is the bringing together of an
object-dependent singular demonstrative sense and an instantiation-dependent
predicational demonstrative sense. Both of these must be available to *S*
independently; and each may individually be involved in a false content.
Indeed, both are involved in the false content expressed after the man turns away
in the case above by the sentence 'that man is thus', regardless of whether this is
the same content as that of *S*'s immediately previous perception or not.
Furthermore, at the moment at which *S* perceives that that (man) is thus (in facial
expression), say, her thought that possibly that man is not thus is clearly true.

The possibility of the falsity of perceptual content plays a key role in (CV)'s
treatment of cases of illusion. Indeed, it is normally thought to be a *strength* of
(CV) that it has available the characterization of illusions precisely as cases in
which perceptual experience falsely represents the way things are in the world
around us. In this respect, (IM), and McDowell's intermediate position, have an
advantage over the most modified version of (CV) given above. A major
motivation for McDowell's qualified application of (IM) to perceptual experience,
though, as I read him, and certainly a large part of what propelled me in
Perception and Reason, is the idea that perceptual experience presents us directly
with the objects in the world around us themselves. This brings with it a
corresponding reduction in scope of the possible falsity of perceptual content,
and therefore threatens to undermine the treatment of illusion as experience with
false content.

I now think that the appeal to false experiential content is not an obligatory, or
even a satisfactory, account of illusion. Furthermore, the reduction in the scope of
the possibility of falsity in perceptual content, as illustrated in the progression
from the initial model, (IM), to the most modified version offered in *Perception
and Reason*, is inadequate as an attempt to capture the sense in which perceptual
experience simply presents us with the objects in the world around us. I consider
these points in turn.

The (CV) treatment of illusion as false perceptual-experiential content can seem obligatory. For the only alternative to characterizing experience by its representational content is to characterize it as a direct presentation to the subject of certain *objects*, which themselves constitute the way things are for him in enjoying that experience. Call these the *direct objects* of experience: the objects which constitute the subjective character of perceptual experience. The argument from illusion is supposed to establish that, at least in cases of illusion, and therefore also in all cases of experience subjectively indistinguishable from some possible illusion, including those of genuine perception, such objects must be mind-dependent ideas, sense-data, or whatever, rather than mind-independent things themselves. For, since cases of illusion are precisely those in which mind-independent things look, say, *other than* the way they actually are, the direct objects of illusory experiences, as defined above, must actually have properties which the mind-independent objects themselves do not; and so the two must be distinct. This appeal to mind-dependent entities as the direct objects of experience is rightly regarded as untenable. Thus, (CV)'s defining characterization of perceptual experience by its representational content appears obligatory, since it allows the only satisfactory description of illusion, as involving false such content.

There is a great deal going on in this argument; and this is not the place for a proper discussion of all the issues raised by illusion.[4] All I can do here is to sketch the form of an alternative approach to illusion which is ignored by the argument, and then go on to explain why I think that the (CV) approach is unsatisfactory.

The alternative approach is inspired by Berkeley's (1975a, 1975b) conception of perceptual illusion as experience of physical objects themselves, which is apt to *mislead* us about their nature, although it is also crucially different in certain key respects. I claim that this allows the characterization of perceptual experience in both illusory and non-illusory cases by appeal to its *mind-independent* direct objects, in precisely the above sense. The error in illusory cases lies in the fact that such objects have the power to mislead us, in virtue of their perceptually relevant similarities with other things (see also Travis 2004). Let me illustrate very briefly how this approach handles an exemplary case: the Müller-Lyer illusion.

Two lines which are actually identical in length are made to look different in length by the addition of misleading hashes. Rejecting any appeal to two mind-dependent items which actually differ in length, as we surely must, the proponent of (CV) insists that we describe this as a case in which the two lines are falsely represented in perceptual experience as being of unequal length. I claim that the subjective character of a person's perceptual experience of the Müller-Lyer diagram is constituted, amongst other things, by the two mind-independent lines themselves, *distributed in space as they actually are*—that is to say, equally extended. Nevertheless, the hashes at the ends of the lines have the power to mislead her as to their relative lengths. It is still controversial what the correct explanation is of the Müller-Lyer illusion; but, whatever this is, where (CV) applies it in explanation of how the subject's perceptual system arrives at a false representation in experience of their length as unequal, I apply it in explanation of how that very diagram, presented as it is in experience, has the evident power to mislead *her*, whether or not this error is actualized in any false judgement. For example, a plausible account along these lines cites the visually relevant similarities between the Müller-Lyer diagram and a configuration of two unequal lines, one longer and behind its plane, the other shorter and in front, projecting equally onto the plane of the diagram itself. These are objective similarities between the direct object of the viewer's experience and a configuration of two unequal lines, which are visually relevant, crudely, in virtue of the similar projection of light onto the plane of the viewer's eyes. They are made salient by the hashes, bringing paradigms of unequal lines to mind. Thus her experience, with the Müller-Lyer diagram as its direct object, is misleading as to the relative lengths of its lines.[5]

(CV)'s appeal to false experiential content is in general unnecessary as an account of illusion, in my view. Certain developments of (CV) also attempt to reduce the scope of the possibility of falsity in perceptual content, given that it is available, by insisting upon the object- and instantiation- dependence of the singular and predicational senses involved. I claim that this is inadequate as an attempt to capture, within the context of (CV), a genuine, and fundamental, insight, that perceptual experience *presents* us with *the objects in the world around us themselves.*

The key insight here again has something of a Berkeleyian pedigree (see esp. 1975a: III), although, again, without any anti-realist implications. The intuitive idea is that, in perceptual experience, a person is simply presented with the actual constituents of the physical world themselves. Any errors in her world-view which result are products of the subject's responses to this experience, however automatic, natural or understandable in retrospect these responses may be. *Error*, strictly speaking, given how the world actually is, is never an essential feature of experience itself. The incompatibility, between this idea that perceptual experience consists in direct conscious access to constituents of the physical world themselves, and the possibility of falsity in perceptual content which is characteristic of any form of (CV), comes out clearly, and to the detriment of the latter, in my view, in the following considerations.

A first issue concerns the determinacy of the purported perceptual representation of inequality in the case of the Müller-Lyer and other similar illusions. Is the line with inward hashes represented as shorter than it actually is; or is the line with outward hashes represented as longer than it actually is; or both; and by how much in each case? That is to say, how *exactly* would the world have to be for the purported perceptual representation to be veridical? (CV)'s talk of perceptual content requires a specific answer to this question.[6] Yet it is far from clear how one is non-arbitrarily supposed to be given. It might be replied that the perception represents the Müller-Lyer lines merely determinably, as one a little longer than the other. This forfeits the (CV) theorist's preferred account of the fine-grainedness of perception, though, as consisting in the maximal degree of *determinateness* in perceptual content, as opposed, often at least, to the more determinable contents which figure in belief (see e.g. Evans 1982: 229; Peacocke

1992; McDowell 1994: Lect. III and Afterword, Pt. II; Brewer 1999: 5.3.1). Thus, we have a tension here, at the very least, between the (CV) account of the Müller-Lyer error as a false perceptual representation that two lines are different in length, although to no determinate degree, and the standard (CV) account of the fine-grainedness of perceptual discrimination, as due to the maximal determinateness of perceptual content. The (CV) assimilation of perceptual presentation to contentful thought is clearly forced.

Second, and relatedly, one might ask where, exactly, in space, the endpoints of the two main lines are supposed to be represented as being. Facing the diagram head-on, in good lighting conditions, and so on, focus on one on these four endpoints: where does your experience place it? Well, mine places it where it actually is, or at least there is no obvious obstacle to its doing so. Similarly with respect to the three other endpoints. So, presumably, according to (CV), my perception represents all four endpoints as where they actually are, which is to say it represents the endpoints of each of the two main lines as at equally separated points in space. In this sense, then, the lines are represented as equally extended. Yet, at the same time, it is supposed to represent them as unequal in length: this is its account of the illusory nature of the experience. So, at best, (CV) is committed to regarding the representational content of the Müller-Lyer experience as *impossible*. It cannot possibly be veridical, not even when faced by the Müller-Lyer diagram itself, in perfect viewing conditions. This strikes me as an unattractive result. There is nothing wrong with entertaining an impossible thought content: 'Hesperus is distinct from Phosphorus' is plausibly such. The difficulty is that (CV) appears committed to the following. Having the Müller-Lyer diagram subjectively presented in perceptual experience is a matter of representing an impossible state of affairs. For one would surely like to be able to say that what is represented in such a case cannot be impossible, since it is actual. One is seeing precisely what is there—lines just where they are and nowhere else—however misleading that very diagram may be. Impossibility in content may be avoided by the suggestion that the content of the (ML) experience conjoins an indeterminate representation of the positions of the four endpoints, as, roughly, in four regions around their actual locations, with the representation of an indeterminate inequality in their relative lengths. Again, though, the fineness of grain in perceptual content, sup-posedly characteristic of its distinction from non-experiential thought content, is lost.

Third, suppose that you are faced with the Müller-Lyer diagram. Gradually the hashes at the ends of each of the two main lines shrink in size, until even-tually they vanish. If you are like me, then you do *not* have a sequence of experiences representing the two main the lines as gradually *changing* in length—one growing and/or the other shrinking—until they coincide, as (CV) presumably contends. Instead, you gradually come to realize that any previous inclination to take them to be unequal in length was mistaken, as the power of the hashes to mislead in this way diminishes. You are *evidently* presented in experience throughout with the very same pair of lines, equally extended in space as they actually are, whose unchanging identity in length becomes gradually more apparent to you, as their similarities with an alternative configurations of unequal lines at different distances become less salient, as any suggestion of depth given by the hashes disappears.

The case is clearly poorly modelled by (IM), which assimilates it to your entertaining the following sequence of thoughts, gradually 'getting warmer', as they say in children's games, with respect to the height of a 5' 6" person you are about to meet: 'Jane is 6"', 'Jane is 5' 11'''', ... 'Jane is 5' 7''''', 'Jane is 5' 6'''''. Your false representation of her height gradually 'improves' until it finally becomes true. Provided you understand her name, you are thinking about Jane all along, and eventually represent her height correctly; but this is quite different from having *her* in view at any stage. This is not essentially a matter of representing anything as being any specific way, which it may or may not turn out to be; but is rather a matter of having that very person presented in conscious experience. Similarly with respect to seeing the Müller-Lyer diagram.

McDowell's insistence that the contents of perceptual experience involve object-dependent singular demonstrative senses is no help in removing this obstacle to (CV), so far as I can tell. For suppose this time that you meet Jane, who then leaves the room. You then think the following series of thoughts: 'That woman is 6"', 'That woman is 5' 11'''', ... 'That woman is 5' 7''''', 'That woman is 5' 6'''''. Still, this is quite different from seeing her before you. Insisting that you simply find yourself saddled, passively, with the sequence of contents in question does nothing to remedy the situation either. This may just happen, as you cannot take your mind off her when she has left.

Insisting further, as I do in *Perception and Reason*, that your experience is not a genuine *perception* of the Müller-Lyer diagram until you represent both lines' lengths accurately and equally—at which point 'those lines are thus (in length)' is the content of your perceptual experience—and that your previous experience is to be assimilated to a hallucination of two unequal lines gradually getting closer to each other in length, caused by that diagram, hardly helps matters either. For, as things are, you are presented in experience with those very lines in the diagram *from the start*, even though their accompanying hashes give them the power to mislead you as to their relative lengths. It is this power to mislead which gradually reduces as the hashes shrink, regardless of whether you are actually mislead by them in your beliefs. The two main lines of the diagram, extended equally in space as they actually are, which have this diminishing power to mislead as their hashes are removed, are presented in experience *throughout*, and (CV), of whatever variety, is hard pressed properly to respect this.[7]

Generalizing somewhat ambitiously from this discussion, I suggest that there is a tension between the (CV) approach to illusion as false perceptual representation and the idea that the physical objects of illusion are genuinely subjectively presented in illusory experience.

I can *think*, of a figure which you hide behind a screen, that it is square, when actually it is circular; but, if we insist on characterizing my perceptual *experience* as a representation of something as square before me, then how can we claim that it is actually a circle which is *subjectively presented*, even if there actually is a circle out there, where I represent a square as being, which is somehow causally relevant to my purported perceptual representation?

Consideration of perceptual illusion brings out, I think, the need for two levels in the subjective character of experience. I would myself accommodate these, first, as the mind-independent direct object itself, just as it actually is, which is constitutive of this subjective character, and, second, as the way in which this object may mistakenly be perceptually taken: the way it has the evident power to *mislead* one into thinking it is. I have been suggesting that (CV) is torn between, either leaving the mind-independent object itself, as it actually is, out of the subjective picture altogether—as in the case of the circle supposedly seen as a square, above—or forcing both into an impossible representational content—as in the case of the Müller-Lyer lines simultaneously represented as extended between equally distant endpoints, and yet unequal in length—which is therefore implausibly never actually veridical, even when faced with the very illusory phenomenon in question.

The basic worry here is really very simple. Its being the case that one's *thought* about the physical world is dependent for its truth or falsity upon the condition of a particular object out there is one thing, having that very physical object subjectively present in *perceptual experience* is quite another. (CV) unacceptably assimilates the latter to the former. Attempting to mimic the Berkeleyian insight, that, in perceptual experience, a person is subjectively presented with such constituents of the physical world themselves, within the context of (CV), by insisting that various, or all, of the elements of *perceptual* content are world-dependent, fails. Perceiving is not a matter of being saddled with representational content, however world-dependent this may be. It is rather a matter of the conscious presentation of actual constituents of physical reality themselves, particular such things, just as they are, which is what makes all contentful representation of that reality in thought even so much as possible.

2. The Involvement of Generality

(CV) characterizes perceptual experience by its *representational content*. In doing so, it retains a key feature of (IM), namely, that content admits the possibility of falsity: the world might not actually be the way a given content *represents* it as being. Indeed, it is often assumed to be a major benefit of (CV) that this feature may be put to use in its explanation of perceptual illusion. I argued, in section 1 above, that this assumption is mistaken, and that the possibility of falsity is a net cost, not a benefit, to (CV). The current section proceeds as follows. First, I explain the sense in which (CV)'s commitment to the problematic possibility of falsity, as I see it, is due to the involvement, in the very idea of representational content, of a certain kind of generality. Second, I argue that it is this way in which such generality is essentially involved in the notion of perceptual content which ultimately obstructs (CV)'s proper appreciation of the Berkeleyian insight that perception is fundamentally the presentation to a subject of the actual constituents of the physical world themselves.

The claim that content involves generality is most obvious in (IM): *S*'s thought that *a* is *F*. Here a particular object, *a*, is thought to be *a specific general way*, *F*, which such objects may be, and which infinitely many qualitatively distinct possible objects are.[8] '*F*' is associated with a specific general condition; and the particular object, *a*, is thought to meet that very condition. McDowell's insistence that the contents of perceptual experience involve object-dependent singular demonstrative senses makes no significant difference at this point. To think that that (man) is *F*, say, is equally to think, of a particular man, that he meets a specific general condition, which he and indefinitely many other, qualitatively distinct, things might, at least in principle, actually meet. Similarly, the doubly demonstrative contents of *Perception and Reason*—such as 'that (man) is thus (in height, facial expression, or whatever)'—again represent a particular thing as being a determinate general way, which, again, infinitely many qualitatively distinct possible objects are.

In the first and second cases, of thought, and of perceptual content according to McDowell, the general condition in question is identified in such a way that the possibility is left open that the particular thing represented might itself fail to meet it, leaving the content actually entertained on that very occasion false. The result is supposed to be some kind of perceptual illusion. In the third case, of my own account of perceptual content in *Perception and Reason*, the possibility of falsity—that (man) might not be thus (in height, facial expression, or whatever)—still exits, as it were, although its actually obtaining is not compatible with the availability to the subject in experience of the particular content representing it. Still, even in this case, the specific general condition ascribed in the content of perceptual experience involves abstracting in one among indefinitely many possible ways from the particular object purportedly perceived to be just that way. This, I contend, is the source of (CV)'s failure properly to respect the Berkeleyian insight that perceptual experience fundamentally consists in the presentation to a person of the actual constituents of the physical world themselves.

Suppose that you see a particular red football—call it Ball. According to (CV), your perceptual experience is to be characterized by its representational content. Let us take it for granted that this content makes singular reference to Ball. Your experience therefore represents that Ball is a specific general way, *F*, which such objects may be. Whichever way this is supposed to be, its identification requires making a determinate specification of one among indefinitely many possible generalizations from Ball itself. Ball has colour, shape, size, weight, age, cost, and so on. So perception must begin by making a selection amongst all of these, according to (CV). Furthermore, and far more importantly for my present purposes, on any given such dimension—colour, or shape, say—the specification in experience of a determinate general way that your perception supposedly represents Ball as being requires further crucial abstraction. Supposing that your experience is veridical, it must be determinate to what extent, and in which ways,

Ball's actual colour or shape might vary consistently with the truth of the relevant perceptual content. This is really just to highlight the fact that (CV) is committed to the idea that your perceptual experience has specific truth *conditions*, which go beyond anything fixed uniquely by the actual nature of the particular red football—Ball—which you see.

According to (CV), then, perception—even perfectly veridical perception, whatever exactly this may be—does not consist in the simple presentation to a subject of various constituents of the physical world themselves. Instead, if offers a determinate specification of the general ways such constituents are represented as being in experience: ways which other such constituents, qualitatively distinct from those actually perceived by any arbitrary extent within the given specified ranges, might equally correctly—that is, truly—be represented as being. Any and all such possible alternatives are entirely on a par in this respect with the object supposedly perceived, so far as (CV) is concerned. Thus, perceptual experience trades direct openness to the elements of physical reality themselves, for some intellectual act of classification or categorization. As a result, (CV) loses all right to the idea that it is the actual physical objects before her which are subjectively presented in a person's perception, rather than any of the equally *truth-conducive* possible surrogates. She may supposedly be referring to a privileged such entity *in thought*, but it is hard to see how it is that thing, rather than any other, which is truly subjectively presented to her.[9]

However automatic, or natural, such general classification may be, it still constitutes an unwarranted intrusion of conceptual thought about the world presented in perception into the (CV) theorist's account of the most basic nature of perception itself. The selective categorization of particular constituents of physical reality enters the picture of a person's relation with the world around her only when questions of their various similarities with, and differences from, other such things somehow become salient in her *thought* about them, rather than constituting an essential part of their subjective presentation to her in perception. Perception itself constitutes the fundamental ground for the very possibility of any such abstract general thought about the physical world subjectively presented in it.

Proponents of (CV) may hope to soften the impression that their characterization of perceptual experience by its content in this way constitutes a mistaken importation of selective intellectual abstraction, or categorization, into the account of perception, along the following lines. Genuine—that is veridical—perception presents a person with various constituents of the physical world themselves; but it must be acknowledged that this always involves less than perfect acuity. There is a determinate range of respects in which those very things might have been different without any relevant difference in the impact made by them upon the subject in question. Thus her perception is bound to involve a degree of generality. The general way that her experience represents such things as being, is precisely that way which would determine the resultant perceptual content as true if and only if the relevant worldly constituents were as they actually are, or were different in any of these respects.

Such hope is in my view misguided. For this proposal faces a number of serious difficulties.

First, it has more than a whiff of circularity. The suggestion is that perceptual experience is to be characterized by its representational content, which is in turn to be identified by a certain procedure which takes as its starting point a worldly situation in which that very content is supposed to be determined as true. That is, the truth conditions definitive of the experiential content in question are to be specified by a kind of generalization from a paradigm instance of its actual truth. Yet how is it supposed to be determined what is to count as such an instance of its truth, for the purposes of generalizing to these truth conditions, in advance of any specification of those very conditions? This proposed procedure for the characterization of perceptual experience cannot even get started unless it has already been completed. It is therefore either useless or unnecessary.

This first objection may be thought to provide further motivation for the idea that perceptual content is both object-dependent and instantiation-dependent demonstrative content. For, in that case, the worldly situation, which provides the starting point for the generalization procedure supposedly definitive of the content of a given perceptual experience, will be the actual situation accessible to the subject at the time. The problem is that this will only generate the right result in cases in which the subject's experience is genuinely perceptual, as opposed to illusory or hallucinatory. For, on this approach, such phenomena are characterized as something like failed attempts at entertaining a (likely non-existent) doubly world-dependent demonstrative content of this kind, accompanied by various relevant descriptive representations. Again, though, it is far from clear how we are supposed to determine whether or not a given case is one of genuine perception, as opposed to illusion or hallucination in this sense, in the absence of a prior specification of the content of the experience in question, which is precisely what we cannot have.

Second, suppose that we have somehow determined that the case before us is one of genuine—that is, veridical—perception, rather than illusion or hallucination; and suppose, further, that we have some way of fixing the actual constituents of the subject's environment which are experientially accessible to her. The proposed specification of the representational content of her experience then proceeds as follows. Its truth conditions are satisfied if and only if, things are precisely as they actually are, or they are different in any of the various respects in which they might have been different *without making any relevant difference to their impact upon her*. This immediately raises the question *which differences are relevant*, in the impact made upon the subject. Any change in the worldly constituents in question makes a difference *of some kind*, even if this is only characterized in terms of her embedding in a different environment. *Relevant* changes, though, transform the world from a condition in which the initial, target, content of her perceptual experience is to be regarded as true, to one in which it is to be regarded as false. So the question of which worldly differences are relevant is clearly crucial. I cannot establish here that no satisfactory account of what makes such differences relevant can possibly be given. So this line of argument is bound to remain a challenge to the present defence of the way in which (CV) imports generality into the characterization of perceptual experience, rather than a conclusive refutation. Still, the following four proposals are clearly problematic.

1. A worldly change is relevant iff it makes an *intrinsic* physical difference to the subject's perceptual system. This is plausibly neither necessary nor sufficient for the world to change its condition from one in which the subject's initial perceptual content is true to one in which it is false, according to (CV). Any trace of that form of externalism in the contents countenanced for perceptual experiences on which these fail to supervene upon a subject's intrinsic physical condition simply consists in the denial of its necessity; and some such externalism is widely endorsed by proponents of (CV) (see e.g. Pettit and McDowell 1986; Burge 1986; Peacocke 1992; and Davies 1997). On the other hand, the idea that an effect on the intrinsic physical condition of the subject's eyes, say, is sufficient to transform any worldly condition in which a given experiential content is veridical, into one in which it is not, surely individuates perceptual contents far too finely. For we are notoriously capable, from a very early age, of representing crucial environmental constancies, such as shape and colour, *as such*, across variations often far more significant than these. The required (CV) response that the overall perceptual content changes in some way in *every* such case strikes me as rather desperate.

2. A worldly change is relevant iff it actually makes a difference to the way the subject believes things are out there. Again, this is arguably neither necessary nor sufficient for a worldly change to be relevant in the required sense. If she is suitably preoccupied with the colour of an object before her, for example, variation in its shape, say, to an extent which would render her perceptual representation of this shape false, may nevertheless make no impact whatsoever on her actual beliefs about it. On the other hand, (CV) must presumably allow for the possibility, at least, that a change in the way things are in the world around her makes a difference to the subject's beliefs about the world entirely independently of the way things are actually represented as being *in her experience*. Indeed, proponents of the present version of (CV) have no alternative that I can see but to appeal to this very idea, of worldly changes affecting a person's beliefs otherwise than by influencing the content of her experiential representations, in explanation of the systematic effects of various masked stimuli, for example.

3. A worldly change is relevant iff it actually does make, or might, without modifying its intrinsic physical effects upon the subject, have

made, a difference to the way she believes things are out there.
Perhaps a possible effect upon the subject's worldly beliefs of this kind
is a necessary condition of any worldly change which renders a
previously veridical experiential content false, although any such
possibility is intuitively causally explanatorily grounded in experiential change rather than constitutively explanatorily of it. Still, since
the current condition upon the relevance of a world difference is
strictly weaker than the previous one, which I argued is insufficient, it
must be insufficient too: rapidly masked stimuli may actually (hence
actually-or-possibly) affect a subject's beliefs about the world without
showing up in any way in experience.

4. The nature of this insufficiency suggests a fourth approach, which is
   surely in the vicinity of what (CV) needs here, although I shall argue
   that it is either circular or independently highly objectionable, for
   precisely McDowellian-Wittgensteininan reasons. The proposal is that
   a worldly change is relevant, in the required sense, iff it makes a
   difference to the subject's *experience* of the world. This immediately
   raises the question, though, of how such differences in experience are
   to be characterized. I can see just two possibilities, neither of which is
   acceptable. First, they are differences in its representational content.
   The idea would presumably be something like this. A person has a
   perceptual experience, and we are presuming, for the sake of the
   argument, both that it is veridical, and that we have identified the
   worldly objects and their features which it concerns. In order to
   determine its specific representational content, we are to consider the
   various ways in which these very objects might have been different
   with respect to such features. The content will be true in all of those
   cases in which such variation does not change its content. In other
   words, in order to carry out this procedure for the determination of
   perceptual content, we have already to have fixed that very content.
   So the procedure is clearly unacceptably circular. Second, the
   differences in experience, by reference to which the required notion
   of relevant worldly variation is to be characterized, are differences in
   its intrinsic phenomenal character, which is prior to, and independent
   of, its representational content. Here, the suggestion is something like
   this. Perceptual experience consists in a presentation to the subject of
   certain specific phenomenal qualities. In order to determine its
   characteristic representational content in any given case, we consider
   the counterfactual changes in the world around the subject, up to the
   various points at which these phenomenal qualities themselves
   change as a result. The truth-condition of the content in question is
   that the world be within that range of possibilities. The result is a
   familiar form of indirect realism, on which certain phenomenal
   qualities are *natural signs* of various worldly states of affairs

(Ayers 1993: vol. I, ch. 7). The extent of the generality introduced into perceptual content corresponds to the degree of acuity in the signing system. This is certainly not the place for an extended discussion of this proposal. It is sufficient for present purposes simply to make two critical points, very much inspired by McDowell's Wittgenstein. First, Wittgenstein's 'private language argument' (1958: §§ 243 ff.) puts serious pressure upon any attempted individuation of subjective qualities prior to, and independently of, the individuation of the worldly things to which they are our experiential responses. Yet some such is essential to the current indirect realist strategy. Second, even if it were possible, the upshot of the strategy would be an account of perceptual experience on which the subject is entirely ignorant as to how it actually is that her experience supposedly represents the world as being (see McDowell 1994: Lect. I, 1998c; Brewer 1999: ch. 3).

   This fourth approach may be in the vicinity of what (CV) needs here, at least in acknowledging that it is the nature of experience which *grounds* the actual and possible changes in belief cited by the second and third proposals above, if they are to be germane to determination of the content of such experience. Unfortunately for proponents of (CV), though, it is circular if it attempts to combine this with a characterization of experience itself exclusively in terms of its representational content; and it collapses into an untenable indirect realism if it attempts to supplement this content-characterization with any appeal to more basic, mind-dependent, subjective qualities of experience. The right response to this impasse, in my view, is to reject (CV) altogether. The course of perceptual experience does indeed provide the subject with the grounds for her actual beliefs about the world, and also for the various other beliefs which she might equally have acquired had she noticed different things, or had her attention instead been guided by some other project or purpose. It does so, though, not by serving up any fully formed content, somehow, both in advance of, but also in light of, these attentional considerations, but, rather, by presenting her directly with the actual constituents of the physical world themselves.
   Of course there are many more possible proposals than the four which I have considered here. Still, I do think that one might perfectly reasonably conclude from this representative sample of failures, that the current attempt to defend (CV)'s importation of the essential generality of representational content into its account of the nature of perceptual experience faces a very serious challenge in explicating its crucial notion of a worldly change which is relevant to the transition from truth to falsity in any given perceptual experience.
   Suppose, finally, though, that we can somehow overcome this second problem of giving an account of which worldly changes are relevant in the required sense. The current version of (CV) proceeds as follows. Perceptual experience is to be characterized by its representational content. The truth-conditions definitive of any specific such content are to be arrived at by abstraction from a worldly

exemplar of its veridicality, as appropriately governed by the given notion of relevant worldly changes: very roughly, admit into the truth-conditions, along with the paradigm exemplar, all and only those alternative possibilities which do not make a relevant difference in that sense. A third serious difficulty is that the intuitive result of this procedure is a specification of the content of perceptual experience, for the subject, along the following lines. Things are as they are—give or take any variation that does not make a relevant difference—*however that may be*. In the absence of any more basic presentation to the subject of the actual constituents of the physical world themselves, as I recommend in opposition to (CV), then, although some determinate way things are represented as being out there may be identified by a specification of content along these lines, the subject herself is quite ignorant in an absolutely fatal sense of which way this actually is. Perception intuitively puts us in a position to discern how the world is around us, and thus continuously to update our world-view accordingly in the beliefs we form given our attention, interests and purposes. The idea that it simply announces that things are *as they are*, give or take any variations which don't make a relevant difference, is clearly quite useless in this regard.

I conclude, therefore, that the almost orthodox Content View, (CV), should be rejected. We should, instead, explore the viability of accounting for the most basic subjective character of perceptual experience by reference to its mind-independent constituent direct objects themselves: the actual elements of the physical world which are subjectively presented in such experience. Content does enter a complete account of our perception of the world around us; but only as the result of an intellectual abstraction, or generalization, from the basic nature of such experience, given the mode of our attention to its constituent direct objects.[10]

Bill Brewer
Department of Philosophy
University of Warwick
Coventry CV4 7AL
UK
b.brewer@warwick.ac.uk

NOTES

[1] It is notoriously difficult to make this sense both precise and plausible, though.

[2] Another approach to the modification of (IM), for application to perceptual experience within the context of (CV), is of course to elucidate a sense in which perceptual content is supposed to be *non-conceptual* (see, e.g, Evans 1982; Peacocke 1992; Cussins 1990; Crane 1992). This approach cannot possibly succeed in my view. For it shares the core errors of (CV), which come under critical scrutiny in the present paper, and it has other objectionable features of its own besides (see, e.g. Brewer 1999: ch. 5, and Brewer 2005).

[3] Although almost orthodoxy, (CV) has been subject to probing critical scrutiny elsewhere recently. For example, Martin (2002) objects that it is inconsistent with the transparency of experience, properly construed; Campbell (2002) objects that it fails to do justice to the intuitively explanatory role of perceptual experience in connection with the very possibility of demonstrative thought about the perceived world; Travis objects, amongst other things, that it is not possible, as (CV) requires, to recover determinate representational content from the truths about how things look, for example, to a person in perception; and Gupta (2006) objects to its basic assumption that perception makes a categorical, as opposed to hypothetical, contribution to the rationality of belief. A complete treatment would compare and contrast these objections with my own argument against (CV) below; but this is not possible within the confines of the present paper.

[4] See my forthcoming (a) and forthcoming (b) for a full treatment.

[5] See my 'How to Account for Illusion' for an extended development and defence of this view.

[6] All I mean here is that there must be a specific answer to the question of what the content of any given experience is. This content itself may be thought determinable or quantificational to some extent. See below.

[7] I now see that this line of objection to my earlier version of (CV) (1999) is very closely related to those urged by Mike Martin (2001).

[8] I focus here on the case of subject-predicate thought, which most explicitly registers the combination of particularity with generality. My own view is that this combination is integral to the truth-evaluability of any content. The 'particulars' involved need not necessarily be persisting material objects, or, indeed, 'objects' of any kind. Even the most abstract formulation of a truth-evaluable content as that things (or the relevant realm of reality) are (is) thus and so (as opposed to some other way), displays the particular/general combination.

[9] An important line of reply at this point would appeal to the direct presentation in experience of the properties of things out there in the world, as a way to capture the generality in perception. These properties are elements of physical reality, it may be said. Hence their presentation in experience does nothing to threaten the idea of perception as a direct openness to the world. Of course physical objects have all the properties which they have. I deny, though, that these are features of the physical world on a par with the objects themselves which have them, in the way in which this reply requires. Thanks to Tim Crane for this suggestion. Far more is necessary than I can provide here adequately to respond to it.

[10] Many thanks to Steve Butterfill, John Campbell, David Charles, Bill Child, Tim Crane, Imogen Dickie, Naomi Eilan, Anil Gupta, Christoph Hoerl, Hemdat Lerman, John McDowell, Jennifer Nagel, Johannes Roessler, Nick Shea, Paul Snowdon, Matt Soteriou, Helen Steward, Charles Travis, Ralph Wedgwood, Michael Williams, and Tim Williamson, for helpful comments on previous versions of this material.

REFERENCES

Ayers, M. (1993), *Locke*. London: Routledge.

Berkeley, G. (1975a), *Three Dialogues Between Hylas and Philonous*, in M. Ayers (ed.), *George Berkeley: Philosophical Works*. London: Everyman.

—— (1975b), *A Treatise Concerning the Principles of Human Knowledge*, in M. Ayers (ed.), *George Berkeley: Philosophical Works*. London: Everyman.

Brewer, B. (1999), *Perception and Reason*. Oxford: Oxford University Press.
—— (2004), 'Realism and the Nature of Perceptual Experience', *Philosophical Issues*, 14: 61–77.
—— (2005), 'Do Sense Experiential States Have Conceptual Content?', in E. Sosa and M. Steup (eds.), *Contemporary Debates in Epistemology*. Oxford: Blackwell.
—— (Forthcoming a), 'How to account for Illusion', in F. Macpherson and A. Haddock (eds.), *Disjunctivism: Perception, Action, Knowledge*.
—— (Forthcoming b), *Perception and its Objects*. Oxford: Oxford University Press.
Burge, T. (1986), 'Cartesian Error and the Objectivity of Perception', in P. Pettit and J. McDowell (eds.), *Subject, Thought and Context*. Oxford: Oxford University Press.
Campbell, J. (2002), *Reference and Consciousness*. Oxford: Oxford University Press.
Crane, T. (1992), 'The Non-Conceptual Content of Experience', in T. Crane (ed.), *The Contents of Experience*. Cambridge: Cambridge University Press.
Cussins, A. (1990), 'The Connectionist Construction of Concepts', in M. Boden (ed.), *The Philosophy of Artificial Intelligence*. Oxford: Oxford University Press.
Davies, M. (1997), 'Externalism and Experience', in N. Block, O. Flanagan and G. Guzeldere (eds.), *The Nature of Consciousness*. Cambridge, MA: MIT Press.
Evans, G. (1982), *The Varieties of Reference*. Oxford: Oxford University Press.
Gupta, A. (Forthcoming), 'Experience and Knowledge', in T. Szabo Gendler and J. Hawthorne (eds.), *Perceptual Experience*. Oxford: Oxford University Press.
McDowell, J. (1994), *Mind and World*. Cambridge, MA: Harvard University Press.
—— (1998a), '*De Re* Senses', in his *Meaning, Knowledge and Reality*. Cambridge, MA: Harvard University Press.
—— (1998b), 'Having the World in View: Sellars, Kant and Intentionality', *Journal of Philosophy*, 95: 431–491.
—— (1998c), 'Singular Thought and the Extent of Inner Space', in his *Meaning, Knowledge and Reality*. Cambridge, MA: Harvard University Press.
Martin, M. G. F. (2001), 'Epistemic Openness and Perceptual Defeasibility', *Philosophy and Phenomenological Research*, 63: 441–448.
—— (2002), 'The Transparency of Experience', *Mind & Language*, 17: 376–425.
Peacocke, C. (1992), 'Scenarios, Concepts and Perception', in T. Crane (ed.), *The Contents of Experience*. Cambridge: Cambridge University Press.
Pettit, P. and McDowell, J. (1986), 'Introduction', in P. Pettit and J. McDowell (eds.), *Subject, Thought and Context*. Oxford: Oxford University Press.
Travis, C. (2004), 'The Silence of the Senses', *Mind*, 113: 57–94.
Wittgenstein, L. (1958), *Philosophical Investigations*. Oxford: Blackwell.

3

McDowell, Sellars, and Sense Impressions

Willem A. deVries

One of John McDowell's central concerns is to understand the relation between mind and world, to understand intentionality. McDowell believes that 'that there is no better way for us to approach an understanding of intentionality than by working toward understanding Kant' (McDowell 1998: 432). McDowell also believes that this conviction is shared by Wilfrid Sellars and that 'coming to terms with Sellars's sustained attempt to be a Kantian is a fine way to begin appreciating Kant, and thereby—given the first belief—to become philosophically comfortable with intentionality' (McDowell 1998: 432). But this is not to say either that Sellars makes understanding Kant easier or that Sellars is a fully adequate guide to the Kantian picture McDowell wants to endorse. Indeed, McDowell believes that 'a fully Kantian vision of intentionality is inaccessible to Sellars, because of a deep structural feature of his philosophical outlook' (McDowell 1998: 432). The reason it is profitable to think about Kant through Sellars's flawed interpretation is that Sellars is straightforward and unembarrassed about his belief that, however brilliant and profound Kant is, he still needs correction, 'rethinking his thought for ourselves and, if necessary, correcting him at points where we think we see more clearly than he did what he should have been doing' (McDowell 1998: 431). Thus, McDowell hopes to reveal the truth about intentionality by coming to grips with Kant and his treatment of intentionality; and he hopes to reveal the true Kantian vision of intentionality by using Sellars's 'corrections' to highlight certain specific themes and moves in a generally Kantian picture of intentionality. A critique of Sellars's corrected Kant, and in particular, the 'deep structural feature of his philosophical outlook', which infects his reading of Kant, will then help the true Kantian vision stand out all the more distinctly.

McDowell's methodology here, then, is quite complex: we are to get at intentionality indirectly through Kant, and to get at Kant indirectly through Sellars. It is, however, essential to McDowell's methodology that his critique of Sellars's corrected Kant has substantive philosophical bite. When we engage in the task of 'reflecting on the difference between what Sellars knows Kant wrote and what Sellars thinks Kant should have written' (McDowell 1998: 432), the objection that Sellars ignores or misconstrues Kant's text holds little force. A corrected Kant cannot be a literal Kant. If we are going to see the true Kant through a critique of Sellars's corrected Kant, then it will have to be the case that the critique of Sellars's corrected Kant reveals substantive philosophical error that the true Kant can avoid. Since McDowell clearly implies that the faults in Sellars's corrected Kant stem from the aforementioned 'deep structural feature of his philosophical outlook', it seems equally clear that McDowell's critique should reveal a substantive flaw in this deep structural feature of Sellars's outlook and a way to do without this feature. It is therefore methodologically important for McDowell's argument that he diagnose the flaw in Sellars's outlook correctly and critique it cogently. Failing those tasks, it will not be clear that Sellars's corrected Kant is not, in fact, the true Kant, and McDowell's 'one long argument' will not be able successfully to motivate the understanding of intentionality he wants to recommend.

The 'deep structural feature' McDowell has in mind seems to be Sellars's attribution of an indispensable role in our theory of mind for the concept of sensation. My purpose in this paper is to argue that though McDowell has correctly identified a deep structural feature of Sellars's philosophical outlook, he has not properly diagnosed why Sellars believes that the concept of sensation is indispensable nor has he constructed a cogent critique of it. My goals are, therefore, modest: McDowell's destination may be the One True Vision of intentionality, but the argument he offers us in 'Having the World in View' does not succeed, for he has not, in fact, 'come to terms' with Sellars. Since McDowell's criticisms of Sellars do not hit their target, they leave Sellars's complex and profound reflections on sensation standing for your independent appraisal. Sellars's corrected Kant might yet be the true Kant, and might even be the truth about intentionality.

In 'Having the World in View' I find five theses that McDowell claims arise out of his reading of Sellars and that he believes are compatible with Sellars's philosophy, although Sellars did not appreciate this fact in every case. These theses are:

1. We need a transcendental justification of the objectivity of thought;
2. Sense impressions are called for (only) in such a transcendental justification of the objectivity of thought;
3. Sense impressions are causally dispensable;
4. A transcendental justification of the objectivity of thought would be a justification from 'sideways on', a justification of the conceptual on the basis of the non-conceptual.
5. Dispensing with sense impressions costs us *nothing* in our ability to understand experience; they are phenomenologically idle.

(Theses 3 and 5, McDowell acknowledges, were not seen by Sellars to be compatible with the Kantian structure of his thought.) I will argue that none of these theses are compatible with Sellars's philosophy; that Sellars's conception of the transcendental is thoroughly misunderstood by McDowell, and that McDowell consequently misunderstands the role of sense impressions or sensations in Sellars's thought. Because of this, the critique McDowell offers of Sellars's relatively robust conception of sensation, which is also a vital part of Sellars's corrected Kant, does not hit the mark. I won't worry about whether Sellars or McDowell is the better Kantian, nor about whether Sellars, McDowell, or Kant is, in the long run, right.

Quine, the Dogmas, and Sellars

But I will not begin with McDowell's relationship to Sellars. His critique of Quine is a clearer place to begin. It *is* sound philosophy and gets us quickly to a place from which we can begin to understand McDowell's relation to Sellars.

According to McDowell, the second dogma of empiricism that Quine criticizes is 'that "empirical significance" can be parcelled out statement by statement among the body of statements that express our view of the empirical world' (McDowell 1994: 129).[1] McDowell accepts Quine's criticism of the dogma. Along with Quine and Sellars, he rejects epistemological atomism.

Quine identifies the root of both dogmas of empiricism as the 'feeling that the truth of a statement is somehow analyzable into a linguistic component and a factual component' ('Two Dogmas of Empiricism', *Philosophical Review* version p. 38). Furthermore, the 'factual component must, if we are empiricists, boil down to a range of confirmatory experiences' (Ibid., pp. 38–39). And finally, Quine suggests that it is 'nonsense, and the root of much nonsense' to believe that the double dependence of truth on language and fact can be separated into individual and isolable components.

McDowell certainly agrees with Quine's conclusion here, but he shows that Quine cannot live up to his own insights. For when Quine speaks of theories confronting the tribunal of experience, he tries to spell that out in terms of a notion of 'stimulus meaning' or 'empirical significance' that, essentially, takes over the role of the 'confirmatory experiences', the factual component of the otherwise discarded dichotomy. Quine hopes to evade being hoist with his own petard by construing his own notion of empirical significance as 'an intellectually respectable notion, because it is explicable entirely in terms of the law-governed operations of receptivity, untainted by the freedom of spontaneity ... ', as something that 'can be investigated scientifically' (McDowell 1994: 132). But Quine's own notion of experience is impoverished, it is the notion of the stimulation of sensory receptors or the irradiation of our sensory surfaces. McDowell's reaction is that:

> The cash value of the talk of facing the tribunal of experience can only be that different irritations of sensory nerve endings are disposed to have different impacts on the system of statements a subject accepts, not that different courses of experience have different rational implications about what system of statements a subject ought to accept. ... Quine conceives experience so that it could not figure in the order of justification, as opposed to the order of law-governed happenings. ... Quine conceives experiences so that they can only be outside the space of reasons, the order of justification. (McDowell 1994: 133)

If experience is something that is neither justified nor justifies, if it does not belong in the space of reasons at all, then, as McDowell proceeds to show, the notion of facing a tribunal makes no sense and the philosophical architecture that

Quine wants to defend cannot stand; indeed, we lose the sense that our concepts have empirical content at all. The world is lost from view, but not well lost.

I begin with the discussion of Quine because it is incisive and because, at least in *Mind and World*, McDowell thinks Sellars is ultimately no better off. Like Quine, Sellars offers us metaphors that promise a proper (Kantian) understanding of experience, but, according to McDowell, he also employs a notion of sense impressions that betrays the promise. For Sellars believes that in order to understand ourselves and our relation to the world, we must have a good theory of sense perception, and a good theory of sense perception will have to posit sense impressions as noncognitive, causal intermediaries between the physical objects that are, normally, the *objects* of our perceptual reports and the conceptual responses to them that *are* our perceptual reports or observation beliefs. Sellars goes to a fair amount of trouble to insist that sense impressions are nonconceptual states (*not* minimally conceptual states, but really *non*conceptual) that have no epistemological role to play, but McDowell thinks he does not succeed, offering the following argument:

> The conception of impressions that is common to Sellars and Davidson does not completely remove impressions from the domain of epistemology, even apart from their indirect relation to what one should believe. The way impressions causally mediate between the world and beliefs is itself a potential topic for beliefs, and these beliefs can stand in grounding relations to other beliefs. Consider a belief that credits an observable property to an object. In the context of a rationally held theory about how impressions figure in causal interactions between subjects and the world, such a belief might be rationally grounded in a belief about an impression. One might be justified in believing that the object has the property by the fact that one has an impression of a type that is, according to one's well-grounded theory, caused in suitable circumstances (for instance the prevailing illumination) by an object's possessing that property. (McDowell 1994: 144)

If this argument is correct, then *everything* is included in the 'domain of epistemology', not just as an *object* of knowledge, but as a *means* of knowledge. The states of our instruments, such as meter readings, obviously fit McDowell's description, but so do tree rings, ice layers, and other clearly natural phenomena. This is not itself a problem, for it is just true (thankfully!) that there are causal relations among many different things in the world that can be exploited to provide evidence for our knowledge.

But it leads us to see what McDowell thinks is the real problem that besets the view of impressions he finds in Sellars and Davidson: like tree rings and ice cores, impressions are not and cannot be 'transparent', by which McDowell means that impressions could *at best* be evidence, but can never be something in which we are simply open to the world. According to Sellars, impressions are normally in the 'explanatory background' of our perceptual openness to the world, but when they are not in that background, and are themselves objects of awareness, they are stubbornly opaque; we cannot glimpse the world *through* them. McDowell seems to assume that if something is ever opaque, it cannot be fully transparent, so Sellars cannot say 'that the belief that an object has an observable property can be grounded in an impression itself: the fact's impressing itself on the subject' (McDowell 1994: 145). McDowell thinks this leads to a conundrum: Sellars claims to be Kantian, and sense impressions are supposed to be 'receptivity in operation' (McDowell 1994: 141). However, if impressions are not 'transparent', then receptivity cannot have the relation to spontaneity that McDowell claims it must have.

> We can have an innocent interpretation of the idea that empirical thinking is rationally responsive to the course of experience, but only by understanding 'the course of experience' to mean the succession of appearings, not the succession of impressions. (McDowell 1994: 141)

There is something right in this, and Sellars would never identify experience with the succession of impressions. But describing it as the succession of appearings is also misleading, for it seems to imply that knowledge gained from experience must either be direct knowledge of appearances or knowledge inferred therefrom. To my jaded ears, the ideas that facts can just impress themselves on subjects and that experience is a succession of appearings smack of the given; the echoes of Chisholm ring strong. We need not accept McDowell's concern over the transparency of impressions. The fact that impressions *can* in some circumstances serve a merely evidential role in knowledge, does not entail that they *cannot* in other circumstances be a means of openness to the world.

The point of my discussion so far is that, in McDowell's view, though Sellars makes a valiant attempt to better understand the relation between receptivity and spontaneity, he is ultimately no more successful than Quine, and for much the same reasons: his scientistic proclivities prevent him from penetrating to the true 'innocent interpretation of the idea that empirical thinking is rationally responsive to the course of experience'. In *Mind and World*, McDowell's view is that Sellars, like Quine, hopes to let science take care of the basic nature and structure of receptivity. And such a view is in principle closed off from a truly Kantian understanding of experience.

The Transcendental Argument for Sense Impressions

McDowell's portrait of Sellars changes in the Woodbridge lectures, and so does his critique. Significantly, McDowell realizes that he was too quick in assimilating Sellars's conception of experience to Quine's. In the Woodbridge Lectures, McDowell draws a distinction on behalf of Sellars between 'above-the-line' and 'below-the-line' characterizations of inner states of people. Above-the-line characterizations place the items they apply to in the logical space of reasons, the conceptual realm; below-the-line characterizations do not.[2] McDowell confesses:

> In *Mind and World* ... I focused on the below-the-line role that Sellars credits to sensibility, and missed the fact that he has an above-the-line conception of perceptual impressions that matches the conception I was recommending (McDowell 1998: 441, n. 15).

But this is only a partial exoneration of Sellars, for Sellars retains the notion of 'sheer receptivity', and that is something that McDowell wants to persuade us to abandon. As he expressed it in McDowell 1994, (though he no longer accepts this formulation) 'We must not suppose that receptivity makes an even notionally separable contribution to its co-operation with spontaneity' (McDowell 1994: 41). McDowell wants to exorcise the line.

It is also significant that 'Having the World in View' focuses to a much greater extent on *Science and Metaphysics* than on 'Empiricism and the Philosophy of Mind'. According to McDowell, Sellars's thought has undergone an evolution in the decade between the two works. The most important change, according to McDowell, is that in EPM, Sellars clearly claims that we are led to a conception of sense impressions, the items below the line, 'in the attempt to explain the facts of sense perception in scientific style' (EPM §7, in SPR: 132–33; in KMG: 211).[3] In SM, according to McDowell, this justification for the belief in sense impressions has been abandoned. There, Sellars remarks that the Kantian 'manifold has the interesting feature that its existence is postulated on general epistemological or, as Kant would say, transcendental grounds, after reflection on the concept of human knowledge as based on, though not constituted by, the impact of independent reality' (SM, I §22: 9).

McDowell makes much of the purported shift from a quasi-scientific to a transcendental argument for sense impressions; it is a key point in his discussion of Sellars. McDowell says very little about what he himself takes the transcendental to be, but the way he interprets Sellars's remark cannot be made consistent with Sellars's own conception of the transcendental, which we now need to look at. Surprisingly, Sellars makes scant use of the term in SM, so we have to look elsewhere to get a real fix on his understanding of the term. Sellars's article 'Some Remarks on Kant's Theory of Experience'—roughly simultaneous with SM—is revealing on this score. There he tells us that 'The task of "transcendental logic" is to explicate the concept of a mind that gains knowledge of the world of which it is a part' (KTE, §13, in KTM: 271). This echoes a similar formulation from Sellars's very earliest essays, so he is clearly not articulating a new conception of transcendental logic here.[4] His most complete statement is also in KTE.

> 40. To construe the concepts of meaning, truth, and knowledge as metalinguistic concepts pertaining to linguistic behavior (and disposi-tions to behave) involves construing the latter as governed by *ought-to-bes* which are actualized as uniformities by the training that transmits

language from generation to generation. Thus, if logical and (more broadly) epistemic categories express general features of the *ought-to-bes* (and corresponding uniformities) which are necessary to the function of language as a cognitive instrument, epistemology, in this context, becomes the theory of this functioning—in short *transcendental linguistics*.

41. Transcendental linguistics differs from empirical linguistics in two ways: (1) it is concerned with language as conforming to epistemic norms which are themselves formulated in the language; (2) it is general in the sense in which what Carnap describes as 'general syntax' is general; i.e., it is not limited to the epistemic functioning of historical languages in the actual world. It attempts to delineate the general features that would be common to the epistemic functioning of any language in any possible world. As I once put it, epistemology, in the 'new way of words' is the theory of what it is to be a language that is about a world in which it is used. (KTE in KTM: 281)

In Sellars's view, then, transcendental logic is concerned with concepts as conforming to epistemic norms that are themselves conceptualized in the framework; it is a metaconceptual discipline aimed at understanding the most general conditions on a conceptual framework's being about the world in which it is used. Transcendental concepts and principles are those meta-level concepts and principles that are essential to understanding how a conceptual framework can be about the world in which it occurs.

Concepts can have both an empirical, object-level use, and a transcendental use at the metalevel; thus Sellars's warning to distinguish those uses in the case of spatio-temporal concepts. But McDowell at one point talks of visual *impressions* playing a transcendental role, and tries to understand the opacity or transparency of sensations in terms of whether a particular sensation is functioning transcendentally. I think this is a confusion. Only concepts and the principles they occur in function transcendentally. There are no meta-level sense impressions, though there are certainly meta-level concepts pertaining to the sensory. So the first important point about Sellars's use of 'transcendental' is that it applies to concepts and principles, not individuals or particulars and not sense impressions.

Second, while the passages I've quoted from Sellars seem to emphasize the distinction between the empirical and the transcendental, in the context of Sellars's overall position, this distinction cannot be taken to be absolute. For Kant, of course, the empirical/transcendental distinction is a distinction between kinds of knowledge that are absolutely distinct. Transcendental concepts and principles are, in the rigid and static Kantian conception, immutable and innate. Because they are necessary conditions of possible experience, actual experience cannot be relevant to their justification. But as Kantian as he may be, Sellars cannot accept this view. Categories, in Sellars's view, are mutable, so are transcendental principles, at least in the sense that their determinate content is not fixed independently of experience; it is only because of such mutability that he can take seriously the idea that the scientific image can challenge the manifest image. The determinate categorial structure of the language/conceptual framework with which we confront the world is, in Sellars's view, subject to revision and correction in the light of controlled experience. One of Sellars's main goals in his philosophical career is to show how crucial features of any recognizable and usable conceptual framework can be general, highly abstract, and *empirically sensitive* yet *also* play a transcendental role. For Sellars, the transcendental/empirical distinction is methodological, not a substantive distinction in kinds of truths or ontological domains. This is the key, in an otherwise deeply Kantian approach, to avoiding Kant's innatism and mobilizing Peirce's insight that the rationality of inquiry rests principally on its self-correcting character.[5] It is also the key to resolving the major problem facing every modern Kantian: what to do about the thing-in-itself, a topic on which McDowell is notably mute.

In this context we can see that if the transcendental grounds on which the manifold of sense is postulated are that it is one of the 'general features that would be common to the epistemic functioning of' any finite, receptive mind like ours, then there has been no important change in his position from EPM, just greater clarity about the relevant level of abstraction and a re-contextualizing of the problematic in explicitly Kantian terms.

We are now clearer about what Sellars meant by his remark, and we can turn to what McDowell thinks he meant. First, McDowell contends that in SM, the explanandum for which Sellars posits sense impressions as the explanans is the very objectivity of thought itself.[6] Second, McDowell contends that the Sellarsian transcendental justification of the objectivity of thought must be from 'sideways on', that is, must attempt to provide us with a justification of the objectivity of the conceptual on a basis that is itself outside the conceptual realm. McDowell is wrong on both counts.

The notion of *receptivity* is important to understanding the objectivity of thought. But the notion of sensation as a purely nonconceptual state does not automatically fall out of the notion of receptivity—otherwise Kant's insight would not be as profound nor his confusions on the issue as understandable. The full force of the idea of nonconceptual sensory states comes through only at a finer-grained level of consideration.

When one looks carefully at Sellars's elaboration of the 'sense impression inference' in SM I, Parts IV and V: §§41–59, it becomes evident that the explanandum that Sellars thinks requires his particularly robust notion of sense impressions is not, as McDowell asserts, the objectivity of thought itself, but why our immediate and (importantly) *minimal* conceptual responses to the world have the structure they do. By 'minimal conceptual representations' Sellars means conceptual representations of the presence of the proper and common sensibles. When Sellars says of the sense impression inference that 'its primary purpose is to explain the occurrence of certain *conceptual* representations in perceptual activity' (SM, I §42: 17), McDowell apparently thinks he means that the sense impression inference is part of an explanation of the conceptuality of these representations, of their very ability to have conceptual content. But Sellars immediately goes on to say that 'The representations I have in mind are those which are characteristic of what we have called "minimal conceptual representations"' (SM, I §42: 17); that means that sensations play a role in explaining why a restricted class of conceptual representations have the particular conceptual content they do. This is a very different matter from justifying the conceptuality of our representations generally. To have conceptual representations of the sensibles is to have representations the content of which is, in part, constituted by relationships to other representations, which relationships trace out the structures of color space, taste space, etc. The structures of our actual and counterfactual minimal conceptual responses, Sellars argues in several places, can be adequately accounted for only by positing ranges of sensory impressions, the structures of which are isomorphic to the qualitative spaces specified by our minimal conceptual responses and the concepts of which are analogous to the concepts of the sensible qualities we report on in our minimal conceptual responses to the world. We have the particular concepts of proper and common sensibles we do, because they map the intrinsic nature and structure of our sense impressions, though it has taken us millenia to realize this. McDowell is prevented from seeing this crucial thesis in Sellars's theory of the sensory, because he believes that sensations are, in fact, causally idle.

Are Sense Impressions Causally Idle?

As you no doubt recall, early in EPM, Sellars claims that the notion of sense impressions, one of the two notions that empiricism has improperly 'mongre-lized', is introduced because of the need for a quasi-scientific explanation of the facts of sensory perception. According to McDowell, however,

> [T]he question that the explanation is to answer seems to be this, to put it in terms that become available during the execution of Sellars's program: How is it that the *same* claim would be 'contained' in, say, each member of a trio of possible experiences of which one is a case of seeing that there is a red and triangular physical object in front of one, one is a case in which something in front of one looks red and triangular although it is not, and one is a case in which it looks to one as if there is something red and triangular in front of one although there is nothing there at all? (McDowell 1998: 443)

It is immediately noticeable that McDowell takes it that the only thing to be explained is why the three different kinds of experiences all 'contain' the same basic claim, even though they seem to be very different kinds of experiences. But that is not consonant with Sellars's view. For instance, in §45 of EPM Sellars restates his problem to be that of understanding the *similarity* of these three experiences, but immediately goes on to say only *part* of the similarity is constituted by the fact that they all involve (roughly) the claim that the object over there is red. 'But over and above this there is, of course, the aspect which many philosophers have attempted to clarify by the notion of *impressions* or *immediate experience'* (EPM §45, in SPR: 175; in KMG: 254–55).[7] One possible point of attack on Sellars here is his assumption that there *is* something 'over and above' the conceptual content of these experiences, and McDowell pushes that line too. I will return to this line of criticism later in the paper.

Sellars clearly thinks that the sameness of the propositional claim in the three experiences is *not* enough. When McDowell asks why Sellars thinks that sensations need to be added to the mix, he points out that Sellars himself says in EPM §7 that 'The core idea is that the proximate cause of such a sensation is *only for the most part* brought about by the presence in the neighborhood of the perceiver of a red and triangular physical object' (EPM §7, in SPR: 133; in KMG: 211). McDowell then asks,

> ...why not suppose a sameness at this level [proximate causes of sensation] will do the explanatory work for which Sellars thinks we need to appeal to sensations? Conceptual episodes of the relevant kind are triggered by impacts from the environment on a perceiver's sensory equipment. If the impacts are suitably similar, there is nothing puzzling about a similarity between the conceptual episodes they trigger.... It seems that what Sellars here introduces as proximate causes of sensations can themselves meet the explanatory need, conceived as he seems to conceive it in 'Empiricism and the Philosophy of Mind'. The sensations look like idle wheels. (McDowell 1998: 443–44)

McDowell is assuming here that the proximate causes of sensations of red will themselves be similar or have something in common. If that were the case, then we could explain the occurrence of a conceptual episode involving the concept of red, not by reference to a sensation that evokes it and is regularly connected to such episodes, but directly by reference to the proximate cause of the sensation. Sensations simply drop out of the equation.

But this assumption is not made by Sellars and cannot be vindicated. McDowell's own suggestion or example of a possible proximate cause of a visual impression is a retinal image, but we know perfectly well that, though illumination of some part of the retina by red light is often (or even *only for the most part*) a cause of conceptual episodes of being under the visual impression that there's something red before one, retinal images are simply not required for visual episodes. The proximate causes of sensations can themselves be many and various: red light impinging on the retina, a sudden blow to the head, ingestion of a bit too much LSD. What they all have in common is only that in given circumstances they cause one and the same effect: a sensation of red. And it is sensations of red that tend to evoke conceptual episodes involving the concept of red. McDowell's argument that sensations are 'idle wheels' is just a bad argument.[8,9]

Indeed, McDowell asserts that it is to counter the objection we have just seen to be mistaken that Sellars shifts, in SM, to a *transcendental* grounding of the sense impression inference, abandoning the claim that sense impressions play a role in a quasi-scientific or empirical explanation of our perceptual capacities. I have already argued against that claim, so here I just want to point out that we've now also removed the purported motivation for such a change in Sellars's view.

Thus, McDowell has misread the motivations behind and the structure of Sellars's 'sense impression inference'. He has not accomplished his purpose of showing by internal critique that Sellarsian sensations cannot have the explanatory or the causal role that Sellars attributes to them, because his arguments are either invalid or simply do not engage the position Sellars actually adopts.

A Sideways-On View from Nowhere

Let me turn to McDowell's second misconstrual of Sellars's 'transcendental turn'. McDowell claims that Sellars 'undertakes to vindicate the objective purport of conceptual occurrences from outside the conceptual order' (McDowell 1998: 445). But this has got to be wrong: This would be equivalent to treating objectivity and objective purport, which are truth-related, semantic conceptions, as relations between the conceptual and the real orders. Sellars systematically denies that semantic conceptions can or should be understood to describe or express relations between the conceptual and the real. They are, uniformly, functional classifications of token classes. The distinction we draw between objective and subjective judgments is a functional distinction concerning the proprieties governing the use of such judgments. Objective judgments, for example, unlike subjective judgments, make claims on the credence of others and are amenable to intersubjectively available evidential support and disconfirmation. In Sellars's view, vindicating the objective purport of the conceptual in general would be a very odd task, since it presupposes forms of speech or thought already presumed to have objective purport. There is *nothing* in Sellars's work that is or can be interpreted to be a transcendental justification of the objectivity of thought from outside the realm of the conceptual.

Let me give some reasons for this assertion. Notice how often in his articles on Kant Sellars emphasizes that Kant is not trying to prove *that* there is knowledge, but rather something about the *structure* of knowledge—namely, that if we have *any at all*, we have a structured and significant amount of knowledge. In seeing his project as that of laying out the essential structures of any language or conceptual framework that is about the world in which it is used, Sellars does not separately address the issue of whether *our* language or conceptual framework *is* about the world in which *it* is used. It is the language we do use here and now. No argument could trump that pragmatic fact.[10]

One could object that Sellars must countenance the task of vindicating the objectivity of a conceptual framework: isn't that what is going on when he defends scientific realism or the ultimate ontological authority of the scientific image? This objection misconstrues the structure of Sellars's thought. He defends scientific realism, not by arguing that scientific theories *are* objective, whereas the manifest image is not, but by arguing that we have *better* reasons to accept scientific theories than their predecessors, that they are, if you want to say it this way, *more* objective than their predecessors. Obviously, claims of greater relative objectivity presuppose an original objectivity to begin with.

We can also see that McDowell's supposition about Sellars's intentions can't be right, if we think through Sellars's Rylean myth. First, pre-Jones Ryleans speak objective truths in an objective language. Interestingly, they lack the notion of subjectivity in the sense of an internal, private realm, and they lack the notion of a sense impression. They do, however, have *a* notion of subjectivity, at least a notion of self and a notion of intersubjective agreement. So Cartesian presuppositions are not built into the notion of objectivity. Second, Sellars does not put Jones's postulation of thought episodes before his postulation of sense impressions by oversight or accident. And there simply *is* no question of the objectivity of the thought episodes Jones postulates. There are certainly questions about the truth of individual thought episodes and questions about what kinds of evidence can be relevant to what kinds of claims, but Jones could not need a further argument to establish that the episodes he has postulated to explain our intelligent behavior in the world are *also* objective, that is, directed upon the objects of the world. Nor does Jones acquire the right to think that the contents he attributes to the postulated inner language-like episodes are directed upon objects in the world only *after* he adds the further postulate that there are sense impressions.

The project McDowell thinks Sellars has set himself in SM, in the course of which he postulates sense impressions, is, in fact, a project that Sellars would not have recognized as either sensible or coherent. There is a tempting diagnosis of McDowell's confusion that I'm sure is oversimple, but might contain a grain of truth. McDowell seems still entranced by Quine's image of a network of beliefs or judgments that impinges on the world only at the outer edges—and sensations would be the boundary points, sitting comfortably neither inside nor outside the net. Furthermore, the idea that there is such a boundary seems to McDowell equivalent to a commitment to a given. Thus, allowing (or requiring) sense impressions to play an important role in knowledge (or giving a transcendental justification of the concept of a sense impression) seems to him to violate the very heart of Sellars's critique of the given. But the Quinean image is misleading here; it does not build into itself the reflective structure of the conceptual realm and is itself too reminiscent of the Cartesian picture of a mind that contacts the world only via sensation. A more appropriate image for Sellars's way of thinking eliminates the idea that there is a distinctive 'outer edge' where the world impacts an otherwise unworldly realm of concepts and judgments. In Sellars's view, any conceptual framework worthy of the name contains, *inter alia*, conceptions of persons, of physical objects, and of the causal intercourse between the two in virtue of which persons know themselves and the world around them. This general categorial structure can be filled in in many different ways, and the determinate form we give these categorial concepts is something we refine in the course of our collective experience. Sellars thinks we are led to believe in non-conceptual sense impressions, not because we need something outside the network of concepts to hold it up or connect it to some outside reality, but because, in filling in the general notion of a causal intercourse between persons and objects in virtue of which they obtain knowledge of those objects, we encounter structures of fact that require a causal mediator: illusions, hallucinations, and the like, even at the conceptually minimal level. It is, I take it, a *contingent* fact about us and the world that we are subject to such episodes, yet it has transcendental consequences, for without a notion of sense impressions, we cannot properly fill in our story about how persons interact with objects. There is no sideways-on view from outside in this imagery, only the requirement that one be able to fill in one's story of the world reasonably, justifiably, and, ultimately, truly. The image to hold on to here is that of *filling in* a story, not a transmission of causal influence from outside to inside a system.

It's time for a little review. So far, we've seen that McDowell attributes to Sellars the following theses:

1. We need a transcendental justification of the objectivity of thought;
2. Sense impressions are called for (only) in such a transcendental justification of the objectivity of thought;
3. Sense impressions are causally dispensable;
4. A transcendental justification of the objectivity of thought would be a justification from 'sideways on', a justification of the conceptual on the basis of the non-conceptual.

I have tried to give you sufficient reason to reject each of these claims as an interpretation (perhaps of the deeper trend) of Sellars's text in SM.

Sensation and the Phenomenology of Perception

I now want to return to another claim McDowell makes that warps McDowell's criticism of Sellars's position. This might be the most serious misinterpretation of Sellars that McDowell commits. McDowell believes that Sellarsian sense impressions are phenomenologically idle.

We have already discarded one leg of McDowell's argument, namely, that sense impressions are *causally* idle. McDowell apparently thinks that, since Sellars has the notion of conceptual episodes such as *being under the visual impression that*, e.g. the ball before one is red, sense impressions, whether causally idle or not, are simply not required in order to explain why there's a difference between thinking about the Eroica symphony and hearing the Eroica symphony, between thinking about a toothache and having a toothache.

> In [Sellars's] view, conceptual episodes of the relevant kind are already, as the conceptual episodes they are, cases of *being under the visual impression* that such-and-such is the case. It is not that as conceptual

episodes they are phenomenologically colorless, so that they would need to be associated with visual sensations in order that some complex composed of these conceptual episodes and the associated visual sensations can be recognizably visual. These conceptual episodes are already, as the conceptual episodes they are, shapings of visual consciousness. (McDowell 1998: 442)

It is not immediately obvious what McDowell means by denying that conceptual episodes of being under a visual impression are phenomenologically colorless. I take him to mean that such episodes are intrinsically qualitative because of and through their conceptuality; in particular, they need no nonconceptual addition to account for or explain their qualitative aspect. Perhaps this is a correct interpretation of being under a visual impression, but I will show that it is not Sellars's interpretation, though McDowell appears to think it is.

There is, of course, *something* right in McDowell's saying that conceptual episodes can be shapings of visual consciousness; Sellars himself remarks in SK that the painter and the musician think in color and sound respectively.[11] But it is not in virtue of their conceptuality that such episodes have a phenomenology, in Sellars's view. It is a recurring theme in Sellars that conceptual episodes, as such, have no particular phenomenology. In EPM this theme is rampant, particularly in parts V and XI.[12] In PSIM it is a crucial part of his strategy to reject the idea that 'in self-awareness conceptual thinking presents itself to us in a qualitative guise' (PSIM: 32). And it is clear from the rest of his argument there that this is not a peculiarity of self-awareness alone, for it is the qualitativeness of sensory states that poses a roadblock to understanding their relation to material reality, a roadblock that Sellars denies exists in the case of conceptual states or episodes.

Furthermore, if conceptual thinking were often qualitative, Sellars's general strategy of attempting to explicate the nature of thought by an analogy to language would be ridiculous, for again and again he makes it clear that the semantic features of language on which the conceptual features of thought are modeled are purely functional in a way that contrasts explicitly with being qualitative.

Still, it can be objected that all the passages I have referred to so far make it clear only that *some*, perhaps even *most* thoughts are not also qualitative experiences, but not that Sellars has to believe that inner episodes, in their very conceptuality, cannot also be qualitative or phenomenologically colorful. Bear with me a bit longer, then.

When Sellars turns to helping us better understand the sense in which being under the visual impression that there's an apple before one is a shaping of visual consciousness, he is extremely careful not to collapse his distinction between conceptuality, on the one hand, and consciousness as a distinctively qualitative presence to us, on the other hand. A constant theme when he turns to such matters is that in the ostensible perception of, e.g., his favorite pink ice cube, *something somehow a cube of pink is present to one other than as believed in*. This, he says, is the result of a sound phenomenology of perception. And the 'other than as believed in' clause is tantamount to saying *other than as (merely) conceived of.* Conceptual awarenesses can be shapings of visual consciousness, but (1) their conceptuality is not *that* visual consciousness is so shaped, and (2) the visual consciousness that is shaped is distinguishable from the conceptualization that shapes it.

A telling and cogent passage is his careful phenomenological analysis of perception and imagination in the opening sections of 'The Role of Imagination in Kant's Theory of Experience', which concludes that:

> Roughly[,] imagining is an intimate blend of imaging and conceptualization, whereas perceiving is an intimate blend of sensing *and* imaging *and* conceptualization. Thus, imagining a cool juicy red apple (*as a cool juicy red apple*) is a matter of (a) *imaging* a unified structure containing as aspects images of a volume of white, surrounded by red, and of mutually pervading volumes of juiciness and coolth, (b) *conceptualizing* this unified image-structure as a cool juicy red apple. (IKTE in KTM: 423)

The visual consciousness shaped is distinguishable from the conceptualization that shapes it.

McDowell's dismissal of sense impressions as something Sellars has not earned a belief in depends on the fact that he has foisted on Sellars the idea that there are conceptual episodes that are *as such* 'phenomenologically colorful'. He has given no argument for this claim that is properly grounded in Sellars's texts. He is disposed to attribute this idea to Sellars because McDowell is himself disposed to accept it, and he believes that Sellars's conception of the 'above the line' states is the same as the view of experience that McDowell was recommending to us in McDowell 1994.

But we now see that this cannot be right, for in McDowell 1994, McDowell proclaims (in several places) that 'We must not suppose that receptivity makes an even notionally separable contribution to its co-operation with spontaneity' (McDowell 1994: 41). McDowell now disavows this formulation, and I am still not sure of just how McDowell wants us to construe the distinction between receptivity and spontaneity, but it is manifestly true that there is nothing in Sellars, who insists on keeping the receptivity/spontaneity distinction strong, that truly corresponds to McDowell's preferred conception of experience: not sense impressions, nor merely conceptual states, which are phenomenologically colorless, and also not experiences as Sellars conceives them, which are phenomenologically rich, imbued with conceptual and categorial structure, but an 'intimate blend' of sense, imagination, and concept.

It is open to McDowell to respond, of course, that if there is nothing in Sellars that corresponds to the conception of experience McDowell wants to persuade us of, then so much the worse for Sellars. Since McDowell fails to demonstrate that when Sellars's position is straightened out, it turns into McDowell's own, McDowell needs to offer us positive arguments that his position is *better* than Sellars's. For the Sellarsian, the relevant standard is fairly clear: Is McDowell's position more likely to be filled in reasonably and persuasively as knowledge expands than the view Sellars offers?

Concluding Remarks

I leave you with two problems McDowell has to face to fill in his position. He thinks that the phenomenology of *being under a visual impression* is a matter of the content, e.g. 'There is a red ball before me' being contained in the experience 'in a distinctive way', e.g. 'as ostensibly required from or impressed on their subject by an ostensibly seen object' (McDowell 1998: 451). According to McDowell, 'in a visual experience an ostensibly seen object ostensibly impresses itself on the subject' (McDowell 1998: 441). This sounds like it is modeled on the fact that in a *seeing*, an object impresses itself visually on the subject. It is natural to construe an object's impressing itself on a subject as a causal relation between an active object and a more or less passive, receptive subject. But an ostensible object's ostensibly impressing itself on a subject is not and cannot be a form of causation. Merely ostensible objects have no causal powers, and merely ostensible impression is not impression itself. The language of ostensibility needs to be related to the broader causal realm.[13]

Second, the content 'there is a locomotive coming' can be contained in a visual experience or an auditory experience. McDowell also needs to fill in the story about how the ways in which this content is contained in the relevant experiences differ, something more than saying that the one experience, if veridical, is a seeing, and the other, if veridical, a hearing.

Notice that this is a demand Sellars can and does say something about. He says that the content 'there is a locomotive coming' can be a conceptual response to a certain set of visual sensations, where visual sensations have certain kinds of intrinsic properties and patterns of resemblance and difference along certain dimensions, or it can be a conceptual response to a certain set of aural sensations, where aural sensations have different kinds of intrinsic properties and different patterns of resemblance and difference along different dimensions from visual sensations. We can even start doing psychophysics to trace the structures of these sensation spaces more adequately. Sellars's story is vague and arm-wavy, but it is vague and arm-wavy in a way that allows for further refinement by empirical investigations, for a causal story is an essential element in it (though not the only element). I do not yet see how to begin refining McDowell's story; perhaps he can help me here.

McDowell thinks that a 'fully Kantian vision of intentionality is inaccessible to Sellars, because of a deep structural feature of his philosophical outlook' (McDowell 1998: 432) and nothing I've said here shows that this claim is false. However, I have pointed to enough problems in McDowell's interpretation of Sellars, that we cannot take for granted that McDowell has correctly identified a 'deep structural feature' of Sellars's thought or drawn its consequences properly. He thinks all of the following are compatible with the general thrust of Sellars's philosophy, though Sellars did not appreciate this fact in every case because he was occasionally blinded by his scientism:

1. We need a transcendental justification of the objectivity of thought;
2. Sense impressions are called for (only) in such a transcendental justification of the objectivity of thought;
3. Sense impressions are causally dispensable;
4. A transcendental justification of the objectivity of thought would be a justification from 'sideways on', a justification of the conceptual on the basis of the non-conceptual.
5. Dispensing with sensations costs us *nothing* in our ability to understand experience.

I have argued that none of these claims are compatible with Sellars's philosophy. My immediate conclusion is that a fully Sellarsian vision of intentionality (or perception) is inaccessible to McDowell because of a deep structural feature of his philosophical outlook.[14]

Willem A. deVries
Philosophy Department
University of New Hampshire
Durham, NH 03824
USA
willem.devries@unh.edu

NOTES

[1] For the sticklers, we should note that this is already a generalization of what Quine says. Quine describes the second dogma as simply 'reductionism', which he glosses as 'the belief that each meaningful statement is equivalent to some logical construct upon terms which refer to immediate experience'. The idea that statements about the world are individually confirmable is described as a way in which the dogma of reductionism 'survives' even among those who would not espouse it explicitly.

[2] Let me remark on the side, for those who were not able to see Sellars teach, that this distinction is by no means foisted on or read into Sellars. In the diagrams that he constructed in his classes, minds were almost always represented by circles divided by a horizontal line; conceptual states, both dispositions and episodes, were entered above the line, sensory states below. And we should note that for Sellars, the above-the-line/below-the-line distinction is not *merely* a distinction of different kinds of characterizations; because the characterizations are irreducibly different, it is a distinction with ontological import.

[3] There is a growing practice among those writing on Sellars of using a standard set of abbreviations for his works. Since I wish to encourage this convenient practice, in this paper I will use this system of references, giving, where applicable, both the relevant section or paragraph number as well as the page number. The list of abbreviations follows; full bibliographical details are given in the list of references.

RNWW	Sellars (1948), 'Realism and the New Way of Words'.
EPM	Sellars (1956), 'Empiricism and the Philosophy of Mind'.
SPR	Sellars (1963), *Science, Perception and Reality.*
PSIM	Sellars (1963a), 'Philosophy and the Scientific Image of Man'.
SM	Sellars (1967), *Science and Metaphysics: Variations on Kantian Themes.*
KTE	Sellars (1967a), 'Some Remarks on Kant's Theory of Experience'.
SK	Sellars (1975), 'The Structure of Knowledge: (1) Perception; (2) Minds; (3) Epistemic Principles'.
IKTE	Sellars (1978), 'The Role of Imagination in Kant's Theory of Experience'.
MGEC	Sellars (1979), 'More on Givenness and Explanatory Coherence'.
KTM	Sellars (2002), *Kant's Transcendental Metaphysics: Sellars' Cassirer Lectures and Other Essays.*
KMG	deVries and Triplett (2000).

[4] In his earliest essays Sellars often described his project as 'pure pragmatics', but in footnote 8 of RNWW he says explicitly that he could just as well call it 'transcendental logic'.

[5] If we think this through, we can see that the image familiar to us from EPM of two 'dimensions' of support between observational and general empirical truths is still too simple. Sellars also requires that there be metaconceptual principles that are brought to bear on the relations between lower level empirical statements. He discusses this some at the end of MGEC.

[6] 'Sellars's sense-impression inference is a piece of transcendental philosophy, in the following sense: it is directed toward showing our entitlement to conceive subjective occurrences as possessing objective import' (McDowell 1998: 445).

[7] This same move is reiterated in §60 as the prolegomena to Jones's postulation of sense impressions. See EPM §60, in SPR: 190; in KMG: 270–71.

[8] See also Coates 2004: fn 28.

[9] The generalizations connecting the proximate causes of sensations with conceptual episodes are examples of the kind of generally good, but not really rigorous empirical generalization, the inaccuracies of which drive rigorous thinkers in philosophy as well as in the sciences to postulate theoretical entities in a framework of more rigorous (though not necessarily more deterministic) lawlike relations. This is the point of §42 in the first chapter of SM, which McDowell has misconstrued as a license to discard sensations altogether. But, in fact, the concept of a sensation of red is cooked so that the occurrence of sensations is more rigorously connected with the occurrence of episodes of being under the visual impression that something red is before one than the various causes that we can identify in the observation vocabulary otherwise available. The 'theory' of sensations is supposed to explain why the empirical generalizations about appearances and environmental conditions are as good as they are, but also why they fail. The general role such posits play in the sophistication of our conceptual scheme is familiar to everyone who has read Sellars on theoretical explanation, though there are some particularities about the positing of sensations that distinguish the theoretical move in their case from other cases of theoretical postulation.

[10] Remember, apparent alternatives are apparent only from the perspective of the language/conceptual framework we do use, so if it is not about the world we're in, we could have no way of assuring ourselves that any other language/conceptual framework is or could be about our world.

[11] See SK, I, §§34–38: 304–5.

[12] The whole of Part V is devoted to distinguishing between ideas and impressions and decrying the tendency to conflate the two; Sellars also explicitly warns against identifying thoughts with verbal imagery and decries the 'mis-assimilation of thoughts to

sensations and feelings' (EPM §47, in SPR: 177; in KMG: 257). In Part XI, he advocates a 'revised classical analysis of our common sense conception of thoughts' that claims 'that to each of us belongs a stream of episodes, not themselves immediate experiences', which are thoughts (EPM §47, in SPR: 178; in KMG: 257–58).

[13] Sellars has a wonderfully prescient discussion of the McDowellian use of 'ostensible' in SK, I §§44–55: 307–10, which I recommend, but won't repeat here.

[14] Thanks are due to Aaron Schiller, Paul Coates, and Carl Godfrey for helpful comments on an early draft, and to the Austrian-American Fulbright Commission for its support during the original preparation of this paper. John McDowell posed significant questions when this paper was presented at a conference at the University of Warwick devoted to his work. I'd like to thank him, the other presenters, and the audience for a very stimulating session. My colleagues at the University of New Hampshire heard a later version and provided further helpful comment. A reviewer for EJP also made valuable comments.

REFERENCES

Coates, P. (2004), 'Wilfrid Sellars, Perceptual Consciousness and Theories of Attention', *Essays in Philosophy: A Biannual Journal*, 5, 1.

deVries, W. A. and Triplett, T. (2000), *Knowledge, Mind, and the Given: Reading Wilfrid Sellars's 'Empiricism and the Philosophy of Mind'*. Indianapolis/Cambridge, MA: Hackett Publishing.

McDowell, J. (1994), *Mind and World*. Cambridge, MA: Harvard University Press.

—— (1998), 'Having the World in View: Sellars, Kant, and Intentionality', *The Journal of Philosophy*, 95, 9: 431–491.

Sellars, W. S. (1948), 'Realism and the New Way of Words', *Philosophy and Phenomenological Research*, 8: 601–34. Reprinted in Herbert Feigl and Wilfrid Sellars (eds.). *Readings in Philosophical Analysis*. New York: Appleton-Century-Crofts, 1949. Reprinted in Wilfrid Sellars, *Pure Pragmatics and Possible Worlds: The Early Essay of Wilfrid Sellars*, Jeffrey Sicha (ed.). Reseda, CA: Ridgeview Publishing, 1980.

—— (1956), 'Empiricism and the Philosophy of Mind', (Presented at the University of London in Special Lectures in Philosophy for 1956 under the title 'The Myth of the Given: Three Lectures on Empiricism and the Philosophy of Mind'), in H. Feigl and M. Scriven (eds.) *Minnesota Studies in the Philosophy of Science*, Vol. I. Minneapolis: University of Minnesota Press, 253–329. Reprinted in SPR with additional footnotes. Published separately as *Empiricism and the Philosophy of Mind: with an Introduction by Richard Rorty and a Study Guide by Robert Brandom*, R. Brandom (ed.). (Cambridge, MA: Harvard University Press, 1997). Also reprinted in W. A. deVries and T. Triplett (2000), *Knowledge, Mind, and the Given: A Reading of Sellars' 'Empiricism and the Philosophy of Mind'*, Indianapolis/Cambridge, MA: Hackett Publishing: 205–76.

—— (1962), 'Philosophy and the Scientific Image of Man', in R. Colodny (ed.) *Frontiers of Science and Philosophy*. Pittsburgh PA: University of Pittsburgh Press, 35–78. Reprinted in *Science, Perception and Reality*. London: Routledge and Kegan Paul: 1–40.

—— (1963), *Science, Perception and Reality*. London: Routledge and Kegan Paul. Re-issued by Ridgeview Publishing Company in 1991.

—— (1967), *Science and Metaphysics: Variations on Kantian Themes*, The John Locke Lectures for 1965–66. London: Routledge and Kegan Paul. Reissued in 1992 by Ridgeview Publishing Company.

—— (1967a), 'Some Remarks on Kant's Theory of Experience', *Journal of Philosophy*, 64: 633–47. Reprinted in J. F. Sicha (ed.) *Kant's Transcendental Metaphysics: Sellars' Cassirer Lectures and Other Essays*. Atascadero, CA: Ridgeview Publishing Co.

—— (1975), 'The Structure of Knowledge: (1) Perception; (2) Minds; (3) Epistemic Principles', in H-N. Castañeda (ed.) *Action, Knowledge and Reality: Studies in Honor of Wilfrid Sellars*. Indianapolis: Bobbs-Merrill, 295–347.

—— (1978), 'The Role of Imagination in Kant's Theory of Experience', The Dotterer Lecture 1978 in H. W. Johnstone Jr. (ed.) *Categories: A Colloquium*. State College, PA: Pennsylvania State University, 231–45. Reprinted in J. F. Sicha (ed.) *Kant's Transcendental Metaphysics: Sellars' Cassirer Lectures and Other Essays*. Atascadero, CA: Ridgeview Publishing Co.

—— (1979), 'More on Givenness and Explanatory Coherence', in G. Pappas (ed.) *Justification and Knowledge*. Dordrecht: D. Reidel, 169–182; reprinted in J. Dancy (ed.) (1998), *Perceptual Knowledge*. Oxford: Oxford University Press, 177–191.

—— (2002), *Kant's Transcendental Metaphysics: Sellars' Cassirer Lectures and Other Essays*. J. F. Sicha (ed.) Atascadero, CA: Ridgeview Publishing Co.

Quine, W. V. O. (1951), 'Two Dogmas of Empiricism', *Philosophical Review*, 60(1): 20–43. Reprinted in *From a Logical Point of View: 9 Logico-Philosophical Essays*. Cambridge, MA.: Harvard University Press; London: Geoffrey Cumberlege, 1953.

4

Three Sorts of Naturalism

Hans Fink

1.

My title, obviously, alludes to the title of John McDowell's well-known and influential paper 'Two Sorts of Naturalism'. His paper first appeared in a Festschrift for Philippa Foot, and it opens with a tribute to her:

> Philippa Foot has long urged the attractions of ethical naturalism. I applaud the negative part of her point, which is to reject various sorts of subjectivism and supernaturalist rationalism. But I doubt whether we can understand a positive naturalism in the right way without first rectifying a constriction that the concept of nature is liable to undergo in our thinking. Without such preliminaries, what we make of ethical naturalism will not be the radical and satisfying alternative to Mrs Foot's targets that naturalism can be. Mrs Foot's writings do not pay much attention to the concept of nature in its own right, and this leaves a risk that her naturalism may seem to belong to this less satisfying variety. I hope an attempt to explain this will be an appropriate token of friendship and admiration. (*MVR*: 167).

McDowell here sets the scene for his discussion by first distinguishing between two sorts of non-naturalism in ethics—subjectivism and supernaturalist rationalism—which he follows Philippa Foot in rejecting. They could both be characterized by their insistence that there is a fundamental discontinuity between the ethical and the natural. At a crucial point, they claim, any attempt to account for ethical values or norms will have to appeal to something in a realm which is not of the same ontological or epistemological order as the natural, either because ethical values or norms are man-made in a way that make them independent of and somehow secondary to and less real or less objective than ordinary natural facts, (as in forms of value-nihilism, anti-realism, subjectivism, relativism, projectivism, error-theory, quasi-realism, non-cognitivism, emotivism, prescriptivism, voluntarism, conventionalism, existentialism etc.) or because at least some ethical values or norms are eternal, absolute or divine in a way that makes them independent of and somehow prior to and more real or more objective than ordinary natural facts (as in forms of Platonism, absolutism, rationalism, intuitionism, divine command theories etc.). An accusation against naturalists for committing a naturalistic fallacy may be issued both from below and from above, as it were, claiming that naturalists take ethical values or norms to be either more or less firm or objective than they really are. Ethical values and norms are used to measure human conduct and there is a pull towards either regarding the measuring rod as something of extraordinary rigidity and stability or regarding it as a matter of personal engagement capable of motivating but ultimately based on mere subjective attitude or more or less parochial convention.

McDowell recognizes the force of both these pulls but finds it necessary to resist them. This brings him within the broad scope of naturalism. An ethical naturalist is someone who insists on a fundamental continuity between the ethical and the natural. Ethical values or norms can and should be accounted for within the realm of nature and in terms of or based on ordinary natural facts. There are several forms of naturalism, however, and it is a main aim for McDowell to argue against one specific form of naturalism which is very common in modern philosophy, but as he sees it, based on an unduly restricted conception of nature and bound to misrepresent the ethical. In the paper, this sort of naturalism is referred to as 'neo-Humean naturalism' (*MVR*: 183, 194) or 'empiricistic naturalism' (*MVR*: 186) and in many places in *Mind and World* (MW) as 'bald naturalism' or 'naturalism of the realm of law' or 'naturalism of disenchanted nature'. This sort of naturalism takes it for granted that reality is 'exhausted by the natural world, in the sense of the world as the natural sciences are capable of revealing it to us' (*MVR*: 173) but claims that the ethical can and must be understood as having a place or being rooted in the natural world even as it is thus understood in abstraction from any specifically human concern. Putative ethical reasons for action need to be grounded in facts of the realm of natural law in order to be in good standing, and at least some ethical reasons for action can be thus grounded. All we need by way of ethics can be grounded in facts about the natural world as 'the province of scientific under-standing' (*MVR*: 182), including, e.g. facts about 'what animals of a particular species need in order to do well in the sort of life they naturally live' (*MVR*: 176). (This is actually a form of naturalism that Philippa Foot comes quite close to exemplifying.) This form of naturalism, in fact, has the same narrow conception of nature as many subjectivist non-naturalists but differs from them in claiming that an understanding of the animal side of human nature can give us sufficient direct ethical guidance without the additional intervention of some personal act of prescribing or endorsing which can be performed or withheld at will.

McDowell regards this sort of naturalism and the underlying conception of nature (which it shares with much subjective non-naturalism) as unduly restricted, and as a dubious philosophical response to the rise of modern science, a piece of 'shallow metaphysics' (*MVR*: 182) or 'philistine scientism' (*MVR*: 72), and he argues that we need not restrict ourselves to a conception of nature which is purged of everything specifically human.

> A scientistic conception of reality is eminently open to dispute. When we
> ask the metaphysical question whether reality is what science can find

> out about, we cannot, without begging the question, restrict the materials
> for an answer to those that science can countenance. (*MVR*: 72)

He insists that this point 'does not involve debunking the scientific way of
understanding nature' (*MVR*: 187). There is nothing wrong with the natural
sciences. They reveal ever-deeper insights into the workings of the natural world.
Their insights are, however, distorted if they are taken not only to reveal
something about the natural world but to define it or to exhaust what it really
contains, thus excluding from the natural world all that the natural sciences have
initially disregarded in order to get going.

It is crucial for McDowell that his criticism of this—his first—sort of
naturalism should not be seen as implying any kind of super-naturalism. He
therefore argues for an alternative position that is a sort of naturalism, too, but in
which the problematic restriction in the conception of nature has been rectified.
This is his second sort of naturalism that he believes has an equal or even a better
right to the name 'naturalism' than that of his opponents. This intellectual
investment in a broader sense of naturalism is an explicit theme throughout
much of his work, not just in ethics, but also in the philosophy of mind and in
other areas of philosophy, prominently so in *MW* and in 'Naturalism in the
Philosophy of Mind' (McDowell 2004). Reality may indeed be exhausted by
the natural world, provided, however, that this is understood in a richer sense of
the natural world that includes all our human potentials including those
necessary for becoming ethically virtuous or, indeed, for becoming a scientist.
McDowell refers to a naturalism based on this richer conception of nature as an
'acceptable naturalism' (*MVR*: 197), a 'relaxed naturalism' (*MW*: 89) and a 'liberal
naturalism' (McDowell 2004: 98). He often introduces it by reflecting on
Aristotle's account of the virtues, and he refers to it as 'Greek naturalism'
(*MVR*: 174), 'Aristotelian naturalism' (*MVR*: 196), 'naturalism of second
nature' (*MW*: 86), or 'naturalized platonism' (*MW*: 91). The richer conception
of nature behind this sort of naturalism is also called a 'partial re-enchantment
of nature' (*MW*: 97) though there is clearly meant to be nothing supernatural
about it.

Basically, I believe I am in rather deep agreement with McDowell, and I should
like to think of myself as joining in the search for ways of formulating and
arguing for an acceptable, radical and satisfying sort of ethical naturalism based
on a not unduly restricted conception of nature—a search that his work helps
along, but which is certainly as yet unfinished and probably open-ended. I shall
do so by paying some further attention to the concept of *nature* in its own right in
order to raise some questions about how, exactly, McDowell's own, second, sort
of ethical naturalism is to be understood. How does he rectify the restriction that
the concept of nature is liable to undergo in our present day thinking? How
broad does he take the concept of nature to be? I shall be distinguishing between
restricted and *unrestricted* conceptions of nature. I shall further show that
restricted conceptions of nature can come in quite different, often competing
versions like materialist or idealist, empiricist or rationalist, subjectivist or

objectivist conceptions of nature. I have chosen to illustrate this by reference to explicit discussions in Plato and Aristotle of materialist conceptions of nature quite similar to the conceptions of nature underlying bald naturalism. In both Plato and Aristotle the outcome of the discussion seems to be an idealist conception of nature that is still a restricted conception. On this basis I shall define three broad sorts of naturalism in ethics: 1) materialist naturalism, 2) idealist naturalism, and 3) unrestricted or absolute naturalism. (It could just as well have been 1) empiricist, 2) rationalist and 3) unrestricted naturalism, but the explicit reference to Plato and Aristotle will allow me to comment on McDowell's credentials to titles like Greek naturalism.) I shall then go on to discuss how to place McDowell's position in relation to schemes like this, given that no form of ethical non-naturalism could be an option for him. Is his position a sort of materialist naturalism, restricted, but somehow less restricted than bald naturalism? Is it an idealist (basically Platonic or Aristotelian) sort of restricted naturalism? Is it an open, unrestricted sort of naturalism? Or are there other options?

I shall introduce my three sorts of naturalism via some elements of a general analysis of the ordinary modern use of the term 'nature' (section 2) and a brief discussion of texts by Plato and Aristotle (section 3). In section 4 I shall then be arguing that nothing short of a completely unrestricted or absolute naturalism would be the acceptable, radical and satisfying sort of naturalism for McDowell's purposes. It is, however, by no means clear that this is his preferred position, but I shall argue that he faces some difficulties on his own terms if he directly rejects that it is. As a minor point, I shall be arguing that McDowell's references to 'Greek naturalism', 'Aristotelian naturalism', 'naturalised Platonism', 'naturalism of second nature', 'relaxed naturalism', 'liberal naturalism', or 'partial re-enchantment of nature' may help loosen the grip of certain reductive forms of naturalism but that they do not really point us in the right direction when it comes to the understanding of a positive naturalism that can provide a convincing alternative to bald naturalism.

2.

Let us begin by noting that the apparently simple structure of super-naturalism/ naturalism/subjectivism has the obvious terminological problem that it involves two rather different discontinuities between the natural and something extra-natural, two discontinuities that are difficult to keep in focus at the same time. However sharply a subjectivist distinguishes between the natural on the one hand and the ethical as man-made, artificial, projected, conventional or whatever on the other, his account of the ethical will nevertheless be naturalistic in the sense that it is surely not meant to appeal to something super-natural. Even the most ardent emotivist anti-naturalist can be seen as some kind of (bald) naturalist in ethics. It is no accident that Hume is regarded both as an arch-naturalist and an arch-anti-naturalist, and that he goes out of his way to stress that in a certain sense nothing is more natural for human beings than the artificial virtues (*THN*: III.II.I). Similarly, however much a super-naturalist emphasizes the exalted status of the roots of the ethical, her account will nevertheless be naturalistic in the sense that it does not see the ethical as man-made and artificial. The whole natural law tradition in ethics with its insistence on the existence of a moral law that is not of human making and yet humanly accessible bears witness to this. It is no accident that Thomas Aquinas is regarded both as a naturalist and a super-naturalist in ethics. On a suitable conception of the natural, there may thus be something naturalistic even about an account of the ethical that is explicitly non-naturalistic on another conception of the natural.

This is a terminological issue, but it is not easy to resolve simply by choosing one's definition of 'nature' and then sticking to it. No account of naturalism should forget the fact that 'nature' is, as Raymond Williams puts it, 'perhaps the most complex word in the language' (Williams 1981: 184), or as Hume puts it, a word 'than which there is none more ambiguous and equivocal' (*THN*: III.I.II.). In this section I shall try to give a somewhat systematic overview of some of this complexity that simply cannot be reduced by philosophical *fiat*.

One general source of ambiguity is that we use the concept of nature in two rather different ways when we are talking about a) the nature of something—e.g. my nature, human nature, the nature of a certain mineral, something being in the nature of things—and when we are talking of b) nature as a realm of its own, the world of nature. Every x has a nature (regarded as something internal to x) and every x has a place in nature or in relation to nature (regarded as something external to x whether x is seen as included in nature or not). The understanding of a) is basic to the understanding of b) so let us begin by considering what it is for an x to have a nature, postponing the question of how the same word can be used both of that which is your innermost self and at the same time, and even in the same sentence, of certain parts of your surroundings where you may or may not choose to go for a walk. Perhaps it is by your very nature that you are a lover of nature.

First, it is worth noting that we may talk about the nature of absolutely everything, any x whatsoever. Individual human beings, mankind, animals, plants, things, materials, properties, relations, events, processes, concepts, ideas—all can be said to have a nature. Even something as elusive as the Japanese reception of Heidegger's philosophy has its own nature. Indeed, it is a deep root of ambiguity that we can talk about the nature of art, law, language, culture, morality, normativity, history, civilization, spirit, mind, God, or nothing-ness even if we otherwise regard these as non-natural, that is, as not belonging to nature as a realm. There is no contradiction in talking about the nature of the unnatural, the super-natural, or the non-natural, just as it is an open question what the nature of the natural is. Our concept of nature has what we could call an over-arching nature: Which ever way we distinguish between a realm of nature and other realms, items on both sides inevitably have a nature.

Everything, any x, can be said to have a nature, but it is a further source of ambiguity that any x has both its own individual nature and the nature of the species or kinds it may be seen as belonging to. The nature of x is both what is special about this x and what makes this x one of the x's as opposed to the y's. When x is defined *per genus et differentiam* both the genus and the differentiating characteristics and their combination could be taken to express what is the nature of x. Our word 'nature' is derived from a Latin word for birth, conception, coming into being. Your nature is something you have from your very beginning both as an individual and as a member of your kin, gender, nation, general kind. (Incidentally, the last five words all have the same etymological root as 'nature'.) Your nature is what differentiates you from all others. It is your own unique and characteristic way of being; your special physiological, physical constitution; your unique genetic code; the deepest and most individuating layers in your personality; the unmistakable tone of your voice. On the other hand, your nature is also what you have in common with certain others. Your nature exemplifies human nature. It takes your sort to make all sorts, but basically you are like the rest of us who each have our own individual nature while sharing in human nature. Our common human nature again is both what is special and what is generic about us as a kind. Human nature is what differentiates us from the animals and the plants. By nature we are rational beings. Our human nature, however, is also that in virtue of which we belong to the animal kingdom and to the living organisms. By nature we are mammals. We may thus use the concept of nature to differentiate rather than include, but also to include rather than differentiate. And we may use the concept of nature to express that differentiation and inclusion should not be seen as incompatible.

Everything, any x, can be said to have a nature, but what is it that x has, when x is said to have a nature? We may try to elucidate this by considering some of the expressions that are often used to explicate the meaning of 'nature'. The nature of x is the essence of x, the constitution of x out of its more elementary constituents, the defining characteristics of x, that about x which explains how x behaves, that which x is ordinarily, that which x is in and of itself prior to and independent of external interference. These common formulae, however, do not mean exactly the same, and they may not be consistent with each other on all interpretations. Terms like 'essence', 'constitution' or 'defining characteristics' are not obviously more perspicuous than the term 'nature' itself. The nature of x is the tautological explanation of the behaviour or conduct of x, but what is demanded and what suffices as explanation under given circumstances may vary enormously. Talking about the nature of x as that which x is in and by itself prior to and independent of external interference raises a lot of questions about what may count as external (human, divine, unusual?) interference, questions that have no resolution on a conceptual level. All such circumscriptions take the nature of x to be something about x that is somehow primary rather than secondary, original rather than later achieved, basic rather than superstructural, necessary rather than accidental or normal rather than extraordinary. Again, these do not mean exactly the same thing, and they are all subject to different interpretations. The primary, for example, may be regarded as separable from and opposed to the secondary, or the primary may be regarded as permeating and allowing the secondary, so that the secondary is an expression of the primary, and similarly with the other contrasts. Again, we find a conceptual pattern where 'the nature of x' may be used both to mark a contrast and to bridge that contrast.

The nature of x is something primary, original, basic, necessary, or normal about x. Rather different aspects of x may, however, with some right be regarded as primary, original, basic, necessary, or normal. The idea of nature as essence may point in an idealist direction, the idea of nature as constitution out of more elementary constituents may point in a materialist direction, whereas the idea of nature as the defining characteristics may point in a formal or rationalistic direction. Your nature may be seen either as something mental, a matter of deep layers of your individual psychology (whether instinctive, emotional or personal), or as something material, a matter of anonymous generic physiology, genetics or physics. Taken this way, these are *contrasting* conceptions of the nature of x prioritizing something we know about x over something else we know about x.

Our concept of nature, however, also allows for a conception of the nature of x identifying it with absolutely everything that is true of x. All we can come to know about any possible aspect of x is knowledge of the nature of x; nothing about x is so inessential, so secondary, or so extraordinary that it does not belong to the nature of x. It would be wrong to leave anything out. The nature of x is the unity in all possible knowledge about x. One could, of course, ask if this identification of the nature of x and the totality of all that can be known about x is really a conception of the *nature* of x? Isn't the nature of x of conceptual necessity something primary, original, basic, necessary or normal about x? Yes, but here is a straightforward sense in which the totality of all that can be known about x is, indeed, primary, original, basic, necessary and ordinary relative to any differentiation within our knowledge of x between primary and secondary, original and later achieved, basic and super-structural, necessary and accidental, or ordinary and extraordinary elements. This would be a *non-contrasting* conception of the nature of x open to any future additional information about x.

A further source of ambiguity that I shall just mention and then leave aside has to do with the ways in which normativity is attached to conceptions of the nature of x. In contrasting conceptions the primary, the original, the basic, the necessary and the normal are often put on the positive side. But not always so; the primary may be the primitive, the original may be the old fashioned, the basic may be the base, the necessary may be the unfree, the ordinary may be the boring. We may use the concept of nature normatively to express a rather low opinion of our nature as merely animal and other than our true self, as in the thought that 'our nature is what we are in this world to rise above', which a Victorian lady has been quoted as saying. We may also use it to express a rather high opinion of our nature as deeply personal and identical with our true—but endangered—self, as in the thought that 'even in what people do for pleasure, conformity is the first thing thought of; (. . .); until by dint of not following their own nature they have no nature to follow;' to quote another Victorian, John Stuart Mill (Mill 1977: 265). We can, however, also use the concept of nature non-normatively to express the thought that our nature is what we cannot help exemplify. We are by nature just the way we are. This non-contrasting, non-normative usage, however, has the normative edge to it that there must be something misleading about both of the quoted Victorian thoughts. On this conception our nature is something we can neither raise above nor lose.

To sum up: Our use of the term 'the nature of x' displays a highly complex combination of excluding and including, contrasting and non-contrasting, restricted and unrestricted uses. The excluding, contrasting and restricted uses may be used to mark many different differences. There is no single contrast that is inevitably being appealed to.

We come now to contexts where we talk about nature in general, the realm of nature. We can approach this by replacing 'x' with 'everything' or 'the world' in the question 'What is the nature of x?' This brings us to questions like: What is the essence, the constitution, the defining characteristic of all there is? What explains how the whole world behaves? How would the world be in and of itself, prior to and independent of any external interference? What are the primary, original, basic, necessary and normal traits of the world we live in? We can then make a conceptual shift from talking about the nature of the world to talking about nature as those parts or aspects of the world that we regard as belonging to the nature of the world. A contrasting and restricted conception of the nature of the world would then identify nature with certain parts or sides of the world. On the other hand, a non-contrasting and unrestricted conception of the nature of x would identify nature with absolutely everything there is. (This conceptual move would give the promised reconstruction of how the same word can come to be used both of that which is your innermost self and of certain parts of your surroundings where you may or may not choose to take a walk, and in which you may or may not be seen as included.)

In ordinary language 'nature' or 'the natural world' is actually understood in a quite bewildering number of different ways which illustrates the different ways in which different parts or aspects of the world in its totality are somehow taken to be external to or other than nature. We can initially distinguish between at least 8 different ways of conceiving of nature as a realm in contrast with other realms:

1. The world prior to or unaffected by human, cultural or social intervention.
2. The world prior to or not under agriculture—the wilderness, the jungle, the desert, as opposed to the cultivated world of the farmland, villages and towns.
3. The world prior to or not subjected to urbanization—the rural, the countryside, the landscape, the outdoors as opposed to life in the cities and indoors.
4. The world prior to or not subjected to industrialization—the organic, the 'green' as opposed to the synthetic and high-tech.
5. The material or physical or external world as opposed to the mental or psychological or inner world.

6. The empirical world as opposed to the intelligible world of the abstract, logical, or mathematical.
7. The earthly world as opposed to the heavenly world—the created (immanent) world as opposed to its transcendent creator.
8. The ordinary world as opposed to a world of the extra-ordinary and mystical.

These are all different versions of restricted conceptions of nature as a realm. They contrast nature with other realms somehow outside or independent of nature. The four first conceptions implicitly identify the world with the surface of the Earth, and then divide this world up according to whether or how much it has been changed by human, cultural, social and industrial activity. Something about human beings and the parts of their surroundings over which they exercise a high degree of control is seen as contrasted with the parts of their surroundings over which they have no or little control. On the first conception there may not be much nature left on earth if one takes the unintended consequences of emissions to the oceans and the atmosphere into account. On the second conception there is still some nature left but increasingly in the form of 'nature parks' or 'national parks' and subject to a fairly benign human control and protection. The third conception is probably the most common understanding of nature in the Western World today (at least in Europe). Here, nature includes the farmland rather than what is left surrounding it, and all plants and animals whether wild or domesticated. The fourth conception allow us to see exquisite cultural products like planed wood, roof tiles, leather, wool, cotton- and silk fabrics as natural materials. The fifth conception takes the human mind to be set over and against the external world of which it receives information and forms its own understanding. The sixth conception takes formal and abstract entities to form a world of their own. On the seventh conception human life and thinking are included in nature but contrasted with a sphere of a higher order of reality with which the human soul may have an affinity both during life and after death. The eighth conception regards nature as law governed and predictable as opposed to phenomena explicitly regarded as defying or being contrary to the ordinary laws of nature.

On top of all those ways of marking contrasts within the totality by help of the term 'nature' our ordinary language also allows a conception of nature as all there is. Such a ninth conception of nature would be an unrestricted conception. It would express the idea that there is one world only, and that that world is the realm of nature, which is taken to include the cultural, artificial, mental, abstract and whatever else there may prove to be. There are no realms above or beyond nature. To be is to be in nature and to be in continuity with everything else in nature. Even the greatest and deepest differences are differences within nature rather than differences between nature and something else.

The list of possible conceptions of nature as a realm could be made longer or be differently structured, but it suffices to show that it does not go without saying what the realm of nature is. Or rather, it shows that it does indeed go without saying but in so many different ways, that some further saying is needed if we want to make it somewhat clearer what we are talking about. On the conceptual level it is systematically unclear whether no human activities, some human activities or all human activities belong to nature as a realm. There is no nature *tout court*.

3.

I shall return to the relevance of all of this for the understanding of McDowell's own sort of naturalism, but first I shall go into some detail concerning the philosophical use of the Greek concept *physis* (which is the direct etymological root of our 'physics' and 'physiology' but standardly translated by 'nature' and highly influential in the formation of both the philosophical and ordinary uses of this concept which is itself derived via Latin from a completely different etymological root). I shall begin by going back to an explicit discussion of *physis* by the old Plato in his last work, *Laws*. I shall also include a brief account of Aristotle's official definitions of *physis* in the *Physics*. It may seem a detour, but it may help us understand the peculiar, hyper-complex logic of our present day concept of nature, and I shall, as mentioned, need it in order to define materialist and idealist naturalism and also to examine to what extent the reference to Greek naturalism can carry the weight placed on it by McDowell.

In *Laws*, Book X, the question of the right understanding of *physis* comes up during a discussion between three elderly gentlemen about how crimes of sacrilege should be dealt with in the laws of a good, but not utopian, polis. In earlier times, they agree, things were easier: every one was brought up to fear the gods, so sacrilege hardly ever occurred, and there was no doubt about how it should be dealt with if it did. Recently, however, written literature has been produced by wise or clever men claiming that there are no gods. These views appeal to the young who thereby come to question not only the notion of sacrilege but also the whole divine foundation of the laws and the established social order. Plato's spokesman—who is here not Socrates but an anonymous Athenian—explains this dangerous modern doctrine—'a very grievous unwisdom which is reputed to be the height of wisdom'—to one of his interlocutors, the Cretan, Clinias. I shall quote at some length.

> Ath.: It is stated by some that all things which are coming into existence, or have or will come into existence, do so partly by nature, partly by art, and partly owing to chance.
> (. . .)
> Ath.: I will explain more clearly. Fire and water and earth and air, they say, all exist by nature and chance, and none of them by art; and by means of these, which are wholly inanimate, the bodies which come next—those, namely, of the earth, sun, moon and stars—have been brought into existence. It is by chance all these elements move, by the interplay of the respective forces, and according as they meet together and combine fittingly,—hot with cold, dry with moist, soft with hard,

and all such necessary mixtures as result from the chance combination of these opposites,—in this way and by these means they have brought into being the whole Heaven and all that is in the Heaven, and all animals, too, and plants (...); and all this as they assert, not owing to reason, nor to any god or art, but owing as we have said to nature and chance. As a later product of these, art comes later; and it, being mortal itself and of mortal birth, begets later playthings which share but little in truth, being images of a sort akin to the arts themselves—images such as painting begets, and music, and the arts which accompany these. (...). Politics too, as they say, shares to a small extent in nature, but mostly in art; and in like manner all legislation, which is based on untrue assumptions, is due, not to nature, but to art.

Clin.: What do you mean?

Ath.: The first statement my dear sir, which these people make about the gods is that they exist by art and not by nature,—by certain legal conventions which differ from place to place, according as each tribe agreed when forming their laws. They assert, moreover, that there is one class of things beautiful by nature and another class beautiful by convention; while as to things just, they do not exist at all by nature, but men are constantly altering them, and whatever alteration they make at any time is at that time authoritative, though it owes its existence to art and the laws, and not in any way to nature. All these, my friends, are views which young people imbibe from men of science, both prose-writers and poets, who maintain that the height of justice is to succeed by force; whence it comes that the young people are afflicted with a plague of impiety, as though the gods were not such as the law commands us to conceive them; and because of this, factions also arise when these teachers attract them towards the life that is right 'according to nature', which consists in being master over the rest in reality instead of being a slave to others according to legal convention. (Plato *Laws*: 888 E–890 B)

The 'modern' scientists here discussed distinguish three types of causes by which something can be brought into existence, nature (*physis*), chance (*tyche*) and human intervention or art (*techné*). To come to exist by nature (*physei*) is to come to exist by inner force or necessity. Each of the four elements fire, air, water and earth possess such an inner force that determines their way of being and their effects on each other. The inner force of the elements in combination with blind chance accounts for the existence of many things in the world. Together they have brought about the existence of the sun, the moon, the earth, the plants and the animals. No intelligent design, divine or human, was involved. Human beings like other animals come to exist by nature and chance, but they have the special power to make new things come into existence by the help of art, law (*nomos*) or nurture (*melete*). The products of these could not have been created by nature and chance alone. That which exists by nature, however, is ontologically primary, original, basic, necessary and normal relative to that which has a secondary and dependent form of existence because it owes its existence not to its own inner force but to human intervention. Human beings may even use their imagination to create patterns of thought that are quite independent of what exists by nature. They may thus invent a whole realm of gods and deities, shown to be merely illusory by being different from society to society. Conventional justice, similarly, does not exist by nature but merely by human invention of laws—often based on appeal to illusory deities or other bad arguments with no proper reference to what really exists by nature. Conventional ethics is thus wholly man-made and without true reality and objectivity. An unconventional ethos of self-aggrandisement, however, would be 'according to nature' (*kata physin*).

What we have here is a completely disenchanted and severely restricted conception of nature excluding not only anything supernatural but much of the human, cultural and social as well. This conception of nature is quite close to the restricted conception of nature behind both subjectivist anti-naturalism and bald naturalism in ethics, so it is underlying the first sort of naturalism both on McDowell's and my reckoning. Of course there are enormous differences between the science that is modern today and the science modern around 350 BC, but I believe we should not underestimate the importance of the availability of such ancient materialism as a live inspiration for the advance of modern science. The possibility of restricting the natural to elementary material forces as governed by blind necessity and chance, and the further possibility of construing the ethical as specifically human and of a precarious ontological and epistemological status potentially undermining its authority in social life has clearly been present since antiquity and has been formative in the early history of our concept of nature. Of course such a restriction took on much greater respectability and became much more influential with the success of modern science, but there is a conceptual continuity that I see reasons to stress, rather than to disregard. At least the example shows that it is not as if all Greeks just had an innocent unrestricted or broad conception of nature that we could simply return to after rectifying the restrictions of a specifically modern conception of nature. This will become clearer as we go on.

The Athenian sets out to refute this dangerous doctrine. He does so by focusing on the concept of *psyche*, which has not been explicitly mentioned so far.

> Ath.: It appears that the person who makes these statements holds fire, water, earth and air to be the first of all things, and that it is precisely to these things that he gives the name of 'nature', while soul he asserts to be a later product therefrom.
>
> (. . .)
>
> Ath.: As regards the soul, my comrade, nearly all men appear to be ignorant of its real nature and its potency, and ignorant not only of other facts about it, but of its origin especially,—how that it is one of the first existences, and prior to all bodies, and that it more than anything else is what governs all the changes and modifications of bodies. And if this is really the state of the case, must not things which are akin to soul be

necessarily prior in origin to things which belong to body, seeing that
soul is older than body?
Clin.: Necessarily.
Ath.: Then opinion and reflection and thought and art and law will be
prior to things hard and soft and heavy and light; and further, the works
and actions that are great and primary will be those of art, while those
that are natural, and nature itself,—which they wrongly call by this
name—will be secondary, and will derive their origin from art and
reason.
Clinias: How are they wrong?
Athenian: By 'nature' they intend to indicate production of things
primary; but if soul shall be shown to have been produced first (not fire
or air), but soul first and foremost,—it would most truly be described as a
superlatively "natural" existence. Such is the state of the case, provided
that one can prove that soul is older than body, but not otherwise. (Plato
Laws: 891C–892C)

This last passage is crucial for the argument and highly interesting. The Athenian
doesn't just leave the concept *physis* to the 'men of science'. He does not first
accept their conception of nature and then confront them with the claim that
there is something extra-natural—the soul or the gods—which they have
disregarded and which is in fact prior to nature. No. Like McDowell the
Athenian is eager to have nature on his side. He therefore challenges the
scientists' right to restrict the term 'nature' to the soulless, partly necessary and
partly accidental combinations of the elements. As he sees it, the common ground
between them is a definition of nature as that which is primary in existence
because caused by its own inner force and not by something else. The men of
science claim that it is something material, the four elements, that fulfil this
definition, but if the Athenian can show that soul is primary in existence, he shall
also have shown that soul has the better right to the name 'nature'. Notice that
the soul is not being introduced as *super-natural*, but as *superlatively natural*, that
is, even more natural (primary, original, basic, necessary and normal) than what
some, or perhaps even most, people call nature.

The Athenian's conception, however, depends on the possibility of proving
that soul is older than body. Here follows a long argument the upshot of which is
this:

Ath.: What is the definition of that object which has for its name 'soul'?
Can we give it any other definition than that stated just now—'the
motion able to move itself'?
Clin.: Do you assert that 'self-movement' is the definition of that very
same substance which has 'soul' as the name we universally apply to it?
Ath.: That is what I assert. And if this be really so, do we still complain
that it has not been sufficiently proved that soul is identical with the
prime origin and motion of what is, has been, and shall be, and of all that

is opposite to these, seeing that it has been plainly shown to be the cause of all change and motion in all things?

Clin.: We make no such complaint; on the contrary, it has been proved most sufficiently that soul is of all things the oldest, since it is the first principle of motion.

(. . .)

Ath.: Truly and finally, then, it would be a most veracious and complete statement to say that we find soul to be prior to body, and body secondary and posterior, soul governing and body being governed according to the ordinance of nature.

Clin.: Yes, most veracious. (Plato *Laws*: 896A–C)

This, I take it, is pretty rampant Platonism but clearly presented as an account of the soul as natural because primary in existence and the only thing with the inner power to make itself and other things move and change. Mind is prior to world. What the men of science call nature the Athenian might call dependent existence or "second nature" relative to the soul-like 'first nature'. Both parties to the discussion have their own restricted conception of nature privileging either the bodily or the soul-like respectively. Nature is identified with either "world-stuff" or "mind-idea" and in both cases to the exclusion or the reduction to secondary status of the other.

If we take a very brief look at one of the most explicit discussions of *physis* in Aristotle there are clear differences to Plato but the conceptual structure is similar. A short selection from the *Physics*:

Of things that exist, some exist by nature, some from other causes.

'By nature' the animals and their parts exist, and the plants and the simple bodies (earth, fire, air, water)—for we say that these and the like exist 'by nature'.

All the things mentioned present a feature in which they differ from things which are not constituted by nature. Each of them has within itself a principle of motion and of stationariness (in respect of place or of growth and decrease, or by way of alteration). On the other hand, a bed and a coat and anything else of that sort, qua receiving these designations—i.e. in so far as they are products of art—have no innate impulse to change. But in so far as they happen to be composed of stone or of earth or of a mixture of the two, they do have such an impulse, and just to that extent—which seems to indicate that nature is a source or cause of being moved and being at rest in that to which it belongs primarily, (. . .)

(. . .)

Some identify the nature or substance of a natural object with that immediate constituent of it which taken by itself is without arrangement, e.g. the wood is the 'nature' of the bed, and the bronze the 'nature' of the statue.

(...)

Another account is that 'nature' is the shape or form which is specified in the definition of the thing. (...) (not separable except in statement). (...)

The form indeed is 'nature' rather than the matter; for a thing is more properly said to be what it is when it has attained to fulfilment than when it exists potentially. (Aristotle *Physics*: 2, 1, (192 b 7–193 b 12))

The discussion is mainly concerned with how to understand the nature of something. Like in Plato, we find here both a definition of the word 'nature' (an inner source or cause of being moved and being at rest) and two competing conceptions of what that source is, namely matter and form (the material and the formal cause in Aristotle's sense). Aristotle himself finds it most satisfying to regard the formal (and the teleological or final) cause as the nature of x. The official theory of Aristotle seems, thus, to be a restricted idealist conception of nature presented with the possibility of a restricted materialist conception of nature in clear view, but for him the underlying contrast is between matter and form rather than between body and soul.

4.

With reference to Plato and Aristotle I have characterized two sorts of contrasting or restricted conceptions of nature, a materialist and an idealist. Each of them could be seen as underlying a sort of naturalism in ethics or in other branches of philosophy. The materialist conception of nature is at the root of bald, empiricist naturalism and of the many different modern forms of naturalism that let one or other interpretation of the results of present day science define what belongs to nature and what not. (A materialist conception of nature is also being taken for granted by most forms of non-naturalism, whether subjectivist or super-naturalist). The idealist conception of nature is at the root of the natural law tradition of naturalism that is still alive. The philosophical impulse behind both these sorts of naturalism is to see the ethical in continuity rather than discontinuity with nature understood as that which is most primary in existence and most objective in experience. They just happen to disagree about what that is.

With reference to the over-arching or all-inclusive use of the concept of nature I have further characterized a non-contrasting conception of nature. This could be taken as underlying a third sort of naturalism that could be called unrestricted or absolute naturalism. This is not the most common sort of naturalism, though it is not unheard of either. There might be something like it in Heraclitus or forms of Stoicism, and there certainly is something like it in Spinoza's conception of *Deus sive Natura*, the *Natura* that is the underlying unity of *natura naturans* and *natura naturata* and which alone could be said to be its own cause, *causa sui*. In modern philosophy I believe that nothing less than this is implied by the concept of natural history in § 25 of Wittgenstein's *Philosophical Investigations*:

—Commnding, questioning, recounting, chatting, are as much a part of our natural history as walking, eating, drinking, playing. (Wittgenstein 1967: 12)

It is even more explicit in the young Adorno when he says:

If the question of the realtion of nature and history is to be seriously posed, then it only offers any chance of solution if it is possible *to comprehend historical being in its most extreme historical determinacy, where it is most historical, as natural being, or if it were possible to comprehend nature as an historical being where it seems to rest most deeply in itself as nature.* (Adorno 1984: 117, italics in original)[1]

The emphasis on the historical character of nature and the natural character of history is important to counter our tendency to think of nature as static and the human as free-floating. Whatever happens happens in nature. I find this sort of naturalism also in Dewey when he uses an example from geology to stress a point relating to aesthetics:

Mountain peaks do not float unsupported; they do not even just rest upon the earth. They *are* the earth in one of its manifest operations. It is the business of those who are concerned with the theory of the earth, geographers and geologists, to make this fact evident, in its various implications. The theorist who would deal philosophically with fine art has a like task to accomplish. (Dewey 1958: 3–4, italics in original)

On this conception the aesthetical (and the ethical) are not independent of nature, but they are not somehow based on nature or supervening on it either; rather, they simply are nature in some of its manifest operations. To think otherwise is both to mystify the aesthetical (and ethical) and to trivialize nature. The man-made, the artificial, the cultural, the historical, the ethical, the normative, the mental, the logical, the abstract, the mysterious, the extraordinary, are all examples of ways of being natural rather than examples of ways of being non-natural. Nature is never *mere* nature. That which is *more* than *mere* is nature, too.

The philosophical impulse behind this third sort of naturalism is a general anti-dualism and anti-reductivism. If there were no anti-naturalists and no reductive naturalists there would be little point in insisting on understanding nature as all-inclusive. This could therefore not be the first form of naturalism to be developed historically. We have to begin with a struggle between different conceptions of what is primary to what, but the fact that there are so many incompatible contrasting and restricted conceptions of nature and the fact that each of them creates formidable difficulties in accounting for that which is regarded as non-natural provides a strong motivation for trying to explicate an absolute conception. Calling that which is at one side of a distinction 'nature' has a metaphysical import that inevitably tends to turn that distinction into a dualism. To take the absolute conception of nature for granted does not by itself solve any problems and it involves problems of its own, but it seems to me the most promising way of avoiding the otherwise endless oscillation between materialist and idealist, empiricist and rationalist conceptions of nature while at the same time keeping in touch with the genuine tensions from which they spring: Something surely at the very centre of McDowell's thinking.

According to this sort of naturalism one should resist any tendency to regard nature as a special realm or domain among other realms or domains. Nature is that which all possible domains are domains of. Nature is all there is, all that is the fact, all that happens. There is nothing above or beyond nature and there is nothing below or besides nature either. On this conception of nature to say that something is natural is not to say something specific about it but merely to deny claims from others that a certain domain could be in discontinuity with or be *sui generis* in relation to nature, given that it has its own nature and belongs to nature in this the broadest possible sense.

On this conception of nature, nothing could be non-natural, unnatural, super-natural or extra-natural. So, of course, the ethical is natural. There is nothing else it could be. Nothing is secondary in an absolute sense. The totality of absolutely everything, however, is primary in an absolute sense which gives room for all kinds of relations of priority between different aspects within the totality.[2] Using the famous quotation from Sellars we could say that to understand nature is to understand 'how things in the broadest possible sense of the term hang together in the broadest possible sense of the term' (Sellars 1963 : 1).

Both materialist and idealist naturalism may be argued for with reference to science. (Emphasizing the mathematical and law-like character of science may be taken to point in an idealist direction.) Unrestricted naturalism can equally claim to be capturing what is important about science. Here, however, it is not particular results or aspects of science that are taken to define what is nature and what is not. It is rather the open, undogmatic character of science combined with its aspiration to account for everything in continuity with everything else that one appeals to. Using another famous quotation from Sellars against himself we could say that where restricted, empiricist naturalism is claiming that 'science is the measure of all things', (Sellars 1963: 173) unrestricted naturalism takes it to be defining of science that all things are the measure of science.

These are my three sorts of naturalism. How do they correspond to McDowell's two sorts of naturalism? As I have already indicated, I find that what McDowell calls bald or empiricistic naturalism is clearly in the tradition of a restricted materialist naturalism, so at least initially one should think that his own second sort of naturalism could not belong to this sort.

How about the idealist naturalism that I believe must be regarded as the official doctrines of Plato and Aristotle in the passages considered? In spite of his references to 'Greek naturalism' it seems quite clear that this could not be McDowell's second sort of naturalism, either. He is explicitly *not* trying to replace a materialist, empiricist conception of nature with an idealist, rationalist conception. He is trying to help us get free of such dualisms. It would thus be wrong to place his second sort of naturalism at the same level as bald naturalism, in the way in which the two conceptions I have extrapolated from the discussions by Plato and Aristotle are on the same level. Idealist naturalism and absolute naturalism are two quite different ways of opposing materialist naturalism while remaining a naturalist.

If this is true McDowell's appeal to 'naturalized Platonism' and 'Aristotelian naturalism' must be somewhat problematic for his own purposes. Talking about 'naturalized Platonism' is, of course, a way of pointing beyond bald naturalism while at the same time distancing oneself from rampant Platonism, but it seems to me rather unclear what 'naturalization' could mean here. If this notion is relying on a restricted conception of nature referring to the results of science, one would need to hear more about exactly how far bald naturalism is being opened up, or exactly how far the 'partial re-enchantment of nature' is supposed to go, and these are questions McDowell, in my view wisely, refrains from trying to answer. When McDowell talks about 'Aristotelian naturalism' or 'naturalism of second nature' it is clearly Aristotle's position in the *Ethics* that he has in mind, but the use of the concept of *physis* there is quite consistent with its use in the *Physics*. When Aristotle says of the moral virtues that they:

> . . .are engendered in us neither by nature nor yet in violation of nature; nature gives us the capacity to receive them, and this capacity is brought to maturity by habit. (Aristotle *Nicomachean Ethics*: 1103a26)

the point is precisely to emphasize that virtues, like beds, are not due to nature and not according to nature though, again like beds, not contrary to nature either. In modern usage, I suppose, the notion of second nature is mainly used about some, but not other, habitual traits that are so firm that they are like nature (considered as permanent) without actually being nature (permanent). Any distinction between first and second nature certainly keeps something like the bald naturalist conception of nature in the picture, and leaves it an open question exactly how far into the ethical (or mental) second nature reaches.

The way I have presented an absolute naturalism based on an unrestricted conception of nature seems to me to be an acceptable, radical, and satisfying sort of ethical naturalism both in itself and for many of McDowell's purposes. This conception is not simply a 'liberal' or a 'relaxed' naturalism, it actually needs a rather careful explanation because it is clearly not as if we would all know what nature is if only we got rid of the misleading bald conception of it. Nevertheless, there is something straightforward about it. McDowell has convincingly shown that what Bernard Williams calls the absolute conception of reality is merely restricted, bald naturalism ideologically presented as absolute (*MVR*: 112–31, esp. sect. 5). Nothing less than a naturalism that deserves to be presented as absolute could help break the spell of bald naturalism without merely replacing one restricted sort of naturalism with another and thus keeping the oscillations going. A naturalism based on the unrestricted, absolute conception of nature seems to me to be the only candidate. There may be restricted conceptions of nature that I have not taken into account, but if McDowell's own, second sort of naturalism should be understood as based on such a conception, perhaps some kind of materialist or empiricist naturalism somehow less restricted than bald naturalism, it seems fair to say that he owes us an account of exactly where and why he draws his line between nature and something else, and in particular what that something else is supposed to be.

Hans Fink
Department of Philosophy
University of Aarhus
DK-8000 Aartus C
Denmark
filhf@hum.au.dk

NOTES

[1] 'Wenn die Frage nach dem Verhältnis von Natur und Geschichte ernsthaft gestellt werden soll, bietet sie nur dann Aussicht auf Beantwortung, wenn es gelingt, *das Geschichtliche Sein in seiner äußersten geschichtlichen Bestimmtheit, da wo es am geschichtlichsten ist, selber als ein naturhaftes Sein zu begreifen, oder wenn es gelänge, die Natur da, wo sie als Natur scheinbar am tiefsten in sich verharrt, zu begreifen als ein geschichtliches Sein'* (Adorno 1973: 354–55).

[2] If anyone should doubt that there is a consistent notion of absolutely everything for nature to be identified with, I can recommend a highly technical paper by Timothy Williamson called 'Everything', where scepticism about absolute generality is shown to be inconsistent though everything is not identified with nature (Williamson 2003).

REFERENCES

Abbreviations:

MVR: McDowell, J. (1998), *Mind, Value and Reality*. Cambridge, MA: Harvard University Press.
MW: McDowell, J. (1996a), *Mind and World*. Cambridge, MA: Harvard University Press. Second edn. (First edn. 1994).
THN: Hume, D. (1969), *A Treatise of Human Understanding*. Harmondsworth: Penguin Books. (First edn. 1739–40).

Adorno, T. W. (1973), *Gesammelte Schriften, Band I*. Frankfurt a.M.: Suhrkamp, 'Die Idee der Naturgeschichte' (1932).
—— (1984), 'The Idea of Natural History', Bob Hullot-Kentor, trans., *Telos*, 60: 111–24.
Aristotle (1962), *Nicomachean Ethics*. London: The Loeb Classical Library, Heinemann.
—— (1963), *Physics*. London: The Loeb Classical Library, Heinemann.
Dewey, J. (1958), *Art as Experience*. New York: Capricorn Books. First published 1934.
Hume, D. (1969), *A Treatise of Human Understanding*. Harmondsworth: Penguin Books. (First edn. 1739–40).

McDowell, J. (1996a), *Mind and World*. Cambridge, MA: Harvard University Press, 2nd edn. (First edn. 1994).

—— (1996b), 'Two Sorts of Naturalism', in R. Hursthouse, G. Lawrence and W. Quinn (eds.) *Virtues and Reasons: Philippa Foot and Moral Theory*. Oxford: Clarendon Press. Reprinted in McDowell 1998.

—— (1998), *Mind, Value and Reality*. Cambridge, MA: Harvard University Press.

—— (2004), 'Naturalism in the philosophy of mind', in M. de Caro and D. Macarthur (eds.) *Naturalism in Question*. Cambridge, MA: Harvard University Press.

Mill, J. S. (1977), *Collected Works of John Stuart Mill vol. XVIII*. Toronto: University of Toronto Press. From *On Liberty*, first published 1859.

Plato (1961), *Laws*. London: The Loeb Classical Library, Heinemann.

Williams, R. (1981), *Keywords: A Vocabulary of Culture and Society*. London: Fontana/Croom Helms.

Williamson, T. (2003), 'Everything', in *Philosophical Perspectives*, 17, 415–65.

Wittgenstein, L. (1967), *Philosophical Investigations*, G. E. M. Anscombe trans. Oxford: Basil Blackwell.

5

Varieties of Nature in Hegel and McDowell

Christoph Halbig

> Wir finden die Natur als ein Rätsel und Problem vor uns, das wir ebenso
> aufzulösen uns getrieben fühlen, als wir davon abgestoßen werden.
> Hegel, *Enz.* § 244Z[1]

1.

The idea of a second nature as the basis for a relaxed naturalism has a fair claim on being the master idea not only of McDowell's richly suggestive *Mind and World* but also of his papers on subjects as diverse as metaethics, epistemology, philosophy of language and the theory of value. Nevertheless the reader will look in vain for an elaborate theory of second nature in McDowell's work. This is no accident, of course: McDowell explicitly disavows the need to provide such a theory as incompatible with the status the concept of second nature carries in his argument: It is meant as a Wittgensteinian ladder which deserves no attention on its own but just serves as a conceptual tool which might help in emancipating us from traditional philosophical impasses. Or, to put it in McDowell's own words: 'Once my reminder of second nature has done its work, nature can drop out of my picture' (R: 277).[2]

This paper's line of argument proceeds in two contrasting stages which include three steps respectively. The first stage is focused on McDowell and tries to substantiate the thesis that the concept of second nature lies at the heart of his philosophical position. In a first step, the way in which McDowell's way out of the epistemological oscillation between the Myth of the Given on the one hand, and frictionless coherentism on the other, presupposes a reconception of nature, and the place of spontaneity within it is analysed. In a second step, McDowell's solution is explored and evaluated in contrast to three competing approaches to the problem discussed by McDowell. Finally attention will be drawn to the metaphilosophical status McDowell attributes to his conception of second nature. In all three steps we will observe that McDowell alludes to the work of Hegel at crucial joints in his line of argument.

Hegel's philosophy in its turn enters centre stage in the second stage of the argument: In a first step, the problem Hegel discusses under the heading of 'second nature' ('zweite Natur') is distinguished from the question at stake in McDowell's distinction between first and second nature. Hegel faces these questions, as will be shown, in his discussion of the relation between Nature and Spirit. The argumentative tools that Hegel develops to cope with them are then outlined by way of an interpretation of § 381 of Hegel's *Encyclopedia* which marks the crucial transition from Nature to Spirit. Relying on the results of this interpretation it will be shown how Hegel's own solution to the epistemological problem discussed by McDowell relies on an elaborate theory of how Nature and Spirit are related, which allows him to make good on the metaphor (also invoked by McDowell) of the 'unboundedness of the conceptual'.

The concluding section of this paper then tries to show that the way in which Nature is sublated into Spirit in Hegel's philosophy allows us to successfully cope with the problems which remain unsolved in McDowell—though the price to be paid for this solution is a metaphilosophical position as far away as possible from the Wittgensteinian quietism at which McDowell aims. Thus the very idea of a naturalism of second nature highlights McDowell's uneasy position between Wittgenstein and Hegel: The problems posed by McDowell's naturalism of second nature and which he himself phrase in a deliberately Hegelian language, call for a solution in terms of an endeavour of constructive philosophy which alienates him from the Wittgensteinian perspective from which, ironically, McDowell claims to have given philosophy peace precisely by means of the idea of second nature. At this point the threat of yet another oscillation looms large for McDowell: The oscillation between a Wittgensteinian quietism which simply has to suppress the substantial philosophical problems posed by his reconception of nature on the one hand and on the other hand a Hegelianism which solves these problems at the price of a hyperbolic system which gives philosophy peace only in the sense that even the conceptual space for any further problems is exhausted.

2.

2.1

In *Mind and World* McDowell approaches the problem of the relation between mind and world via the discussion of two equally unsatisfactory positions which seem to leave us in an impasse: The Myth of the Given is based on the idea that the space of reasons exceeds the limits of the conceptual: Something which is non-conceptually structured could on this picture justify items within the conceptual sphere (for instance perceptual judgements). According to McDowell the Myth of the Given fails because it wrongly assumes that the relations in virtue of which a judgment is warranted, include relations between something conceptual on the one hand, and something non-conceptual on the other, thus providing an external constraint on the use of our concepts.[3] What we get instead are just causal impacts which might serve as exculpations ('I can't help thinking there's a blue table in front of me') but not as normative constraints on our conceptual practices. At this point recoil to the other horn of the dilemma seems inevitable: Once it is acknowledged that justification of items within the conceptual sphere cannot come from outside this sphere, we seem to have lost the idea of an external normative constraint on our thinking altogether. What we are left with is a 'frictionless spinning in the void' which might be subjected to internal norms of consistency but which is no any longer recognisable as bearing on an external reality in an epistemologically relevant sense. At this point a second glance at the Myth of the Given seems tempting—we have entered into an oscillation which threatens to be interminable.

McDowell's strategy for dismounting this seesaw is based on the thesis that an adequate theory of experience has to be based on the observation that the two pairs of oppositions 'receptivity vs. spontaneity' and 'non-conceptual vs. conceptual' are not related in a way that would make the conceptual an exclusive prerogative of spontaneity whereas receptivity has to be considered as *ipso facto* non-conceptual. Instead McDowell opts for conceiving experience itself as imbued with conceptual content. According to McDowell what we are taking in through experience is not a non-conceptual Given which would have to be epistemologically otiose anyway, but something which is essentially of a propositional form ('that there is a blue table in front of me'). But how is this thesis compatible with the idea of a constraint by an external reality which we expect from our experience (on pain of falling back into the coherentist 'spinning in the void')? McDowell's answer is that this compatibility is guaranteed by the fact that in experience our conceptual capacities are exercised in a *passive* way—it simply strikes us that there is a blue table in front of us: 'In experience, one finds oneself saddled with content' (*MW*: 10). This experiential content is conceptual and thus—unlike the Given—able to enter into relations of justification with other members of the conceptual sphere. The problem of how something non-conceptual can constrain our conceptual practices simply disappears: 'the conceptual is unbounded; there is nothing outside it' (*MW*: 44).

Although the deliberately Hegelian metaphor of the unboundedness of the conceptual at this crucial point of McDowell's argument[4] might suggest the threat of a hidden idealism, McDowell interprets his theory of experience in an utterly realistic way: What we take in through experience are facts ('that there is a table'); if we do not go wrong the content of the experience is nothing but a fact that is part of the fabric of reality.

2.2

But is it an even remotely plausible idea that, as McDowell's solution to the epistemological dilemma suggests, conceptual capacities might be at work within the deliverances of sensibility? The following argument suggests that it is not:[5]

P$_1$: Sensibility is part of Nature; it is something human beings share with animals who lack conceptual capacities altogether.

P$_2$: What is part of Nature is what it is by virtue of its position in the realm of law.

P₃: The conceptual deliverances of the understanding as the faculty of spontaneity are characterised by a different kind of intelligibility than that of the realm of law, i.e. that of the space of reasons.

C: The operations of sensibility cannot be shaped by concepts. To suppose otherwise would imply that deliverances of sensibility qua part of nature (P_1) could be what they are by virtue of their position within the space of reasons—which would be incompatible with P_2.

Since the conclusion does follow from the premises and since McDowell is unwilling to revise his basic epistemological idea that conceptual capacities are operative in the very actualizations of our sensibility, he decides at this point to step back and critically examine the basic terms in which the argument is framed. According to McDowell, the problem of how spontaneity relates to nature lies at the heart of the matter. In *MW* McDowell distinguishes four theories of this relation, i.e. bald naturalism, rampant Platonism, Davidsonian naturalism and naturalized Platonism, the position McDowell himself favours.

The aim of my reconstruction is to lay bare the basic topography of the field as suggested by McDowell (which in *MW* seems to me to be a bit drowned out by many illuminating remarks on the various positions under discussion, which do not contribute to the basic line of argument) so that the way in which McDowell implicitly makes room for his own position becomes visible:

a) Bald naturalism (i) equates nature with the realm of law and (ii) denies that there is a *sui generis* intelligibility characteristic of the space of reasons. Bald naturalism must not be confused with eliminativism: Notions like rational justification are not dropped from the picture but can be maintained in so far as it is possible (for instance by reduction) to make them intelligible in terms of distinctive categories of the realm of law.

b) Davidsonian naturalism (i) equates nature with the realm of law (like bald naturalism), but (ii) admits that there is a *sui generis* intelligibility characteristic of the space of reasons which remains irreducible to the concepts which get their point from placing things in the realm of law. Because it accepts the equation of nature with the realm of law Davidsonian naturalism maintains the ontological thesis that the entities which satisfy the *sui generis* concepts can be made intelligible in terms of the realm of law—which appears to be the only way to make safe their place in Nature. The two kinds of intelligibility characterize our conceptual equipment but not the reality it is about.

c) Rampant Platonism (i) equates nature with the realm of law, (ii) admits that there is a *sui generis* intelligibility characteristic of the space of reasons, but (iii) rejects Davidson's monistic naturalism and interprets the existence of two *sui generis* kinds of intelligibility in terms of an ontological dualism: According to rampant Platonism human beings are citizens of two worlds, the natural one as equated with the realm of law and the supernatural one.

What should be immediately obvious from our reconstruction of the three conceptions of how spontaneity relates to nature is that they all depend on the unquestioned assumption (i) which equates nature with the realm of law. Not surprisingly it is this assumption McDowell finds fault with. He concedes that the modern scientific revolution has made an understanding of the realm of law available, which provides us with unique opportunities both to understand and to manipulate natural phenomena.[6] But he refuses to equate nature itself with this realm of law (*MW*: 78) and opts for a reconception of nature as including both a first and a second nature.

McDowell offers us a somewhat confusing array of labels for his position: 'Aristotelian naturalism' (*TS*: 178), 'naturalized Platonism' (*MW*: 91f.), 'naturalism of second nature' (*MW*: 91) and 'relaxed naturalism' (*MW*: 89). But these different labels seem to emphasize only different aspects of one central idea: Once it is acknowledged that nature must not be identified with the realm of law (which McDowell in turn identifies with first nature),[7] one gets conceptual room for an understanding of human potentialities as thoroughly natural: An active exercise of conceptual capacities is as much part of the natural development of human beings as the capacity for intentional action. On such a conception of nature the fact that the notion of spontaneity can only be made intelligible within a framework that differs from that appropriate for the realm of law is no longer incompatible with understanding it as part of the natural powers of man—it is part of his second nature.

At the same time the above-mentioned argument against the possibility of conceptual capacities being at work within the deliverances of sensibility cannot even get started insofar as it relies on the now disproved premise that the deliverances of sensibility as natural goings-on could only be *externally* related to the conceptual powers of spontaneity—simply because these powers resist intelligibility in terms of laws of nature and therefore on a conception which equates nature with the realm of law have to be considered as something non-natural. For this crucial move McDowell appeals again to his affinity with Hegel: According to McDowell both share a 'non-Kantian conception of reason as essentially situated (sc. in human life)' (*R*: 274). Man is a rational animal—his reason is part of what characterises him as a natural being. From this Hegelian perspective trying to bridge a gap between receptivity as something natural on the one hand and spontaneity as the part of man that participates in something non-natural on the other looks like a misconceived project from the start: There is no gap to be bridged in the first place.

But is this reconceiving of nature just a terminological sleight of hand or is it the liberating move which, as McDowell promises us, gives philosophy peace?[8] Before discussing this question there can, if one looks back at the dialectical structure of McDowell's line of argument, be no doubt that it is McDowell's relaxed naturalism that carries the main weight of his argument. McDowell himself admits that his focus on philosophical difficulties about perceptual experience in the first lectures of *Mind and World* 'was not essential',[9] it rather served to exemplify a type of problem which arises once a false conception of the natural is in place. It is this false conception that McDowell tries to replace by his 'relaxed naturalism'. The new perspectives opened by this reconception of the natural are once again mainly illustrated by means of the epistemological problems which have served to set the stage for McDowell's line of argument in *Mind and World*. But there can be no doubt that the consequences of this relaxed naturalism loom large also in other areas of philosophy, as for instance McDowell makes clear in his contributions to the debate on moral realism.[10]

Within McDowell's writings, however, no elaborate theory of second nature and of the relaxed naturalism based on it corresponds to the weight these concepts have to carry within his overall philosophical approach. In the third step of the first part of this paper we will analyse the reasons McDowell himself provides for avoiding theory-building at this point. But what are the problems raised by McDowell's line of argument which could be in need of such a theory?

I suggest distinguishing two basic problems: The first one concerns the unity and internal structure of the natural when conceived along the lines suggested by McDowell (1). The second concerns the ontological status of first and second nature (2).

Re (1): Nature, according to McDowell, seems to comprise both first and second nature. But what holds these two parts together in a way that would justify subsuming them under the heading of 'nature' (1a) and how are they related to one another (1b)? McDowell dismisses question 1a quite quickly:

> . . .the only unity there needs to be in the idea of the natural, as it applies, on the one hand, to the intelligibility of physical and merely biological phenomena [. . .], and, on the other, to the intelligibility of rational activity, is captured by a contrast with the idea of the supernatural, the spooky or the occult. (*RM*: 99)

Everything not supernatural, spooky or occult falls on the side of Nature simply by definition. This move strikes me as too quick in two respects: Firstly in mentioning the supernatural in one breath with the spooky and the occult, it ignores the constitutive role supernatural entities seem to play not just in confused philosophical theories, but in the self-image of common sense itself (take the idea of individual immortality as an example). Secondly it threatens to turn the unity of the natural into a triviality. Bernard Williams has recently drawn attention to a dilemma that faces the naturalist, i.e. that of 'stabilizing the idea of "nature" so that naturalism is not either trivially true or implausible to such an extent as to be uninteresting'.[11] McDowell's relaxed naturalism seems to come dangerously close to the first horn of Williams' dilemma: If entities as different as the denizens of the realm of law on the one hand and, for example, ethical and aesthetical values on the other are yoked together under the common term of the 'natural' simply because neither of them turns out to be spooky, wouldn't the term lose all it's bite? Wouldn't it be less misleading to replace the label of the 'natural' by the neutral 'real' of which the natural would then form one part amongst others? Such a terminological move would have the advantage that 'real' unlike 'natural' does not suggest a homogeneity of the phenomena subsumed under it when all that is meant is that they are not spooky in the sense of metaphysically unacceptable?

This suspicion gets added force from the way McDowell deals with the question of how first and second nature are related to one another (1b). He seems to think that the integration of second nature within first nature as the realm of law is guaranteed by a set of potentialities which form part of the realm of law but are then transformed into second nature by a process for which McDowell avails himself of the notion of *Bildung*:

> Second nature could not float free of potentialities that belong to a normal human organism. This gives human reason enough of a foothold in the realm of law to satisfy any proper respect for modern natural science. (*MW*: 84)

In his essay 'Two Sorts of Naturalism' McDowell provides some further hints which help to clarify the metaphor of the 'foothold'; he distinguishes between two different ways in which first nature matters for second nature:[12] Firstly it acts as a constraint on what passes as an intelligible candidate for the way second nature should be. (1) A configuration of second nature which would system- atically stifle basic human potentialities like that of developing deep social relationships disqualifies for that reason. Secondly it provides input for the reflection which takes place within a formed second nature (2): If a rational wolf, in McDowell's example, who has been accustomed to hunt in a pack comes to ask itself about the rational credentials of this practice it might have recourse to the wolfish need to hunt in a way which is impossible for an individual on it's own.

Unfortunately both these clarifications are of little help in solving the problem at hand, i.e. to make the way in which first and second nature are related to one another intelligible: In (2) first nature figures not as it is in itself qua part of the realm of law, but *as seen from within* the perspective of an already formed second nature. The thesis that any attempt to provide a theory of human nature as the basis for the normative claims of ethics necessarily fails because the claims of reason come into view only from within an already on-going cultural practice lies at the heart of McDowell's critique of competing theories of the foundations of ethics like that of Aristotle in Bernard Williams' interpretation (which McDowell himself considers as a historical monstrosity) or of Philippa Foot.[13] The truths about first nature which are to provide justifications for elements of second nature one finds oneself with are, to use another term forged by McDowell, 'naturally shapeless':[14] If approached via the epistemic means of the realm of law they lose all intelligible shape; they come into view only from within a Neurathian reflection[15] by which a configuration of second nature tries to assure itself of its own credentials.

McDowell's first point does not settle the issue either: The claim that first nature constrains the field of candidates for the way second nature could be, is ambiguous between a normative and a factive reading: On a factive reading it just means that some configurations of second nature would violate laws of nature and are therefore impossible. On a normative reading it would mean that a configuration of second nature like a radical ascetism which looks for salvation in systematically stifling basic human needs should be rejected. But this thesis could, as McDowell himself has to admit, only be intelligibly defended from within an historically evolved space of reasons—on pain of rehabilitating a concept of human nature as an external foundation for ethics.

The foothold of human reason in the realm of law that McDowell had promised us still remains elusive—it seems to get stuck between the horns of the following dilemma:[16]

According to the first horn the constraint exercised by first nature on second nature implies only the claim that configurations of second nature must not be incompatible with laws of nature. Such a reading would empty the thesis of a foothold of second within first nature of any substantial content.

According to the second horn, there are indeed potentialities that are characteristic of human beings qua natural beings which are substantial enough in order to be understood as structuring the process of *Bildung*, e.g. the capacity of leading a happy life by entering into deep human relationships as opposed to the capacity of learning how to keep one's equilibrium in climbing steep walls. But—and at this point a sub-dilemma opens for McDowell—either these potentialities are, strictly speaking, part of second nature since they come into view, as McDowell himself seems to admit, only by means of the intelligibility in terms of the space of reasons characteristic of second nature, or, if they are awarded to first nature, they lead to an implosion of the category of first nature which would no longer be coextensive with the realm of law.

Re (2) This dilemma leads to the second of the two basic problems distinguished above: What is the ontological status of the distinction between first and second nature?[17] On the one hand McDowell seems content to characterise the distinction by purely methodological means while leaving open its ontological implications. For instance he speaks of a:

> ...contrast between two kinds of intelligibility: the kind that is sought by
> (as we call it) natural science, and the kind we find in something when
> we place it in relation to other occupants of 'the logical space of reasons'.
> (*MW*: 70)

The first kind of intelligibility characterises first nature, the second kind characterises second nature. On the other hand McDowell interprets the denizens of first and second nature in a thoroughly realist way: Not only entities of first nature like trees or tables with which we enter into contact through sense experience, but also entities like values which belong to second nature are characterised in the realist way of entities to be discovered: McDowell speaks of 'a human being's eyes being opened' to demands of reason implied by an action's being, for example, cowardly, or of the 'revelation' of such a fact.[18] These metaphors suggest that our initiation into second nature opens our eyes to a different level of reality than that with which we were familiar before. On such a reading the distinction between first and second nature cannot be just the result of a useful methodological distinction but refers to a two-level structure within reality itself. A clarification on this point seems crucial for many aspects of McDowell's philosophy: For instance, part of the attraction of metaethical realism rests on the intuitions inherent in common sense that ethics is not just about finding one's way around a realm of reasons but at least partially about discovering something that is genuinely there. Whether McDowell succeeds in accommodating these intuitions depends crucially on the way the ontological status of second nature is defined.

2.3

The results of the two preceding paragraphs suggest that McDowell owes us a detailed exposition of his 'relaxed naturalism' that would show a way to overcome the problems we have tried to pinpoint. But according to McDowell such a demand already misconstrues the status of his remarks on naturalism:

> 'Naturalized platonism' is not a label for a bit of constructive philosophy. The phrase serves only as shorthand for a 'reminder', an attempt to recall our thinking from running in grooves that make it look as if we need constructive philosophy. (MW: 95)

In the tradition of a Wittgensteinian quietism McDowell aims at dislodging the background of traditional problems, not at providing a solution to them by just another piece of constructive philosophy. The demand for a theory of second nature would deeply involve McDowell in the business of constructive philosophy whereas his recourse to the concept was meant as a ladder which should be left behind after having done it's service:

> When I invoke second nature, that is meant to dislodge the background that makes such questions look pressing, the dualism of reason and nature. (MW: 178)[19]

Now, unfortunately what the argument of this paper so far has tried to show is that an attempt at climbing the ladder of second nature instead of giving us peace from misconstrued problems[20] just convinces us that the ladder is badly in need of repair, if it is meant to lead us anywhere: Instead of freeing us from an endless oscillation it leads us into oscillations of its own. In the next part of this paper an analysis of how Hegel's philosophy allows to deal with the set of problems we have identified in McDowell should corroborate this thesis.

3.

Hegel provides a detailed theory of second nature in his philosophical system. Several philosophers have already alluded to this theory and have contrasted the attention Hegel pays to the subject with McDowell's Wittgensteinian reticence to enter into a detailed discussion of it.[21] Unfortunately these gestures towards Hegel have not been accompanied by suggestions on where to look for such a theory in Hegel. If one simply looks up Hegel's remarks on *zweite Natur*, the German equivalent of 'second nature', it becomes immediately obvious that this problem is everything but trivial: What Hegel discusses under this heading is *not* equivalent to the issues at stake in McDowell's discussion of second nature. In his *Philosophy of Mind*, for instance, Hegel calls *Habit* a second nature:

> Habit is rightly called a second nature; nature, because it is an immediate being of the soul; a second nature, because it is an immediacy created by the soul, impressing and moulding the corporeality which enters into the modes of feeling as such and into the representations and volitions so far as they have taken corporeal form (§ 401). (*Enz.* § 410A)

What Hegel emphasizes in his discussion of *Habit* is the aspect of liberation from immediate sensations: It shares their immediacy (if I have acquired a habit of indifference towards traffic noise, I do not have to struggle any longer and try to ignore it), but this immediacy itself is not immediate, i.e. part of the natural endowment of human beings, but it is created, or, to be more accurate, posited (*gesetzt*) by higher parts of the mind.[22] I might have decided that it would be useful to be indifferent to traffic noise in my rather noisy flat, so I try to form a habit of indifference towards it. If I succeed, my system of attention gets restructured in a way that I could not bring about as a result of a single act of will.

In a related way Hegel employs the category of 'second nature' to analyse processes at the level of intersubjectivity which concern the internalisation of social norms: Ethical life (*Sittlichkeit*) is fully realised only if compliance with the norms which emanate from an analysis of the presuppositions of free will does not require an act of critical reflection every single time, but enters into the very identity of those who share in it. Bringing this about is a process which Hegel also subsumes under the title of acquiring a second nature.[23]

At this point it should be evident that second nature in Hegel's terminology is not coextensive with second nature in McDowell's sense. Phenomena like legal norms as codified in codes of law or in ethical demands, which the individual fails to identify with, but nonetheless feels normatively subject to, for instance, are part of McDowell's second nature but would not qualify as part of it according to Hegel's use of the term. So in order to avoid mislocating the problem under discussion we have to broaden our view to a higher structural level within Hegel's system: The context in which Hegel deals with the problems we have identified in McDowell is, as I am going to argue, the relation of Nature and Spirit. This question in turn is highlighted in Hegel's analysis of the transition of

Nature to Spirit as part of the overall process of the self-unfolding of the Idea. The paragraph in Hegel's *Encyclopedia* which marks this crucial transition deserves to be quoted at length:

> From our point of view Spirit has for its presupposition Nature, of which it is the truth, and for that reason its absolute prius. In this its truth Nature is vanished, and Spirit has resulted as the 'Idea' entered on possession of itself. Here the subject and object of the Idea are one— either is the intelligent unity, the notion. (*Enz.* § 381)[24]

It is impossible to interpret the extremely dense argument in this paragraph in detail.[25] It has to suffice to summarize its main points and relate it to our list of problems: The following three questions seem suitable to structure our discussion:

1. What is meant by Nature being presupposed by Spirit and from which point of view is it thus presupposed?
2. In what sense is Spirit the truth of Nature?
3. What does Hegel mean by the identity he claims for the subject and object within the structure of the idea?

Re 1. At first glance, 'our point of view' could be understood along the lines familiar from the *Phenomenology of Spirit*: It would then refer to a deficient form of consciousness which is still to be superseded by other, more adequate forms. But such a reading is inadmissible within the methodological framework of Hegel's *Encyclopedia* which presupposes that the development of the forms of consciousness have already come to completion. But 'our point of view' cannot signify the philosopher's view either—from that point of view, as the second part of the sentence makes clear, Spirit is the truth of Nature, a thesis which we still have to understand, but which cannot be identical to the thesis that the former presupposes the latter. What is left is, as Michael Quante has convincingly shown, to understand 'our point of view' as the point of view of the common sense.[26] Common sense considers Nature as a presupposition of Spirit. Presupposition here has to be read according to Hegel's terminology as 'external reflection' (*äußere Reflexion*):[27] What is externally presupposed is seen as utterly independent—that it is a term of a relation of presupposition is only visible from the philosopher's point of view. Common sense, as we are now allowed to conclude, considers Nature as independent from the conceptual activities which characterise Spirit; it adopts a naïve realism towards Nature.

Re 2. But the common sense-perspective cannot have the last word on the relation of Spirit and Nature. Instead, Hegel reminds us that Spirit is the truth of Nature. Truth here is meant not as a property of propositions but as an ontological category: According to Hegel's theory of ontological truth, an entity is true insofar as it corresponds to its notion.[28] Hegel's system as a normative ontology structures entities according to evaluative criteria—an entity is deficient inasmuch as it fails to realize its Notion and is therefore *false*.[29] But what is the framework in which Nature and Spirit can themselves be evaluated? It is the

Idea, to which Hegel explicitly refers in § 381: Both Nature and Spirit are moments of the development of the Idea, which, interpreted according to the model of self-consciousness, constitutes the ultimate structure which encompasses all reality. That Spirit is called the truth of Nature therefore means that the structure of the Idea is more fully realized in Spirit than in Nature. Hegel elaborates on this thesis in the *Introduction* to the *Philosophy of Nature*:

> In this externality, the determinations of the Notion have the show of an indifferent subsistence and isolation (Vereinzelung) in regard to each other, and the Notion, therefore, is present only as something inward. Consequently, Nature exhibits no freedom in its existence, but only necessity and contingency. (§ 248)

To understand this passage, two different meanings of necessity have to be distinguished: On the one hand an entity is necessary insofar as it is part of the realisation process of the Idea which is the overall subject of the *Encyclopedia*. The laws which are exhibited by Nature and discovered by physics are called contingent because they lack necessity in this first sense. It takes philosophical study of nature to exhibit the working of the notion even within the data provided by natural sciences.[30] Since Nature, as the object of natural sciences, precisely lacks this necessity in the first sense, Hegel—somewhat confusingly—calls Nature the realm of necessity in a second sense of necessity which is opposed not to contingency, but to freedom. Nature lacks freedom because the notion does not succeed to be as adequately 'with itself in the other' as it does in Spirit: How many species of parrots, to use one of Hegel's stock examples, exist is just a matter of chance. What the elements of a just constitution are, is not.

But, to return to § 381, this fuller realization which the Idea achieves in Spirit only comes about *through* Nature. Spirit has 'resulted' from Nature instead of simply supplanting it. On the other hand, Hegel emphasises that Nature has 'vanished' in its truth, Spirit. The metaphor of vanishing has seduced Robert Pippin to doubt that Hegel could even feel 'the force of this question [sc. what must nature be like for meaning in nature to be possible]'[31] which lies at the centre of McDowell's distinction between first and second nature. Pippin suggests understanding Spirit in Hegel as 'a product of itself'[32] and emphasises the 'non-metaphysical character of the Natur-Geist distinction in Hegel as a better way of leaving first nature behind'.[33] He thus provides an unambiguous answer to the second of the two problems distinguished above which beset McDowell: In Pippin's reading first and second nature are nothing but constructions from within an ongoing practice of Spirit, a model which he also claims for Hegel.

Such a reading however proves incompatible both with the structure of Hegel's system and with the text of § 381. The logic of presupposition implies that the terms of it retain a certain independence. As we have seen, the common sense perspective has been proven wrong only insofar as the independence of Nature cannot be a total one: Nature is part of the realisation process of the Idea and can only be properly understood in its context. This however must not be confused with Pippin's claim that Nature in Hegel's system is nothing but the product of a 'common mindedness'. What vanishes once the level of Spirit has been reached is not Nature itself, but only Nature's claim to be the adequate form of the Idea. But it remains crucial to keep in mind that the more adequate realisation of the Idea in Spirit presupposes that Spirit relates itself to Nature as at least partially independent of itself (partially because in processes like that of habituation, Spirit transforms its own natural basis—but even such a process of course presupposes that there is something to be transformed).

Re 3. The suggested interpretation is further corroborated by the way in which Hegel characterises the level of Spirit. Hegel gives the following paraphrase of what it means that the Idea has entered into possession of itself: 'Here the subject and object of the Idea are one—either is the intelligent unity, the notion'. (§ 381) It is evident that the Notion cannot be understood as the title of a conceptual scheme which would be applied from the outside to some given material. Instead Hegel claims that the Notion is to be found on the side of the subject *and* of the object and that there is a relation of identity among them.

In this sentence, the central thesis of both Hegel's metaphysics and of his epistemology converge: That all reality is nothing but the process of unfolding the set of Notions which Hegel had discussed in the *Science of Logic*, i.e. Hegel's absolute idealism, guarantees that the conceptual capacities which are actively exercised by the cognising subject are directed towards something that is in itself structured by the same Notions the subject relies on in the activity of cognition: In Hegel's *Psychology* the Notion ('Begriff') of cognition is therefore appropriately defined as 'the identity of the subjectivity of the notion and of its objectivity' (*Enz.* § 438). If I know that the table is square, then the content of my act of knowledge is just that—the fact that the table is square. Now within Hegel's holistic metaphysics this fact is a very deficient one and therefore hardly deserves to be called 'true' in the ontological sense of truth. Nonetheless, Hegel clearly defends what would today be classified as an identity theory of propositional truth (which Hegel discusses under the heading of '*Richtigkeit*' instead of '*Wahrheit*', so as to avoid confusions with his far more prominent theory of ontological truth).

Hegel's thesis of 'the unboundedness of the conceptual', towards which, as we have seen, McDowell gestures in his attempt to overcome the epistemological oscillation,[34] has to be understood in this framework: The conceptual is unbounded because reality as the object of cognition is in itself conceptually structured—Nature is the realm of 'objective thoughts' (cf. *Enz.* § 24). Hegel's absolute idealism which does imply a rejection of ontological realism is, however, not incompatible with an epistemological realism; on the contrary: It provides the systematic foundation for it. Since the 'determinations [sc. of the self-consciousness] are no less objective, or determinations of the very being of things, than they are its own thoughts' (*Enz.* § 439) an immediate epistemological access to reality is guaranteed (although of course error remains possible): In its acts of cognition the subject is directed not towards 'mental intermediaries' (Davidson) but towards reality itself which is constituted by the same determinations which structure the cognising activity.

The metaphor of 'objective thoughts' might invite a misconstrual of such a theory as a form of subjective idealism which would make reality dependent on the side of the subject. But Hegel explicitly rejects such a construal; it relies, as he emphasises in *Enz.* § 24 A., on an undue classification of thoughts as something mental. Within the process of the Idea the opposition of subject and object is overcome, because the Notions or thought-determinations which form the subject matter of the *Science of Logic* are analysed both—in the mode of the 'in itself'—as the essence of natural objects (in the Philosophy of Nature) and—in the mode of the 'for itself'—as the determinations of the cognitive and volitional activities of *Geist*.

4.

The best way to summarize the results we have reached in our interpretation of Hegel's analysis of the transition from Nature to Spirit is to apply Hegel's position to McDowell's project of a reconciliation of reason and nature (see *MW*: 86) and to the problems raised by it.

First it is crucial to see that Hegel approaches the project of reconciliation not by a distinction between a first nature which is identified with the realm of law on the one hand, and a second nature on the other. Nature according to Hegel is the object both of sciences and of philosophy of nature. The relationship between these two disciplines can be characterised by three theses:

1. In terms of their methodology and ontological commitments natural sciences on the one hand, and philosophy of nature on the other have to be kept strictly distinct.[35]
2. Hegel refuses to accept a methodological or ontological primacy of the natural sciences over philosophy of nature: Philosophy of nature must be in agreement with the empirical results of the natural sciences, but it is only the philosophy of nature which lives up to Hegel's standard of science: Only the philosophy of nature allows us to understand nature not as governed by a contingent set of natural laws, but as the expression of the necessary process of the self-unfolding of the Idea.[36]
3. The most important aspect of nature, its role as a presupposition of Spirit within the overall structure of the Idea, necessarily eludes natural sciences. The problem of how Nature and Reason are related can therefore be raised only within the philosophical framework of Hegel's system.

Hegel thus agrees with McDowell in his rejection of scientism which assumes that the natural sciences ultimately decide on what there is and thus take care of their own ontology. He disagrees with him in what he tries to put in place of this wrong-headed scientism: Whereas McDowell thinks that philosophy, after completing its negative, therapeutic project of laying to rest the problems which are based on a misguided understanding of nature can be laid to rest too, for Hegel this therapeutic role of philosophy can only be part of a most-ambitious project of system-building. Only once it has been proved that both nature and reason are nothing but steps in the process of the self-unfolding of the Idea, does it become possible to accommodate the claims of the natural sciences and of common sense in their respective, but, as contrasted with the philosopher's perspective, always limited rights.

Because of this crucial difference in the claims Hegel and McDowell respectively make for the role of philosophy in bringing about the reconciliation of Reason and Nature, it will not be sufficient to simply look for Hegelian answers to the two problems we have identified above in McDowell's approach. Instead it might be helpful to see how the Hegelian perspective transforms the very terms in which these problems can be formulated.

(1)   The problem of unity and internal structure of the natural: Hegel does not accept McDowell's opposition of the natural on the one hand, and the supernatural/spooky/occult on the other. On the basis of his metaphysical monism he denies the existence of any supernatural or transcendent entity; there can be no outside to the process of the Idea. In Hegel, however, there is no need to identify anything which is not spooky with the natural. Instead, he keeps the term Nature to signify a deficient stage in the process of the Idea which, however, is still presupposed by the superior level of Spirit: Human beings have to understand themselves as living in a world which is not constructed from their own activities though it is of course malleable by them (in this context, as we have seen, Hegel's discussion of second nature in his sense of the word takes place). By this terminological move Hegel avoids the danger of relaxing the label of the natural in such a way that it comes dangerously close to being trivial. On the other hand he does not run into the dilemma McDowell faces in explaining the internal structure of the natural. Instead of facing the daunting task to make room for a normatively relevant foothold for a second nature within a first nature that is identified with the realm of law, Hegel is able to show why the Spirit feels 'at home' within nature. One the one hand, Hegel has shown within the teleological structure of his Philosophy of Nature how Nature transcends itself into beings who are aware of themselves and their surroundings and who then go on to transform their natural basis into a 'second nature'. On the other hand, and even more importantly, he has tried to show that both Nature and Spirit are instantiations of the same conceptual structure which Hegel had analysed in the *Science of Logic* differing only in the specific way they are doing so. This is where the Hegelian theme of the 'unboundedness of the conceptual' that McDowell has invoked in support of his common sense-realism comes into its own.

(2)   The problem of the ontological status of the distinction between first and second nature: The question whether the distinction between first and second nature is to be understood as an ontological distinction between different levels of reality or as just a methodological one cannot be addressed meaningfully to Hegel's distinction between Nature and Spirit.

According to Hegel the phenomena of Nature and Spirit differ in the kind of intelligibility appropriate to them, but they differ in this way because they are characterised by a different ontological structure. This ontological difference however does not run the risk of tearing Nature and Spirit apart and thus creating the problems which beset a Cartesian dualism because Nature and Spirit are just moments of the movement of the Idea. Although Spirit forms the ontological truth of Nature, it still, as our analysis of § 381 has shown, presupposes that of which it is the truth. Spirit does not accede to Nature from the outside but is already involved in it. Though throughout the Philosophy of Spirit Hegel tends to stress the ways in which the Spirit emancipates itself from it's natural basis, he always reminds us that the Spirit is 'this identity [sc. of subjectivity and objectivity] only in so far as it is a return out of nature' (*Enz.* § 381).[37]

We are, as Hegel remarks in the *Introduction to the Philosophy of Nature*, both attracted to and repelled from looking for the solution to the 'riddle and problem' that nature is.[38] McDowell seems to be repelled from looking for a solution to the problem of nature simply because he tends, in a mood of Wittgensteinian quietism, to deny that there is any problem left once philosophical confusions have been laid to rest: His relaxed naturalism is meant to serve him as a ladder which should be thrown away after having served its purpose. But, as we have seen, McDowell's relaxed naturalism is vexed with structural problems which call for a solution in terms of constructive philosophy—if the concept is to be of any use at all. This throws us back to Hegel: He gives in to the attraction of finding a solution to the problem of nature by assigning nature its place within the overall ontological structure of the Idea. Not only nature in general but also its internal structure is, Hegel claims, ultimately intelligible as a necessary moment of a process in which the Idea realises itself in more and more adequate ways until it reaches its ultimate truth in Absolute Spirit. Hegel's confidence in philosophy's power of coping with the problem of nature is of course the exact opposite of McDowell's quietism—it is therapeutic only in the sense that it claims to be able to prove that after the completion of the system, there is not even conceptual room for any further problems left.

Hegel's solution to the problem of nature might ultimately repel us in its over-confidence in philosophical theorising, but as this paper has tried to show, there *is* a problem of nature which even McDowell's relaxed naturalism has not laid to rest and which is still in need of a solution which, as it seems, only constructive philosophy can provide—a solution which McDowell still owes us.

Christoph Halbig
Westfälische Wilhelms-Universität Münster
Philosophisches Seminar
Domplatz 23 48143 Münster
Germany
abessess@uni-muenster.de

NOTES

[1] The translation of this passage provided by Wallace is inaccurate: 'Nature confronts us as a riddle and a problem, whose solution both attracts and repels us'. It is not, as Wallace's translation implies, the solution to the problem of nature which attracts and repels us, but nature as a problem itself.

[2] McDowell's writings are quoted according to the following scheme: Abbreviation of the title and page number. For a list of abbreviations see references.

[3] See *MW*: 7–9.

[4] McDowell reminds us in this context that 'it is central to Absolute Idealism to reject the idea that the conceptual realm has an outer boundary' (*MW*: 44) and quotes a remark from Hegel's *Phenomenology of Spirit* in support of this idea.

[5] This argument provides the basic framework of McDowell's line of argument in *MW*: 70–72.

[6] McDowell readily acknowledges the conception of first nature as a 'hard-won achievement of human thought at a specific time, the time of the rise of modern science' (*MW*: 70), which has allowed us to make decisive progress in our understanding of the world as compared for instance to the medieval point of view; for this comparison see *TS*: 163.

[7] For this identification of first nature with the realm of law see McDowell's clarification in *RM*: '[...] in *Mind and World*, the only material I provide for a gloss on the idea of first as opposed to second nature is the idea of the realm of law' (*RM*: 97f.).

[8] For this claim see *MW*: 86.

[9] *MW*: 89.

[10] In his writings on metaethics McDowell marks out the scientistic premise that 'natural science has a foundational status in philosophical reflection about truth—that there can be no facts other than those that would figure in a scientific understanding of the world' (McDowell 1997: 222) as the most important obstacle to an adequate theory of moral values. If the notion of reality is thinned out in such a way an error theory or a projectivist theory of value appear to be the only viable options. The refutation of the scientistic theory of reality and its replacement by a 'relaxed naturalism' is thus an inevitable precondition for broadening the field of metaethical options and to make room for McDowell's own theory of moral truth. See McDowell 1985: § 5 & 1997: § 5.

[11] Williams 2002: 22f.

[12] See *TS*: 171–173.

[13] See *TS*, esp. §§ 2–4. According to McDowell these theories converge in feeling the need to provide external foundations for ethics in a conception of human nature that is identifiable without relying on any existing ethical outlooks. Such an anxiety McDowell claims was utterly foreign to the ancients.

[14] The term 'natural shapelessness' has been introduced by McDowell in (1981) in order to characterize the fact that the supervenience-basis for moral properties is discernible only by those who understand the evaluative point of the moral concepts in question. That for instance some natural properties of an act form the supervenience-basis for the moral property of being cowardly is discernible only 'from upside down', i.e. from the perspective of those of see the point of calling something cowardly. Someone who does not share this point would be left with a mere enumeration of natural properties without any unity amongst them that would allow to qualify them as the supervenience-basis for the moral property.

[15] To which McDowell himself alludes in *TS*: 173.

[16] Waters are further muddied here because McDowell in his discussion of the relation between first and second nature uses not only metaphors like *Bildung* that suggest a transformation of first nature in acquiring a second one, but also additive metaphors which seem to imply that developed human nature remains a composite of two at least epistemically separable parts. See for instance: 'our nature is largely (sic!) second nature, and our second nature is the way it is not just because of the potentialities we were born with, but also because of our upbringing, our *Bildung*' (*MW*: 87).

[17] For this problem see also Quante 2000: 962.

[18] See *MW*: 92; *TS*: 174, 178. It is nonetheless a difficult question whether McDowell should be ranked among the defenders of a realist theory of values; see for this problem Gibson 1996 and McDowell's reply to Axel Honneth who attributes a fairly strong metaethical realism to him (*R*: 300–303).

[19] In the same spirit McDowell asks us not to take the question 'What constitutes the structure of the space of reasons' seriously: If we would do so, as he admits, 'my invocation of second nature, sketchy and unsystematic as it is, will seem at best a promissory note towards a proper response' (*MW*: 178).

[20] See McDowell's invocation of § 133 of Wittgenstein's *Philosophical Investigations* in *MW*: 86.

[21] See, for instance, Bernstein 2002: 18: 'It is Hegel who explores in depth the concept of a second nature (including its historical dimensions'. See also Gubeljic *et al.* 2000.

[22] Hegel discusses these issues under the heading of embodiment (Verleiblichung), see *Enz.* § 401 and Halbig 2002, chap. 2.5 & 2.6.

[23] See *Philosophy of Right* (= *MM*: 7), §§4 and 151 and the Introduction to the *Lectures on the Philosophy of History, MM*: 12, p. 56.

[24] In the quotation *Geist* is translated as 'Spirit' not, as in Wallace's translation, as 'Mind'—which strikes me as highly misleading: What is at stake in § 381 is the relationship between Nature and Spirit as two of the three (besides Logic) major parts of Hegel's system. *Geist* comprises both subjective spirit *and* the realm of intersubjecitivity which Hegel discusses in his philosophy of objective spirit. By translating it as 'Mind' Wallace unduly narrows down the meaning of the *Geist* in a way that makes it hard to understand how it could be confronted on the same level with Nature.

[25] For an in depth analysis of this crucial paragraph see Quante 2004.

[26] See Quante 2004: 83–85.

[27] For 'external reflection' see the Logic of Essence (*MM*: 6), pp. 28–30 and Quante 2004, ibid.

[28] A detailed analysis of Hegel's theory of truth is provided in Halbig 2002: chap. 9 and Halbig 2004.

[29] For instance Hegel considers a tyranny as a deficient form of government and therefore as false.

[30] On the relation between the empirical studies of Nature and the philosophy of Nature see § 246 Z.: 'The Philosophy of Nature takes up the material which physics has prepared for it empirically, at the point to which physics has brought it, and reconstitutes it, so that experience is not its final warrant and base. Physics must therefore work into the hands of philosophy, in order that the latter may translate into the Notion the abstract universal transmitted to it, by showing how this universal, as an intrinsically necessary whole, proceeds from the Notion. The philosophical way of putting the facts is no mere whim, once in a way to walk on one's head for a change, after having walked for a long while on one's legs, or once in a way to see our everyday face bedaubed with paint: no, it is because the method of physics does not satisfy the Notion, that we have to go further'.

[31] Pippin 2002: 60.

[32] See ibid. p. 70.

[33] Ibid., p. 60.

[34] See above section 2.1. The interpretation of the unboundedness-thesis offered here implies that McDowell's attempt to domesticate the Hegelian metaphor in a Wittgensteinian spirit as just a truism dressed up in high-flown language (see *MW*: 27) ultimately fails. For an account of the different metaphilosophical approaches to the problem of realism in Hegel and McDowell see Halbig 2005.

[35] Compare Hegel's critique of Schelling in the preface to the *Phenomenology of Spirit* who according to Hegel fails to do so in a way which both compromises natural philosophy and hampers empirical research into nature.

[36] See *Enz.* § 246 A.: 'Not only must philosophy be in agreement with our empirical knowledge of Nature, but the origin and formation of the Philosophy of Nature presupposes and is conditioned by empirical physics. However, the course of a science's origin and the preliminaries of its construction are one thing, while the science itself is another. In the latter, the former can no longer appear as the foundation of the science; here, the foundation must be the necessity of the Notion'.

[37] Thus Pippin's remark 'The plot for his [Hegel's] narrative concerns attempts by human spirit to free itself from a self-understanding tied to nature, and these anthropological elements are understood as intitial, very limited successes' (Pippin 2002: 68f.) which accurately characterizes much of what is going on within Hegel's Anthropology runs the risk of loosing sight of this more fundamental way in which Nature is preserved in Spirit insofar as Spirit is defined as *its* truth.

[38] See *Enz.* § 244 Z.

REFERENCES

Bernstein, Richard J. (2002), 'McDowell's Domesticated Hegelianism', in Nicholas Smith (ed.), *Reading McDowell*. London/New York: Routledge, 9–24.

Gaynesford, Maximilian de (2004), *John McDowell*. Cambridge, MA: Polity.

Gibson, Roger F. (1995), 'McDowell's Direct Realism and Platonic Naturalism', *Philosophical Issues*, 7: 275–281.

Gubeljic *et al.* (2000), 'Nature and Second Nature in McDowell's Mind and World', in M. Willaschek (ed.), *John McDowell: Reason and Nature*. Münster: LitVerlag, 41–49.

Halbig, Christoph and Quante, Michael (2000), 'Absolute Subjektivität. Selbstbewußtsein als philosophisches Prinzip im deutschen Idealismus', in F. Gniffke and N. Herold (eds.), *Klassische Fragen der Philosophiegeschichte*, Bd. 2 Münster: LitVerlag, 83–104.

Halbig, Christoph (2002), *Objektives Denken. Erkenntnistheorie und Philosophy of Mind in Hegels System*. Stuttgart/Bad Cannstatt: Frommann-Holzboog, (= Spekulation und Erfahrung II, 48).

—— (2004), 'Ist Hegels Wahrheitsbegriff geschichtlich?', in B. Merker *et al.* (eds.), *Subjektivität und Anerkennung*. Paderborn: Mentis, 32–46.

—— (2005), 'The Philosopher as Polyphemus? Philosophy and Common Sense in Jacobi and Hegel', *Internationales Jahrbuch des Deutschen Idealismus/International Yearbook of German Idealism*, 3: 261–282.

Hegel, Georg Wilhelm Friedrich: *Werke in 20 Bänden. Theorie-Werkausgabe*. Auf der Grundlage der Werke von 1832–1845 neu edierte Ausgabe, E. Moldenhauer und K. M. Michel (eds.), Frankfurt a.M.: Suhrkamp 1970–1971. (= MM) *The Encyclopedia*

Philosophy of Mind & Philosophy of Nature is cited form the translation by W. Wallace and A.V. Miller, Oxford 1970/1971 (= *Enz.*). Additions to *Enz.* (*Zusätze*) (= *Z*).

Hegel, Georg Wilhelm Friedrich: *Ein Fragment zur Philosophie des Geistes*, in: M. J. Petry (ed.), *Hegel's Philosophy of Subjective Spirit*, Bd 1, Dordrecht: Reidel: 90–139. (= *F*)

Horstmann, Rolf-Peter (1986), 'Logifizierte Natur oder naturalisierte Logik?', in R. P. Horstmann and M. J. Petry (eds.), *Hegels Philosophie der Natur*. Stuttgart: Klett-Cotta: 290–308.

McDowell, John (1981), 'Non-Cognitivism and Rule-Following', in S. Holtzman and C. M. Leich (eds.), *Wittgenstein: To Follow a Rule*. London/Boston: Routledge and Paul: 141–162.

—— (1985), 'Values and Secondary Qualities', in Ted Honderich (ed.), *Morality and Objectivity*. London: Routledge and Paul: 110–129.

—— (1994), *Mind and World*, Cambridge, MA: Harvard University Press (= *MW*).

—— (1995), 'Two Sorts of Naturalism', in R. Hursthouse *et al.* (eds.), *Virtues and Reasons*. Oxford: Clarendon Press: 149–179. (= *TS*)

—— (1997), 'Projection and Truth in Ethics', in Stephen Darwall *et al.* (eds.), *Moral Discourse and Practice*, Oxford: Oxford University Press: 215–226.

—— (2000a), 'Kant ist der Größte. Interview mit Marcus Willaschek', *Information Philosophie*. 1: 24–30.

—— (2000b), 'Responses', in M. Willaschek (ed.), *John McDowell: Reason and Nature*. Münster: LitVerlag: 91–114. (= *RM*)

—— (2002), 'Responses', in Nicholas Smith (ed.) (2002): 269–305. (= *R*)

Papineau, David (1993), *Philosophical Naturalism*. Oxford: Blackwell.

Pippin, Robert B. (2002), 'Leaving Nature Behind: or Two Cheers for Subjectivism', in Nicholas Smith (ed.) (2002): 58–75.

Quante, Michael (2000), 'Zurück zur verzauberten Natur—ohne konstruktive Philosophie?', *Deutsche Zeitschrift für Philosophie*, 48: 953–965.

—— (2004), 'Die Natur: Setzung und Voraussetzung des Geistes. Eine Analyse des § 381 der Enzyklopädie', in B. Merker *et al.* (eds.), *Subjektivität und Anerkennung*. Paderborn: Mentis: 81–101.

Smith, Nicholas H. (ed.) (2002), *Reading McDowell*. London/New York: Routledge.

Williams, Bernard (2002), *Truth and Truthfulness*. Princeton, NJ: Princeton University Press.

6

Thought and Experience in Hegel and McDowell

Stephen Houlgate

John McDowell rightly suggests that some of his thinking is 'Hegelian, at least in spirit'.[1] In this essay, however, I wish to highlight certain ways in which McDowell's thought is non-Hegelian. I shall try to do so by examining a relatively unknown part of Hegel's philosophy: his philosophy of subjective spirit (which forms the first section of his *Encyclopaedia Philosophy of Spirit*). McDowell has written sympathetically about Hegel's *Phenomenology of Spirit* and his essay 'Faith and Knowledge'.[2] It is in Hegel's neglected philosophy of subjective spirit, however, that we find his most detailed engagement with the epistemic issues that concern McDowell.[3]

In what follows my aim is not to defend Hegel's position against that of McDowell. It is simply to point to certain significant differences between the two thinkers that, in my view, have so far been overlooked. Which position is more persuasive, I leave to others to decide.

Hegel on Sensation

In his *Science of Logic* Hegel maintains that thought and language condition all our mature mental activity. 'Logic', he writes, 'permeates every relationship of man to nature, his sensation, intuition, desire, need, instinct'.[4] In this respect Hegel anticipates McDowell's idea that conceptual capacities are operative not only in explicit acts of judgement but also in perceptual experience.[5] In marked contrast to McDowell, however, Hegel insists in his philosophy of subjective spirit that sensation, intuition and thought each make a 'notionally *separable* contribution' to their cooperation.[6] Human beings do not have—or, rather, are never aware of—any raw, unconceptualised sensations. Nonetheless, the distinctive contribution of sensations and concepts to experience can be identified.

Hegel claims, first, that sensations as such do not present us with objects that are clearly distinct from us. 'The soul to the extent that it *only* senses', he contends, 'does not as yet grasp itself as a subject confronting an object'.[7] Second, sensations are not actively produced by the sensing subject itself, but are simply given when the eyes are opened or the fingers extended in a certain direction. In sensation, therefore, we are not freely self-determining beings—as we are in reasoning—but we are determined by what lies outside us. We are passive and receptive, rather than active and spontaneous.[8]

Third, each type of sensation has its own distinctive character. Vision, for example, gives us colours, but no sense of spatial depth. Touch, by contrast, gives us depth and shape, as well as cohesion. The way we come to 'see' depth and shape, therefore, is by learning to associate what we see with what we feel. Echoing Berkeley's *New Theory of Vision*, Hegel states that:

> only in noticing that to the depth we have perceived by touch there corresponds something dark, a shadow, do we come to believe [*glauben*] that where a shadow becomes visible we see a depth.[9]

Hegel understands sensations to be different ways of being 'determined from outside'.[10] Sensations, however, are not to be understood as mere 'impressions' or 'effects' produced by outside 'causes'.[11] Hegel follows Aristotle in holding that in sensation we are not simply 'affected' by objects but we 'take up' (*aufnehmen*) something *of the objects themselves*.[12] The organs of sensation—in particular, the eyes—are thus open to and let in aspects of the world around us.[13]

Yet Hegel's position does not overlap exactly with Aristotle's. For what we take up in visual sensation, for example, is not the *form* of things, but their appearance or *look*. This look is not projected on to things by the mind, but is objective: it is the way things manifest *themselves* in the light.[14] This appearance or look of things—their colour—is carried by the light to the eyes and mind. Visual sensations are thus not mere subjective 'effects' produced by the action of the light on the eyes. In vision we take up (and take in) the look of things themselves. In this sense, Hegel could be said to be a 'direct realist' about colour. He does not deny that colours are partly 'conjured up by the eye': what we see depends on the health of the eyes, as well as the light conditions.[15] In normal circumstances, however, what we see is, indeed, the way things look. Vision, like touch, is thus a form of openness to the world.[16]

Hegel on Consciousness

Sensation alone, however, does not suffice for the concrete experience of things. Experience requires further mental operations. The first such operation Hegel discusses is that of consciousness (*Bewusstsein*).

Consciousness should not be equated with awareness as such. Sensation is also a form of awareness—the highest form thereof attained by non-human animals. Yet no sensation, in Hegel's view, brings with it a clear awareness that we stand in relation to something separate from ourselves. Consciousness, by contrast, understands what is sensed in precisely this way: as something that stands over against the self, as a *Gegenstand*. Consciousness, therefore, differs from mere sensory awareness in being the activity of understanding what is sensed to form a realm of *independent objects*.[17] On earth it is the prerogative of human beings alone.

Such consciousness, for Hegel, involves an irreducible moment of *self-awareness*, because it understands what is sensed to stand over against the self or the 'I'. Hegel reserves the term 'self-consciousness' (*Selbstbewußtsein*) for the particular form of consciousness that is wholly absorbed by itself; but he argues that there must be an element of self-awareness even in consciousness that focuses on objects. For, as he puts it, 'only when I come to apprehend myself as 'I', does the Other become objective to me, confront me'.[18]

All such consciousness of objects, for Hegel, is the result of the free activity of the self. The self actively differentiates the sensed content from itself and places or *posits* that content over against itself.[19] It does so in an act of thought. The self thus *understands* the sensed content to be an object distinct from itself. The sensations of brown, round and hard are given to us, but there being an independent object—for example, a tree—over there is not given. The content we receive in sensation must thus be *set* over there in thought in order for us to be conscious that what we see and feel is a 'tree'.

Though the activity of consciousness is free or 'spontaneous', it is not self-conscious or deliberate. It is not activity of which we are aware. Since consciousness remains blind to the activity through which it distinguishes what is objective from itself, it regards objects as simply *given* to it.[20] As a result, consciousness believes that it simply opens its eyes and *sees* the tree, without further ado.

The act of thought whereby we objectify what is sensed is not performed on sensations that are already present to the mind. We do not first become aware of sensory content and subsequently understand it to be objective. Rather, colours, shapes and textures are taken up into the mind and enter our awareness *only in so far* as they are understood to be objective. Hegel believes that we can isolate the distinctive contributions to experience made by our passive, receptive sensibility and the unnoticed activity of thought. Yet he also insists that in concrete human experience these two contributions are inseparable. As very young children, we can be aware of sensations without an understanding of objectivity.[21] In more mature human beings, however, the (unnoticed) activity of thought confers objectivity on sensory content *as* the latter is being received into the mind.

Consciousness understands its sensuous content to be objective by employing certain categories. Different forms of consciousness employ different categories. Sensuous certainty employs the simplest and least determinate categories, such as 'being' and 'something' (*etwas*). Accordingly, it understands what we see and feel simply to *be there* and to be *something*. It is the bare consciousness that what is sensed, *is*, and is *this* individual thing. In Hegel's own words, sensuous certainty 'separates the material [of sensation] from itself and gives it initially the determination of *being*'.[22]

Perception, by contrast, knows what is sensed not just to *be there*, but to be a thing with manifold *properties* that are shared by other things in different ways. Perception thus goes beyond the immediacies of sensation in ways that sensuous certainty does not: for it understands colours and textures not just to be the individual colours and textures they are but to be instances of universals that extend across a whole range of objects. Furthermore, it understands these objects not to be isolated, individual things but to be *connected* in multiple ways by the various properties they share. While sensuous certainty merely focuses on the simple singularity of things, therefore, perception grasps their 'connectedness' (*Zusammenhang*).[23] This connectedness is not immediately given in sensation, but is understood or posited by the perceiving self using categories such as 'thing' (*Ding*), 'property' and 'universal'.[24]

The third form of consciousness identified by Hegel is understanding proper or *Verstand*. Understanding proper knows the object to be connected with others not just through shared properties but also through causality. Furthermore, such understanding considers objects and their causal relations to obey certain laws. *Verstand* thus knows there to be not just contingent but also necessary connections between things.[25]

Experience, for Hegel, requires all three forms of consciousness and the categories they employ. Together they constitute the *unnoticed* activity through which we understand what we see, touch and hear to constitute an *independent, objective* world. Such activity confers on the content of sensation an intelligible form that does not belong to that content itself. Nonetheless, 'this alteration [*Veränderung*] appears to consciousness as one brought about without its subjective activity, and the determinations it places [*setzt*] in the object count for it as belonging only to the latter, as immediately given in it [*seiend*]'.[26] As far as consciousness is concerned, therefore, it simply finds things, properties and causal relations in the world it encounters and so is a purely receptive consciousness. In fact, however, it is not purely receptive, for it actively *posits* the things we experience and their logical connectedness.

Hegel assigns this (unnoticed) active role to consciousness because sensations alone do not provide the awareness of objectivity that ordinary experience entails. What we take in from the world through the senses does not account for experience as we know it; accordingly, the mind must supply the missing element in experience through its own free activity. If what is sensed is to be experienced as something objective, therefore, it must be *understood* to be such through certain categories. Experience in the ordinary, everyday sense is thus the product of the cooperation of sensibility and various forms of understanding. Such understanding, though freely active, is not conscious and deliberate. Rather, our conceptual capacities are drawn into operation automatically on encountering things. Without the operation of such conceptual capacities, we could—like non-human animals—have sensations, but we could not have the concrete, objective experiences with which we are familiar. We could not see trees or hear cars go by.

Like Kant, Hegel holds that concepts and categories are employed in judgement.[27] If perceptual experience depends on understanding and its categories, therefore, it must also be inseparable from the making of judgements—judgements such as 'that tree is brown' and 'the car made that noise'. These judgements will be tacit and implicit, not explicit; but they are nonetheless the irreducible conditions of objective experience. Experience is thus at one and the same time a conceptually structured seeing and a judging-that . . . or knowing-that . . . (*Wissen, dass* . . .).[28] Indeed, it is the former only in being the latter. Strictly speaking, therefore, we do not *see that* things are thus and so; rather, in seeing we *judge* that things are thus and so. Nor is the fact that things are thus and so taken up in any other way. Colours and textures are indeed taken up directly from the world, but the idea 'that this is something red' is not. It is *posited* in an unnoticed act of judgement.[29]

Hegel on Intelligence

Experience, however, does not just involve sensation and consciousness. It also involves a further form of thought that Hegel calls 'intelligence' (*Intelligenz*). All that is given to consciousness are sensations. The object-character of the things we see and the causal connections between them are not given but are thought or 'posited' by consciousness itself. Yet consciousness takes that object-character and such causal connections to be *given* to it, since it does not notice its own mental activity. As far as consciousness is concerned, all it is doing is passively registering *that* such and such is the case and *that* X causes Y. Intelligence, by contrast, is aware that it is active and that the world it experiences is opened up by its own intelligent activity: 'it is *for* the free spirit that it produces from out of itself [*aus sich hervorbringt*] the self-developing and altering determinations of the object'.[30] Furthermore, intelligence takes the world it encounters to be intrinscially *rational* (*vernünftig*) and it understands its own activity to render that rationality fully explicit.[31]

Such intelligence takes several different forms. Its least developed and least 'intelligent' form, Hegel claims, is intuition (*Anschauung*). Like consciousness, intuition still *finds* itself confronted by things and so does not yet have a clear sense that it is active. Nonetheless, since it is a form of intelligence, it regards what it sees as intrinsically rational. It does not, however, have a fully determinate understanding of the rational character of the world, but has merely what Hegel calls an 'indeterminate certainty of reason'.[32]

For reasons I do not propose to explore here (because they would require close study of Hegel's logic and philosophy of nature), intuition considers the inherent rationality of things to reside in their *spatio-temporal* character.[33] In Hegel's view, the all-encompassing continuity of space and time is not simply *given* in intuition, but is actively posited by intuition (though without its fully realising that it does so). As Hegel puts it, intuition itself 'casts [the content of sensation] out *into space and time*' (*wirft ihn in Raum und Zeit hinaus*).[34] Intuition does not thereby alter the given content of sensation; rather, 'the activity of intuition produces [. . .] a shifting of sensation away from us, a transformation of what is sensed into an object existing outside of us'.[35] Intuition *finds* itself confronted by things, therefore, only by virtue of the fact that it actively opens the space in which they are found.

Note that intuition does not arbitrarily impose a spatio-temporal order on to sensations that are themselves utterly non-spatiotemporal. It does not wilfully assign positions to patches of colour or capriciously project depth just where it wills. Spatial position and depth are in one sense already given in sensation: colours occupy a given position in the visual field; touch is the direct sensing of shape and depth; and shape and depth can themselves be 'seen' by being associated with shadows.[36] Furthermore, all sensations are in themselves 'transitory' (*vorübergehend*) and thus temporal.[37] Intuition does not rearrange or alter the sequence of what is given in sensation. Like consciousness, intuition accepts what is given, but *understands* it in a particular way. In contrast to consciousness, however, intuition understands what is sensed to form not just a set of objects over against us, but a spatio-temporal *totality* that surrounds us and within which we are located.[38] It understands the colours we see and the shapes we feel to belong to, and to fit into, an objective, all-encompassing and fully extended spatio-temporal continuum. It is this awareness of a spatio-temporal continuum—rather than simple depth or transitoriness—that is not given directly with sensation but actively generated or 'posited' by intuition itself.

The specific activity through which intuition casts colours and shapes out into space and time is that of attention (*Aufmerksamkeit*). We do not, therefore, just attend to what is already disclosed to us; rather, it is through attention itself that a concrete, fully extended world of space and time first comes into view. Such attention, Hegel claims, is 'something that depends on my free will [*Willkür*]', albeit one that is habitual and largely unnoticed.[39] It is not, however, an act of will in which we assert ourselves against the world. It is an act in which we open up our field of vision to allow what is seen to be encountered in its full concreteness. It is simultaneously an act in which we allow ourselves to be filled with whatever our now expanded and concretised field of vision contains.[40] Attending is thus an act of self-restraint through which we—literally—*make space* for what is seen, heard and felt. It is an act in which we both *give* to ourselves, and give ourselves *to*, a world of concretely objective things, and without which experience as we know it would not be possible.[41]

Hegel goes on to examine further acts of the mind in which intelligence becomes more overtly active and free. The imagination, for example, produces (via association) 'general representations' which form the basis of our empirical concepts.[42] Imagination also produces the symbols and signs essential for language.[43] Finally, Hegel argues, intelligence takes the form of thought in which conceiving, judging and reasoning are explicitly understood *both* to be our own activities *and* to disclose fully the intelligible, rational character of the world.[44]

Hegel discusses these activities of intelligence separately, but he makes it clear that they are in fact inseparable and together constitute the conditions of mature experience.[45] In particular, he insists that *thought* permeates all our mental activity. 'In all human intuiting' he says, 'there is thinking; similarly, thinking is what is universal in all representations, recollections, and in every spiritual [*geistig*] activity'.[46] Intuition thus not only incorporates consciousness and its categories, it is also inseparable from the explicit activities of conceiving, judging and reasoning. Furthermore, intuition is inseparable from imagination and language. Intuition can open a world of identifiable objects only if it employs empirical concepts; empirical concepts are general representations produced by the imagination and combined with categories of thought;[47] all thought (whether self-conscious or not) requires language.[48] Without the joint activity of imagination, thought and language, therefore, concrete determinate intuition cannot occur.

Hegel does not deny that in one sense experience *precedes* thought: much of our experience calls for further reflection. Indeed, this is what gives rise to science and philosophy.[49] Hegel points out, however, that the experience upon which we reflect and about which we think is itself made possible by thought: because only thought—through its unnoticed and explicit activity—can understand what is given in sensation to constitute a world of objective, identifiable, spatio-temporal things. It is not the case, therefore, that we *first* have bare sensations or intuitions and only afterwards bring thought to bear on what we see. As mature human beings, we have sensations only in so far as we intuit things, and we intuit things only in so far as we employ empirical concepts and general logical categories and so exercise both our imaginative and conceptual capacities.

Hegel concedes that young children can be aware of sensations without the use of concepts: at first, he says, 'the child has only a sensation of light by which things are manifest to it. This mere sensation misleads the child into reaching out for something distant as if it were near'. Yet children acquire the capacity for concrete experience—the capacity to intuit and see *things*—as they learn to attend, imagine, speak and think.[50] Furthermore, our capacity for rich, discriminating and comprehensive experience is enhanced as we develop our ability to attend, imagine, speak and think through education or *Bildung*. Empirical concepts are in principle revisable and in that sense contingent; logical categories, by contrast, are *a priori* and necessary. We can, however, develop a more subtle and profound understanding of those logical categories, and the role of speculative philosophy is precisely to provide such an understanding.[51] Both in our individual lives and through history, therefore, human beings are in the process of conceptual *Bildung*; and with such increasing education comes an enhanced ability not just to think about what we experience but also to see and experience the world in the first place.[52]

Thought and Being in Hegel

Having now sketched (all too briefly) Hegel's understanding of the basic operations of the mind in cognition, we need to address the following question: to what extent, on this understanding, do we know anything of the world, or are we simply caught up in a web of our own concepts?

In sensation we take up directly the look, shape and texture of things, but nothing else that belongs to concrete experience is taken up in this way. The spatio-temporal continuum in which we experience things is projected by intuition; the general representations which underlie our empirical concepts are the product of our imagination; and the object-character or 'thinginess' of things and the causal relations between them are posited by thought in its different forms. When we see a car going by, therefore, we do not actually *see* a car: we see colours that we *understand* and *judge* to be a car.[53] Such judgements make experience possible, but, as deVries points out, they are never firmly grounded in the sensations that prompt them.[54]

Yet this is not to say that our judging activity is wholly indifferent to what we take from the world. What we see and feel has to be compatible with, and fit, the judgements we make; and to the extent that it does not do so, we are required to revise our judgements. As mature human beings, all that we see, feel and hear is *understood* in certain ways: we have no unconceptualised sensations (of which we are aware). Our understanding, however, may require revision if what we see does not allow us to sustain that understanding. In this way, our good judgements take account of what is sensed, even if they are not grounded in it.

Not only is the conceptual structure or 'content' we understand the world to have not taken in by the senses, it is not taken in in any other way: for neither intuition, imagination or thought is a mode of receptivity. For Hegel, therefore, there is no way we can *take up* or *receive* conceptual content from the outside world. All such content is posited by consciousness and intelligence in their various forms:

> That the content or object [*Gegenstand*] is *given* to knowledge, something coming to it *from outside*, is therefore only an *illusion* [*Schein*], and mind, by removing this illusion, proves to be what it is in itself, namely, absolutely self-determining, […] the ideal existence that produces all reality *from itself.* […] Consequently, the activity of mind, far from being restricted to a *mere taking up* [*Aufnehmen*] of the given must, on the contrary, be called a *creative* [*schaffende*] activity.[55]

Hegel maintains, however, that his philosophy, unlike Kant's, is not a 'subjective idealism'.[56] He insists that things are themselves spatio-temporal, independently of intuition, and that the world is itself inherently rational: 'laws', he says, 'are determinations of the understanding [*Verstand*] that is inherent in the world itself'.[57] Yet how can this be? How can thought understand the inherent conceptual structure *of* the world but not take up any conceptual content *from* the world? Hegel's answer is that thought understands the structure of being *a priori* from within itself: 'it knows that what is *thought*, *is*, and that what *is*, only *is* in so far as it is thought [*Gedanke*]'.[58] This does not mean that I can deduce through pure thought that there is tree or car in front of me. It means that thought knows through itself what the general *categorial*, ontological structure of being is. It knows that being comprises spatio-temporal things with properties, causal relations and quantitative determinations. Thought knows, therefore, that what there is before me is a realm of law-governed objects, even if I may be mistaken in judging that this is a cat rather than a dog. Hegel thus shares the pre-Kantian, Spinozan conviction that thought can disclose and determine through itself the nature of the world *an sich*.[59]

Hegel justifies this claim in two ways. The long version is supplied by the *Phenomenology*, a text I do not propose to examine here.[60] The shorter version goes like this: thought has an *a priori* understanding of the nature of being because thought is itself nothing but *being* that understands itself. Thought is not something cut off from being and restricted to entertaining only what is 'conceivable' or 'possible', but it is being itself that has come to know *that* it is. Thought necessarily has it within itself, therefore, to understand *what* being is: the fundamental ontological structure of being itself. Thought can, indeed, go astray in its *a priori* understanding of being; but it can do so, in Hegel's view, only by adhering to one-sided abstractions. If thought eschews such abstractions, it cannot but disclose the true character of being, because it is nothing but *being's own understanding of itself.*[61]

Hegel's philosophical position thus combines both a quasi-Kantian and a quasi-Spinozan component. On the one hand, he argues that thought actively 'posits' the space of things, properties and causal relations that we experience. This is the quasi-Kantian side to Hegel. On the other hand, he contends that there is nothing subjectively idealistic about such positing, because it is rooted in thought's *a priori* understanding that there is being and that it comprises causally related things—an understanding that is in fact being's own understanding of itself. This is the quasi-Spinozan side to Hegel. When thought posits the space of objective 'being' by means of its categories, therefore, it is not simply constructing a world of its own devising. It is bringing explicitly to mind what it knows there actually *to be*.

For Hegel, thought knows the general categorial structure of the world, not because it somehow takes it up from the outside (in the way it takes up the look of things), but because thought is inherently—*within itself*—the understanding of what there is. This does not guarantee that all our empirical judgements are correct; but it does justify us in understanding what we see to be a realm of objectively existing, rationally connected things. It thereby provides us with good reason to understand our perceptual experience to be *of the world*.

Hegel is clear that experience is not simply an openness to things that lets them come immediately before the mind. As he puts it, 'one can bring the qualities of something before the eyes [*vor Augen*], but not the something itself'.[62] Experience is openness to, and takes in directly, the look and shape of, say, this tree, but it does not take in its being 'something', its being an 'object'. That aspect of the tree (along with its belonging to a spatio-temporal continuum and being causally connected to other things) is posited by the mind. Yet the mind posits what it sees as an 'object', *knowing a priori that there is, indeed, a world of spatio-temporal, causally connected objects out there*. It knows, therefore, that it has good reason to understand what it sees and feels to constitute an *object* connected in various ways to other objects. Furthermore, provided that the object looks and feels as a 'tree' should (according to its empirical concept), we have good reason to understand it to be a tree in particular (as opposed to some other thing). Experience is thus not just a series of subjective 'impressions'; it is the encountering of what—with good reason—*we understand to be there*.

In Hegel's view, we do not actually *see* the tree, if 'seeing' is taken in its precise sense: for all we see are the colours and shapes that we understand to form the tree. We do see the tree, however, if 'seeing' is taken in a broader and more everyday sense: that is, if *'seeing'* (*Sehen*) is taken to be the 'concrete habit which *immediately* combines the many determinations of sensation, consciousness, intuition and understanding in one simple act'.[63] In this ordinary, non-philosophical sense, we *see*—directly—all manner of things around us. What it means to see them, however, is not quite what ordinary consciousness and intuition think.

McDowell and Hegel

It is now time to turn to the similarities and differences between Hegel and McDowell. First, neither Hegel nor McDowell believes that experience consists in simply having sensations. Both agree that, in McDowell's words, 'experiences have their content by virtue of the fact that conceptual capacities are operative in them'.[64] The motivation for making this claim, however, is in each case slightly different.

McDowell argues that experiences must provide reasons for our empirical judgements if these judgements are to be *about* the world. At the same time, he insists that only what is 'conceptually shaped' can provide a warrant or justification for belief and judgement.[65] Experience must, therefore, be understood to involve the operation of conceptual capacities, if it is to stand in a rational, rather than merely causal, relation to our judgements, that is, if it is to provide *reasons* or *warrants* for those judgements.[66]

Hegel, on the other hand, maintains that experience must involve understanding because without it no *experience* of 'things' with 'properties' and 'causal' connections would be possible in the first place. In contrast to McDowell, therefore, Hegel is concerned to show what is needed for us to have experience at all, rather than what is required for experience to be able to ground or justify judgements. This is not to say, however, that Hegel would disagree with the claims that 'a bare presence cannot be a ground for anything' and that 'only what is conceptually shaped can justify belief'.[67] Indeed, he appears to hint at precisely this thought when he remarks that sheer sensation does not fall within 'the common field of reasons' (*das gemeinsame Feld der Gründe*).[68]

Second, both Hegel and McDowell accept that our empirical concepts, and the corresponding conceptual capacities, are developed through the historical (and personal) process of education or *Bildung* and so are intrinsically revisable.[69]

Third, both Hegel and McDowell accept the 'unboundedness of the conceptual'. They agree that experience involves the operation of conceptual capacities and that the world itself is intelligibly structured—that there is, in Hegel's words, 'understanding, reason in the world'.[70] As far as I can tell, however, McDowell has a more pared down conception of what such worldly reason involves than Hegel does.[71]

Much more would need to be said on this last point to determine the precise relation between Hegel and McDowell. I shall restrict myself here to comparing what both have in mind by claiming that conceptual capacities are drawn into operation in experience.

McDowell emphasises that the 'capacities that belong to spontaneity are already operative *in* receptivity'. They are not put to work 'on something independently supplied to them by receptivity'.[72] Experience, therefore, is not the result of our intellect's *acting on* something given; rather, it comprises 'states or occurrences of sheer *passivity*' (or receptivity) in which conceptual capacities are operative.[73] Those conceptual capacities thus belong to our receptivity itself. This means that when they are drawn into operation they themselves become distinctively human ways of *passively receiving* what is in the world. As such, McDowell maintains, they allow us to take or let in not just bare sensations but 'conceptual content'. Experience, as McDowell construes it, does not, therefore, put a 'construction on some pre-conceptual deliverances of sensibility'. On the contrary, thanks to the operation of our conceptual capacities in our receptivity 'conceptual content is already borne by impressions that independent reality makes on one's senses'.[74]

More accurately, what we take in from the world in experience are perceptible or observable *facts*, such as the fact 'that things are thus and so'.[75] Such facts constitute the conceptual content of experience and can also become the content of a judgement, 'if the subject decides to take the experience at face value'. Thanks to the operation of our conceptual capacities, therefore, experience is 'openness to the layout of reality' itself: 'in enjoying an experience one is open to manifest facts, facts that obtain anyway and impress themselves on one's sensibility'.[76] These facts that are taken in in experience as 'thinkable contents' constitute 'norms for belief'. That is to say, 'the fact that things are thus and so [. . .] equip[s] one with a warrant for believing that things are thus and so'.[77] In this way, McDowell contends, empirical judgements are grounded in the facts of the world and so are 'under constraint from the world itself'.[78] They are judgements and beliefs that are actually *about* the world rather than beliefs that spin frictionlessly in a void.

The important point to note is that Hegel holds two views that McDowell wants to see as incompatible. McDowell stresses that 'in judgements of experience, conceptual capacities are not exercised *on* non-conceptual deliverances of sensibility. Conceptual capacities are already operative *in* the deliverances of sensibility themselves'.[79] Hegel, however, holds *both* that conceptual capacities are operative in receptivity *and* that our understanding works on the non-conceptual deliverances of sensibility. He agrees with McDowell that human beings do not receive (or, at least, are not aware of) bare sensations: for Hegel, we see nothing without understanding it to be some determinate (or indeterminate) thing. In this sense, understanding is irreducibly operative in receptivity. Yet Hegel argues that, in being so operative, understanding does precisely what McDowell wishes to deny: it 'make[s] experiences of an objective world out of items that are in themselves less than that'.[80]

In Hegel's view, our conceptual capacities are drawn into operation in receptivity in the sense that nothing is received into the conscious mind without their operation. Through their operation, however, we actively *posit* what we see *as* something objective. When drawn into operation, therefore, our conceptual capacities *do not themselves become ways of being receptive*: they do not let us take in more than is supplied by sensation, let us take in facts as thinkable contents. For Hegel, in contrast to McDowell, we can never *take in* or *let in* facts or conceptual content: we take in nothing but sensory content. In taking in that content, however, we actively understand and judge it to be something objective that is there before us.

It should be clear from this that Hegel and McDowell have different conceptions of the role of judgement. For McDowell, judgement is the activity of 'freely making up one's mind' that things are thus and so, and so 'actively exercising control over one's cognitive life'.[81] If it is responsible, such judgement is grounded in experience. Indeed, it 'simply endorses the conceptual content [...] that is already possessed by the experience on which it is grounded'.[82] Judgement, however, is not itself constitutive of experience. As McDowell puts it, 'there is a disconnection between perceptual experience and judging'.[83]

For Hegel, by contrast, active judgement and understanding are constitutive *of* experience, for without them we would not experience a world of *objects* at all. They are the 'conceptual capacities' at work in all experience. We experience what we see as a world of objects only because we employ categories such as 'something', 'thing', 'property' and 'cause'; and we employ such categories, as we employ all concepts, in acts of judgement. Judgement and understanding, therefore, make experience possible. Such judgement is, however, not always deliberate or self-conscious. Indeed, it is more often habitual and automatic. In that sense, Hegel would agree with McDowell that our conceptual capacities are 'passively drawn into operation'.[84] We do, indeed, find ourselves 'passively saddled with conceptual contents': Hegel says of both consciousness and intuition that they *find* themselves confronted with a realm of things.[85] We find ourselves so confronted, however, only because of the (largely unnoticed) active operation of understanding and judgement *on* the sensations we receive.

In Hegel's view, experience does precede many empirical judgements. Yet Hegel argues that such experience itself involves judgement: it involves judging that things are thus and so, and thereby positing a realm of objects. The judgements that are *about* experience are not, therefore, the first judgements we make: they build on judgements already made *in* perceptual experience itself, whenever I 'see' a tree or a car.

For Hegel, we do not passively *take in* facts; we actively judge things to be thus and so. To what extent, then, are our experience and judgement subject to *external* constraint? Our visual and tactile sensations take in directly the look and shape of things. Yet they do not ground the judgements that are constitutive of experience. Such judgements make sense of sensations in terms of empirical concepts and logical categories that are acquired as we learn to speak.[86] Empirical concepts are the inherited (though revisable) products of the imagination; logical categories are generated immanently within thought. Neither, therefore, is derived directly from, or firmly grounded in, our sensory awareness of the outside world. Nonetheless, the judgements we make are the ways in which we make sense of what is given to us in sensation; sensations must thus allow us to understand them in specific ways, even if they do not ground our understanding. As McDowell points out, therefore, Hegel incorporates *receptivity* into reason.[87] Our judgements are to a degree constrained by the world outside, even though, for Hegel (in contrast to McDowell), no conceptual content is taken in from the outside.

Yet external constraint is not the only kind of constraint that the world can exercise on us. In Hegel's view, thought is *internally* constrained by the logical categories that are inherent in being. Thought is constrained in this way because it is being's own understanding of itself. Thought actively opens up for us a space of objects that is not given directly with sensation. The logical-ontological categories in terms of which we understand the world are not, however, arbitrarily chosen by thought; they are immanent in thought because they are immanent in being. Thought is, therefore, constrained internally by the nature of being, by the way the world is.[88] Being constrained internally in this way—being passive in being active—constitutes, for Hegel, true *freedom* of thought.[89]

This, in my view, is the principal difference between Hegel and McDowell. For McDowell, 'we seem to need rational constraints on thinking and judging, from a reality *external* to them, if we are to make sense of them as bearing on a reality outside thought at all'.[90] Or, to put it more bluntly, we know *of* the world only what we take in *from* the world outside (or what can be grounded in what we take from that world). For Hegel, by contrast, we know *of* the world from *within* thought—at least, we know the categorial structure of the world from within thought, if not its contingent empirical features. It is this *a priori* understanding of being that justifies us in understanding what we see to be objectively existing 'things' with 'properties'. This understanding is in one sense a 'projection' on to what we see. But it is a projection that is wrung from us *by the world itself*, by what the world is known to be from within thought.

Perhaps another way to state the difference between McDowell and Hegel is this: for McDowell, the world exercises authority over thought through perceptual experience. For Hegel, by contrast, the world exercises authority over our perceptual experience through thought. Thought is the authority that ensures that our perceptual experience is of the world, not the other way round.

Conclusion

McDowell and Hegel are clearly close in many ways. It seems to me, however, that their positions are significantly different. McDowell seeks to ground our empirical judgements in experience of the outside world. The conceptual capacities operative in experience enable us to *take in* facts—conceptual content— that ground and anchor our judgements. For Hegel, by contrast, experience is made possible by the active employment of empirical concepts and general logical-ontological categories that *introduce* conceptual content into experience. Thought employs general categories, such as 'something', 'cause' and 'object', because it is internally constrained by the world itself to do so. We are justified in understanding what we see to be a world of causally related objects, therefore, because we know *a priori* that the world comprises causally related objects.

Note that this does not justify our use of specific *empirical* concepts, because they are the products of the imagination and are not immanent in thought or being.[91] Empirical concepts are not firmly grounded in perceptual experience, either, for they are the conditions of perceptual experience, inherited when we acquire language. Empirical concepts are, of course, revised in the light of experience and new concepts are sometimes formed. Even in these cases, however, the concepts are not firmly anchored in, or made necessary by, perceptual experience, because they are ultimately the product of our imaginative freedom.[92] New empirical concepts must make sense of our given sensations, take account of past experience and be consistent with the basic categories of thought, but beyond that the activity of the imagination is unconstrained. Even the empirical judgements that are about experience, rather than constitutive of it, lack a firm *foundation* in experience, therefore, because no empirical concept has any such firm foundation.

For Hegel, in contrast to McDowell, empirical judgements cannot be firmly anchored in the outside world. Some aspects of nature can be known a priori and some laws of nature—such as Galileo's law of free fall and Kepler's laws of planetary motion—can be justified by philosophical reason.[93] Our distinctively empirical understanding of nature, however, must be left without ultimate foundation or anchoring. If we want to know what the world really *requires* us to think, therefore, we must look not at our empirical judgements but at the *a priori* categories and concepts of thought. These categories—whose structure Hegel endeavours to clarify in his speculative philosophy—are the fundamental concepts in terms of which thought is internally constrained to think by the very nature of being.

Hegel and McDowell share many important ideas in common. In my view, however, Hegel's conviction that being principally constrains thought internally and immanently—rather than externally through perceptual experience—clearly distinguishes his rationalism (inspired by Spinoza and Kant) from McDowell's 'non-traditional' empiricism.[94] McDowell writes that 'Hegel is not good at making his way of thinking inviting to people who find it alien', and he suggests that some of his own ideas might show outsiders ways of entering into Hegel's work.[95] I think that to an extent this is true. Outsiders should, however, beware: they may find the Hegelian world they are entering to be somewhat less congenial than they had hoped.[96]

Stephen Houlgate
Department of Philosophy
University of Warwick
Coventry CV4 7AL
UK
stephen.houlgate@warwick.ac.uk

NOTES

[1] McDowell, 2002: 269.

[2] See McDowell, 2003, and McDowell, 2004.

[3] It might be thought that Hegel's *Phenomenology of Spirit* should be the main focus of attention in any study of the relation between Hegel and McDowell. In my view, however, the *Phenomenology of Spirit* exposes immanent contradictions in the self-understanding of various shapes of consciousness, but does not set out directly Hegel's own philosophical understanding of the workings of the mind. The latter task falls to Hegel's *philosophy* of spirit, in particular his philosophy of subjective spirit. For my more detailed thoughts on the role of Hegel's *Phenomenology*, see Houlgate, 2005: 48–66. For my views on the principal differences between Hegel's *Phenomenology* and his philosophy proper (including the philosophical 'phenomenology' that forms part of Hegel's philosophy of subjective spirit), see Houlgate, 2005: 101–5, 176–7. The most detailed study of Hegel's philosophy of subjective spirit in English is deVries, 1988. For alternative approaches to the Hegel-McDowell relation, see, for example, Stern, 1999, and Bernstein, 2002.

[4] Hegel, 1969: I, p. 20; Hegel, 1999: 32.

[5] McDowell, 1996: 12.

[6] My emphasis. See McDowell, 1996: 9.

[7] Hegel, 1970c: §400 Addition, p. 100; Hegel, 1971a: 75. See also Hegel, 1970c: §400 Remark, p. 98; Hegel, 1971a: 73: 'in sensation, by contrast [. . .]'. I have occasionally altered the published translation.

[8] Hegel, 1970c: §400 Addition, p. 100; Hegel, 1971a: 75.

[9] Hegel, 1970c: §401 Addition, p. 104; Hegel, 1971a: 78. See Berkeley, 1975: §45, pp. 20–1, and Hegel, 1971b: III, p. 274.

[10] Hegel, 1970c: §401 Addition, p. 102; Hegel, 1971a: 77.

[11] Hegel, 1970c: §445 Remark, p. 241; Hegel, 1971a: 189.

[12] Hegel, 1971b: II, p. 208.

[13] Vision and touch, for Hegel, are the senses that are most open to the independent character of things. In smell and taste, we are more aware of ways in which things *interact* with our body. See Hegel, 1994: 79.

[14] Hegel, 1970b: §320 Addition, p. 265; Hegel, 1970d: 214: 'Colour, therefore, is the physical nature [of body] which has come forth on to the surface, which no longer has anything internal for itself [. . .] but is pure appearance [*reine Erscheinung*]; in other words, everything that it is *in itself* is also *there* [*alles, was sie an sich ist, ist auch da*]'. See also Hegel, 1994: 77: 'the pure being-manifest [*Manifestiertsein*] of objects'.

[15] Hegel, 1970b: §§317 Addition, 320 Addition, pp. 227, 256–7; Hegel, 1970d: 183, 207.

[16] See, for example, Hegel, 1970c: §401, p. 100; Hegel, 1971a: 75: 'What the sentient soul finds within it is, on one hand, the naturally immediate [*das natürliche Unmittelbare*], as "ideally" in it and made its own'.

[17] Hegel, 1970c: §413, p. 199; Hegel, 1971a: 153.

[18] Hegel, 1970c: §413 Addition, p. 201; Hegel, 1971a: 154. For a discussion of Hegel's account of self-consciousness, see Houlgate, 2003.

[19] Hegel, 1970c: §413 and Addition, p. 199; Hegel, 1971a: 153.

[20] Hegel, 1970c: §415 Addition 1, p. 203; Hegel, 1971a: 156.

[21] Hegel, 1970c: §396 Addition, p. 80; Hegel, 1971a: 59.

[22] Hegel, 1970c: §418, p. 206; Hegel, 1971a: 159. See also Hegel, 1994: 151.

[23] Hegel, 1970c: §420 Addition, p. 209; Hegel, 1971a: 162.

[24] Hegel, 1970c: §419, p. 208; Hegel, 1971a: 160.

[25] Hegel, 1970c: §§422–3 and Additions, pp. 210–12; Hegel, 1971a: 162–5. See also Hegel, 1994: 158.

[26] Hegel, 1970c: §415 Addition 1, p. 203; Hegel, 1971a: 156.

[27] Hegel, 1970c: §467 Addition, p. 286; Hegel, 1971a: 226. See also Kant, 1997: B 94, p. 205: 'understanding in general can be represented as a faculty for judging'.

[28] Hegel, 1970c: §445 Addition, p. 244; Hegel, 1971a: 191.

[29] In this respect I understand Hegel's position to be very close to that of Kant. Kant maintains that 'the same function that gives unity to the different representations in a judgment also gives unity to the mere synthesis of different representations in an intuition'. In the following sentence he makes it clear, however, that judging and introducing synthetic unity into intuitions not only employ 'the same function' but also occur together in the same action: 'The same understanding, therefore, and *indeed by means of the very same actions* through which it brings the logical form of a judgment into concepts by means of the analytical unity, also brings a transcendental content into its representations by means of the synthetic unity of the manifold in intuition in general'. See Kant, 1997: B 104–5, pp. 211–12, my emphasis.

[30] Hegel, 1970c: §441 Addition, p. 234; Hegel, 1971a: 182.

[31] Hegel, 1970c: §445 Addition, p. 244; Hegel, 1971a: 191: 'Thus intelligence strips the object of the form of contingency, grasps its rational nature and posits it as subjective'.

[32] Hegel, 1970c: §441 Addition, p. 233; Hegel, 1971a: 182. See also Hegel, 1994: 179.

[33] For a study of Hegel's account of space and time in his philosophy of nature, see Houlgate, 2005: 106–10, 122–31.

[34] Hegel, 1970c: §448, p. 249; Hegel, 1971a: 195.

[35] Hegel, 1970c: §448 Addition, p. 252; Hegel, 1971a: 197.

[36] Hegel, 1970c: §401 Addition, p. 104; Hegel, 1971a: 78. See also Hegel, 1994: 76–7.

[37] Hegel, 1970c: §400, p. 97; Hegel, 1971a: 73.

[38] Hegel, 1970c: §449 Addition, p. 254; Hegel, 1971a: 199.

[39] Hegel, 1970c: §448 Addition, pp. 249–50; Hegel, 1971a: 196.

[40] Hegel, 1970c: §448 Addition, p. 249; Hegel, 1971a: 195: 'Attention [...] must be understood more exactly as the filling of oneself with a content that is both objective and subjective'. See also Hegel, 1994: 195.

[41] See also Houlgate, 1993: 112–14.

[42] Hegel, 1970c: §§455, 456 and Additions, pp. 262–7; Hegel, 1971a: 206–10.

[43] Hegel, 1970c: §§458–9, pp. 270–1; Hegel, 1971a: 212–14.

[44] Hegel, 1970c: §465 and Addition, pp. 283–4; Hegel, 1971a: 224.

[45] Hegel, 1970c: §445 Remark, p. 243; Hegel, 1971a: 190: 'The truth [...] lies in this, that intuition, representation [*Vorstellen*], etc. are not isolated, but exist only as "moments" in the totality of cognition itself'.

[46] Hegel, 1970a: §24 Addition 1, p. 82; Hegel, 1991: 57. See also Hegel, 1970a: §20 Remark, p. 75; Hegel, 1991: 51: 'since I am at the same time in all my sensations, notions, states, etc., thought is present everywhere and pervades all these determinations as [their] category'.

[47] See, for example, Hegel, 1970c: §§466–7, pp. 284–5; Hegel, 1971a: 225, and Hegel, 1994: 229.

[48] See Hegel, 1970c: §462 Remark, p. 278; Hegel, 1971a: 220: 'It is in names that we *think*'.

[49] Hegel, 1970a: §21 and Addition, pp. 76–7; Hegel, 1991: 52–3.

[50] Hegel, 1970c: §396 Addition, p. 80; Hegel, 1971a: 59.

[51] See, for example, Hegel, 1969: I, p. 27; Hegel, 1999: 37: 'the loftier business of logic therefore is to clarify these categories and in them to raise mind to freedom and truth'.

[52] See, for example, Hegel, 1970c: §448 Addition, p. 250; Hegel, 1971a: 196: 'only through the education of the mind [*die Bildung des Geistes*] does attention acquire strength and fulfil its function'.

[53] Hegel, 1970c: §418 Addition, p. 207; Hegel, 1971a: 160: 'the thought-determination [...] in virtue of which [*kraft welcher*] the manifold particular content of sensations concentrates itself into a unity that is outside of me'.

[54] deVries, 1988: 68: 'no sensory episode plays a foundational epistemological role'.

[55] Hegel, 1970c: §442 Addition, pp. 235–6; Hegel, 1971a: 184.

[56] Hegel, 1970a: §42 Addition 3, p. 119; Hegel, 1991: 86.

[57] Hegel, 1970c: §§422 Addition, 448 Addition, pp. 211, 253; Hegel, 1971a: 163, 198.

[58] Hegel, 1970c: §465, p. 283; Hegel, 1971a: 224.

[59] Hegel, 1970a: §24, p. 81; Hegel, 1991: 56.

[60] On the role of Hegel's *Phenomenology*, see Houlgate, 2005: 48–105.

[61] Hegel, 1970c: §465 Addition, p. 284; Hegel, 1971a: 224: 'since this [thinking] knows *itself* to be the nature of the matter [*Sache*]. [...] *Thought* is *being*'. In this respect, the interpretation of Hegel put forward here is similar to that advanced by Christoph Halbig, who maintains that, for Hegel, reality is itself conceptually structured and that 'in *cognition* [*Erkennen*] the structure realised there becomes epistemically transparent to itself' (Halbig, 2004: 157). There is, however, a significant difference between my interpretation of Hegel and Halbig's. Halbig argues—against commentators, such as Robert Pippin—that Hegel's philosophy cannot be understood as a continuation of the Kantian project of transcendental philosophy, because it rests on 'strong metaphysical premises' that, while rationally defensible, are at odds with the epistemic restrictions that Kant imposes on thought (Halbig, 2004: 159; Halbig, Quante and Siep, 2004: 15). On my reading, by contrast, Hegel's rationalist ontology does not rest on 'strong' premises of its own, but results directly from his *suspension* of what he considers to be the unwarranted assumptions about thought that underlie Kant's apparent epistemic 'modesty'. In Hegel's view, Kant simply *assumes* without proper justification that human thought (without sensible intuition) entertains no more than the possibility of things and so necessarily falls short of understanding being itself. If, however, we suspend this unjustified Kantian assumption— together with all other determinate assumptions about thought and being—we are led directly to the recognition that thought is minimally the thought of indeterminate *being* and thus is ontological: 'the beginning must be an *absolute*, or what is synonymous here, an *abstract* beginning; and so it *may not presuppose anything* [...]. The beginning therefore is *pure being*' (Hegel, 1969: I, pp. 68–9; Hegel, 1999: 70). The further course of Hegel's 'science of logic' then demonstrates that such being is intrinsically rational or conceptually structured. Hegel believes that the imperative to begin philosophy by submitting all unwarranted assumptions to radical critique itself stems from Kant's critical thought. He thus understands himself to be taken by Kant's own insistence on philosophical critique to a new, post-Kantian rationalist ontology. For a more detailed discussion of Hegel's 'post-Kantian Spinozism', see Houlgate, 2006: 24–8, 115–43.

[62] Hegel, 1994: 153.

[63] Hegel, 1970c: §410 Remark, p. 186; Hegel, 1971a: 143.

[64] McDowell, 1996: 66.

[65] McDowell, 2002: 293.

[66] See. for example, McDowell, 1996: 68: 'we need to see intuitions as standing in rational relations to what we should think, not just in causal relations to what we do think'.

67 McDowell, 1996: 19, and McDowell, 2002: 293.

68 Hegel, 1970c: §400 Addition, p. 100; Hegel, 1971a: 75.

69 See, for example, McDowell, 1996: 12–13, 88.

70 McDowell, 1996: 24–45, and Hegel, 1970a: §24 Remark, p. 81; Hegel, 1991: 56.

71 McDowell insists that in modernity we should not 'rehabilitate the idea that there is meaning in the fall of a sparrow or the movement of the planets, as there is meaning in a text' (McDowell, 1996: 72, 97). Hegel does not argue that there is 'meaning' in the movement of the planets either; but he does see in their movement the workings of the 'Idea', or reason, which leads eventually to the emergence of life in nature and which is not apparent to the natural scientist. As I understand it, this goes beyond what McDowell would be prepared to accept. On Hegel's account of planetary motion and his derivation of the rationality of Kepler's laws, see Houlgate, 2005: 144–56.

72 McDowell, 1996: 61, my emphasis.

73 McDowell, 1996: 99, 39, my emphasis.

74 McDowell, 1996: 67.

75 McDowell, 1996: 26, and McDowell, 2002: 288–9.

76 McDowell, 1996: 26, 29. See also McDowell, 2002: 291: 'experience at its best [is] openness to how things are'.

77 McDowell, 2002: 276, 295.

78 McDowell, 1996: 43.

79 McDowell, 1996: 39, my emphases.

80 McDowell, 2002: 273.

81 McDowell, 1998: 439, 434.

82 McDowell, 1996: 49.

83 McDowell, 1998: 439.

84 McDowell, 1996: 30.

85 McDowell, 1996: 31, and Hegel, 1970c: §§415 Addition 1, 445, pp. 203, 240; Hegel, 1971a: 156, 188.

86 See Hegel, 1970c: §396 Addition, p. 80; Hegel, 1971a: 59: 'speech [*Sprache*] enables man to apprehend things as universal'.

87 McDowell, 1998: 490.

88 The task of the *Science of Logic*, accordingly, is to show precisely how 'determinations have first to arise from the movement of *being* itself'; see Hegel, 1969: I, p. 80; Hegel, 1999: 79.

89 See, for example, Hegel, 1970a: §238 Addition, p. 390; Hegel, 1991: 305: 'To this extent philosophising is wholly passive [*passiv*]'.

90 McDowell, 1996: 25, my emphasis. See also McDowell, 2002: 285: 'if we could not make sense of the idea that experience discloses the world to us [. . .], how could we think about the world at all?'.

91 Note that concepts such as 'matter', 'gravity', 'light', 'chemical object' and 'life' are not empirical concepts, for Hegel, but a priori concepts of necessary aspects of nature. See, for example, Hegel, 1970b: §§275 Addition, 276 Remark, pp. 111, 117; Hegel, 1970d: 87, 91–2: 'the a priori conceptual determination [*Begriffsbestimmung*] of light' [§275 Addition]. See also Houlgate, 2005: 110–12.

92 Hegel, 1970c: §456 Addition, p. 266; Hegel, 1971a: 210: 'In generating general representations [*Vorstellungen*], intelligence is *self-active* [*selbsttätig*]; it is, therefore, a stupid mistake to assume that general representations arise, without any help from the mind [. . .], that, for example, the red colour of the rose seeks the red of other images in my head, and thus conveys to me, a mere spectator, the general representation of red'.

110 *Stephen Houlgate*

93 See, for example, Hegel, 1970c: §422 Addition, p. 211; Hegel, 1971a: 163. See also Houlgate, 2005: 138–53. See also note 91 above.

94 McDowell's stated aim is 'to defend a non-traditional empiricism that retains the thought, inchoately present in traditional empiricism [...], that the possibility of empirical objective content depends on a rational connection between experience and empirical belief'; see McDowell, 2002: 284. On the relation between Hegel's speculative philosophy and empirical knowledge, see Hegel, 1970a: §6, p. 47; Hegel, 1991: 28–9, and Hegel, 1970b: §246 and Remark, p. 15; Hegel, 1970d: 6–7. See also Houlgate, 2005: 106–21.

95 McDowell, 2002: 277.

96 This paper was given at a conference entitled 'McDowell between Wittgenstein and Hegel' held at the University of Warwick on 13–15 May, 2005. I should like to thank Robert Guay for his comments on an earlier draft of the paper and Jakob Lindgaard for inviting me to write the paper in the first place.

REFERENCES

Berkeley, G. (1975), 'An Essay Towards a New Theory of Vision', in *Philosophical Works*, M. R. Ayers (ed.). London: Dent.

Bernstein, R. J. (2002), 'McDowell's Domesticated Hegelianism', in N. H. Smith (ed.), *Reading McDowell. On Mind and World*. London: Routledge.

deVries, W. A. (1988), *Hegel's Theory of Mental Activity, An Introduction to Theoretical Spirit*. Ithaca, NY: Cornell University Press.

Halbig, C. (2004), 'Das "Erkennen als solches"', in C. Halbig, M. Quante & L. Siep (eds.), *Hegels Erbe*. Frankfurt am Main: Suhrkamp Verlag.

Halbig, C., Quante, M. & Siep, L. (2004), 'Hegels Erbe—eine Einleitung', in C. Halbig, M. Quante and L. Siep (eds.), *Hegels Erbe*. Frankfurt am Main: Suhrkamp Verlag.

Hegel, G. W. F. (1969), *Wissenschaft der Logik*, eds. E. Moldenhauer and K. M. Michel, 2 vols, *Werke in zwanzig Bänden*, vols 5, 6. Frankfurt am Main: Suhrkamp Verlag.

—— (1970a), *Enzyklopädie der philosophischen Wissenschaften im Grundrisse (1830). Erster Teil: Die Wissenschaft der Logik. Mit den mündlichen Zusätzen*, eds. E. Moldenhauer and K. M. Michel, *Werke in zwanzig Bänden*, vol. 8. Frankfurt am Main: Suhrkamp Verlag.

—— (1970b), *Enzyklopädie der philosophischen Wissenschaften im Grundrisse (1830). Zweiter Teil: Die Naturphilosophie. Mit den mündlichen Zusätzen*, eds. E. Moldenhauer and K. M. Michel, *Werke in zwanzig Bänden*, vol. 9. Frankfurt am Main: Suhrkamp Verlag.

—— (1970c), *Enzyklopädie der philosophischen Wissenschaften im Grundrisse (1830). Dritter Teil: Die Philosophie des Geistes. Mit den mündlichen Zusätzen*, eds. E. Moldenhauer and K. M. Michel, *Werke in zwanzig Bänden*, vol. 10. Frankfurt am Main: Suhrkamp Verlag.

—— (1970d), *Hegel's Philosophy of Nature. Being Part Two of the Encyclopaedia of the Philosophical Sciences (1830)*, trans. A. V. Miller. Oxford: Clarendon Press.

—— (1971a), *Hegel's Philosophy of Mind. Being Part Three of the Encyclopaedia of the Philosophical Sciences (1830)*, trans. W. Wallace together with the *Zusätze* in Boumann's text (1845), trans. A. V. Miller. Oxford: Clarendon Press.

—— (1971b), *Vorlesungen über die Geschichte der Philosophie*, eds. E. Moldenhauer and K. M. Michel, 3 vols, *Werke in zwanzig Bänden*, vols 18, 19, 20. Frankfurt am Main: Suhrkamp Verlag.

—— (1991), *The Encyclopaedia Logic. Part 1 of the Encyclopaedia of Philosophical Sciences*, trans. T. F. Geraets, W. A. Suchting and H. S. Harris. Indianapolis: Hackett.

—— (1994), *Vorlesungen über die Philosophie des Geistes. Berlin 1827/1828*, eds. F. Hespe and B. Tuschling. Hamburg: Felix Meiner.

—— (1999), *Hegel's Science of Logic*, trans. A. V. Miller. Amherst, NY: Humanity Books.

Houlgate, S. (1993), 'Vision, Reflection, and Openness. The "Hegemony of Vision" from a Hegelian Point of View', in D. M. Levin (ed.), *Modernity and the Hegemony of Vision*. Berkeley, CA: University of California Press.

—— (2003), 'G. W. F. Hegel: The Phenomenology of Spirit', in R. C. Solomon and D. Sherman (eds.), *The Blackwell Guide to Continental Philosophy*. Oxford: Blackwell.

—— (2005), *An Introduction to Hegel. Freedom, Truth and History*, 2nd edn. Oxford: Blackwell.

—— (2006), *The Opening of Hegel's Logic, From Being to Infinity*. West Lafayette, IN: Purdue University Press.

Kant, I. (1997), *Critique of Pure Reason*, trans. and eds. P. Guyer and A. W. Wood. Cambridge: Cambridge University Press.

McDowell, J. (1996), *Mind and World*, paperback edn., Cambridge, MA.: Harvard University Press.

—— (1998), 'Having the World in View: Sellars, Kant, and Intentionality', *The Journal of Philosophy*, 95,9: 431–91.

—— (2002), 'Responses', in N. H. Smith (ed.), *Reading McDowell. On Mind and World*. London: Routledge.

—— (2003), 'The Apperceptive I and the Empirical Self: Towards a Heterodox Reading of "Lordship and Bondage" in Hegel's *Phenomenology*', *Bulletin of the Hegel Society of Great Britain*, 47/48: 1–16.

—— (2004), 'Selbstbestimmende Subjektivität und externer Zwang', in C. Halbig, M. Quante and L. Siep (eds.), *Hegels Erbe*. Frankfurt am Main: Suhrkamp Verlag.

Stern, R. (1999), 'Going Beyond the Kantian Philosophy: On McDowell's Hegelian Critique of Kant', *European Journal of Philosophy*, 7,2: 247–69.

7

Practical Reason and its Animal Precursors

Sabina Lovibond

1.

A number of contemporary philosophers who have sought to resist the claims of ethical non-cognitivism, and to vindicate the thought that one can sometimes be straightforwardly right or wrong about questions of value, have formulated their views by reference to the idea of *practical reason*. Thus Philippa Foot has abandoned her earlier, well-known account of morality as a 'system of hypothetical imperatives' in favour of the view that moral goodness is a particular instance of *being good at making the kinds of practical choice that arise for human beings, given the natural circumstances of their existence.*[1] Similarly, John McDowell in *Mind and World*[2] proposes to reintegrate reason with nature on the basis of a 'naturalized Platonism'—a conception of human beings as equipped with a 'second nature' that enables them to appreciate the claims of objective reasons, both practical and theoretical; and in doing this he provides a friendly philosophical environment for ethics, construed as the critical study of certain constituents of our 'second nature'. Such a study would represent, I take it, one species of the genus of critical enquiry in which McDowell says at the end of his book that we have a 'standing obligation' to engage;[3] it would involve scrutinizing our habits of feeling and choice and asking, 'All things considered, are we satisfied that such and such a disposition should figure in the "second nature" of someone who has received a standard ethical upbringing?'

In this paper, then, I shall be concerned with the idea of 'second nature' and with the contribution it can make to an ethics of practical reason. My main interest will be in the distinctively human character of our 'second nature' and, relatedly, in why moral philosophy has regarded human beings as the uniquely ethical species of animal. I am not going to argue that it has been wrong to do so, but it seems to me that there is a lack of clarity in our thinking about what it is that separates humans (ethically) from other species, and I want to pursue this question by looking at some critical remarks by Alasdair MacIntyre[4] about McDowell's account (in *Mind and World*: Lecture VI) of the human-animal divide. Briefly, I think MacIntyre is right to draw attention to a stress on discontinuity or rupture at the expense of continuous development in this part of the philosophical scene of *Mind and World*; but that rather than discrediting the idea of human 'second nature' as a unique attribute, his discussion should prompt us instead to work towards a better understanding of what this uniqueness consists in—a topic to which McDowell has returned in at least one recent paper.

2.

The point on which McDowell and MacIntyre are in agreement is that the rational subjectivity of humans should be understood as emerging, in an evolutionary sense and also within the lives of individual human beings, from a 'proto-rational' precursor which we can see in operation in other animal species and in human children.[5] I borrow the prefix 'proto-' from McDowell, who uses it to introduce a concept of animal 'proto-subjectivity' in contrast to full (human) subjectivity.[6]

However, there is at least a major difference of emphasis here between McDowell and MacIntyre. This difference corresponds to the different dialectical backgrounds against which the two writers' thoughts on non-human animals are presented. McDowell's discussion is prompted by the threat of a certain intellectual embarrassment on the subject of animals—a threat originating in his project of incorporating into a naturalized epistemology the Kantian notion of the mind's 'spontaneity'. Since McDowell throws in his lot with Hegel in rejecting as unintelligible the very idea of an objective reality, or domain of 'things in themselves', external to the sphere of concepts, he is led to picture our being in a 'world' at all as a consequence of our ability to engage in the conceptually articulated thought which records *how things are* in that world, and hence of our possessing something like the Kantian 'faculty of spontaneity', the locus of a 'rationally organized network of [conceptual] capacities for active adjustment of one's thinking to the deliverances of experience'.[7] But this commits him to rather an austere position on the subject of other animal species. For if, as McDowell holds, '[i]t is the spontaneity of the understanding, the power of conceptual thinking, that brings both the world and the self into view',[8] it will follow that '[c]reatures without conceptual capacities lack self-consciousness and—this is part of the same package—experience of objective reality'.[9] And the only 'creatures with conceptual capacities', in McDowell's idiom, are ourselves. 'Mere animals . . . do not have the spontaneity of the understanding. We cannot construe them as continually reshaping a world-view in rational response to the deliverances of experience; not if the idea of rational response requires subjects who are in charge of their thinking, standing ready to reassess what is a reason for what, and to change their responsive propensities accordingly'.[10] So, on McDowell's account of what it is to 'experience' objective reality (or to enjoy 'outer experience', as he also puts it), other animal species cannot be party to such 'experience' at all. 'And that can seem to commit me to the Cartesian idea that brutes are automata'.[11]

This is where McDowell seeks help from a certain application of the Aristotelian side of his account of knowledge. He holds that the rational capacities called into play in human knowledge are those of a particular animal species which has evolved, over time, from other species by a process describable in principle—if we knew enough—without any violence to the modern scientific world-view; that is, without positing any 'transcendence of biology'.[12] So it would be incredible that—as the 'Cartesian' view implies—there should just be *nothing* in the life of other species that we could point to as an evolutionary precursor of what, in our own form of life, constitutes the fully fledged 'experience' of reality. In order to explain what there is (but in a way consistent with the paradoxical claim that it is only humans who have 'outer experience' or inhabit a 'world'), McDowell makes use of the contrast drawn by H.-G. Gadamer in *Truth and Method*[13] between a 'world', in the relevant theory-laden sense, and an 'environment'—which is the counterpart of a 'world' in the life of animals that lack (Kantian) spontaneity. The crucial difference which grounds the contrast between 'world'-dwellers and (mere) 'environment'-dwellers is that 'a merely animal life is shaped by goals whose control of the animal's behaviour at a given moment is an immediate outcome of biological forces. A mere animal does not weigh reasons and decide what to do';[14] whereas '[t]o acquire the spontaneity of the understanding is to become able . . . to "rise above the pressure of what impinges on us from the world" . . .—that succession of problems and opportunities constituted as such by biological imperatives—into a "free, distanced orientation"'.[15]

McDowell also draws on the early writings of Marx for the idea of *nature* (potentially, at least—within a 'properly human life', as McDowell puts it)[16] as the 'inorganic body of man':[17] something not alien to us, since we can reorder the natural world through our own intelligent activity, and so come to *recognize ourselves in it*. This is in contrast to the character that an animal's natural environment has for it, namely, not something that expresses its own being but something that keeps on impinging on it from outside, throwing up situations that it has to *cope with*. The animal is not an automaton, it has its own 'alert and self-moving life';[18] but this life contains no activity beyond that of 'responding to a succession of biological needs'.[19] The human being is emancipated from this condition of unfreedom into one of genuine agency, which itself depends on the possession of conceptual capacities, as McDowell has argued earlier: 'movements of limbs without concepts are mere happenings, not expressions of agency'.[20] (I take it, though, that he would not consider it obligatory to mark the distinction that interests him by way of this stipulative restriction on the notion of agency, any more than he wants to make it obligatory—in a recent discussion of the work of Wilfrid Sellars—to mark out the class of occupants of the 'space of reasons' by the specific device of a restriction on the concept of the conceptual, or of *being a possessor of conceptual capacities*.)[21]

Of course, as McDowell reminds us,[22] a human being remains an animal and is not emancipated from *having* an environment; but humans alone develop beyond the stage of 'enslavement to *immediate* biological imperatives',[23] since they alone acquire the capacity for a continual *active adjustment* of their beliefs and intentions to the 'deliverances of experience'—a process of adjustment that engages our powers of self-criticism ('Perhaps *p* isn't true after all . . . Perhaps *a* would not be the best thing to do . . .', etc.), and so exhibits our Gadamerian 'free, distanced orientation' to the input we receive from our senses from moment to moment, or to our emotional responses to this input. And the sensitivity to reasons that is expressed in the workings of our 'spontaneity', or in the continual active correction of our thinking, can be seen as providing the content of the 'second nature' that we acquire through ordinary human upbringing. For the distinctively human thing that we get from our upbringing, the thing that goes beyond mere habituation to various routines, is an ability to find our way around within the 'space of reasons' established by the culture into which we are being initiated—an ability, then, to treat that culture as a 'repository of tradition, a store of historically accumulated wisdom about what is a reason for what'.[24] And one important part of this 'accumulated wisdom' would be the part that discloses to us the existence of distinctively practical reasons: reasons deriving either from prudential considerations such as safety, or from distinctively ethical ones such as loyalty, honesty, kindness and the like.

3.

McDowell, as I have tried to show, presents us with an account of the relation of humanity to the rest of animal nature in which the theme of evolutionary continuity—essential as it is in order to distinguish his own 'naturalized Platonism' from the 'rampant' kind that threatens to place human beings outside nature altogether—is in the end subordinated to that of separation, or of the *specialness* of the human. McDowell's reconciliation of reason with nature has to be consistent with his own picture of human knowledge: consistent, I mean, with the idea that although what we call our 'knowledge' is indebted to the peculiar modes of expression evolved by the human animal, it is nevertheless an effect (at any rate when things go well enough) of the openness of human beings to various aspects of the 'layout of *reality*'.[25] Conversely, anything that can count (for us) as 'reality' must be such as to reveal itself to creatures with just the range of conceptual capacities reflected in these modes of expression; it must be an inherently *thinkable* reality.[26]

For MacIntyre, on the other hand, this aspect of McDowell's thinking places him in a tradition which has done European philosophy more harm than good. Where McDowell refers admiringly to Gadamer, MacIntyre speaks critically of Heidegger with his conception of the human being as 'world-forming' (*weltbildend*), in contrast to the animal, which is 'poor in world' (*weltarm*)— half-way, as it were, to the condition of a 'worldless' (*weltlos*) inanimate object such as a stone.[27] MacIntyre offers no detailed discussion of McDowell, but he complains that on the Gadamerian view of animal life as 'structured exclusively by immediate biological imperatives' it becomes mysterious how the distinctively human mode of agency could ever have emerged, or rather how it *can* ever emerge, in the course of individual human development, from the equally 'unfree, undistanced' orientation of human infants to *their* surroundings. McDowell, he says, fails to do justice to those features of the life of other animals that make such a transformation intelligible at all—to the fact that 'mere animals', as McDowell calls them, 'are already guided by a kind of practical reasoning that is exhibited in their taking *this* to be a reason for doing *that*, one that is to be characterized by *analogy* with human understanding'.[28]

The particular kind of imaginative failure that tends to conceal this fact from philosophers is entrenched by the habit of contrasting our own species, as I have been doing so far, with an undifferentiated category of 'other' animals, instead of paying attention to the massive differences that exist, in respect of purposive behaviour, between earthworms or crabs on one hand and creatures such as dogs, gorillas, chimpanzees and bottle-nose dolphins on the other.[29] Drawing on a wide range of research literature on these more intelligent species, MacIntyre argues that on the evidence available, it seems to be wrong to say with Heidegger that non-human animal perception, as such, lacks the 'as-structure'[30]—i.e. the recognition of objects *as* being of a certain kind, as opposed to a more primitive perceptual awareness of their presence. For a dolphin or a gorilla, *pace* Heidegger, 'recognizes individuals, notices their absences, greets their returns, and responds to them *as* food or *as* source of food, *as* partner or material for play, *as* to be accorded obedience or looked to for protection and so on'.[31] And because there are goods internal to the form of life of dolphins, gorillas, and so forth as distinct natural species—that is, because there are more or less determinate conditions under which a dolphin (etc.) will or will not *flourish*—we can also see the behaviour of individual dolphins, when directed towards the relevant goods, as exemplifying after all the phenomenon of *action for a reason*. (Note that the link between 'good' and 'reason' here depends on the idea that to give someone's *reasons* for doing something is to specify the *point* or *value* of it in their eyes. This is the sort of answer Elizabeth Anscombe has in mind when she says that an intentional action is one 'to which a certain sense of the question "Why?" is given application', the sense being 'that in which the answer, if positive, gives a reason for acting'.)[32]

This claim about the nature of motivation in the species that interest MacIntyre is, I think, best understood as relating to the resources we draw on in order to interpret their behaviour. Returning from the case of 'other' animals to that of human infants, there are, so far as I can judge, no strong inhibitions about attributing various kinds of rational motivation to children at an age when, descriptively, there might well be as good a case for saying that their lives are 'structured exclusively by immediate biological imperatives' as there is to say this about an adult bottle-nose dolphin. If we experience no problem here, that is presumably because we interpret young children proleptically, in the light of their *future status* as creatures possessed of the fully fledged subjectivity described by McDowell and Gadamer. (Of course, this proleptic or anticipatory mode of relating to babies and children is an essential element in the business of upbringing: we are enabled or helped to make the transition to a fully human mode of behaviour, sensitive to reasons 'as such',[33] by the willingness of adults to use their imagination in treating us—sometimes at least—as being further along the path towards this mode of behaviour than is actually the case. A version of this process is noted by Bernard Williams when he writes: 'The institution of blame is best seen as involving a fiction, by which we treat the agent as one for whom the relevant ethical considerations are reasons'; he adds that this fiction helps to sustain 'a process of continuous recruitment into a deliberative community'.)[34]

MacIntyre, then, wants to warn us against any tendency—resulting, perhaps, from a dogmatically rationalist view of the relationship of human beings to the rest of the natural world—to deny or overlook the workings of a similar (though not in this case proleptic) play of imagination over dogs, chimpanzees, dolphins, and the like. Only under the influence of a somewhat intrusive bit of *theory*, of the kind represented by the Gadamerian opposition of human 'world' to animal 'environment', might we be led to forget that much of the conceptual apparatus we use in interpreting human behaviour—the attribution of purposes, of action with one intention rather than another, of the ability to see a situation in one way or another and to correct mistakes, of the perception of a reason as sufficient, or again as insufficient, to deflect one from one's present course—that much of this, to repeat, is carried over into our interpretation of the behaviour of other intelligent animal species. (One philosopher who I take it would agree with all this is Simon Glendinning, who cites a certain game he has played with a dog as an instance of human-animal interaction relying on (nothing less than) 'mutual *intelligibility*').[35] So the lesson MacIntyre would like to convey to McDowell seems to be that when we contrast animal 'proto-subjectivity' with (full) human subjectivity, we should take care not to let our appreciation of the discontinuity here suppress the awareness of continuity implicit in the term 'proto-'. We should be willing to recognize members of certain other species as 'prelinguistic rather than nonlinguistic',[36] as party to the 'as-structure' and hence, in a limited way, as possessing conceptual capacities,[37] and in general as located (in common with *all* animal species) on a 'scale or spectrum', rather than on the far side of 'a single line of division between "them" and "us"'.[38]

4.

However—to recall a phrase I used in §1 above—MacIntyre doesn't contest the traditional view of human beings as the uniquely *ethical* species. And, in fact, he has a good deal to say about the *sui generis* character of human practical rationality that would justify us in thinking of his own views as closer to McDowell's than his glancing criticism suggests. For MacIntyre too, as it turns out, takes human beings to be set apart by more than a quantitative difference from (even) such high-level non-human company as that of dolphins and chimpanzees. Despite his rejection of the reductive picture of non-human animals as being set in quasi-mechanical motion by their environment, he agrees with Heidegger that '[s]uch animals cannot grasp the world as a whole. They cannot stand back from their immediate environment', nor do they experience the present in relation to a 'remembered past' or an 'envisaged future'.[39] And above all, '[t]hey do not have to go through a stage in which they separate themselves from their desires, as humans do',[40] so as to gain access to the kind of practical thinking within which *acting on a particular desire* means that 'I either make or presuppose a judgement that it is *best* for me here and now to act so as to satisfy this particular desire'.[41]

This occurrence of the word 'best' brings out the point of MacIntyre's concessions to Heidegger, and more remotely, to the humanist tradition at large. To 'stand back from one's immediate environment', to 'grasp the world as a whole' or as unfolding, surveyably, in time—all these marks of our humanness seem to express a single underlying characteristic, which is the ability or disposition to concern oneself with the nature of one's *life* 'as a whole', with how things are going for one 'not in some particular respect' (as Aristotle puts it)[42] 'such as health or strength, but in respect of living well in general' (πρὸς τὸ εὖ ζῆν ὅλως, *pros to eu zên holôs*). To do things because one perceives them as conducive to some good—to something one wants or values—and, accordingly, to act *for reasons* may indeed, as MacIntyre argues, be a feature common to the lives of humans, dolphins, gorillas, and various other creatures. But to select something as *the* (best) thing to do, here and now, in the light of *everything* that matters to one, or of *all* the values that one would wish an (imaginary) observer to find expressed in one's life—this is something that does genuinely appear to be reserved for humans, not just by our inherited rationalist prejudices, but by phenomenological considerations about what it makes sense to say. (Just as Wittgenstein points out that a dog can believe his master is at the door but not that his master will come the day after tomorrow,[43] so we might say that although a caged gorilla can show signs of depression, it cannot show signs of feeling that its life has been wasted; this is not the sort of feeling we attribute to any non-human animal.) What is coming into view here, I take it, is the 'dimension of freedom' which McDowell continues to insist 'is required if behaviour is to be in a proper sense informed by rationality'—the freedom to 'step back' from our inclinations and to evaluate them critically.[44]

These concessions with regard to the discontinuity of human and animal existence are only what one would expect to find in any writer influenced by the ethics of Aristotle, since they reflect the idea which Aristotle expresses by saying that although children and other animals act *voluntarily*, or have a 'principle of movement' within themselves,[45] only adult human beings share in προαίρεσις (*prohairesis*), or (as the standard translations have it) in 'rational' or 'preferential' choice'.[46] However, MacIntyre's animal evidence does help to sharpen our understanding of what *prohairesis* is, and to bring out the difference between properly human 'practical wisdom' and the kind we attribute, by analogy, to other animals. (Aristotle says we do this in the case of those animals that seem to have an 'ability to take thought for the future',[47] so presumably it would cover, say, nest-building in birds or winter food storage in squirrels.) What MacIntyre's evidence reveals is that even the propensity to behave in ways that can be interpreted as *choosing a rather than b for a reason*, or because of the superior good one sees in it, is not yet enough to place one within the class of *ethical* beings—those capable of 'practical wisdom' in the core (not merely analogical) sense.

This kind of behaviour seems, admittedly, to be present in some intelligent non-human animals, as illustrated by MacIntyre's description of a situation that arises among dolphins hunting for fish: '... bottlenose dolphins who have first tried to drive a school of fish towards the shore, in order to pen them in, but who are failing to do so, will then instead drive the fish out to sea towards the rest of the herd'.[48] (In other words: the dolphins can be understood as choosing one hunting strategy in preference to another, and as doing so for a reason arising from one of the goods internal to their form of life, namely getting fish to eat.) But such behaviour (which is also observable, *mutatis mutandis*, in young children) does not, in itself, qualify the subject of the behaviour as 'having an ethics', because in order to satisfy *this* description one must be interpretable as making choices with a view to the over-arching aim of 'living well all things considered' (Aristotle's *eu zên holôs*). That is, one must be the sort of subject who can be credited with this as an *intentional* object of pursuit—an object implicitly present, I suppose, in all of one's voluntary actions, at least in the negative sense that by performing the action one provides *prima facie* (though certainly defeasible) evidence that one does not believe there to be any objection to it from the *eu zên holôs* point of view. (Note that the idea of *to eu zên holôs* is not a specifically 'ethical' one in the modern sense of 'ethical', since it is not the case that we can attribute a concern with it only to people who are recognizable as living more or less conscientious, law-abiding lives. For example, the 'licentious' person— someone who has the vice contrasted with Greek σωφροσύνη (*sôphrosunê*), 'temperance' or 'self-control'—is still, if we ignore the possibility of mental abnormality or subnormality, an 'ethical' being in the sense that concerns us here: their 'licentious' way of life expresses what *they* take *to eu zên holôs* to consist in, though of course mistakenly by Aristotelian standards.)[49]

Occasionally *to eu zên holôs* emerges from the background position I have suggested it normally occupies in our practical thinking, and becomes an explicit rather than a merely implicit object of reference; such cases would be those we might think of, outside philosophy, as calling for 'moral choices' or 'life choices'. Most of the time, no doubt, somewhere fairly deep in the background is the right place to keep it, or we risk succumbing to a kind of moral pretentiousness, loading the trivia of life with an intolerable burden of significance. (Someone once told me that Virginia Woolf said of the literary critic John Middleton Murry that he 'couldn't fry a sausage without thinking about God', which captures something of what I mean here, though unfortunately I can't provide a source for it and don't know how far it is fair to Middleton Murry.) But by its mere presence, and by the constraint it exerts on the behaviour of a normal, mature human being from moment to moment, the idea of the 'good life as a whole'—however indeterminate in detail—establishes a boundary between human beings and other animal species, a boundary which seems to be the one we have to cross in order to achieve the Gadamerian 'free, distanced orientation' to our world.

Although MacIntyre's book is centrally concerned with the place of dependence and disability in human life, and with the way moral philosophy has been pulled out of shape by ignoring this side of our experience, one theme on which he is surprisingly quiet is that of the distinctively human awareness of death. It seems to me that there was room here for a further concessionary gesture towards Heidegger, from whom we get the idea of 'being-toward-death' as a defining feature of *Dasein*. Although the knowledge that each of us has that we are going to die some day may be 'fugitive',[50] it seems nevertheless to be this knowledge that opens up the necessary logical space in which to ask: when I die, how might an intelligent observer assess *my life as a whole?*—and that, in doing so, condemns us (as it were) to that 'freedom', that 'distance' from one's life as lived from moment to moment, which places each of us at risk of feeling that we are wasting our time or turning out badly.[51]

5.

So: do MacIntyre's considerations about the animal world disclose a flaw in McDowell's 'naturalized Platonism'? Do they show that there is anything wrong with it that might cast doubt on its claims to supply the appropriate epistemological backdrop for an (updated) ethics of practical reason?

What they seem to me to show is, at most, that McDowell's account of the 'animal/human', or 'environment/world', opposition fails to take much notice of the kind of transitional phenomena on the basis of which some animal species, given their 'perceptual and intentional achievements',[52] might be said to inhabit an environment which is also a 'proto-world'. That is, McDowell does not dwell on those elements in the life of other species which stand out as the evolutionary ancestors of our own exercises of Kantian 'spontaneity'. But there is nothing here that should cause embarrassment to anyone who wishes, as McDowell does, to locate 'spontaneity' in a ('relaxed') naturalistic setting, since to believe that human beings have *evolved* is precisely to suppose that features present at a pre-human level of development have been taken up, by one of those Hegelian processes that convert successive quantitative changes into a qualitative one, into a form of life marked by this unique new attribute of a *second* nature—the attribute displayed in our critical monitoring of our own thoughts and actions in the light of a 'store of *historically accumulated* [and hence culturally informed] wisdom about what is a reason for what'.[53]

It is true that when, in his Afterword to *Mind and World*, McDowell reaffirms that on his view 'we are animals too, not beings with a foothold outside the animal kingdom' (as in 'rampant Platonism'), and that '[i]f someone wants to work out a conception of orientation towards the world that [would make] the language of world-directedness available for talking about the mentality of brutes, that is, so far, perfectly all right'[54] with him, his main emphasis is on the ways in which adult human beings are still animals rather than on those in which some other species exhibit behaviour that points, in evolutionary terms, to a future *beyond* the condition of a 'mere' animal. But to look at the facts of evolution from this different, MacIntyrian angle surely does no more than fill out a story that is already before us in essentials in McDowell (or in McDowell's Gadamer). If the human capacity for 'spontaneous' thought and action really did evolve—if it did not 'drop from the sky' in the manner of a Platonic soul-substance—then nothing, surely, could be more natural than the discovery of some 'mere' animal capacities that foreshadow it. The case for setting human life, in some respects, radically apart from that of other species depends not on our success in dishonestly pushing such discoveries out of sight but on the plausibility of the idea that human life is marked by *some* qualitatively new beginning in practical rationality, albeit in the midst of a great deal that is old. The 'environment/world' contrast, as I understand it, is meant to celebrate (or, anyway, take the measure of) the new without any snobbery towards its humble origins. It expresses a kind of dualism, but a dualism in the 'non-rampant' style.

Embracing this view, moral philosophy can reaffirm the Aristotelian idea that human beings are a species of animal which, like other species, needs certain conditions—not of its own choosing—to be fulfilled if it is to flourish. Where humans differ from other species is in their expectation of attaining, in normal or favourable cases, to a life characterized at least some of the time by that 'free, distanced orientation' to the world which entails that for them—for us—it is a *question* what these conditions are; something that we need to keep under continual review. Indeed, being the kind of creatures we are, we cannot even hope to 'flourish' or live well unless we *do* keep it under review, through the maintenance of a public sphere of discussion in which values and the plans of action they inspire can become objects of reasoned criticism.[55] The underlying idea here is that human beings are, as Aristotle claimed, naturally ethical (and political) creatures, not—except in certain clearly delimited contexts—creatures to be managed or administered. In the end, I think it is this conviction more than any other that gives the ethics of practical reason its subversive character in relation to the normal way of life of post-industrial consumer society, and that makes it worthy of the attention of philosophers.[56]

Sabina Lovibond
Worcester College
Oxford OX1 2HB
UK
sabina-mary.lovibond@worc.ox.ac.uk

NOTES

[1] Foot 1978; contrast her 1995 and 2001.

[2] McDowell 1994, esp. Lecture IV.

[3] Ibid.: 126.

[4] MacIntyre 1999, esp. chs. 5–7.

[5] The theme of childhood—more prominent in MacIntyre than in McDowell, who tends to stick to a rather abstract notion of 'upbringing'—is also of keen interest to Rosalind Hursthouse, who commends Aristotle for 'never forget[ting] the fact that we were all once children', whereas '[t]o read almost any other famous moral philosopher is to receive the impression that we, the intelligent adult readers addressed, sprang fully formed from our father's brow' (Hursthouse 1999: 14).

[6] McDowell 1994: 117.

[7] Ibid.: 29.

[8] Ibid.: 114.

[9] Ibid.

[10] Ibid.

[11] Ibid.

[12] Ibid.: 115.

[13] Gadamer 1979.

[14] McDowell 1994: 115.

[15] Ibid.: 115–116; the words quoted by McDowell are from Gadamer.

[16] Ibid.: 118.

[17] Quoted, ibid.

[18] Ibid.: 116.

[19] Ibid.: 117.

[20] Ibid.: 89.

[21] McDowell unpublished: §4.

[22] McDowell 1994: 118.

[23] Ibid.: 117, emph. added.

[24] Ibid.: 126.

[25] Ibid.: 26, emph. added.

[26] Ibid.: 28.

[27] MacIntyre 1999: 43.

[28] Ibid.: 60.

[29] Also worthy of inclusion in this list may be parrots. The BBC News Online website reported on 26th January 2004 on a captive African grey parrot called N'kisi, which apparently has a vocabulary of 950 words of English, 'uses words in context, with past, present and future tenses, and is often inventive'.

[30] MacIntyre 1999: 48.

[31] Ibid.: 47.

[32] Anscombe 1963: 9.

[33] See McDowell unpublished: §4.

[34] Williams 1985: 193.

[35] Glendinning 1998: 142, emph. added.

[36] MacIntyre 1999: 37.

[37] Ibid.: 55.

[38] Ibid.: 57.

[39] Ibid.: 47.

[40] Ibid.: 68.

[41] Ibid.: 69, emph. added.

[42] Aristotle, *Nicomachean Ethics*: 1140a27–8.

[43] Wittgenstein 1967, Pt II: 174.

[44] McDowell unpublished: §4.

[45] Compare Aristotle, *Nicomachean Ethics*: 1110a17–18.

[46] Ibid.: 1111b8–9.

[47] Ibid.: 1141a26–28.

[48] MacIntyre 1999: 26.

[49] Compare McDowell 1980 : §§7–8.

[50] See Inwood 1997: p. 102, quoting Heidegger 1962.

[51] Milton draws attention to the (possibly paradoxical) absence of this feature from the life of Adam and Eve in Eden before the Fall, when he has Adam say to Eve that all God requires of them is '. . . not to taste that only Tree/Of Knowledge, planted by the Tree of Life,/So near grows Death to Life, whate'er Death is,/Some dreadful thing no doubt . . .' (*Paradise Lost* IV: 423–426).

[52] MacIntyre 1999: 46.

[53] McDowell 1994: 126; emph. added.

[54] Ibid.: 183. McDowell also says, in response to those who find him too dismissive of 'dumb animals': 'The point is just that [they] do not have Kantian freedom. That is perfectly compatible with acknowledging that they can be, in their ways, clever, resourceful, inquisitive, friendly, and so forth' (ibid.: 182).

[55] MacIntyre (1981: 204) once made this point—more hyperbolically than McDowell—by stating that 'the good life for man [= humanity] is the life spent in seeking for the good life for man'.

[56] I am grateful to John McDowell and to everyone else who commented on this paper when it was delivered at the conference on 'McDowell between Wittgenstein and Hegel' (Sandbjerg section) in May 2005. Earlier efforts on the same topic were presented to a seminar on virtue ethics which Martha Klein and I gave at Oxford in 2001, and to an audience at Middlesex University in the same year, and I would also like to thank those groups for their responses.

REFERENCES

Anscombe, G. E. M. (1963), *Intention*. Oxford: Basil Blackwell.

Foot, P. (1978), 'Morality as a System of Hypothetical Imperatives', in her *Virtues and Vices*. Oxford: Basil Blackwell.

—— (1995), 'Does Moral Subjectivism Rest on a Mistake?', *Oxford Journal of Legal Studies*, 15: 1–14.

—— (2001), *Natural Goodness*. Oxford: Oxford University Press.

Gadamer, H-G. (1979), *Truth and Method*, trans. William Glen-Doepel, 2nd edn. London: Sheed and Ward.

Glendinning, S. (1998), *On Being with Others: Heidegger, Derrida, Wittgenstein*. London: Routledge.

Heidegger, M. (1962), *Being and Time*, trans. J. Macquarrie and E. Robinson. Oxford: Basil Blackwell.

Hursthouse, R. (1999), *On Virtue Ethics*. Oxford: Oxford University Press.

Inwood, M. (1997), *Heidegger*. Oxford: Oxford University Press.

MacIntyre, A. (1981), *After Virtue: A Study in Moral Theory*. London: Duckworth.

—— (1999), *Dependent Rational Animals: Why Human Beings Need the Virtues*. London: Duckworth.

McDowell, J. (1980), 'The Role of *Eudaimonia* in Aristotle's Ethics', in A. O. Rorty (ed.) *Essays on Aristotle's Ethics*. Berkeley: University of California Press.

—— (1994), *Mind and World*. Cambridge, MA: Harvard University Press.

—— (unpublished), 'Sellars and the Space of Reasons'.

Williams, B. (1985), *Ethics and the Limits of Philosophy*. London: Fontana Press.

Wittgenstein, L. (1967), *Philosophical Investigations*, trans. G. E. M. Anscombe, 3rd edn. Oxford: Basil Blackwell.

8

Contemporary Epistemology: Kant, Hegel, McDowell

Kenneth R. Westphal

1. Introduction

John McDowell and I agree that the fundamental task of contemporary epistemology is to achieve a cogent philosophical understanding of human knowledge that affords conjoint, affirmative answers to these three questions:

1. Is there a way the world is that does not depend upon what we say, think or believe about it? (Realism.)
2. If the ordinary realism involved in (1) is correct, can we know anything about how the world is? (Anti-scepticism.)
3. Is human knowledge a social and historical phenomenon? (Moderate collectivism.)

In sum, McDowell and I agree that we require a socio-historically grounded epistemological realism. We further agree that Kant's and Hegel's theories of knowledge are of great contemporary importance because they contribute to understanding how a realist account of human knowledge can recognise and build on the deep and pervasive socio-historical dimensions of human knowledge.[1] We also agree that 20th-century epistemology, especially in the Anglo-American analytic tradition, has been impoverished by neglecting or misunderstanding Kant's and Hegel's epistemologies, and by adhering to pictures of 'experience' that make it something internal to us or to our minds, rather than being our access to the natural and social world.[2]

McDowell's remarks about the content and abiding importance of Kant's and Hegel's theories of knowledge in *Mind and World* (1994a) provoked by turns excitement, bewilderment and consternation. Such effects were inevitable, for his remarks were oblique and required much careful development. Fortunately, McDowell (2003a, 2001b/2003b) has revisited these issues recently, in order to 'retrace, more carefully' some of those preliminary remarks (2003a: 76).[3] Here I examine McDowell's views in relation to those of Kant and Hegel, focussing on his recent statement of his own views regarding their epistemologies. Analysing McDowell's recent statements shows, however, that he has not yet identified some key points in Kant's and Hegel's epistemologies, points that are important for his own 'transcendental' project, largely because McDowell's theraputic aims preclude examining Kant's and Hegel's views in sufficient detail. These points include: the co-extensiveness of understanding and sensibility (§2), identity and predication (§3), objective purport and Kant's transcendental deduction (§4), and proving mental content externalism transcendentally (§5).

2. The Co-extensiveness of Understanding and Sensibility

One could write a complete history of epistemology by examining the relation between what Kant called our understanding and our sensibility. McDowell poses his critique of empiricist versions of 'the given' in terms of this relation. According to empiricism, our sensibility delivers unto us—*gives* us—purely sensory data; subsequently our understanding exercises our conceptual capacities by subsuming this data in empirical judgments (p. 76). Against this two-step view of the relation between our two basic cognitive capacities, McDowell contends our conceptual capacities are involved in 'the receptivity of sensory consciousness' (p. 77, cf. 1994a: 67, 72). For this reason, McDowell agrees with Sellars, Kant, and Hegel that 'there is no empirical immediacy, no experiential intake without conceptual consciousness' (p. 77). Sellars' rejection of givenness involves rejecting *atomistic* entry-level epistemic episodes, regardless of whether they are merely sensory or expressly conceptual (e.g. in the form of isolated, mutually independent empirical judgments).[4] McDowell's statement of the rejection here clearly discards non-conceptual sensory states, though it does not reject atomism about such states in the way Sellars stressed. Presumably, McDowell's endorsement elsewhere of the interdependence of empirical judgments with our other empirical knowledge, concepts and principles must be taken here as understood.[5]

McDowell recognises that there are various ways to argue for this rejection of givenness. He criticises Kant's way of arguing against givenness, in order to recommend Hegel's way, which he finds closer to his own. According to McDowell, Kant rightly recognised that 'there is no experiential intake without conceptual mediation' (p. 77). McDowell contends that Kant erred in two significant ways, by overstating the centrality of free rational judgment in sensory intuitions (pp. 80–1), and by adopting transcendental idealism. Transcendental idealism has two unfortunate implications, according to McDowell: that our forms of intuition happen to be space and time is a brute, if transcendental, given (p. 83; 2004/2005: §4), and the objectivity of Kantian empirical objects falls short of 'real objectivity' (p. 85, cf. p. 84; 2004/2005: §4). Hegel avoids these pitfalls by 'rejecting the frame' of Kant's transcendental idealist account of space and time (McDowell 2001b/2003b: §5), by regarding space, time, and fundamental concepts as 'indifferently subjective and objective' (p. 88) and by reconceiving the empirical world, not as an 'external constraint', but as the context for 'the free self-development of reason' (pp. 87, 88; cf. 2004/2005: §7). This is to paint the philosophical and historical picture with extremely broad strokes. Moving from such imagery to philosophical analysis shows that McDowell misunderstands these central issues.

McDowell's criticism of Kant's rejection of givenness only focuses on Kant's way of involving our judgmental capacities in sensory experience, and disregards whether Kant recognised the epistemic interdependence among individual episodes of sensory experience. According to McDowell, because Kant overstated the centrality of freedom to his own account of sensory intuition, Kant cannot say what McDowell thinks Kant could and should say, namely, that:

> ...unlike judgments, intuitions do just happen, outside the control of their subjects. The right point is not that [intuitions] result from spontaneous understanding, but that they exemplify kinds of unity that cannot be understood except in terms of the fact that such unity also characterises acts of the spontaneous understanding. (pp. 80–1)

The premise of McDowell's criticism is that judging is under our control, it is a free cognitive activity, and we are responsible for how we make up our minds about whatever we judge (p. 80). McDowell is right that freedom is central to Kant's account of rational judgment. Yet he urges 'that intuitions should not be seen as themselves the product of intellectual activity' (p. 82).

I agree with McDowell (1998c: 431–2) that the best approach to understanding intentionality is by working through Kant; I don't believe McDowell has capitalised sufficiently on this approach. McDowell, not Kant, overstates the role of free rational judgment in Kant's account of empirical intuitions. This is because McDowell misunderstands Kant's theory of perception (see below). McDowell seeks:

> ...a conception of perceptual experience whose point is to exemplify how subjective states can make gap-free contact with genuinely objective reality. (p. 78, cf. p. 77)

To develop this conception, McDowell proposes that:

> we should make sense of the objective import of intuitions and the objective content of judgments together. Each is supposed to cast light on the other. (p. 80)

To make sense of McDowell's proposal requires great care specifying exactly what kinds of 'subjective states' are supposed to make 'gap-free contact with ... objective reality'. On Kant's view (discussed further below), concepts and sensory intuitions are *components* of cognitive judgments in virtue of which we know spatio-temporal objects and events. According to Kant, singular cognitive reference, achieved in cognitive judgment, is parasitic upon singular sensory presentation, achieved in perceptual synthesis of sensory intuitions, which in turn is parasitic upon the singular reference of the sensory intuitions synthesised out of (typically sub-conscious) sensations. To make sense of the objective import of sensory intuitions, on Kant's view, requires making sense of the most basic level of synthesis in Kant's account, the synthesis of any group of sensations (which lack referentiality) into a sensory intuition by what Kant calls the transcendental power of imagination (*not* 'understanding', *pace* McDowell, pp. 80–1, quoted just above).

Thus to 'make sense of the objective import of intuitions and the objective content of judgments together', as McDowell suggests, requires careful analysis of the character and cognitive status of sensations. If our sensations are 'original existences', as Hume said about sensory impressions, or if our sensations are the sole direct *objects* of our awareness—as some Stoics, many Modern philosophers (e.g. Descartes, Locke), and most sense-data theories held—then Sextus Empiricus is right that we cannot have and cannot demonstrate any knowledge of any world or objects alleged to exist outside our awareness and ideas.[6]

To follow McDowell's suggestion about Kant thus leads quickly into complex issues in philosophy of mind, the likes of which McDowell's therapeutic aims seek to avoid. Indeed, these issues in philosophy of perception are far from McDowell's repeated stress on the importance of singular thoughts, especially for understanding how our 'subjective states' are directly world-involving in ways that enable the world itself to exercise suitable rational constraint on our thinking. This line of thought has considerable merit, and can be developed without engaging in philosophical *cum* cognitive psychology (see, e.g. Hyman 2003, Travis 2005).

Unfortunately, McDowell repeatedly flirts with philosophical *cum* cognitive psychology, to the detriment of his much more austere positive, if therapeutic views. For example, McDowell slides from the answerability of our beliefs or judgments to the world, under the guise of 'world-directedness' (1996a: 231, cf. 1996b: 292–4) to 'answerability to impressions' (1996a: 235–8). We cannot be 'answerable' to impressions, in any sense that preserves McDowell's conviction that cognitive judgment is a free act, unless we are self-consciously aware of these (alleged) impressions. Yet if we are aware of these impressions, then we lose the direct experiential involvement with *the world* that was to be the cornerstone of McDowell's realism and his account of singular thoughts. If 'impressions' have any suitable role to play, it is as vehicles or conduits, *not* as objects or contents, of our self-conscious awareness. Substituting sensory impressions as objects of our express awareness (so that we could be 'answerable' to *them*) puts McDowell back into the representationalist 'veil of perception' exposed by Sextus Empiricus. Understanding our cognitive answerability to the world in terms of our answerability to any causal or intensional intermediaries is epistemologically doomed, for just the reason McDowell himself identified:

> If we suppose that rational answerability lapses at some outermost point
> of the space of reasons, short of the world itself, our picture ceases to
> depict anything recognizable as empirical judgment; we have obliterated
> empirical content altogether. (1994a: 42–3)[7]

Kant knew this, and wisely rejected the representationalist 'new way of ideas' in favour of sensationism, which treats sensations (roughly) as information conduits rather than as objects of our self-conscious awareness.[8] Kant's epistemology involves direct realism about the objects of perception, whilst also providing a rich and insightful cognitive psychology of perception. This division of Kant's philosophical labour maps onto his distinction between the 'objective' and 'subjective' deductions (discussed below).

According to sensationism, whilst sensations relevant to perception typically are caused by objects in our surroundings, such causal relations do not suffice for sensations to represent anything. To represent anything, sensations must be integrated into (what we would now call) percepts. The main advances of sensationism are two: No longer to assume that representation is a brute feature of sensory input, and to recognise that sensations are components in our perceptual awareness of objects in our environs; typically, sensations are not themselves *objects* of our awareness. The main challenges facing sensationist theories of perception is to explain how such integration occurs, how this integration affords representation, and what epistemic status this integration and its resultant representation can have.

Kant was the first philosopher to resolve these sensationist challenges. This is a key task of Kant's account of perceptual synthesis. Very briefly, according to Kant, the relevant kinds of integration are all guided by the basic forms of judgment of which we are capable.[9] A first level of integration forms an empirical intuition out of several sensations.[10] Such an intuition is an '*Erkenntnis*', which in contemporaneous philosophical usage meant primitive cognitive *reference* (not ascription) to an object (George 1981). Translating '*Erkenntnis*' (in the distributive singular) into English as 'cognition' is nearly unavoidable, but understanding Kant's view requires understanding *his* use of his term. To have such an 'intuition' of an object is not yet to have a percept of it, nor any self-conscious awareness of it. McDowell claims that Kant claims that empirical 'intuitions' are 'cases of sensory consciousness of objects' (p. 79, 1998e: 414). Kant says this, but does not mean by it what McDowell presumes it to mean. Sensations and sensory intuitions are states of consciousness, according to Kant, though they are not (as such) states or components of *self*-conscious awareness (cf. e.g. A122). This reflects Kant's version of Leibniz's distinction between merely perceptive and apperceptive consciousness; only the latter involves self-conscious awareness. On Kant's view, 'enjoying [sensory] intuitions' is *not* 'having objects in view' (*pace* McDowell 1998e: 414). A second stage of cognitive activity integrates a set of empirical intuitions into (roughly) a percept of an object. Both of these stages of integration Kant ascribes to the 'transcendental power of imagination', that 'blind though indispensable power of the soul' without which we could experience nothing (A78/B103). Both of these stages are prior to self-conscious experience or empirical judgment, which is effected by our understanding integrating all the empirical intuitions of any one object (both concurrent and successive) over some period of time, which alone affords self-conscious experience of the object in question.[11] Closely conjoined with Kant's views on perceptual judgment are his transcendental requirements for self-ascription of experiences (Westphal 2004a: §2.3), and his solution to what is now called the 'binding problem' in neurophysiology of perception: How is it possible, how do our minds determine which among the plethora of any full set of concurrent sensations are sensations of any *one* object or event, both within any one sensory modality, and even more so, across our sensory modalities?[12]

This summary only touches on some key points of Kant's complex and sophisticated philosophical psychology of perception. Fortunately it suffices for three observations. First, Kant insists that the two basic levels of integration effected by our transcendental power of imagination are spontaneous, without being 'free' in the way expressed judgments are; this is why Kant calls it 'blind'. Transcendental imagination acts *spontaneously* because its activities are occasioned, though not caused,[13] by sensory intake, and they can be neither explained solely by, nor reduced to, purely causal processes. This is because the processes and products of transcendental imagination involve *proper* functioning, where its proper functions are specified normatively in terms of facilitating the generation of veridical experience, which itself is a component of justified empirical knowledge. Kant's discussions of the perceptual synthesis effected spontaneously by our transcendental power of imagination do not describe this process as a 'free' one.[14] *Pace* McDowell, there is nothing 'awkward' (p. 80; 2004/2005: §2) about ascribing spontaneous, though sub-conscious proto-cognitive activities to the transcendental power of imagination. McDowell's supposition to the contrary appears to be due to his unwarranted equation of 'spontaneity' with 'freedom' in Kant's account of perceptual judgment and his unwarranted ascription of the relevant forms of spontaneity to Kant's 'understanding', rather than to transcendental imagination (pp. 80–1, quoted above; 1994a: 5). According to Kant, rational freedom does require spontaneity, though not all forms of spontaneity require rational freedom.[15] Kant's profound anti-Cartesianism involves many externalist aspects in his transcendental account of human experience and knowledge (Westphal 2004a, 2006c). Sub- or non-conscious cognitive processes are among these externalist aspects. It is perplexing that McDowell does not recognise them for what they are. Perhaps this is why McDowell repeatedly underestimates what Kant allegedly 'needs' (p. 80).

Has McDowell inherited too much epistemic internalism, or lingering Cartesian infallibilism? An affirmative answer is suggested by McDowell's assertion that '. . . we cannot really understand the relations in virtue of which a judgment is warranted except as relations within the space of concepts: relations such as implication or probabilification . . .' (1994a: 7). This unargued premise is required to support McDowell's key contrast between frictionless coherentism and the Myth of the Given. Only excessive epistemic internalism or lingering Cartesianism make sense of McDowell's (1998c: 467) surprising worry about Sellars's contention that there are subconscious 'guides' to conscious episodes of awareness or judgment, or analogously about Evans (McDowell 1994a: 47–65), or his fixation on Davidson's exclusive contrast between reasons and causes. Yet these kinds of internalist worries are inconsistent with McDowell's (1994a: 72f., 1998e: 429 note 14) appeal to our 'second' cognitive or epistemic 'nature' in order to pave a *via media* between 'bald naturalism' and Davidson's coherentism, because (*inter alia*) the acquisition, development and proper functioning of our second nature is only possible for beings like us on the basis of our properly functioning 'first' (physio-neuro-psychological) nature.[16]

Secondly, McDowell has underestimated what he himself needs. McDowell is mistaken to claim that, on Kant's view, the objective purport of experience is solely a function of the categorial structuredness of sensory intuitions (p. 81). On Kant's view, the categorial structuring that converts sensations, which lack objective purport, into empirical intuitions, which have objective purport (in the form of primitive referentiality), involves exploiting the primitive information embodied in sensations in order to incorporate sensations into *acts* (not objects) of referential and (ultimately also) ascriptive awareness of surrounding objects. The categorial structure of empirical judgments cannot achieve this alone; Kant knows that this also requires an account of the roles of sensations in reference and ascription to particulars.[17] So far, McDowell lacks an adequate, corresponding account of sensations.[18] Without such an account, McDowell cannot follow out his suggested clue, that 'we should make sense of the objective import of intuitions and the objective content of judgments together' (p. 80). McDowell's non- if not anti-theoretical therapeutic aims are deeply at odds with his continued flirtation with psychology of perception.

Third, this very brief excursus into Kant's philosophical psychology of perception reveals a point of great strategic importance. To argue about sensory 'receptivity' and judgmental 'spontaneity' in the way McDowell does is to flirt with deep issues in the cognitive psychology of perception, both philosophical and empirical. Yet Kant stressed that his primary issue lies in the success of his 'objective deduction', his proof *that* we can and do make legitimate cognitive judgments. Compared to this, Kant's 'subjective deduction', his philosophical *cum* cognitive-psychological explanation of *how* we make such judgments, is secondary (Axvii). Kant knew that sceptics and empiricists—and for that matter, rationalists, too, all of whom took far too much for granted about singular cognitive reference—had to be addressed directly, and that mixing these two tasks can only generate confusion. The cogency of McDowell's views would benefit greatly from keeping these two tasks distinct. Nevertheless, considering some core features of Kant's direct reply to skepticism shows that much more can be achieved in these regards by analysis and argument than by McDowell's broad therapeutic strokes.

3. Identity and Predication

Much more important than the exegetical and strategic philosophical mis-steps just noted is that McDowell overlooks the most important ways in which Kant and Hegel argue for the rejection of givenness. More surprising yet, the way Kant and Hegel argue for this thesis provides a crucial link between Kant's and Hegel's epistemologies and contemporary views, especially those of Gareth Evans, for they bear directly on the character and preconditions of singular thoughts.

In his penetrating critique of Quine in 'Identity and Predication', Evans argues *inter alia* for the following conclusion:

> ...the line tracing the area of [ascriptive] relevance delimits that area in relation to which one or the other, but not both, of a pair of contradictory predicates may be chosen. And that is what it is for a line to be a boundary, marking something off from other things. (Evans 1985: 36, cf. 34–37)

It is implicit, and very nearly explicit, in Evans' analysis, that specifying the relevant boundary for the use of either member of a pair (or set) of contrary (mutually exclusive, though not necessarily 'contradictory') predicates is only possible by specifying the region relevant to the manifest characteristic in question, and vice versa, and (for reasons Evans provides) this region will be either co-extensive with or included within the spatio-temporal region occupied by some physical particular. More generally, Evans proves—even if he only implicitly argues—that predication requires conjointly specifying the relevant spatio-temporal region and some manifest characteristics of any particular we self-consciously experience or identify. These conjoint specifications may be rough and approximate; the key point is that spatio-temporal designation and ascription of manifest characteristics are *conjoint, mutually interdependent* cognitive achievements that integrate sensation ('sensibility') and conception ('understanding'). I shall call this the 'Evans thesis'.

This conjoint designation of an object's region and at least some of its manifest characteristics requires thorough co-operation between and integration of sensibility and understanding: Sensibility is required (though not sufficient) for sensing the various manifest characteristics of the sensed particular, and in directing us to its location; Understanding is required (though not sufficient) for explicitly identifying its region and its manifest characteristics, thus enabling us to be self–consciously aware of this particular. Arguments for this conclusion can be made on semantic grounds, as Evans does, at least in response to Quine's views on the alleged inscrutability of reference. Sound arguments for this conclusion can also be made on epistemic, indeed on transcendental grounds, as Kant and Hegel did.

Kant's arguments for the Evans thesis are both semantic and epistemic, for it is justified by Kant's semantics of cognitive reference (Westphal 2004a: esp. §§7–9, 33, 62–63.2). Kant's semantics of cognitive reference is basically a two-stage theory. According to Kant, concepts have 'meaning' or content as predicates of possible judgments (as determinables), and yet no concept has fully determinate meaning unless and until it is referred to some actual particular in a candidate cognitive judgment, whether about an object or an event.[19] Given our forms of judgment and of sensibility, the only way we human beings can refer concepts as possible predicates in judgments to actual particulars is to locate those particulars in space and time.[20] One important joint implication of Kant's Transcendental Aesthetic and Transcendental Analytic of Concepts is that genuine, determinately meaningful judgments are possible for us only through conjoint spatio-temporal designation of, and predicative ascription of characteristics to any experienced particular. Kant's semantics has been widely neglected by commentators, though it is central to Kant's lead question:

> How does it come about that we posit an object for these representations, or attach to them, beyond their subjective reality as modifications, some kind of an objective reality? (A197/B242).

This is how Kant officially formulates his lead question to Herz.[21] If it can indeed be proven that recognising any particular requires conceptual identification of both the region it occupies and of at least some of its manifest characteristics, then both sensibility and understanding are required, concurrently and conjointly, in any and every experience we have of any particulars. Thus, in brief, does Kant justify the Evans thesis. (The Evans thesis is a joint conclusion of Kant's Transcendental Aesthetic and Transcendental Analytic.)

I noted above (§1) that rejecting givenness requires rejecting the epistemic independence of entry-level cognitive episodes. Kant rejects this as well, by arguing that causal judgments are required to identify and to locate any spatio-temporal particular (see below: §§4, 5), and that the causal judgments required for this are interdependent because they are *discriminatory*; they discriminate among various objects and events in one's surroundings, and they discriminate the causal processes in which any one object participates from alternative causal processes in which it does not partake. Because these causal judgments are required to identify and to locate any spatio-temporal particular, they are likewise required to refer any of our *a priori* categories to such particulars (Westphal 2004a: §36). Thus does Kant reject givenness in the form of mutually independent basic claims or judgments.

These two points form the nub of Kant's proof that sensibility and understanding, or put otherwise, the roles of sensation and conception, are coextensive and mutually integrated throughout the entire scope of our experience of the objects and events surrounding us. Kant's proof is much more clear and cogent than McDowell's suggestions that, e.g.,

> We can dismount from the seesaw [between the Myth of the Given and coherentism] if we can achieve a firm grip on this thought: receptivity does not make an even notionally separable contribution to the co-operation between receptivity and spontaneity, understood as the involvement of conceptual capacities (1994a: 9, cf. 41, 51),[22]

or that,

> there is no distance from the world implicit in the very idea of thought (1994a: 27),

or that,

> we must not picture an outer boundary around the sphere of the conceptual, with a reality outside the boundary impinging inward on the system (1994a: 34),

or that,

> we can effect this deletion of the outer boundary [of the conceptual] without falling into idealism, without slighting the independence of reality. (1994a: 34)

In sum, Kant knows better than McDowell how to execute the 'transcendental task of entitling ourselves to see conceptual activity as directed toward a reality that is not a mere reflection of it' (McDowell 1998c: 473).

Yet here is a point at which Hegel's epistemology clearly advances on Kant's, not because Hegel argues for a different conclusion, but rather that he argues much more directly for the Evans thesis. Starting with a paradigmatic exponent of the thesis that sensation is sufficient, and conception not at all necessary to identify and thus to know sensed particulars, Hegel argues (in 'Sense Certainty') by strictly internal critique that sensation is necessary but not sufficient for knowledge of sensed particulars. Cognitive reference to particulars also requires correctly and justifiedly using *a priori* conceptions of space, spaces, time, times, self, and individuation in order to designate the known particular by locating it in space and time. Consequently, predication requires jointly specifying the relevant spatio-temporal region and some manifest characteristics of any particular we self-consciously experience. Thus (in brief) does Hegel defend the Evans thesis.

I have examined Hegel's analysis of these issues and his proof of this conclusion in detail, and have determined that they are sound (Westphal 2000). Although Hegel's examples all concern spatio-temporal particulars and our experiences of them, because his analysis focuses strictly on the central epistemological issues, his critique holds equally of alleged 'ego-centric' particulars, whether Russellian sense data (Westphal 2002b) or Hume's sensory impressions. Indeed, a careful internal critique (of the kind Hegel advocates and practices) of Hume's own account of abstract ideas reveals that Hume was not only the classic proponent of the 'copy theory' of impressions and ideas, he was also its first and still one of its most profound *critics*: ultimately, if unwittingly, Hume shows that the qualitative resemblances among impression and ideas that we name, we identify by acts of judgment that are linguistically based, and made by the understanding by using distinctions of reason (Westphal 2005a). Furthermore, Hegel rejects givenness through his moderately holistic account of epistemic justification (Westphal 2003a), which emphasises (*inter alia*), like Kant, the discriminatory character of the empirical judgments by which alone we identify any one particular.

McDowell (1998a: 214–74) is much concerned with singular thoughts, and with defending Evans' account of them against various misunderstandings. In this regard, it is puzzling that McDowell (1994a, 1998a, 1998b, 1998c, 2003a) does not cite Evans' 'Identity and Predication', for in it Evans identifies crucial semantic and conceptual conditions that must be satisfied if we are to have any singular thoughts at all, because the satisfaction of these conditions is required to identify any object of any singular thought (the Evans thesis).[23] Furthermore, these conditions must be satisfied in order to exploit self-consciously (cognitively) any of the 'dynamic thoughts' required to sustain any singular thought across time and changes in place. Hence these conditions and their satisfaction are crucial preconditions for McDowell's (1998a: 214–74; cf. 1994a: 56–58) own interpretation and defence of singular thoughts. McDowell has not yet sufficiently probed the requirements for our having singular thoughts.[24] Third, it appears that the Evans thesis provides sufficient grounds for maintaining the kind of conjoint exercise of sensibility and understanding central to McDowell's rejection of givenness. Indeed, Evans' stress on the use of discriminatory judgments in identifying the spatio-temporal boundary of any particular may suffice to show that our basic identifications of particulars are significantly interdependent. Finally, addressing head-on the epistemological issues involved in givenness—especially in the way that Hegel does—suffices to prove that sensibility and understanding must and can only function conjointly in human experience and cognition, without losing this proof in secondary concerns involving philosophical psychology.

4. Objective Purport and Kant's Transcendental Deduction

McDowell contends that Kant sets up his solution to the problem of objective purport within his transcendental idealism in a way that thwarts Kant's own best insights on this issue, and reveals Hegel's advance beyond Kant's analysis (p. 81). Stated very generally like this, I agree. However, McDowell has not fully identified the issues underlying, nor the proper reasons for this contention.

McDowell notes that Kant's problem in the Transcendental Deduction is to show that the categories are objectively valid because they can be correctly and justifiedly used to judge and thus to know spatio-temporal particulars. This task is not addressed by the Transcendental Aesthetic, which only concerns the transcendental conditions under which particulars can be given to us; the Aesthetic does not concern the transcendental conditions under which particulars can be thought, and thus judged or known. McDowell claims (p. 82; cf. 2004/2005: §3) that Kant re-wrote the second half of the B Deduction in order to solve this problem, by contending that the formal intuitions of space and time themselves are generated by combining spatial and temporal manifolds into the two unities that *are* space and time. This combination is effected by 'the unifying powers of the understanding'. Consequently, any objects that conform to the requirements of sensibility must per force also conform to the requirements of the understanding.

McDowell is right that Kant indicates, for the first time, in the infamous note to B160, that the formal intuitions which are space and time are generated by synthetic acts of the understanding. However, McDowell is mistaken to claim, as he does (p. 82; cf. 2004/2005: §3, and below: note 27), that the Kantian doctrine stated in this note solves the problem of the Transcendental Deduction. If McDowell's claim were correct, Kant could have simply put his note into the body of the *Critique*, and omitted at least the second half of the B Deduction. That Kant did not do so, especially knowing he must not over-extend the length of the B edition, and must above all avoid obscurity and misunderstanding, strongly suggests that Kant understood his problem, and especially his solution, rather differently than McDowell does.

Kant's note to B160 expressly distinguishes our spatial and temporal forms of intuiting from space and time as formal intuitions, and expressly indicates that the formal intuition of space is required for geometry. Exactly whether or how the formal intuitions of space and time as singular infinite manifolds pertain to human empirical knowledge or even to experience, which are generated in part through our forms of intuiting, is not obvious.[25] What is clear, however, is that the two formal unities, space and time, are generated by the understanding by using only the quantitative categories (unity, plurality, totality). None of the other categories are required for their generation. Consequently, showing that the quantitative categories undergird the formal intuitions of space and time as singular infinite manifolds shows nothing, and can show nothing, about whether spatio-temporal objects can, do, or must meet the judgmental requirements for using any of the remaining categories, especially the dynamic (causal) categories so central to Kant's objective deduction. Kant's note to B160 cannot and does not solve Kant's transcendental problem, of showing that *all* of our *a priori* categories can be used in legitimate cognitive judgments about spatio-temporal particulars.

To show that our categories of judgment do pertain to spatio-temporal objects given to us through our sensibility, Kant argues in the Transcendental Deduction along these lines: To ground the very possibility of the 'I think' accompanying our representations (so far as we can become self-consciously aware of them), including those representations involved in our experience or knowledge of spatio-temporal substances or events, requires showing that we cannot be self-conscious unless we are aware of and distinguish ourselves from spatio-temporal substances, and from our various experiences of them. Ascribing representations or experiences to ourselves requires that we can identify ourselves as the subjects of what we experience or represent. The key premise for Kant's argument is not the bare Cartesian *cogito*, but the richer premise that, for each of us, 'I am aware of my own existence as determined in time' (B275). By this Kant means that we are each aware of ourselves as being aware of apparent sequences of events in which some events appear to us before, during or after others. These events may be mere changes in representations or they may be objective changes of spatio-temporal states of affairs. Kant's thesis is that we can identify no such sequences at all, not even apparent ones, unless we can and do identify at least some objective sequences among spatio-temporal substances. Sequencing such events requires us to determine the time order in which they occur. This we can do only if we successfully identify *their* causal interactions in ways that allow us to 'derive' the subjective order in which these events happen to appear to us from the objective order in which they in fact transpire, even in those cases in which these two orders coincide (A193, 195, 349–50/B238, A240). If we cannot identify any such objective, causally grounded sequences of spatio-temporal events, then we cannot identify any merely subjective sequences of appearances either, because in such a case there would be no distinctive, identifiable relations among any mere appearances to us (A112, A194–5/B239–40).

Kant's Transcendental Analytic provides two proofs of what we now call mental content externalism, in the sense that (1) many basic 'mental' contents are what they are and have whatever content or manifest character they do only due to their relations to spatio-temporal objects and events in our environs, and (2) that for human beings, no 'mental' contents of self-conscious awareness are possible for us without our having some of the basic contents indicated in (1).[26] Kant's proofs of mental content externalism entail that, if we are self-consciously aware of some events appearing to occur before, during or after others, then we in fact have at least some empirical knowledge of our physical surroundings. This is the nerve of Kant's objective deduction. If this proof succeeds (I have argued elsewhere that it is sound; Westphal 2004a), then any apparent 'gap' between our 'subjective states' and the world itself must and can only be an artifact of our misunderstanding *how* we have such worldly experience and empirical knowledge. This can only mean, we must still understand, complete or replace what Kant called his 'subjective deduction'. McDowell has not completed his version of a subjective deduction, and has not even attempted the much more important objective deduction. Because he has not clearly distinguished these two tasks (above: §2), he has thwarted his prime objective of relieving us of our need for an objective deduction.[27] Reviewing Kant's problem and aims in the objective deduction highlights the extent to which McDowell focuses on issues pertaining to the 'how' question, central to Kant's subjective deduction, and why this focus cannot have the anti-sceptical, world-opening realist implications McDowell seeks, in trying to explain how the world just *is* open to us, if we would but open ourselves to it by getting our philosophical pictures straight by adopting McDowell's new picture of intentionality. McDowell's new picture of intentionality remains too elusive either to diagnose our alleged philosophical plight, or to provide a constructive alternative (cf. above: §2).

5. Proving Mental Content Externalism Transcendentally

McDowell shares Hegel's concern that, within Kant's transcendental idealism, the very guarantors of objective validity—the categories—nevertheless appear to be a mere subjective imposition by us on whatever we experience, and that this must be our 'imposition', or at least a failure to obtain genuine objectivity, because Kant contends that space and time are nothing but our human forms of sensibility (pp. 83–85).

This concern is based on Kant contending that objects as we sense, intuit or perceive them are radically different from the way they are 'in themselves', unintuited by us. This is a strongly metaphysical interpretation of Kant's phenomena/noumena distinction. Strawson (1966) held such an interpretation, but charged that Kant's view was incoherent. One response has been to reject the charge of incoherence by rejecting any metaphysical interpretation of Kant's phenomena/noumena distinction. Most prominently, this has been argued by Bird (1962, 1982), Prauss (1974), Allison (1983, 2004), and Buchdahl (1992), all of whom contend that Kant's transcendental idealism is not a metaphysical view. McDowell (1994a: 41–44 *passim*) initially accepted Strawson's view that Kant's transcendental idealism is metaphysical, though he shows signs of giving in to his critics on this count (p. 87; 1998c: 469 note 23). Nevertheless, McDowell's diagnosis of Kant's shortcomings, and of Hegel's advance, hews to a metaphysical interpretation of Kant's account of our forms of sensibility (cf. McDowell 2001b/2003b: §§4, 5). In this regard McDowell is correct; I have argued elsewhere in detail that Kant's distinction between phenomena and noumena is strongly metaphysical, although (*pace* Strawson 1966 and others) Kant's semantics renders it coherent.[28]

If the genuine objectivity of our empirical judgments is restricted in Kant's account by the transcendental ideality of space and time, can this restriction be surmounted? If so, how? On this question, McDowell's remarks are, as he says, 'programmatic' (p. 88). In 'Hegel's Idealism as a Radicalization of Kant', McDowell (2001b/2003b: §5; cf. 1994a: 44) suggests that Hegel's advance lies in 'discarding the frame' of Kant's transcendental idealist account of space and time. In 'Hegel and the Myth of the Given', he suggests somewhat more positively that Hegel's emphasis on the 'free self-development of reason' provides the right kind of alternative, in part because this free self-development of reason can include our engagement with empirical reality, because the empirical world is 'the medium in which the freedom of reason is exercised' (2003a: 87, cf. 88, McDowell 1998c: 466, 2004/2005: §7). On this central issue, we need more thorough analysis.

Fortunately, Hegel provided a powerful reply to the question, What is to be done about Kant's view that space and time are nothing but transcendentally ideal (even if also empirically real) forms of human sensibility? One obvious approach is to assess Kant's justification for claiming that our spatio-temporal forms of intuition are transcendentally ideal (Westphal 2004a: 118–23). Kant contends that objects acquire their spatio-temporal characteristics through our intuiting them. Kant further contends that this is the only possible explanation of our knowing *a priori* that any objects or events we can experience are spatio-temporal. Kant defends this claim by arguing against the only alternatives he could identify, Newton's and Leibniz's accounts of space and time. The question has always been whether we could identify an additional coherent, humanly possible alternative. Hegel did so. Indeed, Hegel did better than this: Hegel realised that a neglected alternative of the right kind is entailed by Kant's transcendental proof of the affinity of the sensory manifold. Kant notes, in accord with the central problem of the Transcendental Deduction (above: §§2, 4), that our sensations might be so fleeting and chaotically irregular that even the most acute human understanding could find no identifiable regularities, whether similarities or differences, among them. In this case, we could not exercise our understanding *at all*, and so could not be self-conscious (A121–3, A653–4/B681–2). Conversely, we can only achieve self-consciousness (or consciousness of our own existence as determined in time, above: §4) if the contents of our sensations or the objects we sense (Kant uses both terms) provide us a sufficient minimum, humanly detectable degree of regularity and variety. This is the principle of the transcendental affinity of the sensory manifold (Westphal 2004a: §§15–23).

Though it has profound ramifications, this insight generates a dilemma Kant's transcendental idealism cannot resolve (Westphal 2004a: §§24–29). Kant attempts to prove that only transcendental idealism can account for the satisfaction of the principle of the transcendental affinity of the sensory manifold. This is to say, Kant contends that this principle is satisfied because our understanding structures our experience according to this principle. However, Kant's contention is unjustified for two key reasons. First, for this claim to hold, our minds would have to generate more than just the structure of our experience, they would also have to generate at least some of its content; otherwise the structure and functioning of our minds could not guarantee that the principle of the transcendental affinity of the sensory manifold was satisfied. This implication directly violates a defining feature of transcendental idealism, namely, that the matter of experience is given us *ab extra*, while only the form of experience is generated by us. Second, Kant's arguments for his transcendental idealist account of the satisfaction of the principle of transcendental affinity conflate the *ratio cognoscendi* of the satisfaction of this principle with its *ratio essendi*. We know on transcendental grounds provided by Kant that this principle must be satisfied, if we are to be self-conscious, although this bit of *a priori* knowledge cannot explain why or how this principle is satisfied. Rather, Kant's analysis of transcendental affinity proves a *conditional* necessity: We human beings can only be self-conscious in a world which in fact presents us with a humanly detectable degree of similarities and differences among the contents or objects of sensation. In this way, Kant in fact provides us a genuinely transcendental proof of mental content externalism.[29]

The discovery that Kant's transcendental proof of the affinity of the sensory manifold provides a genuine proof of mental content externalism also proves the soundness of at least one version of the 'neglected alternative' objection to Kant's direct arguments for the transcendental ideality of space and time. The alternative Kant neglected there is this: Granting that we can know *a priori* that any and all objects we can experience are spatio-temporal (I submit that this is the case, in part due to the Evans thesis), the alternative realist explanation of this fact is that our forms of sensibility are only receptive to stimulation by spatio-temporal objects and events. If so, then objects or events have whatever spatio-temporal characteristics they have, regardless of our 'intuiting' or sensing them. There may be (not: are) entirely non-spatio-temporal objects, though we could not sense such objects all. Thus only spatio-temporal objects and events are possible candidates for objects of our human form of experience. The general point is that Kant's transcendental analysis of the *a priori* conditions that must be satisfied if we are to be self-consciously aware of ourselves as being aware of some appearances occurring to us before, during and after others (B275) unwittingly identifies several such conditions that are transcendental, formal, and also *material*. Such conditions are inconsistent with Kant's transcendental idealism (Westphal 2004b).

By his own methodological lights, Hegel owes us a thorough internal critique of Kant's transcendental idealism. He did not provide one. However, by 1802 Hegel clearly saw two key points in such a critique. First, the principle of transcendental affinity entails mental content externalism, and thus the falsehood of transcendental idealism (Westphal 1996). Second, Hegel recognised that Kant's *Metaphysical Foundations of Natural Science* (1786; hereafter '*Foundations*') fails to prove *a priori* that all motions of matter are inertial. Hegel recognised that this is no mere detail. This failure marks the failure of Kant's transcendental idealist effort to prove that every event we can experience must have a cause.[30] A key problem with Kant's analysis of causal judgments is that the only principle he states or defends in the first *Critique* is that 'every event has a cause'. However, the Analogies of Experience require the specific principle that 'every physical event has an external physical cause'. Kant first recognised this distinction in the *Foundations*. There he recognised that this specific causal principle cannot be proven on transcendental grounds alone, but requires 'metaphysical' proof of the kind licensed by Kant's Critical metaphysics in the *Foundations*. Yet even Kant's metaphysical proof of the specific causal principle in the *Foundations* fails, as Kant himself later recognised. This is to say, Kant's official Critical epistemology, including his Transcendental Idealism, fails to prove that the events we can experience in space and time have external physical causes.

Despite that failure, Kant's analysis of self-ascription, time-determination and the mutual interdependence of the three principles of causal judgment defended in the Analogies of Experience *do* provide a sound, genuinely transcendental proof that we human beings can only be aware of ourselves as being aware of some events appearing to occur before, during or after others only if and insofar as we correctly identify at least some causally interacting perceptible substances in our physical environment. How prevalent such objects and events are in our world remains a matter for empirical inquiry. That there are some, and that we identify some, can be proven transcendentally. This more restricted argument is, strikingly, a second, genuinely transcendental argument for mental content externalism. This pair of arguments proves that any world in which human beings can be aware of themselves as being aware of some events appearing to occur before, during, and after others, is a world that presents us with a significant degree of humanly identifiable regularities and varieties among the spatio-temporal substances and events we experience, both in their manifest characteristics and in their causal dispositions and interactions.

These two proofs of mental content externalism execute McDowell's (1998c: 473) 'transcendental task' of 'entitling ourselves to see conceptual activity as directed toward a reality that is not a mere reflection of it', and do so much more directly and cogently than McDowell's proposals.[31] Furthermore, both of Kant's transcendental proofs of mental content externalism entail that any world in which we can be self-conscious is one structured by humanly identifiable kinds. This provides all the proof we need that the world we live in provides us, as

McDowell says, 'thinkable contents' (1994a: 28). Finally, once we realise *that* we must have at least some empirical knowledge, because these two kinds of mental content externalism are true of us, and must be true if we are so much as self-consciously aware of even apparent sequences of events, then we can and should stop subverting our inquiries into *how* we have such knowledge by confusing this question with the question *whether* we have any empirical knowledge (cf. above: §4).

These insights into the key insights and oversights of Kant's Critical epistemology are fundamental to Hegel's development of his entire epistemology, beginning with the *Phenomenology of Spirit*. The route forward from Kant to Hegel does not lie in slogans about 'the free self-development of reason'.[32] The route forward from Kant to Hegel lies in detailed internal critical assessment of Kant's analyses and arguments, in just the ways required by Hegel's philosophical methods.[33] My research shows that this route is very fruitful philosophically. Once we understand Kant's and Hegel's genuine achievements in epistemology, we can recognise the distinctive, conjoint roles of spatio-temporal designation and ascription of characteristics in identifying particulars, and we can recognise the distinctive roles played by sensed determinates and by conceptual determinables in such identification, whilst knowing that these roles and components do not typically come apart in our experience, and cannot altogether come apart if we have experience at all, because externalism is true for many key mental contents, and it must be true if we are to think, experience or have anything in mind at all.

I conclude that McDowell is right that he has found himself 'impelled' to say things with an 'Hegelian sound' to them (p. 76). However, it is an important step to convert these 'Hegelian' sounds into determinate thoughts. If McDowell's approach is either common-sensist or merely theraputic (or both), then it shouldn't flirt with 'sensibility' and 'understanding', nor with 'spontaneity' and 'receptivity', which are Kant's terms of art; as mere English words they are far removed from commonsense discussion of belief or knowledge. Either McDowell must use these terms in Kant's sense, *or* he must establish his own sense of these terms of art, and establish their philosophical credentials and significance. He does neither, and cannot do so without constructing, analysing and defending a positive philosophical view of the kind officially proscribed by his therapeutic approach. Yet once we replace McDowell's 'Hegelian' sounds with informed, determinate thoughts about Kant's and Hegel's genuine epistemological achievements, it is not obvious that we need either McDowell's therapy, or his new though nascent 'picture' of intentionality.[34]

Kenneth R. Westphal
School of Philosophy
University of East Anglia
Norwich, NR4 7TJ
UK
k.westphal@uea.ac.uk

NOTES

[1] On the social and historical dimensions of Hegel's epistemology, which cannot be discussed here, see Westphal 2003a: §§11, 16, 20, 24–37, and forthcoming b.

[2] I have argued for the great contemporary importance of Kant's and Hegel's epistemologies in several places; most importantly in Westphal 1989, 2003a, 2003b, 2004a, 2006a. The three questions just posed are the key to understanding Hegel's epistemology (Westphal 1989: 1). Harris 1997 (see Westphal 1998d) and Beiser 2005: 177 agree that Hegel espouses a socio-historically grounded realism in epistemology. Halbig 2002: 19 agrees that Hegel holds epistemological realism, but disregards Hegel's *Phenomenology* and so omits Hegel's account of the social and historical dimensions of human knowledge.

[3] Unless otherwise noted, parenthetical page references are to McDowell 2003a.

[4] Sellars 1963: 147–8, 164–70; DeVries & Tripplett 2000: *xx*, 7.

[5] For example, McDowell 1994a: 12, 29, 31–2; 1998c, 464, 475; 2003d. Nevertheless, McDowell 2001a shows the same tendency as McDowell 2003a to focus on the integration of sensation and conception as the key to rejecting givenness, while neglecting Sellars' focus on whether entry-level cognitive states are mutually independent. McDowell 1994a: 23 contends that misunderstanding the relation between sensibility and understanding has caused repeated oscillations in epistemology between foundationalism and coherentism. Many other factors also contribute to these oscillations; see Westphal 1989, 2002c, 2002d, 2003a, §§16–24.

[6] 'Nor, again, is it possible to assert that the soul apprehends external realities by means of the affections of sense owing to the similarity of the affections of the senses to the external real objects. For how is the intellect to know whether the affections of the senses are similar to the objects of sense when it has not itself encountered the external objects, and the senses do not inform it about their real nature but only about their own affections . . . ?' (Sextus Empiricus 1933: 2: 74.)

[7] Cp. 1994a: 55 and McDowell's (1994b) parallel point about 'sub-personal' states or processes.

[8] 'Sensationism' was first developed by Condillac; Kant adopted it from Tetens. Kant's commitment to sensationism is highlighted by George 1981, Harper 1984 and Westphal 2004a: 13, 44–5, 60, 88–9.

[9] Both the content and the completeness of Kant's Table of Judgments have been widely disparaged, though Kant's view is defensible, even in contemporary terms (Wolff 1995, 1998, 2000, 2004). Wolff's brilliant work cannot be recommended too highly. It (together with Longuenesse 1998) would save McDowell 1998c: 457–62, 467, 472, 476 from misreading Kant's 'Clue to the Discovery of all Pure Concepts of the Understanding' (A74/B104–5).

[10] McDowell (p. 79) cites Kant's important remark that the unity of representations in a judgment and the unity of representations in an intuition have the same source (namely, our judgmental functions of logical unity, A79/B104–5), without inquiring what sorts of 'representations' are unified within empirical intuitions. These are sensations, on Kant's view. McDowell 1998c: 454 note 3, 456 notes Kant's distinction between sensations and intuitions, without examining it. McDowell 1988: 460 mistakes Kant's line between the merely conscious and the apperceptive.

[11] In this regard, Kant draws the 'line' between sub-conscious and self-conscious episodes, and between the non-conceptual and the conceptual, differently from each other, and differently from the way McDowell 1998c: 451 ascribes to Sellars. Neglecting these differences leads McDowell astray.

[12] Although this 'binding problem' (Roskies 1999) is embedded in the core of the Modern 'new way of ideas' and the entire sense-data tradition, it was recognised only by Hume, Kant, and Hegel (Westphal 1998a, esp. §§3.5, 4, 5, 6.5). Only very recently have analytic philosophers begun to address this problem (Cleeremans 2003). Hegel, too, espouses sensationism (DeVries 1988: 108–9; Westphal 1998a).

[13] Kant contends that we cannot make legitimate causal judgments about psychological events (Westphal 2004a: §61).

[14] Kant links perceptual synthesis with spontaneity at B102–3, 130, 149–52, and A97. He further discusses perceptual synthesis at B133, 142, 160–2, 164, 184, 202–3, 207–8, 212, 218, 221–3, 237, 246, 255, 257–9, 283–4, 286–7, 510–12, 747–8, 792, and A98–110, 115–6, 120, 123, 128. 'Freedom' and its cognates or equivalents appear in none of these passages.

[15] McDowell may appear to come close to this view, e.g. when he states that, in Kant's co-operation between receptivity and spontaneity, ' "spontaneity" can be simply a label for the involvement of conceptual capacities' (1994a: 9). Yet assimilating this statement to Kant's view requires a stronger reading of 'simply' than McDowell allows, for he insists that 'freedom [is] implicit in the idea that our conceptual capacities belong to the faculty of spontaneity' (1994a: 10).

[16] Elsewhere McDowell (1996b: 289, cf. p. 296) states, '. . . reliability must be present in the conceptual surroundings of the very idea that someone has a capacity to see (for instance) that things are thus and so. That seems obvious to me, even though I had no occasion to mention it in my book'. Unfortunately, McDowell does not examine any potential links between perceptual reliability and 'probabilification' within the 'space of concepts'.

McDowell 1998d may appear to set up this basic opposition differently, but there, too, the issue of—though not the phrase—'bald naturalism' appears in his concern that '. . . we should not allow the logical space of scientific understanding to hijack the very idea of the natural' (McDowell 1998d: 367; cf. 1998e: 420–21, 428). (For an illuminating account, diagnosis and critique of this hijacking, see Rouse 2002.) Likewise, McDowell 1996a: 234 may appear to set up the basic opposition otherwise, but bald naturalism is still central to his problematic (1996a: 235–6). The link between bald naturalism and the Myth of the Given appears to be this: bald naturalism assimilates sensations to mere causal effects of nature, and so excludes them from any normative realm required for reasoning or justification, whether it be the express 'space of reasons' or the normative biological realm of proper sensory functioning (on which see, e.g., Sellars 1981).

Apparently McDowell is led to these internalist worries, in part, by having come to these epistemological issues via semantics and philosophy of mind, rather than epistemology (cp. above: note 5). This is due in part to his engagement with Davidson, who continues the logical empiricist effort, begun by Carnap, to supplant epistemology by semantics. This effort has been highly informative, though so far unsuccessful. On Carnap's failure, see Westphal 1989a: 50–67; on Quine's, see (in this order) Haack 1995, chapter 6; Hanna 2001; Wallgren 2006, chapter 4 and Westphal 2006b: §4. On Brandom's failure, see McDowell 1996b: 294–96, 1998c: 491 note 22, 1998e: 407–09, 2003d. Davidson's effort fails, in part, because it assumes that, unlike us mere mortals, the radical interpreter knows much about the environment of whomsoever's beliefs are interpreted, on the basis of which assumption alone the translator (allegedly) can determine that most of whomsoever's beliefs are true—having already somehow ascertained that whomsoever *is* a believer and has beliefs (cp. Westphal 2006b: §4, about the parallel failure in Quine). Whatever may be the significance of Davidson's radical interpretation for semantics or philosophy of mind, it has no anti-sceptical implications in epistemology because his semantic 'coherence theory' is not a theory of *knowledge* precisely because it omits the justification condition of an individual's knowledge, without which there is no proper basis for distinguishing between that person's lucky guesses, reasonable beliefs (along a long continuum of justificatory supportiveness), and knowledge, nor any basis for avoiding Gettier problems. Sceptics can accept that we may (not: do) generally have true beliefs; so long as none of them is justified for individual believers, none of them count as knowledge. Davidson's insistence that only beliefs can provide reasons for (rather than causes of) other beliefs limits him to epistemic internalism. Conversely, externalist accounts of the epistemic justifiedness of perceptual beliefs do not need Davidson's semantics to show (allegedly) that most of anyone's beliefs are true; externalist accounts of justification (whether pure or mixed) can assess the truth-values and justificatory status of beliefs piece-meal rather than wholesale.

McDowell recommends rejecting 'the whole approach to knowledge that structures epistemology around the Argument from Illusion' (1995: 880). How we are to reject this approach while recognising the 'permanent possibility of having to decide we were wrong', which is required to maintain a suitable realism about the objects of empirical knowledge (1996a: 284–5), he does not explain.

More significant, in the present context, is that McDowell neglects, on the one hand, the role of infallibilism in his recounting and rejection of the argument from illusion ('unless reason can come up with policies or habits that will *never* lead us astray . . .'; 1995: 880, emphasis added), and neglects on the other hand Kant's brilliant strategy in the objective deduction of the Categories, which blocks the skeptical generalisation from the universal possibility of perceptual error to the possibility of universal perceptual error. If Kant's objective deduction is correct, universal perceptual error would undermine the very possibility of us being aware ourselves as being aware of some sensory appearances occurring to us before, during or after others. Kant's objective deduction affords a brilliant critique of global perceptual skepticism, including Stroud's, and provides a suitably fallibilist account of empirical cognitive judgment (Westphal 2004a: §63).

[17] This brief summary of Kant's intricate analysis is necessarily schematic. On Kant's account of the transcendental syntheses of imagination see Longuenesse 1998. On Kant's account of perceptual synthesis see Brook 1994 and Rosenberg 2005, chapter 5. Very important for the particular issues discussed here are Milmed 1969, Sellars 1978 and Strawson 1970, 1979.

[18] McDowell 1998c is his best effort to date to provide an adequate account of sensations. DeVries 2006 and Williams 2006 expose some serious difficulties with McDowell's view in those lectures. My observations here show that neither did McDowell there grasp Kant's view of sensations. Kant's closest contemporary heir regarding the role of sensations in empirical knowledge is Dretske's 1981 information theory, which involves a very Kantian distinction between the way information, which always has a propositionally structurable and hence conceptually formulable content, is embedded in analog form in sensation, whilst being decoded in digital form conceptually in human cognition. (Dretske's theory also provides yet another alternative to the allegedly exclusive but hardly exhaustive dichotomy McDowell 1994a: 24, 25, 26, 40, 46, 66–69 seeks to escape between givenism and coherentism; Haack 1993, too, shows that McDowell's dichotomy isn't exclusive. In this regard, McDowell's view is itself 'one of those set-ups that are familiar in philosophy, in which a supposedly exhaustive choice confers a spurious plausibility on a philosophical position'; 1995: 885.) The kind of justificatory externalism involved in information channels can be identified and ratified through philosophical

reflection (and empirical enquiry), though this higher-level justificatory ratification cannot replace the contribution of sensory information channels to the justifiedness of reliable sensations and their role in generating veridical experience. (I discuss some of these points in Westphal 2003a, chapter 9.) McDowell 1998c: 475 adverts to Evans' suggestion that perceptually demonstrative thoughts involve an information link—though no thought of that information link—between the object thought of and the subject who thinks of that object, though without developing this important externalist insight. Gettier 1963 ultimately persuaded epistemologists that our actual cognitive processes must be taken into philosophical account (Kitcher 1992: 59). Those attempting to replace epistemology by semantics (above: note 16) appear not to have learned this lesson, though Kant already knew it (Westphal 2004a: 16–7, 19–22, 76–7). Regarding McDowell's neglect of externalist factors, also see Grundmann 2003.

[19] McDowell interprets Kant's statement, that 'thoughts without content are empty' (A51/B75), to mean that '[f]or a thought to be empty would be for there to be nothing that one thinks when one thinks it; that is, for it to lack what I am calling "representational content" ' (1994a: 3–4). Kant however means by this that the thoughts in question lack reference to particular objects or events and so remain determinables. Nevertheless, as conceptual determinables they retain a genuine and legitimate conceptual content as determinable predicates of possible judgments; only thus are they mutually distinct determinables (Westphal 2004a: §§7, 8). McDowell's appeal (1994a: 4) to 'bits of experiential intake' to supply content is too broad to formulate the key points of Kant's cognitive semantics.

[20] Kant's critique of Leibniz's doctrine of the identity of indiscernables led him to realise that no description, however specific, can identify itself as definite, rather than as empty or ambiguous. Descriptive specificity cannot secure particularity (singularity) of reference, because particularity of reference is as much a function of the features or contents of the world as it is of the description (or concepts) in question.

[21] 'On what ground rests the relation of that in us which is called representation to the object?' (Kant 1902, 10: 130.6–8).

[22] At the Warwick conference, McDowell acknowledged that the phrase 'receptivity does not make an even notionally separable contribution to the co-operation' is an unfortunate and misleading formulation of his view.

[23] One obvious place where McDowell could have brought the Evans thesis to bear on perceptual demonstrative thoughts is in his discussion (1998c: 475–6) of how his account of ostensible perceptions aligns with Evans' account of such thoughts. Recognising Kant's and Hegel's defense of the Evans thesis also would have much improved McDowell's 2003a: 85–88 analysis. McDowell said to me that 'Identity and Predication' is not his favourite piece of Evans' because it 'is so obvious that such claims would have to have that structure'. Obvious to whom? Not to proponents of the myth of the given. More importantly, even if it is 'obvious' that such claims must have such a structure, it is far from obvious to most philosophers, including McDowell, what is required for us to be able to make and use claims having this basic predicative structure. In this regard, McDowell fails to identify and exploit some of Kant's and Hegel's central, genuinely transcendental insights.

[24] I submit that the Evans thesis also pertains directly to our having demonstrative thoughts about quite specific sensed qualities, such as a quite specific shade of color. However, this issue cannot be explored here; cf. McDowell 1998e: 415–17.

[25] The role is fundamental and fascinating. Certainly it concerns figurative synthesis (B150–3, 160–1), though the role of figurative synthesis in instances of our experience of

particulars and in empirical knowledge is barely suggested by Kant when he speaks of our 'outlining' the figure of the house we perceive (*'ich zeichne gleichsam seine Gestalt . . .'*; B162). Kant's point and phrasing resonate strikingly with Evans' 1985: 36 point about our demonstratively delineating the region within which only one of a set of contrasting predicates properly describes a perceived particular or at least one of its aspects (quoted above: §3).

[26] The ligaments of Kant's main proof are summarised in Westphal 2004a: §65; the book reconstructs and defends Kant's proof. The press misprinted an 'inference line' on p. 272; please omit the line between premises (8) and (9) and insert a line between premises (9) and (10). For a conspectus of the constructive argument developed in Westphal 2004a, see Westphal 2006a.

[27] McDowell claims that 'With this move [in B160 note], Kant takes himself to be entitled to say that the categories apply to "whatever objects may *present themselves to our senses*" [B159]' (p. 82). Kant does not say this. On B159 Kant does not claim that he has already solved the problem of the Transcendental Deduction by appealing to the doctrine of figurative synthesis mentioned in a note he has not yet provided. (Note the page order of McDowell's references.) Rather, Kant here states the problem to be solved by the Transcendental Deduction: *'Jetzt soll die Möglichkeit, durch Kategorien die Gegenstände, die nur immer unseren Sinnen vorkommen mögen, und zwar nicht der Form ihrer Anschauung, sondern den Gesetzen ihrer Verbindung nach a priori zu erkennen, also der Natur gleichsam das Gesetz vorzuschreiben und sie sogar möglich zu machen, erklärt werden. Denn ohne diese ihre Tauglichkeit würde nicht erhellen, wie alles, was unseren Sinnen nur vorkommen mag, unter den Gesetzen stehen müsse, die a priori aus dem Verstande allein entspringen'* (B159–60). The third clause of the first quoted sentence is Kant's only mention on these pages of 'our senses', which McDowell italicised. Kant's note to B160 concerns figurative synthesis and its role in generating the formal intuitions that are (according to Kant's Transcendental Idealism) space and time as unified manifolds so structured as to admit of a metric. These formal intuitions are, in Kant's view, distinct from both our forms of sensibility, space and time as forms of human intuiting, and from the spatial or temporal form of anything we intuit in space or time; on this three-fold distinction, see Paton 1936, 1: 101–6 and Allison 1983: 96–97. *Pace* McDowell, Kant's note to B160 does not concern, broadly speaking 'the way our sensibility is formed'.

Can McDowell have made such an error? At the Warwick conference, McDowell recognised that this cannot be Kant's view. Yet consider what McDowell wrote about Kant's infamous note to B160 to which I object:

> So the way our sensibility is formed, the topic of the Transcendental Aesthetic, cannot after all be understood independently of invoking the unifying powers of the understanding, the topic of the Transcendental Analytic. The Aesthetic does not after all lay down independent conditions for objects to be available to our senses, in a way that would leave it still open whether the objects conform to the requirements of the understanding.

> In 'Glauben und Wissen', Hegel appreciatively describes Kant's move like this: 'Here [in the Transcendental Deduction], the original synthetic unity of apperception is recognised also as the principle of the figurative synthesis, i.e. of the forms of intuition; space and time are themselves conceived as synthetic unities, and spontaneity, the absolute synthetic activity of the productive imagination, is conceived as the principle of the very sensibility that was previously characterised only as receptivity' [Hegel 1977: 69–70; *GW* 4: 327].

With this move Kant takes himself to be entitled to say the categories apply to 'whatever objects may *present themselves to our senses*' [B159]. He takes himself to have averted the threat that, by his own lights, objects might be able to be present to our senses but not conform to the requirements of the understanding. The threat seemed a live one when it seemed that there were two independent sets of conditions, those relating to sensibility and those relating to understanding, but Kant has unmasked that as a misleading appearance. (McDowell 2003a: 82)

In 'Faith and Knowledge' (*GW* 4: 327–8) Hegel celebrates the integrity of sensibility and understanding revealed by Kant's note to B160, and insists that they both must have a common root in our original synthetic power of cognition, thus alluding to Kant's suggestion that there may be a common root of our sensibility and understanding (B29). Unlike McDowell, Hegel does *not* claim that Kant's note to B160 solves the problem of the Transcendental Deduction. McDowell does claim this, both before and after his quotation from Hegel (in the first and third paragraphs just quoted), by unjustifiably juxtaposing Kant's note at B160 with Kant's *prior* remark from B159, in which Kant in fact refers to the previous §§20 and 21 of the Transcendental Deduction, *not* forward to a footnote (i.e. B160 note), for the solution to the problem of the (objective) Deduction stated at B159. Regrettably, the quoted passage is not isolated: McDowell has published this same account in two other articles in a total of five publications, *viz.*, McDowell 2003a: 82; 2001b/2003b: §§3, 4; 2004/2005: §3. Moreover, omit his account of B160 note, and McDowell has not charted any route forward from Kant to Hegel. This is a key example of how the general level of McDowell's discussion fails to grasp Kant's views, Hegel's views, and the important debates between them. Yet the general level of McDowell's discussion is not required for an effective therapeutic approach to philosophy; see Wallgren 2006.

[28] See Westphal 2004a, chapter 2; 1998e, 2001. Metaphysical interpretations of Kant's phenomena/noumena distinction are also defended by Adams 1997, Ameriks 1992, Greenberg 2001, Guyer 1987 and Watkins 2005. To respond effectively to his critics requires digging into Kant's texts and issues to develop an informed and justifiable interpretation of Kant's infamous distinction; McDowell has not yet done so.

[29] Regretably, here I can only state the main thrust of Kant's proof. For a concise statement of this proof, which connects it with a very important though neglected aspect of Wittgenstein's later philosophy, see Westphal 2005b. For full details, see Westphal 2004a, chapter 3.

[30] For details, see Westphal 2004a: §§30–59. I do not claim that Hegel worked out or saw all of these details, though Hegel did see that this problem serves to refute Kant's transcendental idealism, and bolsters the grounds for realism, and indeed for the transcendental proof of mental content externalism based on the transcendental affinity of the manifold of sensory intuition discussed above (Westphal 1998c). These are key tenets of Hegel's epistemology in the *Phenomenology of Spirit* (Westphal 2003a, 2003b, 2004b).

[31] McDowell 1998c: 490 (cf. 1994a: 34) states that 'The key question for understanding Kant, and thereby seeing how to become comfortable with intentionality, is just the question brought into focus by Sellars: Can the transcendental project be acceptably executed from within the conceptual order, or does it require a sideways-on point of view on the directedness of the conceptual at the real?' Kant's key question for understanding Kant lies in understanding why his method of transcendental reflection (Westphal 2004a, chapter 1) is required in order to answer his own question to Herz (above: §3). Kant's

reasons for adopting transcendental reflection as his method show that the dichotomy McDowell uses to formulate his own key question is itself a major roadblock to understanding intentionality. McDowell still seeks a purely 'conceptual' analysis to solve his transcendental problem, and seeks to find one in Kant, despite Kant's insight that no purely analytic argument could succeed in this endeavor (B263–5, B810; Baum 1986: 1, 175–81), so that we must use transcendental reflection to identify our key cognitive capacities and their attendant incapacities (Westphal 2004a, chapter 1). Kant's methods and analysis require and provide a cogent third alternative to the only two options McDowell considers.

[32] In this section I have summarised my main grounds for rejecting the notion that Hegel's idealism is any kind of radicalisation of Kant's transcendental idealism. Elsewhere I show that Hegel's 'idealism' is a form of ontological holism that is, and is intended to be, consistent with ordinary realism (Westphal 1989a: 140–8, forthcoming c). Hegel's own phenomenological 'deduction' of our categorial concepts takes a very different form from Kant's (Westphal 1989a: 154–88). (Westphal 1989a: 150–3, is in the main superceded by Westphal 2002a.)

[33] It also requires at least approximating the standards for adequate interpretation, namely: providing a complete philosophical reconstruction of an historical text, within its historical and philosophical context, which provides good philosophical sense for both the structure and the details of that text, down to individual lines, phrases, and terms (Westphal 2003: 1–2). These exacting standards can be satisfied; doing so clears away much mythology about and misunderstanding of Hegel's views.

[34] Be this as it may, the genuinely Hegelian alternative to *Mind and World* is available, for whomever may be interested; see Westphal 2003a. I thank John McDowell for his discussion of these issues and for providing his original English texts of McDowell 2001b/ 2003b, 2003d, 2004/2005; Charles Travis for discussing various points raised herein, and Bill deVries for very prompt, helpful comments on the first draft of these remarks and for subsequent advice. I also thank an anonymous referee, Jakob Lindgaard and Bob Stern for their constructive suggestions, and above all Jakob for his kind invitation for me to formulate these remarks for the Warwick conference on McDowell's work. Finally, I thank Jason Leddington, Cinzia Ferrini, and George Di Giovanni for prompt and very helpful comments on my penultimate draft.

REFERENCES

Adams, R. M. (1997), 'Things in Themselves', *Philosophy and Phenomenological Research*, 57, 4: 801–25.

Allison, H. (1983), *Kant's Transcendental Idealism: An Interpretation and Defense*. New Haven: Yale University Press.

—— (2004), *Kant's Transcendental Idealism: An Interpretation and Defense*, Revised and enlarged edition. New Haven: Yale University Press.

Ameriks, K. (1992), 'Kantian Idealism Today', *History of Philosophy Quarterly*, 9: 329–40.

Baum, M. (1986), *Deduktion und Beweis in Kants Transzendentalphilosophie*. Königstein/Ts: Hain bei Athenäum.

Beiser, F. C. (2005), *Hegel*. New York: Routledge.

Bird, G. (1962), *Kant's Theory of Knowledge*. London: Routledge & Kegan Paul.

—— (1982), 'Kant's Transcendental Idealism', in G. Vesey (ed.), *Idealism Past and Present*. Cambridge: Cambridge University Press, pp. 71–92.

Brook, A. (1994), *Kant and the Mind*. Cambridge: Cambridge University Press.

Buchdahl, G. (1992), *Kant and the Dynamics of Reason*. London: Blackwell's.

Cleeremans, A., (ed.), (2003), *The Unity of Consciousness: Binding, Integration, and Dissociation*. Oxford: Oxford University Press.

DeVries, W. (1988), *Hegel's Theory of Mental Activity*. Ithaca, NY: Cornell University Press.

—— 2006, 'McDowell, Sellars, and Sense Impressions', *European Journal of Philosophy*, 14, 2: 182–201.

DeVries, W. and Tripplett, T. (2000), *Knowledge, Mind, and the Given*. Cambridge, MA: Hackett Publishing Co.

Dretske, F. I. (1981), *Knowledge and the Flow of Information*. Cambridge, MA: MIT/Bradford Press.

Evans, G. (1985), *Collected Papers*. Oxford: The Clarendon Press.

George, R. (1981), 'Kant's Sensationism', *Synthese*, 47, 2: 229–55.

Gettier, E. (1963), 'Is Justified True Belief Knowledge?', *Analysis*, 23, 6: 121–23.

Greenberg, R. (2001), *Kant's Theory of A Priori Knowledge*. State College, PA: Pennsylvania State University Press.

Grundmann, T. (2003), 'Perceptual Representations as Basic Reasons', in: R. Schumacher (ed.), *Perception and Reality. From Descartes to the Present*. Paderborn: Mentis, pp. 286–303.

Guyer, P. (1987), *Kant and the Claims of Knowledge*. Cambridge: Cambridge University Press.

Haack, S. (1993), *Evidence and Inquiry*. Oxford: Blackwell.

Halbig, C. (2002), *Objektives Denken. Erkenntnistheorie und Philosophy of Mind in Hegels System*. Stuttgart-Bad Cannstadt: frommann-holzboog.

Hanna, R. (2001), *Kant and the Foundations of Analytic Philosophy*. Oxford: The Clarendon Press.

Harper, W. (1984), 'Kant's Empirical Realism and the Distinction between Subjective and Objective Succession', R. Meerbote and W. Harper (eds.), *Kant on Causality, Freedom and Objectivity*. Minneapolis, MN: University of Minnesota Press, pp. 108–37.

Harris, H. S. (1997), *Hegel's Ladder*, 2 vols. Cambridge, MA: Hackett Publishing Co.

Hegel, G. W. F. (1968–). H. Buchner and O. Pöggeler (eds.), *Gesammelte Werke*. Published by the Rheinisch-Westfälischen Akademie der Wissenschaften in association with the Deutsche Forschungsgemeinschaft. Hamburg: Meiner. Cited parenthetically as '*GW*' by volume: page number.

—— (1801), 'Differenz des Fichte'schen und Schlling'schen Systems der Philosophie', *GW*, 4: 3–92.

—— (1802), 'Glauben und Wissen. Oder die Reflexionsphilosophie der Subjektivität, in der Vollständigkeit ihrer Formen, als Kantische, Jacobische, und Fichtische Philosophie', *GW*, 4: 315–414.

—— (1807). *Die Phänomenologie des Geistes*, *GW* 9.

—— (1977), *Faith and Knowledge*, Cerf, W. and Harris, H. S. (eds. and trs.), Albany, NY: SUNY Press.

Hyman, John (2003), 'The Evidence of our Senses', in H. J. Glock (ed.), *Strawson and Kant*. Oxford: The Clarendon Press, pp. 235–53.

Kant, I. (1902–), *Kants Gesammelte Schriften*, Königlich Preußische (now Deutsche) Akademie der Wissenschaften, Berlin: G. Reimer (now De Gruyter). Cited by volume: page numbers.

—— (1781, 1787), *Kritik der reinen Vernunft*, in Kant (1902), 3 and 4: 1–252. Cited by the usual designations of the first ('A') and second ('B') edition pages.

—— (1786). *Metaphysische Anfangsgründe der Naturwissenschaft*, in Kant (1902), 4: 456–566.

Kitcher, Philip (1992), 'The Naturalists Return', *The Philosophical Review*, 101, 1: 53–114.

Longuenesse, B. (1998), *Kant and the Capacity to Judge*. Princeton, NJ: Princeton University Press.

McDowell, J. (1994a), *Mind and World*. Cambridge, MA: Harvard University Press.

—— (1994b), 'The Content of Perceptual Experience', *The Philosophical Quarterly*, 44, 175: 190–205.

—— (1995), 'Knowledge and the Internal', *Philosophy and Phenomenological Research*, 55, 4: 877–93.

—— (1996a), 'Précis of *Mind and World*', *Philosophical Issues*, 7: 231–39.

—— (1996b), 'Reply to Gibson, Byrne, and Brandom', *Philosophical Issues*, 7: 283–300.

—— (1998a), *Meaning, Knowledge, & Reality*. Cambridge, MA: Harvard University Press.

—— (1998b), *Mind, Value, & Reality*. Cambridge, MA: Harvard University Press.

—— (1998c), 'Having the World in View: Sellars, Kant, and Intentionality', *Journal of Philosophy*, 95, 9: 431–91.

—— (1998d), 'Precis of *Mind and World*', *Philosophy and Phenomenological Research*, 58, 2: 365–68.

—— (1998e), 'Reply to Commentators', *Philosophy and Phenomenological Research*, 58, 2: 403–31.

—— (2001a), 'Comment on Richard Schantz, "The Given Regained" ', *Philosophy and Phenomenological Research*, 62, 1: 181–4.

—— (2001b), 'I'dealismo di Hegel come radicalizazzione di Kant', *Iride*, 34: 527–48.

—— (2002), 'Knowledge and the Internal Revisited', *Philosophy and Phenomenological Research*, 64, 1: 97–105.

—— (2003a), 'Hegel and the Myth of the Given', in W. Welsch and K. Vieweg (eds.), *Das Interesse des Denkens. Hegel aus heutiger Sicht*. München: Fink, pp. 75–88.

—— (2003b), 'I'dealismo di Hegel come radicalizazzione di Kant', rpt. of *idem*. 2001b in L. Ruggiu & I. Testa (eds.), *Hegel Contemporaneo: la ricezione americana di Hegel a confronto con la traduzione europea*. Milano: Guerini, pp. 451–477.

—— (2003c), 'Reason and Nature', in M. Willascheck (ed.), *John McDowell: Reason and Nature. Lecture and Colloquium in Münster 1999*. Münster: LIT press; http://web.uni-frankfurt.de/fb08/PHIL/willaschek/mcdowellkolloq.pdf.

—— (2003d), 'Hyperbatolokikos Empeirismos' ('Transcendental Empiricism'), *Defkalion*, 21, 1: 65–90.

—— (2004), 'Selbstbestimmende Subjectivität und externer Zwang', in C. Halbig, M. Quante and L. Siep (eds.), *Hegels Erbe*. Frankfurt a.M.: Suhrkamp, pp. 184–208.

—— (2005), 'Self-determining subjectivity and external constraint', *Internationales Jahrbuch für deutschen Idealismus/International Yearbook for German Idealism*, 3: 21–35; (Slightly revised version of *idem*. 2004).

Milmed, Bella K. 1969, '"Possible Experience" and Recent Interpretations of Kant', in L. W. Beck (ed.), *Kant Studies Today*. LaSalle, IL: Open Court, pp. 301–21.

Paton, H. J. (1936), *Kant's Metaphysic of Experience*. London: George Allen & Unwin; New York: Humanities, 2 vols.

Rosenberg, J. (2005), *Accessing Kant: A Relaxed Introduction to the Critique of Pure Reason*. New York: Oxford University Press.

Roskies, A. (ed.), (1999), 'The Binding Problem', *Neuron*, 24.

Rouse, J. (2002), *How Scientific Practices Matter*. Chicago, IL: University of Chicago Press.

Sellars, W. (1963), *Science, Perception, and Reality*. London: Routledge & Kegan Paul.

—— (1978), 'The Role of Imagination in Kant's Theory of Experience', in H. W. Johnstone (ed.), *Categories: A Colloquium*. University Park, PA: The Pennsylvania State University Press, pp. 231–245.

—— (1981), 'Mental Events', *Philosophical Studies*, 39: 325–45.

Sextus Empiricus (1933), *Outlines of Pyrrhonism* in Works, 4 vols. Rev. R. G. Bury (tr.), Cambridge, MA: Harvard University Press, vol. 1.

Strawson, Peter F. 1966, *The Bounds of Sense*. London: Methuen.

—— (1970), 'Imagination and Perception', in L. Foster and J. W. Swanson (eds.), *Experience and Theory*, (Amherst, MA: University of Massachusetts Press; London: Duckworth), pp. 31–54; rpt in Strawson, *Freedom and Resentment and Other Essays* (London: Methuen, 1974), pp. 45–65.

—— (1979), 'Perception and its Objects', in G. F. MacDonald (ed.), *Perception and Identity*. Ithaca, NY: Cornell University Press, pp. 41–60.

Travis, C. (2000), 'Taking Thought', *Mind*, 109, 435: 533–57.

—— (2005), 'A Sense of Occasion', *The Philosophical Quarterly*, 55, 219: 286–314.

Wallgren, T. (2006), *Transformative Philosophy: Socrates, Wittgenstein, and the Democratic Spirit of Philosophy*. Lanham, MD: Rowman & Littlefield/Lexington Books.

Watkins, E. (2005), *Kant and the Metaphysics of Causality*. New York: Cambridge University Press.

Westphal, K. R. (1989), *Hegel's Epistemological Realism*, Philosophical Studies Series, vol. 43. Dordrecht: Kluwer.

—— (1993), 'Hegel, Idealism, and Robert Pippin', *International Philosophical Quarterly*, 33, 3: 263–72.

—— (1996), 'Kant, Hegel, and the Transcendental Material Conditions of Possible Experience', *Bulletin of the Hegel Society of Great Britain*, 33: 23–41.

—— (1998a), *Hegel, Hume und die Identität wahrnehmbarer Dinge*. Frankfurt a.M.: Klostermann.

—— (1998b), 'Hegel's Solution to the Dilemma of the Criterion', revised version in J. Stewart (ed.), *The Phenomenology of Spirit Reader: A Collection of Critical and Interpretive Essays*. Albany, NY: SUNY Press, pp. 76–91.

—— (1998c), 'On Hegel's Early Critique of Kant's *Metaphysical Foundations of Natural Science*', in S. Houlgate (ed.), *Hegel and the Philosophy of Nature*. Albany, NY: SUNY Press, pp. 137–66.

—— (1998d), 'Harris, Hegel, and the Spirit of the *Phenomenology*', *Clio*, 27, 4: 551–72.

—— (1998e), 'Buchdahl's "Phenomenological" View of Kant: A Critique', *Kant-Studien*, 89: 335–52.

—— (1999), 'Hegel's Epistemology? Reflections on Some Recent Expositions', *Clio*, 28, 3: 303–23.

—— (2000), 'Hegel's Internal Critique of Naïve Realism', *Journal of Philosophical Research*, 25: 173–229.

—— (2001), 'Freedom and the Distinction between Phenomena and Noumena: Is Allison's view Methodological, Metaphysical, or Equivocal?', *Journal of Philosophical Research*, 26: 593–622.

—— (2002a), 'Kant, Hegel, and the Fate of "the" Intuitive Intellect', in S. Sedgwick (ed.), *The Reception of Kant's Critical Philosophy: Fichte, Schelling, and Hegel*. New York: Cambridge University Press, pp. 283–305.

—— (2002b), ' "Sense Certainty", or Why Russell had no "Knowledge by Acquaintance" ', *Bulletin of the Hegel Society of Great Britain*, 45/46: 110–23.

—— (2002c), 'Rationality and Relativism: The Historical and Contemporary Significance of Hegel's Response to Sextus Empiricus', *Esercizi Filosofici, (Trieste)*, 6: 22–33.

—— (2002d), 'Razionalità e relativismo: Il significato storico e contemporaneo della risposta hegeliana a Sesto Empirico', C. Ferrini (tr.), *Etica e Politica*, 4, 1; http://www.units.it/~etica/2002_1/index.html (Italian translation of previous item).

—— (2003a), *Hegel's Epistemology: A Philosophical Introduction to the PHENOMENOLOGY OF SPIRIT*. Cambridge, MA: Hackett Publishing Co.

—— (2003b), 'Hegel's Manifold Response to Scepticism in the Phenomenology of Spirit', *Proceedings of the Aristotelian Society*, 103, 2: 149–78.

—— (2003c), 'Can Pragmatic Realists Argue Transcendentally?', in J. Shook (ed.), *Pragmatic Naturalism and Realism*. Buffalo, NY: Prometheus, pp. 151–75.

—— (2004a), *Kant's Transcendental Proof of Realism*. Cambridge: Cambridge University Press.

—— (2004b), 'Must the Transcendental Conditions for the Possibility of Experience be Ideal?', in C. Ferrini (ed.), *Eredità Kantiane (1804–2004): questioni emergenti e problemi irrisolti*. Napoli: Bibliopolis, pp. 107–26.

—— (2005a), 'Hume's Commitment to, and Critique of, "Knowledge by Acquaintance": Some Hegelian Reflections', *Bulletin of the Hegel Society of Great Britain*, 51/52: 28–55.

—— (2005b), 'Kant, Wittgenstein, and Transcendental Chaos", *Philosophical Investigations*, 28, 4: 303–23.

—— (2006a), 'How does Kant Prove that We Perceive, and not merely Imagine, Physical Objects?', *The Review of Metaphysics*, 60: 781–806.

—— (2006b), 'Science and the Philosophers', in H. Koskinen, S. Pihlström and R. Vilkko (eds.), *Science: A Challenge to Philosophy?* Frankfurt a.M.: Lang, pp. 125–52.

—— (2006c), 'Consciousness and its Transcendental Conditions: Kant's Anti-Cartesian Revolt', in S. Heinämaa, V. Lähteenmäki and P. Remes (eds.), *A History of Consciousness*. Dordrecht: Springer.

——(forthcoming a), 'Kant's Two Proofs of Mental Content Externalism'.

——(forthcoming b), 'Rational Judgment and Mutual Recognition in Hegel's Theory of Justification'.

——(forthcoming c), '*Intelligenz* and the Interpretation of Hegel's Idealism: Some Hermeneutic Pointers'.

Williams, M. (2006), 'Science and Sensibility: McDowell and Sellars on Perceptual Experience', *European Journal of Philosophy*, 14, 2: 303–326.

Wolff, M. (1995), *Die Vollständigkeit der kantischen Urteilstafel*. Frankfurt a.M.: Klostermann.

—— (1998), 'Erwiderung auf die Einwände von Ansgar Beckermann und Ulrich Nortmann', *Zeitschrift für philosophische Forschung*, 52, 3: 435–59.

—— (2000), 'Nachtrag zu meiner Kontrovers mit Ulrich Nortmann', *Zeischrift für philosophische Forschung*, 54, 1: 86–94.

—— (2004), *Abhandlung über die Prinzipien der Logik*. Frankfurt a.M.: Klostermann.

9

Science and Sensibility: McDowell and Sellars on Perceptual Experience

Michael Williams

Introduction

I want to discuss John McDowell's account of perceptual experience in relation to that of Wilfrid Sellars. McDowell generously acknowledges his debts to Sellars, while nevertheless offering some sharp criticisms. So I shall pose three questions: how close are McDowell and Sellars really? Does McDowell get Sellars right? And are his criticisms well-aimed? The answers will turn out to be, respectively, 'Not as close as we might think', 'Not entirely', and 'No'. Central to my arguments in support of these answers will be a claim to the effect that McDowell fails to take heed of one of Sellars's most important epistemological insights, an insight that any account of perceptual knowledge ought to take on board. But we are not dealing with mere oversights here. The differences between McDowell and Sellars run deep, reflecting divergent conceptions of the task of philosophy in our time.

1. McDowell

I shall begin with a brief recapitulation of McDowell's views in *Mind and World*.[1] There are three main components to *Mind and World*: a problem, its solution, and an explanation ('McDowell's diagnosis') for why the solution can be so difficult to see or accept.

First the problem. In modern philosophy, according to McDowell, there is an endless oscillation between the Myth of the Given and 'frictionless coherentism'. This oscillation is the expression of a (possibly inchoate) transcendental anxiety: how can thought be about an objective world? Or as McDowell likes to say, how can thought have 'objective purport'? The problem can be explained (in Kantian terms) as follows. Conceptual activity—thought—belongs to the 'realm of freedom'. What this means is that we are responsible for thoughts: for example, we can be criticized when we get things wrong, or accept things without proper justification. Thus:

> 'The space of concepts' is at least part of what Wilfrid Sellars calls 'the space of reasons'. When Kant describes the understanding as the faculty of spontaneity, that reflects his view. . .[that] rational necessitation is not

just compatible with freedom but constitutive of it. In a slogan, 'the space
of reasons is the realm of freedom' (*MW*: 5).

As this suggests, freedom isn't doing whatever you want. Rather, thought
demands constraint: not anarchy but freedom under law. Now some kinds of
constraint (e.g. consistency) are internal to thought itself and so unproblemati-
cally 'rational'. But if it is to have objective purport, thought also demands
constraint that is external (i.e. influence from outside thinking itself). Such
constraint can only be provided by experience, for it is through experience that
we encounter the world. External constraint is thus empirical constraint. Lacking
empirical constraint, 'thought' would lack empirical content: that is, it would lack
content altogether and so would not really be thought at all. But now the problem
arises. The demand for external constraint—as the demand for constraint by an
external reality disclosed in experience—easily comes to seem like a demand for
constraint by something 'outside the conceptual sphere': that is, by something
outside the space of reasons. McDowell:

> [I]f our freedom in empirical thinking is total, in particular if it is not
> constrained from outside the conceptual sphere, that can seem to
> threaten the very possibility that judgments of experience might be
> grounded in a way that relates them to a reality external to thought. . . .
> What we wanted to conceive as exercises of concepts threaten to
> degenerate into moves in a self-contained game. (*MW*: 5)

Here, according to McDowell, is the source of the temptation to appeal to the
experiential Given:

> . . .when we have exhausted all the available moves from one
> conceptually organized item to another, there is still one more step we
> can take: namely, pointing to something that is simply received in
> experience. It can only be pointing, because *ex hypothesi* this last move in
> a justification comes after we have exhausted the possibilities of tracing
> grounds from one conceptually organized, and so articulable, item to
> another. (*MW*: 6)

Traditionally, (though, unlike Sellars, McDowell does not remark on this at the
initial stage of his argument) the items 'received in experience' have been identified
with sensations (or their non-conceptual contents). But this is not an essential
feature of the Myth. Rather, at the heart of the Myth lies the demand for thought's
being constrained by something that is radically external: that is to say, something
that is 'outside the conceptual sphere' but nevertheless somehow present to us.
However tempting it may be, the appeal to the Given is useless:

> The idea of the Given is the idea that the space of reasons, the space of
> justifications or warrants, extends more widely than the conceptual
> sphere. The extra extent of the space of the space of reasons is supposed

to allow it to incorporate non-conceptual impacts from outside the realm
of thought. But we cannot really understand the relations in virtue of
which a judgment is warranted except as relations within the space of
concepts: relations such as implication or probabilification, which hold
between potential exercises of conceptual capacities. (*MW*: 7)

The constraint on thought offered by the experiential Given is external all right,
but unfortunately it is not rational. And if it is not rational, it will not constrain
thought in the right way. Why? Because the alternative to rational constraint is
'brute impact'. And while perhaps we cannot be blamed for judging as we do
when our judging is the product of brute force, this does not make such a
judgment justified. Thus 'the idea of the Given offers exculpations where we
wanted justifications' (*MW*: 8).

Eschewing the appeal to the Given leads us to demand rational constraint:
constraint by items involving the exercise of conceptual capacities. But if
conceptual capacities are paradigmatically exercised in judgments, we seem to be
in danger of losing the essential element of externality. Thoughts, it now seems,
can be rationally constrained only by further thoughts. Some thoughts may
indeed be provoked by brute impacts, but this does nothing to show why they
should have any special epistemic status. From an epistemic standpoint, we seem
free to adjust the web of belief any way we like, so long as we preserve
consistency (and any other internal constraints). This is as good as to say that we
are not under external constraint at all: in recoiling from the Myth of the
Given, we have embraced frictionless coherentism. We need understanding
(spontaneity) to be constrained by sensibility (receptivity). But it is hard to see
how this is possible. So back and forth we go. This is the problem.

The solution, McDowell thinks, is simple. Conceptual capacities are 'drawn on
in receptivity', not 'exercised *on* an extra-conceptual deliverance of receptivity'
(*MW*: 9). Thus (the content of) experience is conceptual through and through:

> In experience, one takes in, for instance sees, that things are thus and so.
> That is the sort of things one can also, for instance, judge. (*MW*: 9)

However, whereas judgment is an active making up of one's mind, in experience
our conceptual capacities are exercised passively. So experience constrains our
freedom right enough; but because it is thoroughly conceptual, it does so
rationally. Experiential contents are conceptual but non-judgmental justifiers.
Crispin Wright calls this insistence on 'content-sensitive justifiers', McDowell's
'quasi-inferential conception of empirical justification' (Wright 2002: 148). It is the
pivot of McDowell's epistemological outlook.

Now experience sometimes misleads: how things appear is not how they are.
However, in McDowells' eyes, it would be a serious mistake to see the mere
possibility of error as compromising the externality of experiential constraint. Of
course, we can be misled. Sometimes, we take things to be as experience presents
them, when in reality they are not that way. But according to McDowell, 'when

one is not misled, one takes in how things are' (*MW*: 9). In experience, then, we are open to the layout of reality. Thus, through experience, our judgments become subject to rational constraint *by the world*. The constraint comes from outside our *thinking*, but not from outside what is *thinkable*: how things are. The tendency to oscillate between the appeal to the Given and frictionless coherentism is shown to be avoidable.

Why is this solution so hard to see or, if seen, accept? McDowell answers this question by pointing to a 'deep-rooted mental block': the identification of Nature with the realm of law. This identification, encouraged by the rise of modern science, tempts us to see Nature as inhospitable to rational connections: in Nature, nomological connections alone hold sway. McDowell's view of experience as conceptually informed openness to facts (as thinkables) finds no place in such a conception of Nature.

Some philosophers—Descartes perhaps—react by taking the mind out of nature. In so doing, they fall into the supernaturalism of 'rampant Platonism'. Rampant Platonism hypostatizes concepts, which must then be thought to inhabit some realm beyond Nature. To avoid such supernaturalism, many philosophers today try to demystify the space of reasons by reducing epistemic and semantic notions to concepts that are physicalistically (or otherwise scientifically) acceptable. However, McDowell rejects this 'bald naturalism'. Rational justification and subsumption under law constitute distinct modes of intelligibility, neither being reducible to the other. But this does not mean that he falls in with rampant Platonism. We can avoid both rampant Platonism and bald naturalism, he argues, if we resist 'the naturalism that equates nature with the realm of law' (*MW*: 77). Thus:

> To reassure ourselves that our responsiveness to reasons is not super-natural, we should dwell on the thought that it is our lives that are shaped by spontaneity, patterned in ways that come into view only within an inquiry framed by what Davidson calls 'the constitutive ideal of rationality'. Exercises of spontaneity belong to our mode of living. And our mode of living belongs to our way of actualizing ourselves as animals. ... This removes any need to see ourselves as peculiarly bifurcated, with a foothold in the animal kingdom and a mysterious separate involvement in an extra-natural world of rational connections. (*MW*: 78)

So according to McDowell's 'naturalized platonism', the space of reasons is immanent in acquired patterns of human action, which are themselves visible only when human doings are viewed *sub specie rationis*. This is not to denigrate natural science as such, but only to refuse to make it the measure of all that there is. Nor is it to supernaturalize human beings. The self-actualization McDowell refers to is not the result of mere maturation: we have no mysterious inner essence, from which responsiveness to reasons somehow emanates. Rather, initiation into a human form of life is the business of education, 'bildung', through which we acquire a second nature.

There we have it, in capsule form: McDowell's problem, solution, and diagnosis.

2. Sellars and McDowell: Convergence

Turning to Sellars, we can easily find what seem to be counterparts for all three components in McDowell's outlook. This makes it easy to think that McDowell and Sellars are really very close.

Beginning with McDowell's problem, McDowell wants to help us dismount from the seesaw, the oscillation between the myth of the Given and frictionless coherentism. Sellars, too, would like to help us avoid what can easily seem to be a forced choice. Thus, he tells us, in trying to understand human knowledge,

> One seems forced to choose between the picture of an elephant which rests on a tortoise (What supports the tortoise?) and a picture of a great Hegelian serpent of knowledge with its tail in its mouth (Where does it begin?). Neither will do. (*EPM*: 170)[2]

The horns of Sellars's dilemma are foundationalism and the coherence theory, not coherentism and the Myth of the Given. But we should not make too much of this. Sellars argues that the attempt to think through foundationalism, in its empiricist version, brings us 'face to face with givenness in its most straightforward form' (*EPM*. 167).

What about McDowell's solution? In *Mind and World*, McDowell criticizes Sellars for not taking the way out that he (McDowell) recommends. In 'Empiricism and the Philosophy of Mind', Sellars offers a defense of a notion of sensory impressions, in which he insists that impressions not be assimilated to the traditional sensory Given. But for Sellars, this means keeping impressions sharply separated from thoughts. An impression of a red triangle is a state of the perceiver that is common to his seeing that the object over there is red and triangular, that object's looking to him to be red and triangular, and its looking to him that there is a red and triangular object over there. Thus for Sellars, an impression is not a cognitive state at all. This means, McDowell concludes, that the epistemic significance of impressions can only be indirect. Without them, there could not be such directly significant episodes as its appearing to one that things are thus and so. But in so far as experience bears directly on justification, the course of experience must be identified with the succession of appearings—tentative or otherwise qualified perceptual judgments, which for Sellars are thoughts—and not with the succession of impressions.

Although I am not altogether happy with the way McDowell conceives the indirect epistemic significance of Sellarsian impressions—there is a clear sense in which their significance is not *epistemic* at all—I think that he is right to find Sellars and himself at odds. However, in his Woodbridge Lectures, McDowell modifies his *Mind and World* discussion in ways intended to bring about a rapprochement.[3]

McDowell makes four moves. First, he identifies what he calls Sellars's 'master thought' in 'Empiricism and the Philosophy of Mind': that 'in characterizing an episode or state as one of knowing, we are not giving an empirical description of that episode or state; we are placing it in the logical space of reasons, of justifying and being able to justify what one says' (*EPM*: 169). Sellars's point, which McDowell endorses without reservation, is that (in McDowell's words):

> . . .the conceptual apparatus we employ when we place things in the logical space of reasons is irreducible to any conceptual apparatus that does not serve to place things in the logical space of reasons. So the master thought as it were draws a line: above the line are placings in the logical space of reasons, and below it are characterizations that do not do that. (*HWV*: 433)

The master thought is of more than narrowly epistemological significance. Sellars draws a line between epistemic and non-epistemic characterizations and, according to McDowell, takes 'epistemic' to amount to something like 'concept-involving'. As he notes, Sellars refers to the 'epistemic' character of the thought of a celestial city, where all Sellars can mean is its intentionality. I think McDowell is right about this. For Sellars, concepts figure in the propositional contents expressed by beliefs and judgments; and beliefs and judgments are essentially caught up in what Brandom calls 'the game of giving and asking for reasons'. Meaning and justification are thus not separate topics. In drawing his line, Sellars appears to express a thought close in spirit to McDowell's thought concerning the mutual irreducibility of the space of reasons and the realm of law.

McDowell's second move is to remind us that Sellars expresses a measure of sympathy for empiricist foundationalism. Sellars writes,

> There is clearly some point to the picture of human knowledge as resting on a level of propositions—observation reports—which do not rest on other propositions in the same way as other propositions rest on them. (*EPM*: 170)

In insisting that all knowledge is based ultimately on perceptual knowledge, traditional empiricism is not wholly wrong. Its error is to suppose that, to be genuinely foundational, each piece of perceptual knowledge must in principle be capable of being acquired independently of one's possessing any other knowledge, basic or non-basic. It is this second claim—traditional empiricism's commitment to epistemic atomism—that Sellars repudiates. He continues:

> On the other hand, I do wish to insist that the metaphor of 'foundation' is misleading in that it keeps us from seeing that if there is a logical dimension in which other empirical propositions rest on observation reports, there is another logical dimension in which the latter rest on the former. (*EPM*: 170)

For Sellars, no one can acquire knowledge of any kind unless he knows how claims are to be evaluated. In the case of observation-reports, this means (for example) knowing how we can be misled, how things are not always as they seem. Unless one knows when and how observation-reports may need to be corrected, they will not be properly embedded in the space of reasons, and so will not be exercises of conceptual capacities at all. They will at best be vocal responses *to* the environment, not verbal reports *about* it. It follows that one can acquire knowledge through perception only in the context of an extensive world-view, comprising knowledge that would be non-basic by anyone's standards.

If his rejection of foundationalism is not to commit him to a coherence theory, Sellars must hold that his semantic holism (the necessary embeddedness of particular reports in an extensive body of belief) does not imply epistemic (justificatory) holism. So he does: the idea that 'knowledge...which logically presupposes knowledge of other facts must be inferential...is itself an episode in the Myth' (*EPM*: 164). This must mean that the knowledge expressed by observation-reports is non-inferential in an epistemological and not merely a psychological sense. In 'Empiricism and the Philosophy of Mind', Sellars does not explain this aspect of his position as clearly as he might have done.[4] I shall have things to say about the matter in due course. But for now, I shall simply note that, on McDowell's revised reading, Sellars is advocating a version of the reformed empiricism (minimal, but still transcendental) that McDowell himself defends.

This is not all. We might suppose that there is a regress in Sellars's view. Where, after all, does the background knowledge come from, if not observation, which presupposes further background knowledge, and so on? Sellars's reply is that in being trained to make observation-reports (and thus observations) we receive a concomitant initiation into the world-view in which such reporting is necessarily embedded. This training is an aspect of the *Bildung* McDowell insists on. Here we find another point of convergence.

McDowell's third move is to remind us that Sellars's starting point in 'Empiricism and the Philosophy of Mind' is a consideration of a notion central to unreformed empiricism: that of a sense-datum. This notion, Sellars argues, is 'A mongrel resulting from the cross-breeding of two ideas':

> (1) The idea that there are certain inner episodes—e.g. sensations of red or of C# which can occur to human beings (and brutes without any prior process of learning or concept formation); and without which it would *in some sense* be impossible to see, for example, that the facing surface of a physical object is red and triangular, or *hear* that a certain physical sound is C#.
> (2) The idea that there are certain inner episodes which are the non-inferential knowings that certain items are, for example, red or C#; and that these episodes are the necessary conditions of empirical knowledge as providing the evidence for all other empirical propositions. (*EPM*: 132)

In McDowell's terms, the conflation involves assimilating above-the-line exercises of conceptual capacities to below-the-line episodes of merely 'having' a sensation. Sellars's programme in 'Empiricism and the Philosophy of Mind' is thus one of undoing the conflation, with a view to seeing what survives from each.

We already know what survives from the second idea: perceptual knowledge indeed plays a distinguished role in justification, though such knowledge cannot be understood in the atomistic way that the mongrel leads us to suppose. McDowell fully endorses this aspect of Sellars's thinking. For although Sellars's initial discussion of the special role played in justification is conducted in terms of an account of observation-reporting, Sellars goes on to vindicate the idea of inner episodes, which include for example 'seeings'. Sellars wants to make room for experiencing the world, not just for reporting on it.

This brings us to McDowell's fourth move. In the Woodbridge Lectures, he gives much more attention to Sellars conception of experiences, 'ostensible seeings', as 'so to speak making an assertion or claim' which, when the experiences are veridical, is 'so to speak, evoked or wrung from the perceiver by the object perceived' (*EPM*: 144). In a genuine (as opposed to *merely* ostensible) seeing, we are simply made aware that things are thus and so. We see, then, that Sellars has an above-the-line conception of impressions that foreshadows McDowell's own understanding of experience as conceptual through and through, though with our conceptual capacities brought passively into play.

We have found reason to think that Sellars's views anticipate McDowell's both with respect to McDowell's problem and solution. What about McDowell's diagnosis?

Like McDowell, Sellars is inclined to see modern science as the source of many of our current philosophical problems. The deep background to Sellars's thinking is always and everywhere what he sees as the tension between the 'manifest' and 'scientific' images of man-in-the-world. At the heart of this tension lies the difficulty of understanding how the person, as a conscious and rational subject, fits into a world of particles constrained only by natural laws. So the parallel between McDowell and Sellars looks to be complete. But I want to leave the diagnostic issue for the moment, asking instead whether the other points of convergence are as unproblematic as they first seem.

3. Sellars and McDowell: Divergence Above the Line

Sellars's treatment of experiences (which, sticking with Sellars's terminology in 'Empiricism and the Philosophy of Mind', are *not* to be identified with impressions) may seem to foreshadow McDowell's. But taken *au pied de la lettre*, Sellars's way of stating his view differs from McDowell's in at least one significant respect. McDowell draws a sharp distinction between experiences and judgments: though propositionally contentful, experiences are nonjudgmental justifiers. This is a view that McDowell is inclined to find in Sellars too: 'The conceptual episodes Sellars is concerned with, when he speaks of visual experiences as 'containing' claims are not as such cases of judging' (*HWV*: 439). But Sellars says that when we say that an experience is a seeing that something is the case, we characterize it as 'so to speak, making an assertion or claim'. And a few sentences further on, he speaks of the propositional claim 'this is green' as 'an occurrence' (*EPM*: 144). For Sellars, it seems, experiences contain claims in the sense of claimings, not claimables; not judgeable contents, but something like judgments, though perhaps of a special kind.

Sellars' views here are subtle and we must be sensitive to qualifications. Experiences do not *strictu sensu* make assertions or claims, but only 'so to speak'. Characteristically, Sellars does not spell out the qualifications he has in mind, though I think it is clear enough what they are. For a start, experiences don't do things, people do. But more importantly, experiencing isn't a doing: in Sellars's terms, it is an act rather than an action. (I shall say more about this shortly.) Carefully stated, Sellars's point is that experiencings are mental episodes with assertional force. They are like claimings, but they are not produced on purpose. This reading needs defense.

Sellars thinks that talk of experiences as 'containing claims' may be dismissed out of hand. However, he promises to 'put it on the gold standard before concluding the argument' (*EPM*: 144). This promissory note looks forward to his vindication of talk of inner episodes: the myth of Jones. Sellars argues that we can understand the logic of inner-episode talk by treating such episodes as analogous to theoretical entities, introduced for explanatory purposes. He develops the analogy by imagining our 'Rylean ancestors'. The Ryleans have a rich vocabulary for describing behaviour, including dispositional terms, subjunctive conditionals etc.; they also go in for a good deal of thinking-out-loud, intending-out-loud and so on: but they do not yet have the idea of an inner mental life. The 'theory' of inner episodes is introduced by the genius Jones, in the form of a 'model plus commentary'. A model allows theoretical entities to be defined in terms of predicates expressing properties analogous to those of the entities on which they are modeled. The commentary sets limits to the completeness of the analogy. So for example, atoms might be modeled on billiard balls: they will behave like billiard balls in crucial respects, obeying the same dynamical principles. But the commentary will remind us that, unlike billiard balls, they are strictly indestructible, colourless, etc. In the case of thought-episodes (thinkings) the model is candid overt speech: the making of assertions. Thoughts are analogous to assertions primarily in respect of sharing their semantic properties. By postulating thoughts—saying-like episodes that are not actually vocalized—we are able to understand and anticipate each other's actions far better than we could in our Rylean days. But notice: thoughts are modeled on claimings, not on propositional contents.

Of course, we must not forget the commentary, which explains how thoughts differ from their model. For examples, thoughts need not involve verbal imagery: they are not 'the wagging of a hidden tongue' (*EPM*: 187). However, nothing in the commentary suggests that thoughts—and this includes experiences—are non-assertional. Quite the contrary, for experiencings the relevant counterparts in overt speech are observation-reports, the semantics and epistemology of which

Sellars has put in place (*EPM*, Section VIII) before turning to their inner analogues.

Sellars's treatment of observation-reports—the overt analogues of experiencings—provides further evidence for the assertional character of experiences. While reporting certainly involves claiming, reports need not be actions. To be sure, in ordinary parlance, reporting is something that one does. But Sellars makes it clear that he does not think of observation reports in this way. On the contrary, treating reports as actions is a mistake characteristic of traditional empiricists (such as Schlick); and unlike them, '*we* shall not assume that, because "reports" in the ordinary sense are actions, reports in the sense of Konstatierungen are also actions' (*EPM*: 166).[5] Observation reports are *responses* to environmental circumstances: they are actualizations of trained reporting dispositions. That is part of what is involved in their being acts rather than actions. But their not being actions does not mean that they lack assertional force.

We find the same line taken in *Science and Metaphysics*. Seeings, Sellars tells us, are perceptual 'takings': episodes in which a perceiver, under constraint by an object, takes it that, say, there is something red and triangular in front of him.[6] There is a lot to be said for taking Sellars's line. For one thing, doing so allows us to make clear sense of talk of representation. Perception involves representation in the sense that the perceiver *takes it that* things are a certain way. The only representation involved is what Charles Travis calls 'autorepresentation'.[7] Like Travis, Sellars finds no place for the problematic idea that 'experience' itself represents things as being this way or that.

In saying that experiences involve claimings, rather than mere claimables, which may or may not be endorsed, I am not attributing to Sellars the view that the claims involved cannot be overridden by the perceiver's considered judgment. This would leave no room for a thought's being suggested by the perceptual situation but not actually being accepted. Of course perceptual takings can be suggested but overridden. A reporting disposition can be triggered but inhibited. One finds oneself inclined to judge that things are thus and so, but unwilling or unable quite to do so. In the Muller-Lyer illusion, I still find myself inclined to take it that one line is longer than another, even though I know that this is not so. However, cases in which a claiming is overridden or inhibited are not straightforward experiences, since they involve events that take place 'in a higher court'.

On Sellars's account, the function of talk of its (merely) looking to someone that things are thus and so is to withhold endorsement of a claim, just as the function of seeing-talk is to offer it. In Sellars's words, 'the statement that "X looks green to Jones" differs from "Jones sees that x is green" in that whereas the latter both ascribes a propositional claim to Jones's experience *and endorses it*, the former ascribes the claim but does not endorse it' (*EPM*: 145). However—and this is the crucial point—both 'sees' talk and 'looks' talk operate at a higher level than the claims contained in perceptual experiences. If I report only that x looks green,

> ...the fact that I make this report rather than the simple report 'X is green' indicates that certain considerations have operated to raise, so to

speak in a higher court, the question 'to endorse or not to endorse'. I may
have reason to think that x may not be green after all. (*EPM*: 145)

But ordinarily, the higher court does not get involved. Straightforward
experiencing is taking it that things are thus and so, without more ado. It is
not the presentation of a content, which might be endorsed or not. Endorsing (or
withholding endorsement) is a higher level affair; and even then, what we
endorse are claimings, not claimables.

Now McDowell is well aware that Sellars is inclined to speak of experiences as
involving assertions. But he thinks that his own view captures what Sellars
meant, or perhaps should have meant, to say. He has, he says,

> ...charitably discounted 'evoked or wrung *from the perceiver'* in the
> formulation Sellars uses in 'Empiricism and the Philosophy of Mind'.
> A claim evoked from a perceiver would surely be a claim that the
> perceiver makes. But it seems wrong to imply that a perceiver makes the
> claim that his experience contains even before we widen the focus from
> seeings to ostensible seeings. ... We can correct Sellars on this without
> posing a threat to something he wants to insist on: that one gets to have
> conceptual episodes (representations) of the relevant kind occur in one's
> life only by acquiring the capacity to make the claims they 'contain'.
> (*HWV*: 440, n.14)

But charity is not the issue here. As I hope to have shown, Sellars takes the
assertional character of experiences very seriously. The fact is that Sellars and
McDowell have a real difference of opinion.

That said, Sellars would not deny that McDowell is on to something in
attempting to drive a wedge between perception and judgment. But he would
charge that McDowell ignores or mishandles the distinction, already touched on,
between acts and actions. According to Sellars, to construe mental acts as mental
actions would be 'a radical mistake':

> There are indeed mental actions; thus, there is deliberating, turning one's
> attention to a problem, searching one's memory, to mention some clear-
> cut cases. An action is the sort of thing one can decide to do....But
> mental acts, in the basic sense, though they may be elements of mental
> actions, are not themselves actions. Thus perceptual takings, e.g. taking
> there to be a book on the table (and I have in mind not the dispositional
> but the occurrent sense of 'taking' to which there corresponds the
> achievement word 'notice') are not actions. It is nonsense to speak of
> taking something to be the case 'on purpose'. Taking is an act in the
> Aristotelian sense of 'actuality' rather than in the specialized practical
> sense which refers to conduct. (*SM*: 74)

This distinction is closely aligned with one of Sellars' most important ideas: that
the epistemic standards binding conceptual activity are, in fundamental cases,

'ought to be' rather than 'ought to do' rules. Standards are indeed things of which we must be aware. Our thinkings, including our seeings, are rationally constrained. But the constraints are not set by procedural rules—'rules for doing'—that we are bound to follow, if our thoughts are to be epistemically appropriate. Precisely not, since mental acts are not generally doings at all. Rather, if I am to be justified in taking things to be thus and so, I and my circumstances *ought to be* a certain way.

In 'Empiricism and the Philosophy of Mind', the first mention of this distinction occurs when Sellars chides the traditional empiricists for supposing that observation reports must be actions. They are, as Sellars's alternative account of observation-reporting makes clear, more like responses. But what makes them more than mere responses (in the sense of 'responses' in which animals can be trained to make responses) is that, while not produced by the self-conscious following of rules, they are nevertheless subject to critical evaluation. For my reports to be authoritative, I need to be a suitably reliable reporter, so that my reportings and takings are actualizations of a reliable, trained responsive capacity. As for circumstances, in non-standard conditions I cannot simply see how things are, no matter how well-trained I am: this is because things are not as they ought to be for non-inferential knowing to be possible. This need not mean that, generally speaking and in the normal run of things, there is anything that I ought to be doing to guard against error. But I need to be aware of how I can go wrong, and be sensitive to indications that circumstances may not be all they should be. Some circumstances ought to give rise to events in a higher court that inhibit ordinary perceptual takings. In general, if I *do* find reason to think that conditions are or were inappropriate, I may need to re-examine any beliefs formed on the basis of perception. Ought-to-be conditions are thus the basis of 'rules for criticizing' (*SM*: 76): rules for forcing the inhibition, withdrawal, suspension or defence of claims that can normally be made without demurral. This distinction between the two kinds of rules is the key to Sellars's thought that semantic holism can be made compatible with episodes of genuinely non-inferential knowing.

The case of perceptual takings brings us back to the 'second logical dimension', in which even non-inferential reports, or their inner-episode analogues, depend on background knowledge. As we noted, background knowledge need not function in a directly justifying role, compromising the claim of observation reports to be genuinely non-inferential. But this does not seem that its significance is semantic *rather than* epistemic. Not at all. The epistemic function of certain kinds of background knowledge is to render reports and perceptual takings subject to criticism (and of course, when appropriate, to contribute to their defence).

A measure of the importance Sellars attaches to the ought to be/ought to do distinction is that it figures not only in his positive account of perceptual knowledge but, as I briefly mentioned above, in his diagnosis of the Myth of the Given. Traditional empiricists explain how basic experiential judgments can be both empirical and incorrigible by treating semantic rules as 'ought to do' rules. Thus, the semantic rule for 'red' is to say or think 'red' in the non-conceptual presence-to-consciousness of redness. This is 'givenness in its most straightforward form' (*EPM*: 167). As we know, traditional empiricists think that sensation provides us with just such a kind of awareness. Here we see the mongrel doing its work. Of course, we can resist the mongrel; and an important element in so doing is recognizing that epistemic or semantic rules can take the form of 'ought-to-be'.

The importance of the distinction between the two kinds of rules should also make us wonder whether McDowell's argument against the appeal to the given—that causes can exculpate, but cannot justify—is really Sellars's argument at all, even in capsule form. For once we appreciate that ought-to-be rules provide genuine normative constraint, we see that there is no reason why mere causal connections to objects cannot be epistemically significant. Indeed, that is exactly how they do function for Sellars. Perceptual takings involve claims wrung from the perceiver by objects. As reflecting an ought-to-be condition, this causal condition is partly the source of their authority. Causes do not just exculpate: they contribute to justification, though of course only for a being whose performances are subject to epistemic evaluation. (Sellars is not a pure reliabilist.)

I think that McDowell's 'correction' of Sellars's position is related to another misreading. In *Mind and World*, McDowell takes Sellars to countenance 'appearings', which, when veridical, justify beliefs. Even in the Woodbridge Lectures, he continues to read Sellars this way. Sellars' program is to see what survives in the two elements involved in the mongrel concept of a sense-datum; and in the course of carrying out this programme for the case of vision, McDowell tells us, Sellars 'expands the topic from seeings to a wider class of experiences, which he initially introduces as ostensible seeings' (*HWV*: 438). But Sellars does no such thing. Sellars introduces the phrase 'ostensible seeing' in his account of what he calls an 'unfortunate but familiar line of thought'. (It is not a phrase he uses when speaking *in propria persona*.) According to this line of thought, to suppose that 'the non-inferential knowledge on which our world-picture rests consists of such ostensible seeings, hearing, etc., as *happen* to be veridical is to...open the door to skepticism by making a mockery of the word *knowledge* in the phrase "empirical knowledge"' (*EPM*: 133). After all, the concept of knowledge is that of belief that is *non-accidentally* true. But, according to Sellars's interlocutor, who is of course a traditional empiricist, 'the possibility that any given ostensible seeing, hearing, etc., is non-veridical can never be entirely eliminated'. At least, this is so when the ostensible seeings etc. concern objects in the world. What we must do, then, is to set the foundations at a level of awareness at which the possibility of non-veridical takings does not arise. And now the mongrel rears its head again, in the guise of the thought that '*sensations of red triangles* have exactly the virtues that *ostensible seeings of red and triangular physical surfaces* seem to lack' (*EPM*: 134). We cannot be wrong about them. But in Sellars's view, this is because they are below-the-line items. While sensations cannot be unveridical, they cannot be veridical either. They contain no claims. They are not conceptual representations at all.

McDowell takes Sellars to task for treating the issue of what singles out genuine seeings (as veridical ostensible seeings) as if it were settled by appealing to the truth of the contained claim. According to McDowell, 'it was surely wrong to imply that veridicality is all it takes for an ostensible seeing to be a seeing'. He makes the point by way of a Gettier-like counter-example. Suppose that I am presented with 'a successful *trompe l'oeil* painting in which an indistinguishable red cube is depicted as being precisely where [an] unseen red cube actually is'. The claim contained in my experience (say, 'There is a red cube in front of me') will be true, but this will not be a case of seeing that there is a red cube in front of me. McDowell thinks that Sellars came to feel this deficiency and tried to repair his view by adding the condition that, in a genuine seeing, the perceiver must know that conditions are normal. (See *HWV*: 474.) He thinks that Sellars would have done better to have concentrated on the idea that veridical seeings are *seeings*: episodes in which we have the world directly in view, rather than ostensible seeings meeting further conditions. Here we see that McDowell has not revised his view of Sellars quite as much as we might have thought: he still sees Sellars as treating seeings as involving appearings that are, as it were, sworn to veracity. But this is simply not Sellars picture. For Sellars, seeings are just that: perceptual takings wrung from the perceiver by the object (an 'ought to be' condition). That is not all they are, but they are at least that.

Now McDowell is right: Sellars did come to think that, if we are to say correctly that a person sees that such and such, that person must know that the conditions are normal. If Sellars does not accept the picture McDowell criticizes, why insist on this? Let us recall Sellars's claim that 'the statement that 'X looks green to Jones' differs from 'Jones sees that x is green' in that whereas the latter both ascribes a propositional claim to Jones's experience *and endorses it*, the former ascribes the claim but does not endorse it' (*EPM*: 145). What I think Sellars came to realize, however, is that there is really a kind of double endorsement here: one endorses not only the truth of the claim, but also the perceiver's perceptually-based entitlement make it. This means endorsing the presupposition that the claim was wrung from the perceiver *in the appropriate way*, which is not what happens in Gettier-type situations. So while Sellars does add the condition that, in cases of seeing, the perceiver must *know* that conditions are normal, his idea is not that, given an appearing and knowledge that conditions are normal, the perceiver acquires entitlement inferentially. His point is rather that the claim contained in a seeing is an instance of non-inferential knowledge, *provided that circumstances are as they ought to be*. And while some of these ought-to-be conditions are 'external', others relate to the perceiver's collateral knowledge. For an experience to be a case of seeing, there need be nothing that the perceiver need do. In particular, he need not call to mind his knowledge that conditions are normal, in order to endorse the claim his experience contains: to do that would be to raise issues in the higher court. Rather, Sellars's point is that, in the absence of such knowledge, the perceiver's epistemic situation will not be as it ought to be. If he is not entitled to take conditions to be normal, he *should* be raising higher-court issues. If he is not entitled to suppose that things are as they ought to be, there is indeed something that he ought to do. In such a situation, an otherwise straightforward perceptual taking will not amount to knowing, even if it happens to be veridical and even if conditions happen to be normal.

I find McDowell's reading of Sellars unsatisfying because it directs our attention away from some of Sellars's most cherished distinctions. With those distinctions in place, we can see that Sellars neither recognizes nor needs to recognize the non-judgmental justifiers that McDowell takes experience to provide.

It is important to note that McDowell's problem is a kind of skeptical problem. Of course, McDowell's problem is 'transcendental' rather than narrowly epistemological. That is, the problem concerns intentionality, or 'objective purport', rather than knowledge. The problem is, how can any thinking—knowledgeable or not—so much as *be about* an objective world? This is one reason why McDowell highlights the oscillation between coherentism and the Myth of the Given, rather than the more familiar dilemma between coherentism and foundationalism. Fair enough. But his problem is skeptical for all that. It is a 'How possible?' problem.

We should not place too much weight on the distinction between the transcendental and the narrowly epistemological. For a start, we should broaden the narrowly epistemological a little, to encompass justification (and not just the special kind of justification that underwrites knowledge). Gettier isn't the problem here; and radical skepticism was always about justification rather than some narrowly defined notion of knowledge. In any case, McDowell's account of the temptation to appeal to the Given is surely about justification. In fact, it articulates a standard theme in the dialectic surrounding what I like to call 'the Agrippan problem', the problem that attempts to justify any belief that threaten us with an infinite regress that can be escaped only by making a brute assumption of reasoning in a circle. On the assumption that the regress of justification is truly vicious, this problem generates the traditional dilemma between foundationalism (the postulation of terminating judgments that are not mere assumptions) and the coherence theory (which distinguishes between mutual support, or systematic integration, and simple circularity).

This dialectic indeed generates a transcendental problem, given a broadly inferentialist conception of meaning. (Such a conception is reflected in the way Sellars treats intentionality as an 'epistemic' matter.) But the sceptical dialectic itself depends on an evidentialist (quasi-inferentialist) conception of justification. That is, the threat of vicious regress is generated by the tacit requirement that justification always depends on content-sensitive justifiers, rather than external conditions. This conception is exactly what Sellars's idea of epistemic constraints as fundamentally rules of criticism, rooted in ought-to-be conditions, invites us to repudiate. Justification does not depend on causation alone. But the background knowledge that must also be present does not function as extra premises in a justifying inference. Rather, it allows us to criticize our perceptual takings when we suspect that things are (or were) not as they need to be. At bottom, McDowell and Sellars are very different.

4. ...and Below It

Sellars thinks that his remarks on experiences as 'so to speak containing claims' is incomplete. A more complete account must also make room for visual sensations: non-conceptual inner episodes. McDowell is sharply critical of this aspect of Sellars's position.

As McDowell notes, Sellars is trying to determine what survives from the first element in the mongrel conflation: the idea that there are inner episodes, somehow involving (say) redness, without which it would be 'in some sense' impossible to see that the facing surface of an object is red. According to Sellars, this idea arises:

> ...in the attempt to explain the facts of perception in scientific style. How does it happen that people can have the experience which they describe by saying 'it is as though I were seeing a red and triangular physical object' when either there is no physical object there at all, or, if there is, it is neither red nor triangular? The explanation, roughly, posits that in every case in which a person has an experience of this kind, whether veridical or not, he has what is called a 'sensation' or 'impression' 'of a red triangle'. (*EPM*: 132–3)

Sellars connects this idea with a deficiency in his account of 'looks' talk as withholding endorsement from a claim contained in an experience. What this account lacks is an explanation of the way in which 'looks' statements are also reports. As reports, looks-statements are not used to make straightforward reports on the world around me. That kind of reporting has been short-circuited by developments in the higher court. For Sellars, explaining what looks-statements might be reporting on is a major problem. The 'common propositional content' of seeing-statements and looking-statements is unproblematic. It is the claim that the one statement endorses and the other does not: for example, the claim that there is something green over there. But what is it that seeings and lookings have in common as experiences, which we can also report on? What is the 'common descriptive content' of seeings and lookings? It is to answer this question that Sellars's introduces the non-cognitive states he calls 'impressions'.

Now the mongrel conflation makes 'immediate experiences' the foundations of empirical knowledge. There are two critical mistakes here.

First, experiences-as-sensations are definitely below McDowell's line. But although they are not conceptual episodes at all, many philosophers have been tempted to treat them as such. This reason is that 'sensation of a red triangle' shares the logical feature of intensionality (note the 's') with 'thought of a celestial city': that is, one cannot infer from someone's having a sensation of a red triangle that a red triangle exists. However, this intensionality results from the fact that sensations of red triangles are states of the perceiver usually but not invariably brought about by the presence of objects with red and triangular facing surfaces

It does not arise because sensations are *about* something. 'Sensation of.,' is intensional but not intentional.

The second mistake is that by taking 'sensations' as not only epistemic but foundational, traditional empiricists are led to see immediate experiences as 'the most untheoretical of entities, indeed, as *the* observables *par excellence*' (*EPM*: 151). However, to separate the explanatory role of sensations from their supposed epistemic role, we must recognize that sensations or impressions have a logical status akin to that of *theoretical entities*. Far from being 'given', sensations are *postulated*. Or more precisely, their logical status, like that of thoughts, can be illuminated by treating them *as if* they had been deliberately introduced, as in the myth of Jones. The myth has to be extended from thoughts to impressions.

Where thoughts were modeled on speech-episodes, sensations are modeled on replicas. For example, the model for a sensation of a red triangle is a red and triangular surface. What this means is that the properties of sensations are expressed by analogically-formed predicates such as 'of red' or 'of a triangle'. Such predicates inherit crucial inferential powers from their models: for example, just as no surface can be red and green all over, no sensation can be 'of' both red and green. The virtue of treating sensations as characterized by such analogically-formed predicates is that it allows them to have intrinsic properties. Thus sensations or impressions, as Sellars approaches them, are not characterized *solely* in terms of their functional role as causal intermediaries, common to cases of seeing and (mere) looking. However, according to the commentary, sensations are not objects (like the surfaces they are modeled on) but episodic states of the perceiver. It is particularly important to note that the model is a coloured surface, not the seeing of such. Sensations are not a screen between the perceiver and the world. We don't have to swear them to veracity. (Not that they have anything to say.)

How do sensations, thus conceived, explain the 'common descriptive content' of looks-statements? We were looking for something to identify with the traditional empiricist's 'immediate experiences': in detaching impressions from their foundational-epistemological role, haven't we deprived them of their 'immediacy'? We have found something for a perceiver to report on, when he considers his seeings and lookings as experiences; but we have not provided for his special access to it.

In introducing the idea of inner episodes, Jones first deals with thoughts. According to Sellars's story, it turns out that the vocabulary of the theory proves capable of acquiring a reporting use: when people spontaneously say 'I was just thinking that such and such', we do well to take their utterances at face value. So although inner episodes of thinking are introduced for explanatory purposes, it turns out to be a good idea to give each person's spontaneous reports special authority. This is all that privileged access requires. Remember, for Sellars, thoughts have no connection with verbal imagery: so in this case, we should not be tempted to think of privileged access as dependent on a kind of inner seeing.

Sellars thinks that the same account will do for our privileged access to our own sensations. Although sensations are not typically 'apperceived'—they are mental states of which we are usually not aware (conceptually aware) of being in—they *can* be the objects of non-inferential reports (on their intrinsic character). They become such, for example, when we find ourselves in the 'higher court' to which talk of seeing and looking belongs, and in which we switch our attention from the object of our experience's contained claim to its character as an experience. This conception of sense-impressions detaches immediacy (as being a potential object of a non-inferential report) from any kind of irreducible logical privacy. Because sensations are introduced by a functional role that logically connects them with external circumstances, and accorded intrinsic properties modeled on the properties of public objects, they are essentially describable in inter-subjectively intelligible terms. In explaining how we were misled, in a particular perceptual situation, we can talk about our experiences in language that is fully public.

McDowell is sharply critical of all this, wondering why the explanatory role of sensations might not be equally well met by 'patterns of light impinging on retinas'. Sensations, he says, 'look like idle wheels' (*HWV*: 443–4). But this criticism ignores the importance of the intrinsic properties of sensations, properties that no one yet knows how to reduce to (or even correlate with) states picked out in the language of neurophysiology. Impressions belong to what Sellars calls 'molar behaviour theory'. What, if anything, they may turn out to correspond to in a 'micro-theory of sentient organisms' is an open question, though we can be certain that it will not be anything as simple as patterns of retinal irradiation. (See *EPM*: 193f.)

Now McDowell thinks that Sellars himself became worried that sensations were not doing much work. Accordingly, in *Science and Metaphysics*, he casts them for a genuinely transcendental role: explaining how thought obtains objective purport. On this new view, impressions serve to guide 'the flow of one's conceptual representations' (*HWV*: 450). They thus function as 'external' checks on conceptual activity: that is, as checks from outside the conceptual order. As Sellars remarks, distinguishing 'the receptivity of sense from the guidedness of intuition' is necessary, if a Kantian picture of knowledge is to avoid collapsing into Idealism (*SM*: 16).

Sellars denies falling into the Myth of the Given. In finding a transcendental role for sensations, he is not suggesting that conceptual activity is *consciously constrained* by episodes of non-conceptual awareness. That *would* be the Myth. But as McDowell makes admirably clear, Sellars has nothing of the sort in mind. Sensations are indeed states of consciousness, in that they are apperceivable states of the perceiver. But when playing their transcendental (guiding) role, they are not apperceived. They are, as it were, transparent: we see through them to the conceptualized objects of perception proper. They become opaque only if we shift our attention to impressions themselves, focusing not on the world but on the character of our experience as experience. Still, even if Sellars's thinking here does not exactly relapse into the Myth of the Given, McDowell finds that it comes 'dangerously close' (*HWV*: 467). According to McDowell, not only is Sellars's appeal to below-the-line sensations unnecessary, it stands in the way of an unproblematic conception of having the world in view. Such a conception should allow us to see how external constraint on our thinking is 'exerted, in intuition, by objects themselves, the subject matter of the conceptual representations involved in perceptions' (*HWV*: 468). In McDowell's eyes, Sellars's picture does not offer such an understanding.

I think that this criticism depends on misrepresenting the explanatory significance of the guiding role that impressions play. Let us recall that, for Sellars, the claims 'contained' in experiences are modeled on assertions: claimings, not claimables. In the case of non-inferential knowings—experiences that are seeings—these claims are guided ('wrung from us'). This causal influence saves us from Idealism, without a mention of impressions. However, Sellars finds this causal connection problematic. This is where impressions play their part: they help make intelligible the way that perception is controlled by objects. This is another aspect of their explanatory role.

In *Science and Metaphysics*, Sellars takes note of a longstanding tendency, on the part of philosophers concerned with perception, to see our experience of the world as essentially bound up with the occurrence of certain *minimal* representations. According to this tradition, there are, say, impressions of red triangles, but perhaps not impressions of pigs or trees. Still less are there impressions of mu-mesons, though there might be non-inferential reports of them. As Brandom emphasizes, Sellars's account of non-inferential perceptual knowledge puts no principled restrictions on the richness of our observational vocabulary: anything we can be trained to report on reliably is a potential object of non-inferential knowledge. But it is not plausible to think of everything we can report on as something that we *experience*.

Now some (perhaps most) philosophers in the tradition Sellars is examining have tended to think of impressions as minimal *conceptual* representations. For Sellars, this is a mistake. As we have seen, sensations are intensional but not intentional. However, according to Sellars, the idea of *minimal* representations is a good one, provided we are clear that they are non-conceptual.[8] What this means for is that the analogical predicates that express the intrinsic properties of sensations are formed from a restricted range of predicates corresponding to the genuinely *sensible* properties of objects.

What is so good about this idea? Here we can take note of a phrase that McDowell happily uses but that would give Sellars pause: 'glimpses of reality'. The idea of a glimpse suggests the momentary registering of a passing phase in the career of an object: a recording of the here and now. But ordinary observation reports—given the rich vocabulary that Sellars allows them—characterize objects in terms that go way beyond anything strictly available to momentary inspection. They are extensively 'iffy', attributing causal powers that cannot in any very obvious sense be 'glimpsed'. Objects can look solid, heavy, hard to reach, etc. (As Sellars likes to say, borrowing the phrase from Ryle, many of the predicates in terms of which we characterize ordinary objects are 'mongrel-categorical'.) On Sellars's view, this conceptual richness does not compromise the claim of ordinary observation-reports—and the experiences that are their inner analogue—to be non-inferential. But it does raise the question, with respect to observing, of how we do it. This is where impressions come in: they are minimal representations, in that they register the austere cues that guide the rich conceptual episodes exemplified in perceptual takings. (Empirical psychology investigates their detailed character.)

Are there alternative explanations? Sellars suggests two. The first is that the capacity for making rich conceptual responses to objects present to the senses is innate. Sellars says that he will simply ignore this possibility. A more serious suggestion is that the capacity is socially transmitted, *via* training. This is the option Sellars takes in 'Empiricism and the Philosophy of Mind'. However,

> ...the ability to teach a child the colour-shape language game seems to imply the existence of cues which systematically correspond...to the colour and shape attribute families, and are also causally connected with combinations of variously coloured and shaped objects in various circumstances of perception. (*SM*: 19, § 47)

Thus the appeal to social transmission supplements rather than replaces the explanation in terms of consciously encoded cues. This must be so: the existence of such cues is implied by the possibility of training.

To sum up, the 'transcendental' issue of avoiding Idealism is dealt with by insisting on our causal connectedness to our surroundings: this connectedness is all that we need in the way of external constraint. Impressions play a secondary role, explanatory rather than epistemic, in showing how this connectedness is induced and maintained. But this is not quite the end of the story. McDowell's full account of the transcendental role that he thinks Sellars finds for non-conceptual impressions brings in what Sellars sees as the clash between the 'Manifest' and 'Scientific' images of man-in-the-world: roughly, man as a thinking and feeling being and man as a complex physical system. So in closing, I would like to say a few words about this clash of images.

5. Philosophy and Modern Science

McDowell and Sellars both think that our philosophical agenda is set by modern science. However, they conceive the character of the problems we face in quite different ways. McDowell starts from a kind of skeptical problem, and his aim is to identify and remove the misconceptions that generate philosophical anxiety. This project is diagnostic and therapeutic: By contrast, Sellars thinks that the task of philosophy is 'to understand how things in the broadest possible sense of the term hang together in the broadest possible sense of the term'.[9] Specifically, this means combining the Manifest and Scientific images of man-in-the-world in a 'synoptic vision'. This is a constructive, and in some measure speculative, metaphysical undertaking.

According to Sellars, the need for a synoptic vision arises because there is a genuine tension between the images. The tension stems not just from the fact that the images are different, but from the fact that each is quite naturally taken 'to constitute *the* true and in principle *complete* account of man-in-the-world' (*PSIM*: 25). There are various points at which the tension makes itself felt, but one that especially interests Sellars involves the way in which ordinary objects, as they show up in the Manifest image, present us with continuous coloured surfaces. Such surfaces find no obvious place in the Scientific Image, which presents physical objects as systems of particles.

Contrast this idea of the clash of images with McDowell's thought that modern science contributes to a transcendental anxiety by suggesting an identification of nature with the realm of law. Sellars would not see relieving this anxiety as dissolving his problem of the clash of images. The Manifest Image already contains the idea of natural law. The Manifest Image grows out of the Original Image. In the Original Image, *all* things are persons. In the Manifest Image, certain erstwhile persons become 'truncated', thus mere objects. But persons and mere objects peacefully coexist. The category of mere objects does not threaten the category of persons.

The situation is very different when the Scientific Image comes on the scene, and does so as more than a speculative flight of fancy. What distinguishes the Scientific Image is the introduction, *via* the postulational method, of micro-structural entities as the ultimate furniture of the Universe, a development threatens the basic *categories* of the Manifest Image. In the Scientific Image, persons seem to find no place at all: not even a derivative place as complex systems of particles. Now as Sellars says, it is perfectly possible for complex systems to have properties that their parts lack: pieces of wood can form a ladder. But this is a matter of the parts being related in some appropriate way; and the perceptible qualities of objects in the Manifest Image do not reduce, in any obvious way, to relational properties of their micro-structural constituents. If the Scientific Image is to be complete, it must find room for colours and colour-experiences, not to mention conceptual thinking.

While inclined to dismiss these concerns as expressions of an unfortunate scientism, McDowell recognizes their importance for Sellars. However, he connects them with what he takes to be Sellars's account of the 'transcendental' role played by impressions. I claimed in the previous section that the transcendental guiding function is really fulfilled by objects, *via* their causal impacts on our sensory systems. But McDowell thinks that Sellars's concerns about the supposed clash of images leads him to retreat from this view. Thus, he tells us:

> In 'Empiricism and the Philosophy of Mind', Sellars himself talks of conceptual representations evoked by perceived objects. But he would relegate the appropriateness of such talk to the manifest image, and he would urge that we need to give it a transcendental vindication by showing how it correlates with the scientific image. Otherwise, the putative objective purport that figures in the manifest image would be a mere illusion; the apparently perceived objects—such things as red cubes—do not really exist. (*HWV*: 473)

But note what goes immediately before:

> The transcendental task is entitling ourselves to see conceptual activity as directed towards a reality that is not a mere reflection of it. (*HWV*: 473).

The problem set by this conception of the transcendental task is that of averting a collapse into Idealism. As Sellars tells his story, this problem is fully tractable within the confines of the manifest image. It is solved by the element of causal constraint in non-inferential knowledge (perceptual 'takings'), a constraint exerted ultimately by objects. To be sure, these objects may not, in themselves, be exactly as we take them to be, according to the way of thinking that belongs to the Manifest Image. But even if this is so, the element of external constraint provided by objects, even when they are inadequately conceived, ensures that our thinking is not merely a reflection of itself.[10] I think, then, that in connecting Sellars's concerns about the clash of images with his own 'transcendental'—i.e. skeptical—anxieties, McDowell changes the idea of the transcendental problem in ways that Sellars would resist: from vindicating objective purport (at the level of particular judgments)—that is to say, from avoiding Idealism—to underwriting representational success in the quite different sense of vindicating the Manifest Image. Such a way of returning us to common sense is entirely consonant with McDowell's therapeutic conception of philosophy. But it is no part of Sellars's project.

One reason why Sellars would not take McDowell's therapeutic approach to philosophy—an approach that culminates with an untroubled return to the Manifest Image—is that he regards the Manifest Image as itself involving a kind of paradox, independently of any clash with the Scientific Image. Here we turn from colours and the like to conceptual thought. In the Manifest Image, it is no merely accidental feature of human beings that they have a conception of the world and their place in it. Rather, man is essentially a being endowed with self-understanding. Since self-understanding implies understanding, it follows that an essential feature of human beings is the capacity for conceptual thought. But anything worth calling conceptual thought must occur in a framework in which thoughts can be criticized and evaluated, according to standards of evidence. This gives conceptual thinking the holistic character that McDowell stresses and which invalidates the empiricist idea of atomistic foundations. This means that we must learn the game of giving and asking for reasons in large chunks: we must be trained by adults who are already skilled players. But such players cannot have always existed: so how could the whole thing ever have got off the ground? According to Sellars, it is this paradox that supports 'the last stand of Special Creation' (*PSIM*: 6), a doctrine that must be wholly unacceptable to anyone with a naturalistic turn of mind. Here is one reason why Sellars thinks that we cannot rest content with philosophies that recall us to common sense. Sellars does not think that common sense is discomfort-free, at least for those with naturalistic proclivities. McDowell's appeal to second nature and *Bildung* is of no help here. The problem is to understand, in ways that eschew appeals to the supernatural, how the holistic practices that *Bildung* inculcates arose at all.

I cannot trace in detail how Sellars supposes that the two images might be reconciled, or even why he supposes that they need to be. Let me just say this: confronted with McDowell's arguments, Sellars would see McDowell as the latest in a long and distinguished line of philosophers who expound the *philosophia perennis*, making explicit the complex contours of the Manifest Image. But whereas for McDowell, this is the end of philosophy, for Sellars, it is barely the beginning.[11]

Michael Williams
Department of Philosophy
Johns Hopkins University
Baltimore, Maryland 21218
USA
mwilliams@jhu.edu

NOTES

[1] McDowell 1994. References given in the text by '*MW*' and page number.

[2] '*EPM*' is used as the abbreviation for Sellars 1963a.

[3] McDowell 1998. Subsequent references given in the text by '*HWV*' and page number.

[4] For more detailed discussion of the issues involved, see Williams 2002.

[5] Internal evidence strongly suggests that, in discussing empiricist foundationalism, Sellars has in mind Moritz Schlick's classic treatment in 'The Foundations of Knowledge'. This paper is reprinted in Ayer 1959. '*Konstatierungen*' ('confirmations') is Schlick's term for basic observation-reports.

[6] Sellars 1968: see pp. 73–4. Subsequent references given by '*SM*' and page number.

[7] Travis 2004: 57–94.

[8] 'Representation' here is no more than indication.

[9] Sellars 1963b: 1. Subsequent references given by '*PSIM*' and page number.

[10] The idea that such takings are guided by minimal non-conceptual episodes also belongs here. This idea is a sophisticated addition to the manifest image—and to our understanding of it—that both makes causal constraint by objects intelligible and prepares the way for the fusing of the images in a synoptic vision.

[11] This paper was presented at a conference, *McDowell between Wittgenstein and Hegel*, held at the University of Warwick, June 2005. I want to thank fellow participants, and especially John McDowell and Charles Travis, for much useful discussion of the issue broached here. I also thank two anonymous reviewers for this journal, whose pointed criticisms forced me to clarify some central points.

REFERENCES

Ayer, A. J. ed. (1959), *Logical Positivism*. New York: Macmillan.

McDowell, John (1994), *Mind and World*. Cambridge, MA: Harvard University Press.

—— (1998), 'Having the World in View', *Journal of Philosophy*, XCV: 431–491.

Sellars, Wilfrid (1963a), 'Empiricism and the Philosophy of Mind', in Wilfrid Sellars, *Science, Perception and Reality*. London: Routledge.

—— (1963b), 'Philosophy and the Scientific Image of Man', in Wilfrid Sellars, *Science, Perception and Reality*. London: Routledge.

—— (1968), *Science and Metaphysics*. London: Routledge.

Travis, Charles (2004), 'The Silence of the Senses', *Mind*, 113: 57–94.

Williams, Michael (2002), 'Knowledge, Reasons and Causes: Sellars and Scepticism', in James Conant and Andrea Kern (eds.) *Scepticism and Interpretation*. Amsterdam: Elsevier.

Wright, Crispin (2002), 'Human Nature?', in Nicholas H. Smith (ed.), *Reading McDowell*. London and New York: Routledge.

10
Reason's Reach

Charles Travis

Experience (notably perception), one would have thought, makes our surroundings bear on what we are to think. In it, we are aware of some of how these surroundings are, or what is in them. We are thus aware of what bears on what is so: what settles the question whether P, or makes P likely, or is evidence for P, or is, or would (*ceteris paribus*) be reason to think P. Sometimes we are aware of such bearing. In which case some of *our* questions what to think are settled. If we are aware that what we are aware of settles, say, affirmatively, whether Sid is sitting, then that Sid is sitting is the thing for us to think.

But all this has been challenged. The skeletal thought is this. There is a certain condition on standing in a rational relation, that is, on bearing, as per above, on what is so; so being capable of bearing in the above way on what we are to think. What I experience, notably perceive, fails this condition. So it does not bear on what is so of, or in, my surroundings, so nor on what I am to think of them. For the moment I will use 'The Condition' as a placeholder for this supposedly failed condition. The first section will discuss what it might be.

A thought of so-and-so that he drives is about Sid just in case its truth turns suitably on how Sid is. A thought (that such-and-such is so) is about our environment just in case its truth turns on how that environment is. If our surroundings do not bear on whether P, then P is not about them. Suppose our surroundings could not bear on whether to think P so. Experience could not make them. So, no matter how things went, one might just as well either think P or think not. So if one thought P, there would be nothing it would be to treat the world accordingly, or to shape one's thought and agency accordingly. There would be no identifiable shape that thinking P would give to thought. Which threatens the idea that P is really something one could think so or not at all. (Nor would one *be* thinking that P, or that not, while seeing how nothing does, or ever could, make this what you *ought* to think (to think what is so).)

If the skeleton is right, this is how it is for everything we might have thought we thought as to how things are around us. That red meat on the white rug, for example, cannot settle for me, in my seeing it, whether there is red meat on the white rug. The skeleton merits no more allegiance than that idea about the meat. It would be bad faith to mouth what states it, claiming for our words some special sense. *That* it is mistaken can thus be clear enough without our seeing *how* it is.

John McDowell's *Mind and World* (1994, 1996) is a response to some fleshings of the skeleton. Appealing to a Sellarsian distinction between a 'logical space of nature' and a 'logical space of reasons', he describes one fleshing out as follows:

Whatever the relations are that constitute the logical space of nature, they are *different in kind* from the normative relations that constitute the logical space of reasons. The relations that constitute the logical space of nature, on the relevant conception, do not include relations such as one thing's being warranted, or—for the general case—correct, in the light of another. ... Suppose we want to conceive the course of a subject's experience as made up of impressions, impingements by the world on a possessor of sensory capacities. Surely such talk of impingements by the world is 'empirical description'; or, to put the point in the variant terms I have introduced, the idea of receiving an impression is the idea of a transaction in nature. ... On these principles, the logical space in which talk of impressions belongs is not one in which things are connected by relations such as one thing's being warranted or correct in the light of another. So if we conceive experience as made up of impressions, on these principles it cannot serve as ... something to which empirical thinking is answerable. (1996: xv)

In sensory experience the world impinges. That it so impinged is a fact of nature. So, the idea is, it belongs to 'the logical space of nature', hence *not* to 'the logical space of reasons'. Normative relations belong to 'the logical space of reasons'. Hence the world's impingements cannot stand in rational relations; so nor bear on what to think. What one *is* to think is a normative question. The world's impingements, natural occurrence, leave *such* questions open. This sketches one way with the skeleton.

If there is a problem here, it is, for McDowell, only an apparent one. *Mind and World* will show why no fleshing out of the skeleton, so not this one, could be right. But there are two tacks one might take in so aiming. One would be to accept The Condition and show how (some of) experiential intake meets it. That is McDowell's tack. The other is to reject The Condition. That is mine. So I will aim to identify objects of experience—things in our surroundings, and in their being as they are—which fail The Condition, but all the same bear, in specific ways, on what one is to think. I will, in fact, argue that The Condition is incompatible with genuine thought full stop. All of which remains programmatic until, in section 1, The Condition is identified.

1. The Condition

What might The Condition be? McDowell tells us,

A normative context is necessary for the idea of being in touch with the world at all, whether knowledgeably or not. (1996: xiv)

The relations that constitute the logical space of nature, on this conception, do not include relations such as one thing's being warranted, or—for the general case—correct, in the light of another. (1996: xv)

If we are to speak of two spaces as Sellars does, and if we locate the relations between perceiver and what is perceived (perceiver and the world's impingements on him) in the logical space of nature, then (the idea is) such relations will not include *warranting* thinking such-and-such, or making so thinking correct. For *such* relations normativity is needed. Perceptual experience so viewed has no room for perceiving what *bears* on what to think. Thus the apparent problem.

Nothing *warrants* red meat being on a white rug. It just happens when you toss a steak around. Something may warrant your putting the meat there—if, say, your family honour called for it. What did so would stand in a rational relation to your so doing. So it would satisfy The Condition (if valid). So, to, for whatever made it called for for you to *think* such-and-such. Thinking something so engages with normativity: one may thus think truly or falsely. *Perhaps* liability to that sort of correctness is what engagement with normativity requires. *Representing* is what is liable to be true or false. If The Condition demands such liability, then there had better be representing in what we experience of things if the skeleton is to prove wrong.

McDowell speaks of experiences as such that in them things appear to be, and thus are represented as, a certain way. (See, e.g. 1996: 11.) But he does not think anything along the lines just outlined. On the contrary, he assures me emphatically that he could drop all such mention of representing as so without changing his defusing of the apparent problem. So far as I can see, he is right in this. So I will not pause to explain why the notion of representing as so does not fit perceptual experience (but see my 2004a).

In any case, being liable to correctness of some sort (being, say, truth-evaluable) is not, and cannot be, the only way of engaging with normativity. For where there is such liability there is also such a thing as bearing on it—e.g., making for the relevant correctness in a given case. There is the thought that the meat is on the rug. *That* the meat is on the rug is things being precisely such as to make that thought correct. It is *so* that there is precisely where it is true to think so. Meat's being on the rug is neither true nor false. But it is a way things count as being just where a certain thing counts as true to think. If the latter is something normative (whatever that comes to), then so is the former. One can say: the meat's being on the rug is such that for things to be that way is for a certain thought to be true. *Thus* do the meat's being on the rug, its being so that it is, and so on, also engage with normativity. There are at least two routes to engagement. I will call this The Clue (to reason's reach).

McDowell says, 'the space of reasons does not extend further than the space of concepts' (1996: 14). Perhaps this is another clue to The Condition: a term of a rational relation must belong to the space of concepts. What might it be to do that? Perhaps to be conceptually *structured*. But that idea, in turn, admits of understandings. A strong version of it is suggested by this:

> Consider, say, judging that there is a red cube in front of one. There is a conceptual capacity that would be exercised both in making that judgement and in judging that there is a red pyramid in front of one,

and another conceptual capacity that would be exercised both in judging that there is a red cube in front of one and in judging that there is a blue cube in front of one. In judging that there is a red cube in front of one, one would be exercising (at least) these two capacities together. What does 'together' mean here? Not just that one would be exercising the two capacities in a single act of judgment; that would not distinguish judging that there is a red cube in front of one from judging, say that there is a red pyramid and a blue cube in front one. In a judgment that there is a red cube in front of one, the two conceptual capacities I have singled out would have to be exercised with a specific mode of togetherness: a togetherness that is a counterpart to the 'logical' or semantical togetherness of the words 'red' and 'cube' in the verbal expression of the judgment, 'There is a red cube in front of me'. Here we see the point of the idea that non-overt conceptual episodes are to be understood on analogy with linguistic acts. . . .

. . . Now we can say that in an ostensible seeing that there is a red cube in front of one—an experience in which it looks to one as if there is a red cube in front of one—the same conceptual capacities would be actualized with the same mode of togetherness. (1998: 438–440)

A statement that there is meat on the rug is in particular words, and thereby deploys particular concepts in a particular structured way ('mode of together-ness'). The *suggestion* here is that thoughts, one's awareness of the environment in a perceptual experience, and thus the object(s) of such awareness follow this model. To belong to the conceptual, on this idea, would be to be conceptually structured in this sense.

The idea here is Tractarian. (For one of Wittgenstein's expressions of it see Waismann 1979: 89–90.) A representation-as-so, the idea is, has one particular structure. The elements of such a structure are some definite battery of concepts, or atomic representational devices (names). The structure deploys each in a particular logical role within the whole it forms. Within the structure each element bears a particular structural relation to the others. It is essential to the thought, or representation, to be precisely *so* structured. For its structure determines what it represents as so: that the elements *its* elements represent are structured in precisely the way its elements are in it. A different structure would thus represent a different thing as so. In which case what a representation represents as so *must* share its structure. That it takes just *that* structure to represent just *that* as so just is a sense in which what would thus be so has that structure. So to be aware, in experience, of things being so is, *ipso facto*, to be aware of conceptually structured things. An ostensible seeing is then at least seeming awareness of this. On this idea, it is not, *pace* Frege (1892), just *Aussagen*, but equally *Gedanken*, that are each built in a particular way of particular concepts.

Suppose that things being as they are did not articulate into conceptually articulated *ways* things are as per the Tractarian idea. Then a given way things

were—a given thing so—would not require a given structuring of concepts to say
it to be so. It might be reported in words that structured concepts in any of many
ways. In that sense it would be *structurable* in many ways. Would *this* block
experience making the world bear on what to think, where the Tractarian idea
would allow it? Or in making what we see bear on what to think would we
simply be spoiled for choice? I defer the question.

For McDowell does not, he assures me, avow the Tractarian idea. The
Condition, as he reads it, asks conceptual structure only in the weaker sense of
being of the form *That things are thus and so* (or perhaps its grammatical cousin,
things being thus and so). McDowell's response to the skeleton is thus that we
perceive (see, hear, feel, etc.) things of the form *that such-and-such. Perhaps* he
thinks all we perceive to have that form. ('In a particular experience in which one
is not misled, what one takes in is *that things are thus and so*' (1996: 26).) What
matters here is that, in any event, *such* things are what make the world bear on
what to think.

McDowell tells us,

> Any impingements across ... a ... boundary [between the conceptual
> and something else] could only be causal, and not rational; that is
> Davidson's perfectly correct point.

So if there *is* rational bearing, through experience, on what to think, then:

> The facts that are made manifest to us in [impressions on our senses] ...
> are not beyond an outer boundary that encloses the conceptual ... and
> the impingements of the world on our sensibility are not inward
> crossings of such a boundary. (1996: 34)

Something non-conceptual, the idea is, *could not* impinge rationally on what one
is to think. It *could* not stand in a rational relation. Hence the condition. But,
though facts *that* belong, truistically, to the conceptual, and though there is *a*
notion of perceiving on which one can sometimes see a fact (to be one), there
precisely *must* be rational relations between the conceptual (what satisfies the
condition) and something *else* if we are to make sense of experience bearing on
what one is to think. Or so I am about to argue.

2. Frege's Line

Frege writes:

> But don't we see that the sun has set? And don't we thus also see that this
> is true? That the sun has set is no object which sends out rays that reach
> my eyes, no visible thing as the sun itself is. That the sun has set is
> recognized on the basis of sensory impressions. For all that, being true is
> not a perceptually observable property. (1918: 61)

The remark occurs within a discussion of Frege's insistence that only what lacks perceivable features can make questions of truth arise. *Very* briefly, what is perceivable—a sentence, say—admits interpretation; so *it* does not raise some *one* question of truth. There is an objection to what Frege here insists on. We see that the sun has set. We thus see that this is true. So we can see the truth of at least some things. So truth *can* be, a perceivable feature of a perceivable thing. In response to this objection, Frege draws a distinction. Things like the sun (*inter alia*, things which, like it, reflect or emit light into one's eyes) fall on one side of it. Things like *that the sun has set* fall on the other. I will call the distinction *Frege's line*, and the first side of it the *left* side, the second the *right*. To draw the distinction will also be to provide a sense in which things to the right (so things which make questions of truth arise) are not perceivable.

What has visual, auditory, or spatial, properties, Frege tells us, can represent as so only insofar as an intention attaches to it (Frege 1918: 59). That is, only insofar as it *is to be taken* as representing in a particular way (as opposed to others in which, for all its perceivable features, it might). If that painting represented Chartres cathedral as looking thus and so, that is in part because that blue patch in it, on the image of a wall, is to be taken as mattering in a certain way to what one would see in viewing the cathedral if it were as represented (whether, say, the wall would be coloured, or merely in shadow). We need a *way of taking* what is perceivable for the way things are (the world) to matter in some determinate way to whether things are as it represents them. An intention's function here would be to make the world matter in one definite way rather than others. For a question of truth to arise just is for the world to matter in some such way. What *raises* such a question, in the case of perceivable representing (e.g., words or pictures) is how the perceivable is to be taken. That something is to be taken in such-and-such way (so as to make the world matter *thusly*) is not itself perceivable, where this means: something with perceivable, or spatial, features.

It is in this sense that what is perceivable is excluded from 'the domain of things for which truth can come into question at all' (1918: 61). The Clue suggests a converse point. The roast needs no *intention* attaching to it for it to be so that it is on the rug. But for it to be so that the roast is on the rug is for a particular question of truth to have an affirmative answer; for representing to which the world mattered in a particular way to be true. The relevant representing would be just that which is to be taken in a certain way: as representing things as thus and so. If for the roast to be as it is is for it to be on the rug, then its being as it is is one thing which ought to count as *being as thus represented*; one thing which *belongs* within the range of what would count as being as thus represented. That its being as it is *ought* so to count, that this belongs within a certain range of cases, those of being the way in question, is no more perceivable—no more an item with perceivable, or spatial, features—than that a representation *is to be taken* in such-and-such way. This points to a sense in which *that the sun has set*, along with *that it is true that it has* are not perceivable things. To work out this converse will be to see what distinction Frege's line draws.

Seeing the sun, or its trajectory, or the roast on the rug, or the dog carrying it off, or its oxidized condition, is seeing what is *in* one's surroundings. One sees what is at a particular location. One sees that location in the condition it is in. That the sun has set (in Rostock) may be, in some sense, *about* a location. But *it* has none. The sun, perhaps, is in the sky. That it has set is not. So, it seems, what lies to the right of Frege's line has no location. But location is not the crucial point.

I will now assign a sense to *conceptual*. A concept, as I will speak, is always *of* (being) such-and-such. As such it has a certain sort of generality. There is a generality it need not have. It may be, necessarily, of just one thing. There may even be one thing it is necessarily of. Still, there is a sort of generality it has. Suppose a concept were of being Frege. To fit that concept one could stop nowhere short of being him. But suppose (if you can) Frege had taken to wearing a beret. Or had devoted his life to sailing. He would have been different than he was. Still, he would have fit that concept. Suppose, again, Brahms had not visited Breslau, or that Bismarck had not resigned. Still, Frege would have fit that concept. So there are a variety of circumstances that would count as someone's fitting that concept (and here a variety of circumstances which would not so count). There being at least one such range of cases is one thing one might mean by generality. It is what I will mean here by the generality of the conceptual.

The concept of being red meat is general in a sense in which a concept of being Frege is not. It might have fit other than what it does, were the world but different. But it is also general in the present sense. What fits the concept *red meat* might still have done had it had a bit more gristle, or, while older, were not overly oxidized, and even if Texans were all vegetarians.

The key feature of the conceptual, on its present understanding, is that for anything conceptual there is a specific form of generality intrinsic to it. There is then a range that is the range of cases, or circumstances, which would be ones of something instancing that generality (or, again, a range of things not instancing it). The range is indefinitely extensive: for any list of things belonging to it, there are (one can find) more. So for given circumstances to belong is not just for them to be as they are, but for them to satisfy some intelligible demand on membership.

In particular, a representation as so is conceptual in this sense. Sid might represent it to Pia as so that he has been driving. Perhaps he has: things being as they are counts as things being as he said. But suppose they were not quite as they are. Suppose he lacked the lipstick on his collar, or he drove the Fiat and not the Lexus. For all that, they might still have been as he represented them. So there is a range of cases which are the ones in which things would be as Sid represented them. Which is to say there is a specific form of that sort of generality that marks the conceptual in the present sense.

Now we can apply The Clue. If a representation of it as so that Sid has been driving is conceptual, then so, equally, for its being so that he has. For it is so that he has precisely where things are such as to make that representation true. So there is an indefinitely extendible range of cases that would be ones of Sid's having been driving. It is just those cases that would make the corresponding representation true. Its being so that Sid has been driving thus has a specific form of that generality which marks the conceptual. Representation does not exhaust the conceptual. A role for the conceptual—say, in experience—is not *per se* a role for representations. A need for the conceptual—say, so as to bear on what to think—is not *per se* a need for representing.

To the right of Frege's line is the conceptual. What is there to the left? What *instances* (first-order) conceptual generalities. Such as that piece of meat. A piece of meat is not in the business of being instanced. So treating it would be bad grammar. *A fortiori* there is no range of cases that instance it. It is not conceptual. Of course, for any given piece of meat, there is a concept of being it. Being a concept, this does have its range of instances: the meat in the butcher's case, the meat in butcher's paper, the meat on the rug, etc. If we so think, then, entering the salon, seeing the meat on the rug, what one sees is one instance of that range: the meat as it there, and then, is. At least in sublunary affairs, it is the meat, in being as it is, that instances one generality or another—oxidizing, staining the rug. Its being as it is is, *inter alia*, its bleeding rapidly into the rug. So the meat in being as it is, and, if we like, its being as it is, instance generalities. (The latter instances the generality of the zero-place predicate *the meat being on the rug*.) Nor is the meat's being as it is in the business of being instanced, any more than the meat is. Correspondingly, there is no range of cases of the meat being as it is. Nor to be as it is need it satisfy some demand on being a certain way. It is the way it is *however* that may be. What did all that was required for being the meat as it is would simply be the meat, as it is—one way for something to be that piece of meat, but the only way for something to be that meat as it now is. That for which there is thus no range of cases I will call the *non-conceptual*.

It is the non-conceptual that occupies the left of Frege's line. We can now work out Frege's point. To see the meat on the rug is just to be suitably sensitive, or responsive, to it as it then is—to the non-conceptual. Similarly for seeing its condition (how it is), or its movement or changing. Sensitivity to the presence or absence, coming or going, of what is there, literally before me, is enough. To see that the meat is on the rug I must register something else: the instancing by things being as they are of a certain way for things to be, meat being on a rug. I must recognize things being as they are as belonging to a certain range of cases, as what *such* cases would be. The range in which I thus fit things being as they are is not something visible, nor (present case aside) is what would fit in it. My access to these things is not by sight. For a range, on present use, to be the one it is is for it to *require* what it does for membership; for it to make such-and-such matter, other things not, to this (as there is what matters, and what not, to being meat). (As for Frege (1904) it is what matters to being the value of a function for a given argument that identifies the function.) One does not *see* (observe) a range *requiring* one thing or another, any more than one literally *sees* being meat requiring something for so being.

Some have spoken of something called 'non-conceptual (representational) content'. On the present idea of the conceptual, that idea makes no sense. Representing as so is essentially conceptual. One represents *something* as so where there is something it would be for things to be as represented, so what matters to so being, so a range of cases of what would *be* things so being. With no such range there could be no *question* of truth without things being as they are, but then no way for such a question to turn on *how* they are. This is Frege's point in saying,

> A thought always contains something reaching out beyond the particular case, by which this is presented to consciousness as falling under something general. (Frege 1906?/2001: 175)

A representation may be arbitrarily *specific*—arbitrarily definite, say, as to just how something must be coloured where. But specificity is no the particularity, the concreteness, of the non-conceptual. The concreteness of perceptual experience cannot be located to the right of Frege's line. But we can find it if we follow Frege.

McDowell speaks of such things as *that the meat is on the rug* as part of 'the layout of reality'—to which experience is, he tells us, openness (1996: 26). But there are various conceptions of *layout*. Here, too, there are echoes of the *Tractatus*. There is the layout of the furniture in my room: chairs *there*, sofa *there*, etc.—a geometrical arrangement. Such a layout is something visible, and also non-conceptual, just as the roast is. Some such conception of a layout *may* have inspired Wittgenstein's idea that a proposition represents its structure as the structure of reality. But if the meat's being on the rug is part of the layout of reality, that would have to be in things being as they are instancing meat being on a rug; in the meat being on the rug being *one* of the ways things are in being as they are. The layout of reality would consist in all such instancing there is. That would be a very different notion of layout.

Conflating one sort of layout with the other, one might try to model seeing that on seeing the arrangement of a room. So modelled, seeing that would show up as seeing what is *in* one's surroundings, things being as they are at the various locations in them. That might seem to allow our surroundings, when (suitably) experienced, to bear on what to think merely by virtue of relations between what belongs to the conceptual. But if seeing that were seeing an item visible as meat is, one could say: 'Sid saw *that there was meat on the rug*, though clueless as to what it was he saw', 'Sid saw that there was meat on the rug, but mistook it for that the Lexus was in the garage'; and if Sid were asked 'What are *you* looking at?', an intelligible (though perhaps not advisable) response would be: 'I haven't the faintest idea. Perhaps it's that there's red meat on the rug. But it may be that I have been driving'. Such things make no sense. Reason to be wary of the idea that 'perceptual intake' is, *per se*, conceptually structured in so much as McDowell's weak sense.

3. Expertise

The meat, in being as it is, instances being meat. Its so being is *one* thing, among indefinitely many, that would so count; one way of so counting. The meat *fits* within a certain range of cases. If you judged it not to fit (it being as it is), you would be wrong. Its being as it is *dictates* that verdict. (So that it can be *judging* that you thus did.) Following Frege, one *recognizes*, on the basis of what one sees of the meat, that it is meat. 'Recognize' here is *'erkennen'*, not *'anerkennen'*. It is registering what is so; what is *shown* so by what one sees *in* one's surroundings. So there is a *rational* relation between the meat's being as it is and its being meat. The first *bears* on the second. Its bearing is a matter about which one can *judge*. The Condition is thus mistaken.

To judge is to be liable to a particular kind of error, over which things being as they are holds sole sway. Judging that there is a roast on the rug incurs a particular form of such liability: things being as they are decides correctness precisely in deciding whether there is a roast on the rug. One thus judges truly precisely where the surroundings, in all their particularity, instance that generality. If rational relations held only between generalities (bits of the conceptual); if what instanced those generalities (what is non-conceptual, such as some bit of the surroundings being as it is) bore no such relations to those generalities, then things being as they are could not render verdicts as to when one had succumbed to, when escaped, the sort of error liability to which makes judging *judging*. There would then be no judgement.

But the non-conceptual—things being as they are, or a thing being as it is—can settle *our* questions what to think only if we can appreciate, grasp, its bearing on what is so. Where it is the conceptual that bears on the conceptual, grasp of bearing *can* consist in knowing a generalization. The meat on the rug bears on Pia's mood this way: if there is meat on the rug, she will be furious. Knowing this and seeing that there is meat on the rug, one has reason to think she will be furious. One might also think: where one thing means another, for it to bear as it thus does on what is so is for some such generalization to hold. For that lipstick to mean that Sid has been driving, say, is for it to be so that if there is lipstick on Sid's collar then he has been driving. Austin (1946) explained why this is wrong. If that beast's snout is too *retroussé* for a peccary, it is not *that* it is *retroussé* that means it is not a peccary. If *that* barking means the dog will not bite, this is hardly because barking dogs do not bite. If that grunting means the boar are in the wild yams, well, you just have to know the right grunting.

Telling a peccary's snout, innocuous barking, when grunting means the boar are in the wild yams, admits of expertise. One can learn, and be recognizably able, to tell such things. One can tell how given barking, or grunting, bears on what is so. Its so bearing lies within the scope of reason—is a rational relation to what is so—insofar as it actually settles questions, or provides evidence, or etc. Barking, to one who can tell when it is threatening, a snout to one who can tell when it is a pig's, does bear, when he hears, or sees, it, on what he is to think. Where one so skilled takes it to be the bark of a dog about to bite, that the dog will bite just is what it is rational for him to think. He *can* think no other; nor should he. Such is one thing rationality is like.

Ti-Jean hears the grunting and can tell the boar are in the wild yams. He sees how the grunting bears on that. That he can tell reduces his options. It is not as if, despite what he hears, he might decide to believe the boar have all gone south. His position is Lutheran: he sees how things are; he can think no other. But his lack of options does not make it less rational for him to think the boar are in the yams. It does not change the bearing of the grunts on what *he* is to think; so nor the rational relation in which they stand to, first, the boar being in the yams, and, second, his so thinking.

Seeing the bearing of the non-conceptual on the conceptual cannot consist in seeing that when things are such-and-such way they are also such-and-such other. That would be seeing a relation between the conceptual and the conceptual. But one can be expert as to the bearing of the non-conceptual on the conceptual in given matters—even if 'expert' may be a rather grandiose term. One can know red meat, or meat on a rug, when one sees it, or a peccary when one sees one. Or one can know when to say that meat is red, or on a rug, or that something is a peccary. 'I know a peccary when I see one' may *answer* the question, 'How do you know that's a peccary?'

Correspondingly, if, knowing a peccary when you see one, you now say of the beast before you, 'That's a peccary', you have (though it sounds grandiose) exercised expertise. You take it to be a peccary in grasping how its being as it is bears (thus far) on *what* it is. You grasp—can tell—how it does bear. That is what expertise here is. You thus take it to bear as it does. The beast's being as it is thus bears, for *you*, on what to think—on the right thing to think in this matter. Thus may the non-conceptual bear a rational relation to what one is to think.

Knowing a peccary at sight, or when to say that something is one, is the kind of expertise we can acquire through experience. It is the kind we may *recognizably* have. As Frege also taught us, that such expertise can be shared, and recognized by one thinker in another underlies there being such a thing as judging, along with rational relations between the non-conceptual and the conceptual. (Here see my forthcoming) For this reason, too, The Condition is simply a mistake.

Where we see that the meat is on the rug—whether in seeing it there, or otherwise (in Pia's face, in the dog's behaviour)—that the meat is on the rug thereby bears, for us, on what to think. That is not in doubt. But nor does it account for the world's bearing as it does, through experience, on what we are to think. What cannot be right is that it bears only through relations within the space of the conceptual. Nor can it be that experiential intake is conceptually structured. Passivity makes more than a notionally separable contribution to spontaneity. The Condition must be disallowed.

4. Occasion Sensitivity

I have so far followed Frege. I now go where he may not care to. But *he* made the space I will now occupy. My aim is to work out what is really wrong with thinking of *that such-and-such* as visibly before us—in view—as, say. the meat is. Or, again, what that 'as the meat is' might mean.

The core idea so far is: for it to be so that such-and-such is for things being as they are to belong to a particular range of cases. Frege speaks of recognizing such belonging: *here* is a case of being (one way to be) thus and so. German marks two notions of recognition: *erkennen* and *anerkennen*. On the first notion, one registers how things anyway are. On the second, one accepts, or accredits, something as something, lends one's authority to its so being. In the citation Frege speaks of *Erkennung*—the first notion. But belonging, above, is a normative notion. So there is sense to be made of the second as well in the present context.

To you Sid is a great striker. I agree he has moments, but would not call him great. One of us may be demonstrably wrong. You cannot, perhaps, score *that* many own goals and be called great. But perhaps not. There is room to be impressed differently by a given style of play. Sid is what you call great, not what I do. You recognize him as first class; I do not. That is recognition in something like the sense of *Anerkennung*. If one of us were demonstrably wrong, there would be no room for it. Insisting that Sid is a great striker if he could not score on an empty pitch is a bit much. But if it is all a matter of what style of play impresses you—what you think proper football should be like—then there is such room. When it comes to the greatness of a striker, there are two ways one might reasonably think.

Handing you a packet from the butcher's I say, 'Here's the meat I bought for dinner" You open it and find the kidneys. 'I don't call that meat', you say. 'Meat, for me, is muscle'. 'Well, I do', I say helpfully. Again one of us may be demonstrably wrong. Lamb's kidneys are no more meat than wool is, to one who knows what meat is. But perhaps not. In fact, there are various understandings one might have of being meat, consistent with what being meat is a such. In that sense, being meat admits of understandings. We sometimes distinguish (e.g., in good markets) between meat and offal. Then if the kidneys wound up in the meat section they are in the wrong place. On the other hand, one would not (usually) serve kidneys to a vegetarian with the remark, 'I made sure there would be no meat at dinner'. Similarly, brains or spinal column, however delicious fried, gristle, however tasty stewed, would count as meat on some occasions for so counting, but not on others. There are various ways being meat *admits of* being thought of.

The point so far: if for things to be thus and so is for them to *belong* to a certain range of cases, there may be two or more (sometimes) reasonable ways of sorting cases into those which do belong and those which do not, with different results for things as they are. Implicit in the making of that point is this: where a notion admits of understandings, as that of being meat does, a particular occasion for deploying it may impose some given one. Where we are planning a vegetarian meal, kidneys are likely to count as meat on the understanding on which we would then speak of (something) being meat. In the market you may just misunderstand the sign if you look in the meat counter for offal. Conversely, where you have promised to spare me Pia's ubiquitous tofu, I will be thankful indeed for the stewed gristle, will consider your promise kept. If, perchance, I am ungrateful, issues of *Anerkennung* again arise: 'For the purpose, this ought to count as meat'. 'No', I reply, removing the steak from my inner pocket, '*This* is what ought to count'.

Where a notion admits of understandings, and, as above, would bear different ones on different occasions for deploying it, I will say that it is *occasion-sensitive*.

How might occasion-sensitivity matter? For one thing, to this question: Does the world—the *way* things are—articulate absolutely into one particular range of *ways* things are? Or again, does things being as they are partition all the ways there are for things to be into those ways things in fact are and all the others?

Compare: Does colour articulate absolutely into some one range of colours: *the* colours? In a sense not. There are various possibilities for dividing up colour space. But none *excludes* any other. Let shmurple be a colour that (only) some shades of purple, and some shades of blue, are. Then something may both be blue and be shmurple.

But I mean something else here by 'absolutely'. There are things (such as those kidneys) which, in things being as they are, are meat on some ways of thinking of being meat, but not on others. If we do count them as meat, then, so thinking, one of the ways things are in being as they are is: there is meat on the rug. If we do not, then this is *not* among the ways things are. Neither way of factoring the way things are into ways things are is right *tout court*, though either may be right on some occasions for the factoring. Nor is there any occasion on which it counts as so that there is meat on the rug, and (moreover) there is not. ('There is and there isn't' normally says something else entirely.) In that sense, the way things are factors differently (and in mutually incompatible ways) into *ways* things are on different occasions for the factoring.

Donald Davidson has taken Hilary Putnam to task:

> My form of realism . . . is not internal realism because internal realism makes truth relative to a scheme, and this is an idea I do not think is intelligible. A major reason, in fact, for accepting a coherence theory is the unintelligibility of the dualism of a conceptual scheme and a 'world' waiting to be coped with. (1984: 309)

Putnam now rejects 'internal realism'. But explicitly not all of its elements (see Putnam 1993). Specifically *not* the present idea: that there are competing, mutually exclusive, *correct* ways of dividing things up into ways things are. The history of science, I think, led Putnam to that view. Mundane considerations show it correct. This is the idea that makes no sense to Davidson. Such different articulations would, for him, deploy (or be) different conceptual schemes, each capturing a way things were anyway, independent of either. That would be Davidson's 'dualism of scheme and content'. And he cannot see what that might come to.

But we only need Frege to show us what this might be. Conceptual schemes (of course) belong to the conceptual. What they capture—what falls under, or fits, them—belongs to the non-conceptual. If they are adequate, what they are adequate to is things being as they are, which *admits* of being articulated in the ways they call for. The idea of occasion-sensitivity exploits Frege's insight in one way it admits of. I have suggested that the insight, and with it a dualism of scheme and content, is a good idea, without which we can make no real sense of thought. It just comes with the dualism of the left and the right of Frege's line. McDowell subscribes to Davidson's rejection of such dualisms. Perhaps it is this that makes his response to the skeleton too late.

5. Seeing That

Where one sees the meat, what one is thus aware *of* is the meat. Where one sees that there is meat on the rug, what one is *thus* aware of is its being so that there is meat on the rug (or there being meat on the rug). So if we parse 'see that there is meat on the rug' into 'see' and 'that there is meat on the rug', then the object of the verb is not the object of awareness, as it is in 'see the meat'. (We speak of being aware of the fact that such-and-such, but then not of seeing the fact that such-and-such. 'See' in such a construction would call for an object that the fact that such-and-such could not be—something, like the roast, to the left of Frege's line.) What is grammar trying to tell us here?

For one thing, this: The meat is *in* the surroundings. To see it, look where it is. Look there, too, to see the condition it is in. You can watch the meat—watch it change (in condition or position), watch *for* changes. To see that the meat is on the rug, you *might* look where the *meat* is. You might also look elsewhere—in Pia's face, say (the horrified look). You cannot look 'where that the meat is on the rug is'. There is no such place. You cannot *watch* that the meat is on the rug, nor watch for, nor see, changes in it. It is not eligible for such changes. (You can watch only what you can look for changes in.) Vision affords sensitivity to the goings on in one's surroundings, and to what undergoes them. What one is *thus* sensitive to is not that such-and-such is so. One's visual sensitivity to what is going on may gain one sensitivity to things being thus and so. Such depends on your sensitivities to things before you being, or not, particular ways they may be. (What sensitivities, and how it so depends, remain to be explored.) This was Frege's point in disallowing *that the meat is on the rug* as an object of visual awareness.

Wittgenstein describes thinking otherwise:

> The idea of a general concept being a common property of its particular instances connects up with other primitive, too simple, ideas of the structure of language. It is comparable to the idea that *properties* are *ingredients* of the things which have the properties; e.g., that beauty is an ingredient of all beautiful things as alcohol is of beer and wine ... (1958: 17)

Alcohol, if in fact odourless, *might* smell. One can feel it in the nose, or in the gut, or see it burning blue, or evaporating, or freezing. It is the sort of thing one might watch, or perceptually keep track of. Along with the meat (or the wine) it is *in* our surroundings, what we may recognize to instance generalities. To think of properties on the model of alcohol in wine would be to take being alcoholic (or that wine was) for alcohol. One could see being alcoholic, or that wine was, where seeing was occasion for watching, keeping track of, what was seen. There is a red glow in the sky just after sunset. *It* is not the property of being coloured red, nor that something is so coloured. One can watch it fade, as those other things cannot.

If one conflated properties with ingredients, it would be pointless to insist that for something to be red is for it to fit within a certain range of cases. One could say so. But an item's so fitting would be observable, something one saw before him, just as its red colouration is. There would be nothing normative about it. Seeing it would not be a matter of grasping what belongs where (with what range of cases), or when to say that something was a case of something—just as one sees a peccary if it is, in fact, a peccary before him, independent of any grasp of when it would be a *peccary* that was there. This erases Frege's line. That the sky is red now has all the features of what falls on either side of it. Which erases the need for rational relations between the conceptual and the non-conceptual. That things are thus and so is now both (perhaps visibly) *in* the surroundings, literally before us, and part of how they are. Nothing *else*, not in the surroundings—no range of cases, no requirement—need bear on whether things are a given way, or be part of their so being. But what allows this is patent nonsense.

Wittgenstein was not concerned with this solecism as such. His interest, in the *Blue Book*, was in a sense in which *our* concepts leave it open what their proper applications would be—what ought to count as fitting them. His point was: the *same* way things were might be counted as fitting a certain concept—as things being thus and so—or as not, for all the concept dictated as such. It might so count on some occasions for, or ways of, applying the concept, but not on others. His concern, thus, was with occasion-sensitivity. But occasion-sensitivity just is the idea that things being as they are—something to the left of Frege's line— might be taken to bear in different ways on whether things were thus and so—for each way, *correctly* so taken on some occasion for the taking. Things to the left must bear on—stand in rational relations to—*distinct* things on the right. It needs Frege's distinction. Erasing that distinction, as above, erases room for occasion-sensitivity; for the idea that the same thing may sometimes count, and sometimes not, as things being thus and so.

How, then, does occasion-sensitivity bear on seeing that? In the salon, plainly visible, on the white rug, is the raw meat. Pia enters. What is there for her to see? For one thing, that meat. That would be a right answer on any occasion for giving one. It is a relative fixed point across occasions for answering that question. I referred to the meat in speaking of it as meat. There is no guarantee that one could always do that across all such occasions. If I am speaking now of kidneys, then there are occasions on which one could do that and ones on which one could not. But one could always speak of *it*. Across a *very* broad range of occasions, what one thus spoke of would count as something there to be seen in that scene.

Suppose we decided to restrict rational relations to the conceptual. Then, for one to see what bore on what he was to think, he would have to see things that belonged to the conceptual. So there would have to be such things to be seen; things which became visible to one, say, on entering the salon and looking at the rug. One would see these things on a different notion of seeing than the one on which one sees a piece of meat. One might, e.g., see that the meat was on the rug. What one thus saw would not be literally *in* the surroundings. It could not have a location. But (in the present case, at least) we might settle for the fact that it becomes visible (to one suitably qualified to see it) when he looks where the meat is. (It is an accident of the example that this one place seems privileged as it does. To see that Sid has left the room one *might* look at the room, or equally at Sid, outside it. Either might work if, or only if, one knew to make the right thing of what one thus saw.)

Occasion-sensitivity makes for a contrast here between that there is meat on the rug and the meat. Suppose we ask the question just asked for seeing on the notion on which Pia saw the meat. *What* of the conceptual is visible in the scene in the salon? A prior question: what of it is *present* in things being as they (there) are? Here we lose the stability there was for what is present, and visible, of the non-conceptual. That that meat is present is relatively insensitive to occasions for saying so; that it (or some facing part) is visible roughly equally so. Not so with such things as *that there is meat on the rug*. For what is on the rug is liable to count as meat on some understandings of being meat, but not on others (e.g., if it is kidneys). In which case it will sometimes count as so, and sometimes not, that there is meat on the rug. It will so count on, but only on, occasions where, in speaking of meat one speaks on a suitable understanding of being it. So it will inevitably be for the scene's relation to at least many bits of the conceptual. So what would be, on some occasions, a true, if only partial, answer to the question 'What is there to see?', 'see' taking as objects conceptual items, would, on other occasions, be not so much as true. Which conceptual items are so much as part of the scene being as it is varies with occasions for saying which. There is not in this case such a thing as 'that which is to be seen', where what this is remains stable across occasions as what is to be seen of the non-conceptual (e.g., the meat) remains stable across occasions. What is to be seen *of the conceptual*, in viewing a scene, is not what is to be seen simply in the scene being as it is.

Here we run up against the difference in grammar between the two sides of Frege's line. Occasion-sensitivity belongs to the conceptual. It concerns the leeway there is *intrinsically* in sorting cases under rubrics. For any way there *is* for things to be, things being as they are *may*, in point of grammar, count as that way on some understandings of so being, and as not that way on others. It is just bad grammar to speak of the meat, as it is on an occasion, as counting as it thus is on some, but not other, understandings of it so being. Its being in the condition it is does not (so far) call for understandings. They are not to the point. (Again, it might be *that* meat in any of many further conditions. What it would be for something to be *that* does call for understandings. (Is it *that* meat as mince?))

The scene in view articulates (so good as) absolutely into items literally in it. It may thus articulate in many ways; but where one way does not exclude another (as being shmurple does not exclude being purple). The scene does not thus articulate (even nearly) absolutely into ways things were in being as they were in it. Not just that there are many such articulations. Whether something *is* an articulation—which is to say, *which* ways for things to be things are in that scene—has no right answer independent of an occasion for asking.

How does the stability that thus goes missing matter? Pia enters the salon and sees what she does. What she sees in fact bears on what it would be right to think, both in ways she appreciates and in ways she does not. Insofar as she does appreciate how it bears, it bears on what she is to think. So, for example, if she knows meat on a rug when she sees it, then what she sees bears on what she is to think as to whether there is meat on the rug. How her experience thus bears on what she is to think does not seem to vary with occasions for saying how it bears, or at least not in the way it would vary if how it bore depended on whether or not she saw that there was meat on the rug. The bearing remains (relatively) stable across occasions for describing it. I mean by this that it remains constant across occasions which vary, the one from the other, in what there was in the scene, by way of the conceptual, that might be seen—which vary, e.g., as to whether that there was meat on the rug was part of how things were, thus part of what someone might see. But if the bearing is indifferent to that kind of variation, then for there to have been the bearing there was cannot be just for it to have been visible that P, that Q, and so on, for fixed substitutes for those place-holders. It cannot be for there to have been such-and-such things to be seen, or that Pia did in fact see, where those things are that things are such-and-such way, or things being some such way. This can be right neither for the bearing there in fact was on what it would be right for one to think, nor for the bearing there was for Pia, present in her experience, on what she was to think. For her experience to have made the world bear on what she was to think as it did cannot be for her to relate, either in seeing them, or in any other way, to such-and-such conceptual items so conceived.

Might the wanted stability be found while reason reaches no farther than the conceptual? Pia, entering the salon, sees what she does as to how things are there. She appreciates what she does as to how what she thus sees bears on what to think. If one spoke on a suitable understanding of meat being on the rug, one could, perhaps, capture some of this in saying her to see that there is meat on the rug. One could, for one thing, if she were sufficiently sensitive to how things being as they are bore on whether there was meat there; on how it could be right, or wrong, to say so, given things as they were. So far as her appreciation so extends, thus far does what she sees as to how thing are in fact bear on what she is to think (and will). If rational relations start with the conceptual, perhaps her seeing what she did of how things were was her seeing things to be a certain way (such-and-such way), where that belongs to the conceptual. What way? On different occasions there will be different ways of naming it. What names it on one may not do so on another. Perhaps nothing names it full stop. Sometimes one might name it in mentioning *being meat*, and *being on a rug*. Sometimes one may need to mention (say) *being edible animal parts* in place of *being meat*. And so on. *Being meat*, e.g., works when, but only when, one speaks on the right understanding of things so being. The posited way for things to be which so relates to names for it, we hope, will be stably present in the way things are (in the scene Pia views) in just the way the meat is.

If the scene in view does bear stably on what it would be true to think (that there is meat on the rug on the understandings on which there is, that there is not on the understandings on which there is not, etc.), and if it bears as stably as it does on what Pia is to think, occasion-sensitivity calls for a story on these lines. To what does it commit us? On it, the scene came to bear on what Pia was to think in her seeing it to be a certain way. One might ask: What would name it when? When, for example, would one name it in speaking of meat as being on the rug? When one spoke on a suitable understanding of meat being on a rug. Different understandings of meat being on a rug are different understandings as to how particular cases of things to the left of Frege's line sort into those belonging to that range of cases and those not. An understanding would be *suitable* where the cases which count as meat being on a rug on that understanding are those which would instance the generality of that supposed occasion-invariant way Pia saw things to be. Which would be just when things being as they *thus* were (in that particular case) would bear on what Pia was to think in just the way she saw things being as they were (in the scene before her) to bear on what she was to think. With these observations we see that to answer the question which arise on the present story we need to recognize rational relations between things to the left and things to the right of Frege's line. For answers rest on the facts as to when particular cases of things being as they are *are rightly taken* to instance this or that generality (e.g., that of meat being on a rug), and on what Pia can recognize about this. In which case the story has failed of its purpose—if that purpose was to confine rational relations to the realm of the conceptual.

In which case we do not need the story. Pia seeing what she did as to how things were need not be her seeing things to be such-and-such way. We may simply think of her experience as follows. Pia saw what she did of things being as they were, in the scene before her; thus saw what she did as to how they were (notably, though possibly not only, how the scene before her was). She was thus enabled to recognize the instancing of an indefinite variety of bits of the conceptual, within the limits of her grasp of what instancing them requires; and to treat the world accordingly within the limits of her appreciation of what difference it would then make that such-and-such generality was instanced. What she saw of how things were need no more (nor less) be that there was meat on the rug than that there were edible animal parts there—even though for things to be the one way is not in general for them, *ipso facto*, to be the other. There need be no particular repertoire of conceptual items which, in the scene's being as it was, just were those present and (all going right) visible—not even an infinite repertoire—nor any such repertoire which just were, as such, the ones Pia saw. A grasp of what meat being on a rug is, for thinkers like us, includes, as a rule, an ability to see how various particular cases might, or might not, count as that. If Pia has such a grasp, then she will be sensitive to the various understandings on which one might speak of meat being on a rug, thus to those on which that is how things were (when occasion for having those understandings arises). But that there was meat on the rug is not (independent of some particular such understanding) either a way she saw things to be, or not one. Nor need there be any other way for things to be—e.g., one tied to no particular name for it—which does play that role in the shaping of her thought by her experience of that scene.

Pia, like most of us, can adjust her way of saying what she saw to fit the occasion for saying it, so that, in the words she chooses, she will say the right thing. She may speak of meat as on a rug, when so doing would be saying the right thing. When it would not, then, seeing that, she can speak of something else—say, edible animal parts. What she saw is no more what she speaks of in some one such way than what she speaks of in another. Her experience is no more of any one such structuring of concepts than of any other.

How *can* she thus fit what she says to her audience, always saying what, in fact, she saw? One answer might be: for each two such different ways of (sometimes) saying what she saw, there are two different things she in fact saw *tout court*; two different items visible in viewing the scene, each seen, and registered, independent of the other. Another would be that some one thing which is what she *really* saw—that things were F; where speaking of being F is at most sometimes, perhaps never, a way of *saying* what she saw She translates from talk of F to other renderings (e.g., that there was meat), each adequate to its occasion, conforming to the (supposed) correct canons of saying the same.

Neither of these views is plausible—especially if, for the second answer, canons of correct translation (of the sort envisioned) must refer only to relations that hold between different bits of the conceptual *as such*, and not to any rational relations between what belongs to the conceptual and what does not. No relation that holds *per se* between being meat and being an edible animal part makes speaking of the one a good way of saying what one says in speaking of the other. What *may* make for this is a relation that holds between speaking of one *on one occasion* and speaking of the other on another which holds by virtue of what would count, on each occasion, as instancing the generality thus spoken of. There is no escaping reason reaching beyond the scope of the conceptual. Without our seeing how it thus reaches, experience could not rationally shape our thought.

If the non-conceptual lies without the reach of reason, we are not entitled to the idea of occasion-sensitivity. For it cannot then be that instances—items to the left of Frege's line—are *rightly* placed in ranges differently, on different occasions and for different purposes; that they in fact *belong* where they are thus placed. We must then conceive seeing what is before you as visually confronting some given battery of conceptual structures, in the present sense of that term. To see that such-and-such is to see some one of these; which, in turn, is to make it out for what it is. One confronts these things not in being literally before them (or vice-versa); but in *some* other way they are available as objects of sight. To see what one does of how things are is thus to see *that* they are such-and-such ways.

Conversely, with the idea of occasion-sensitivity in play we may conceive seeing that as seeing what is literally in view (the non-conceptual) and grasping some of its bearing on the conceptual. Crediting someone with seeing *that* such-and-such would then be part of a particular way of articulating his visual awareness of how things were into awareness of particular aspects of their so being—just as saying that things are thus and so is part of a particular way of articulating the *way* they are into *ways* they are.

6. Givens

Is the 'Myth of the Given' a myth? *Not* if the Given is nothing but the non-conceptual—such familiar bits of our surroundings as a roast and a rug. But for sure if it is certain other things it is sometimes said to be. It is then a quite familiar myth. McDowell says this about it:

> The idea of the Given is the idea that the space of reasons, the space of justifications, or warrants, extends more widely than the conceptual sphere. . . . The extra extent of the space of reasons is supposed to allow it to incorporate non-conceptual impacts from outside the realm of thought. But we cannot really understand the relations in virtue of which a judgement is warranted except as relations within the space of concepts: relations such as implications or probabilification, which hold between potential exercises of conceptual capacities. The attempt to extend the scope of justificatory relations outside the conceptual sphere cannot do what it is supposed to do. (1996: 7)

> We must not picture an outer boundary around the sphere of the conceptual, with a reality outside the boundary impinging inward on the system. Any impingements across such an outer boundary could only be causal, and not rational; that is Davidson's perfectly correct point . . . (1996: 34)

> According to the Myth of the Given, the obligation to be responsibly alive to the dictates of reason lapses when we come to the ultimate points of contact between thinking and reality; the Given is a brute effect of the world, not something justified by it. (1996: 42)

The Given as first portrayed (1996: 7) need only be the non-conceptual. We have seen how reason reaches that far. McDowell tells us that we cannot conceive of relevant rational relations—such things as warranting or making correct—except as between what belongs to the conceptual. As we have seen, this is simply not so. In the second passage McDowell endorses Davidson's view that the non-conceptual, since it could not stand in a rational relation to anything, must only bear causally on what we in fact happen to think. The last passage (1996: 42) again depends on the claim that the non-conceptual cannot stand in rational relations to things. If not, then in dealing with *it* obligation to be rational (alive to the dictates of reason) trivially lapses: there are no such dictates. But if so, there is no lapse, nor cause to think there is.

So innocuous becomes myth on an assumption: reason is confined to the conceptual. Why make it? One *could* be led to in misunderstanding Frege's idea that laws of logic unfold the concept truth. (1918: 59.) Laws of logic of course concern *thoughts* and their relations. As Frege saw them, they reflect the most general structure of any system of thoughts. Nor could one think *counter* to them. There is no *such* exemption. It is not as if they touch on only *some* thoughts. If they were the full unfolding of the concept truth, questions of truth could arise only for what they governed. So, too, for rational relations.

But there is another half to Frege's story. Judging is exposure to error (so, too, correctness) decidable *solely* by things being as they are. For Frege, laws of logic arise out of this feature of that rather special attitude, and, correspondingly, apply precisely to it. For a given judging, things being as they are may *be* their being as judged, or, again, their being otherwise. When they would be which must be decided by the particular nature of the judgement—the particular way in which, in so judging, one exposes oneself to error. But what matters here is that such things *are* (sometimes) decided. It can be, and sometimes is, that things being as they are *settles* that a given judgment is correct (or, again, incorrect). It can be that this would remain (or cease to be) so if such-and-such changes were worked on how things are. Where there were no such facts there would simply be no judgement. There is a determinate way in which things being as they are thus matters to a judgement's truth. That truth *can* depend on how things are in that way—in the way how things are settles whether there is meat on the rug, e.g.—is also part of the unfolding of the concept truth: of what it is and may be. Yet it is not laws of logic which settle that, or when, this is so. Nor do they touch on the relevant relata. Things being such as to make it true to say that there is meat on the rug is *not* a relation between one conceptual item and another—though, of course, if they are such, then it is so that there is meat on the rug. This is just, once again, the lesson of Frege's line.

So reason's reach is not the same as logic's reach; and could not be if logic is to have any reach at all. The assumption crucial to the idea of a *myth* is not *so* justified. Something *else* in Davidson makes for an entirely different myth. Davidson excludes *perception* entirely from his picture. The Given, conceived merely as the non-conceptual, is such things as roasts and rugs. By contrast, The Given in Davidson's picture could not be something we *perceived*—saw, heard, etc. (As Frege noted, it would be something one *had*.) A roast could not be a bit of it. If there are any roasts, they are *visible* items, what *one* would see by looking in the right place. Here is Davidson on what our senses deliver:

> We have been trying to see it this way: a person has all his beliefs about the world . . . . How can he tell if they are true . . . ? Only, we have been assuming, by connecting certain of his beliefs with the deliverances of the senses one by one, or perhaps confronting the totality of his beliefs with

the tribunal of experience. No such confrontation makes sense, for of course we can't get outside our skins to find out what is causing the internal happenings of which we are aware. (1984: 312)

So the objects of sensory awareness—the deliverances of our senses—become *internal happenings*—in the best case sensations, but not (like a muscle cramping) what one might *perceive*. It is internal happenings, so conceived, which he holds cannot stand in logical relations—which, succumbing to the confusion just scouted, he equates with standing in *rational* relations.

> The relation between a sensation and a belief cannot be logical, since sensations are not beliefs or other propositional attitudes. What then is the relation? The answer is, I think, obvious: the relation is causal. (1984: 311)

I bracket the question whether a sensation could bear rationally on *anything*, since that lies outside present concerns. Anyway, having a sensation as of falling over backwards, or as of being bloated, is not yet feeling oneself falling over or being bloated, even if one also feels sensations. Feeling oneself falling over is enjoying awareness of a going on in one's surroundings—of one's body moving floorwards. Feeling (having) a sensation as of falling over is feeling nothing but the sensation. A sensation is not *of* the objects, or events, around one. My body's moving bears on what is so of my surroundings as a sensation could not.

Perception just *is* of one's surroundings; of what is in them, of how they are. Of, e.g., the meat perching on the plinth. Which bears on whether there is meat perching on the plinth. Sensation is not of one's surroundings; not of what stands to there being meat on the plinth as the meat on the plinth does. If the senses delivered only sensations, and not perception, they would supply no awareness of that in our surroundings which bears on what to think of them. If the Given were what was thus delivered, it would be a myth that *that* was *any* grounding for our beliefs about the world.

McDowell accuses Quine, correctly, of leaving no room in his official view of experience for us to experience what bears on what to think, or even for us to respond to experience with so much as a *belief* 'about the empirical world— something correctly or incorrectly adopted according to how things are' there (1996: 138-139). He adds,

> The point does not turn on the detail of Quine's conception of experience, as stimulation of sensory surfaces. There can be less resolutely anti-mentalistic conceptions of experience that nevertheless match Quine's conception at a more abstract level, in that they take experiences to be deliverances of receptivity. (Footnote p. 138)

Conceiving experiences as 'deliverances of receptivity', as that idea is meant here, would be conceiving them as *of* what lay 'outside the bounds of the conceptual'. That would leave no room for experience to bear on what one is to think, so no room for belief at all—*if*, but only if, the conceptual were co-extensive with reason's reach. But, we have seen, it is not. Which makes 'stimulation of sensory surfaces' more central to the predicament. The root of Quine's problem is that his official view abolishes *perception*. On it, *any* experience is compatible with the truth or falsity of any proposition (see my 2004b). 'Stimulations', or 'irritations, *might* preserve that idea. Ideas (*Vorstellungen*), as explained by Frege (1918: 67–68) would. Just Frege's point (see my forthcoming). It is another matter if what Pia experiences is meat on the rug. Such an experience is incompatible with the truth of the proposition that there is no meat on the rug. One can recognize this of the experience, in having it, in seeing the bearing of something outside the conceptual—the meat, as it is—on something there is to think—that there is meat on the rug. The point holds more generally if there are things *in* the environment that we sometimes *perceive. That* is the right answer to Davidson's claim that experience, 'understood as what receptivity provides us' is *eo ipso* removed from the space of reasons.

If we do not so much as experience our surroundings, then thoughts about what we do experience (if such thoughts there be) are not thoughts about our surroundings. Nor could our experience reveal how those surroundings were. All that is orthogonal to the question whether there are rational relations between the non-conceptual and the conceptual. I have argued that reason reaches, and had better reach, that far.[1]

Charles Travis
Department of Philosophy
King's College, London
Strand
London WC2R 2LS
UK
c.s.travis@gmail.com

NOTES

[1] The person I am far and away the most indebted to in this essay is John McDowell. He has been incredibly generous with his time, and has shown infinite patience trying to get me to see what it is that matters. We have spent many hours in discussion, over an extended period of time. The result, of course, is my responsibility. I am also very thankful to Guy Longworth, Dawn Phillips, and M. G. F. Martin.

REFERENCES

Austin, J. L. (1946/1979), 'Other Minds, reprinted in *Philosophical Papers*, 3rd edn. Oxford: Oxford University Press.
Davidson, D. (1984), 'A Coherence Theory of Truth and Knowledge, reprinted in *Truth and Interpretation: Perspectives on the Philosophy of Donald Davidson*, ed. E. Lepore. Oxford: Basil Blackwell 1986.

Frege, G. (1892), 'Über Begriff und Gegenstand', *Vierteljahrschrift für wissenschaftliche Philosophie*, 16: 192–205.

—— (1904), 'Was Ist Eine Funktion?', *Festschrift Für Ludwig Boltzmann*. Leipzig: Barth: 656–666.

—— (1906?/2001), '17 Kernsätze zur Logik, *Schriften zur Logik und Spraachphilosophie aus dem Nachlass*, ed. G. Gabriel. Hamburg: Felix Meiner.

—— (1918), 'Gottlob Frege, 'Der Gedanke: eine logische Untersuchung'', *Beiträge zur Philosophie des deutschen Idealismus*, 2: 58–77.

McDowell, J. (1994, 1996), *Mind and World*. Cambridge, MA: Harvard University Press. (Roman numerals refer to 1996 edition.)

—— (1998), 'Having the World in View: Sellars, Kant, and Intentionality', *The Journal of Philosophy*, 95: 431–491.

Putnam, H. (1993), 'The Question of Realism', *Words and Life*. Cambridge, MA: Harvard University Press, 295–312.

Travis, C. (2004a), 'The Silence of the Senses', *Mind*, 113: 57–94.

—— (2004b), 'The Twilight of Empiricism', *Proceedings of the Aristotelian Society*, 104: 245–270.

—— (forthcoming), 'Frege, Father of Disjunctivism, *Philosophical Topics*, ed. Edward Minar Fall, 2005.

Waismann, F. (1979), *Wittgenstein: Conversations with the Vienna Circle*. Oxford: Basil Blackwell 1979.

Wittgenstein, L. (1958), *The Blue and Brown Books*. Oxford: Basil Blackwell.

11

Responses

John McDowell

Bill Brewer

1. Brewer thinks holding that 'perceptual experience consists in direct conscious access to constituents of the physical world themselves' is incompatible with acknowledging 'the possibility of falsity in perceptual content'. I think he is wrong about that. I agree with him that the experience we enjoy in perceiving, as opposed to merely seeming to perceive, 'presents us directly with the objects in the world around us themselves'. So far from accepting that this is inconsistent with taking perceptual experience to have content, which is, *qua* content of experience, possibly false, I think the idea of conscious access to objects, of a sort that can enable knowledge about them, positively requires us to conceive the consciousness in question as contentful. The alternative is a form of the Myth of the Given. (See 'Avoiding the Myth of the Given', and my response to Charles Travis.)

Talk of content as possibly false fits most easily with taking content to be propositional. I now think it is better to think of the content of experience as intuitional rather than propositional. (See 'Avoiding the Myth of the Given'.) But intuitional content is still content. And it is, we can say, all but propositional. One arrives at propositional content by simply articulating what are already elements of intuitional content. So in commenting on Brewer's paper I am going to stay with the Sellarsian idea that the content of a perceptual experience is propositional content, the sort of thing that could be the content of a claim.

2. Brewer thinks he can make trouble for the content view by exploiting a requirement that the content of perceptual consciousness (if it had a content) would need to be determinate. Thus, considering the Müller-Lyer illusion, he writes:

> Is the line with inward hashes represented as shorter than it actually is; or is the line with outward hashes represented as longer than it actually is; or both; and by how much in each case? That is to say, how *exactly* would the world have to be for the purported perceptual representation to be veridical? [The content view's] talk of perceptual content requires a specific answer to this question.

His idea is that the content view is required to say 'Yes' to one of the first three questions, and to provide a corresponding answer to the fourth. But that is simply wrong. Suppose I say, of two lines that are in fact the same length, that one, say A, is longer than the other, say B. In saying that, I am representing A as longer than B. It does not follow that I am saying that A is longer than it is, or saying that B is shorter than it is, or saying that both of those things are the case. One of those things would have to be so if what I say were true, but I am not saying of any one of them that it is so. A 'by how much?' question does not arise. Just so with an experience that represents one line as longer than the other.

There does need to be an answer to the question how the world would have to be for a Müller-Lyer experience to be veridical. And there is an answer. The relevant answer, for these purposes, is just that the line with outward hashes would have to be longer than the line with inward hashes. (Of course for any actual Müller-Lyer experience, there will be more to be said about how the world would have to be for it to be veridical: for instance, just to begin with, that the lines would have to be, say, white on a black surface.)

I am insisting that a Müller-Lyer experience can leave some questions unanswered about how the world would have to be for it to be veridical, just as a saying can. Brewer thinks this will not cohere with the content view's account of the fine-grainedness of perception. But perceptual content need not be more determinate than it is. Insisting that a Müller-Lyer experience can leave those questions unanswered is perfectly consistent with holding that normal colour experience, for instance, represents the colours of objects in a more fine-grained way than could be expressed by any usual colour vocabulary.

A similar response works for Brewer's second attempt to embarrass the content view with Müller-Lyer experiences. There is a sense in which a Müller-Lyer experience places the endpoints of the two lines where they are in the objective world. And one of the facts about where they are is that the two pairs of endpoints are the same distance apart. But the aspect of the experience's content that pertains to the spatial position of the four endpoints does not include its being the case that the distances are the same. To suppose it does, just because the experience places the points where they are, would be like supposing that if I say something that places four points determinately where they are in the objective world (perhaps uttering words on the lines of 'This one is *there*, that one is *there*, . . . ', with four pointing gestures), and the distance between one pair of points is the same as the distance between the other pair, I say that the distances are the same.

Brewer's third attempt to embarrass the content view over the Müller-Lyer illusion depends on the phenomenology of a dynamic version, in which the hashes gradually shrink until they disappear. He suggests that the content view would need to model its account of this on a series of increasingly accurate thoughts about the relations in length between the two lines. That would certainly be unsatisfactory. But the idea that the content view would need to describe the case like that depends on the same faulty assumption that vitiates the first attempt. Brewer is suggesting that at each stage the experience would have to warrant a different answer to a question on the lines of 'How much longer does the experience *now* represent the line with outward hashes as being?' But the right thing to say is just that it gradually ceases to be the case that one line looks longer than the other. There need not be answers to questions like 'How much longer does that line look?'; it makes no difference if we add 'now'. And to press the question 'Exactly when does it first look as if the two lines are the same length?' would merely be another attempt to apply Brewer's false assumption about a determinacy in content required by the content view.

3. Those arguments of Brewer's are supposed to bring out that one cannot acknowledge a possibility of falsity in experiential content without threatening one's right to hold, with common sense, that perceptual experience directly presents us with objects. Brewer thinks this puts pressure on an adherent of the content view, at any rate one who wants to stay as close as possible to that common-sense idea, to reduce 'the scope of the possibility of falsity in perceptual content'. Brewer used to accept the content view, and he offered, in his *Perception and Reason*, a version that maximized this supposedly needed reduction by construing experiential content not only as object-dependent in its referential aspects but also as instantiation-dependent in its predicational aspects. But even that version, he argues, did not eliminate the possibility of falsity altogether.

But in so far as Brewer's version of the content view was an attempt to equip experience with a kind of content that comes as close as possible to being immune to the possibility of falsity, it was wrongly motivated all along.

The content of an experience in which one sees something to be the case can be grouped together with the content of an experience in which one merely seems to see something to be the case. Those are two sorts of experiences in which one at least seems to see something to be the case. And if we specify some content by saying what someone seems to see to be the case, we leave open a possibility that it is false. For all we have said, the seeming may be a mere seeming. If all we know is that someone seems to see that things are a certain way, we do not yet know whether things are that way.

But suppose an experience is one in which the subject *sees* something to be the case. That is not consistent with supposing that the content of the experience may be false. This is an elimination—not just a reduction in scope—of the possibility of falsity. If 'content of a seeing' singles out a kind of content, it is a kind of content that admits of no possibility of falsity.

Brewer thinks the content view needs a conception of the content of, say, visual experiences that reduces the scope of the possibility of falsity, independently of whether the experiences in question are experiences of seeing how things are. But that is wrong. Experiences in which one seems to see how things are can be experiences in which one *merely* seems to see how things are. So if we explain the idea of visual experiences by saying they are experiences in which one seems to see something to be the case, we conceive something's being the content of a visual experience as consistent with its being false. But that leaves it beyond dispute that if an experience is one of seeing things to be a certain way, it follows that things are that way.

There is no need to invoke object-dependence, let alone instantiation-dependence, to make the point I am making here. Consider an experience, at least seemingly one of seeing, whose content can be partly articulated by saying 'There's a red cube over there'. (Perhaps what would be meant by 'over there', if one uttered those words in a suitable context, is a case of object-dependence. But I want to focus on the fact that those words, as uttered in a suitable context, would specify a content that does not depend on the existence of a red cube for its thinkability, but only for its truth.) I left it undetermined whether the experience we are considering is one of seeing or one of *merely* seeming to see. If it is one of merely seeming to see, the bit of its content that can be articulated by saying 'There's a red cube over there' may be false. (If it is true, that is a lucky chance.) But suppose the experience is one of seeing how things are. It follows that there *is* a red cube at the place indicated by 'over there'. And there is nothing to prevent us from holding that that red cube is directly present to the subject of the experience when she enjoys the experience.

If a red cube is directly present to her in her experience, she is in a position to refer to it demonstratively, in expressing object-dependent thoughts about it. But we do not need to credit the experience itself with anything but content that can be articulated in existential terms. The point of insisting that demonstratively expressible content is object-dependent should never have seemed to lie in the project Brewer thinks the content view needs to go in for, reducing the scope of the possibility of falsity in perceptual experience.

4. Brewer's second argument against the content view involves the *generality* implied by the very idea of representing something to be a certain way. Brewer thinks this can be acommodated only at the price of 'an unwarranted intrusion of conceptual thought about the world presented in perception into the [content view] theorist's account of the most basic nature of perception itself'. He thinks that according to the content view 'perceptual experience trades direct openness to the elements of physical reality themselves for some intellectual act of classification or categorization'. I think this is confused.

In a typical case of seeing, one sees something to be a certain way. (Many ways, actually; but we can focus on just one.) In a corresponding case of merely seeming to see, one merely seems to see something to be a certain way. In both cases one at least seems to see a thing to be a certain way; that is, as the content view would have us put the matter, one's experience represents the thing as being that way. *How* the thing has to be, if it is to be as one seems to see it to be, is *there* in an experience describable in those perfectly intuitive terms. The thing has to be the way one seems to see it to be. There is no question of needing an intellectual step from what one's experience presents to one, or seems to present to one, to enable one to arrive at a specification of the content of one's experience, its truth-conditions.

How one seems to see something to be can be dependent on one's perceptual acuity. For instance, one cannot seem to see something to have a colour individuated more finely than colours are individuated by one's capacity to discriminate colours.

Consider an experience in which one sees something to have a certain colour. Brewer apparently thinks the content view would need to credit such an experience with a content whose truth-conditions, so far as the seen thing's colour is concerned, are as follows: *either* the seen thing is coloured the way it visibly is, *or* it is coloured in any way that would be indiscriminable from that way given the acuity of the subject's capacity to discriminate colours. It is the second disjunct that he takes to reflect the intrusion of an intellectual act of generalizing. He thinks the content view needs to go beyond what is there in the subject's visual consciousness, exploiting the subject's level of acuity to determine all the ways the seen thing might be, consistently with the content's being true.

But the second disjunct is otiose. The way the object visibly is—can be seen to be—in respect of colour cannot have a determinacy that outruns the acuity of the subject's capacity to discriminate colours. Brewer writes as if the colour that is visually present to the subject figures in the subject's consciousness in such a way that an intellectual step of generalizing would still be needed in order to determine truth-conditions for the subject's experience. But that makes no sense. The colour that is visually present to the subject already determines truth-conditions for the experience. The experience is veridical just in case the colour that figures in the subject's visual consciousness is the colour the object has.

The point carries over to cases in which one merely seems to see something to have a certain colour. For the content of one's experience to be veridical the thing one sees would need to have the colour one seems to see it to have. The colour one seems to see it to have is there in one's visual consciousness, not something one would need to arrive at by taking an intellectual step beyond what is there in one's visual consciousness.

5. Brewer suggests that the arguments he gives here against the content view bring out the core errors lying behind its vulnerability to a dilemma he does not here discuss directly. He thinks the dilemma is ultimately fatal to the view. He describes the dilemma like this:

> [C]onsider the content of any particular perceptual experience. Is this very content also the content of a possible non-experiential thought or belief by the subject? If so, then what is added to it, in perception, to produce the characteristically conscious, subjective nature of the experience? If not, then how are we to explain its status as an *essentially experiential* representational content—a genuine content, which nevertheless cannot be the content of anything other than perceptual *experience*?

But I have urged that the arguments Brewer gives in this paper do not work; they do not expose core errors. This dilemma raises interesting questions, but so far from being fatal to the content view, they leave it unthreatened.

If we are considering the whole content of a perceptual experience, we can comfortably occupy the second horn of the dilemma. Consider an experience of seeing. Its content cannot in its entirety be the content of a belief one could have with one's eyes shut. To suppose it could would be to fail to accommodate the fact that experiences of seeing make objects visually *present* to one. That is a feature of the kind of content they have. (This is easier to see if we take experiential content to be intuitional.)

An experience of merely seeming to see merely seems to make objects visually present to one. But since it seems to do that, seeming visual presentness is a feature of its content.

Any explicit articulation of the content of a visual experience will only partly articulate it, and such partial articulations need not include an implication of visual presentness. In connection with such partial articulations we can comfortably occupy the other horn of Brewer's dilemma. A visual experience might disclose to me that there is a red cube a short distance in front of me. That is something that in another case I might believe without even seeming to see it to be the case, let alone seeing it to be the case—perhaps because I remember how things are arranged in a room I am picking my way through in total darkness. There is nothing problematic about this. Brewer's dilemma poses no problem for the content view.

Willem A. deVries

1. I suggested that an authentically Kantian view of intentionality is inaccessible to Sellars because of a deep structural feature of his philosophical outlook. DeVries surmises that the feature I meant is the role of sensations in Sellars's theory of mind. But I meant something more deeply seated in Sellars's thinking: namely, the scientism he expresses in the claim that 'in the dimension of describing and explaining the world, science is the measure of all things, of what is that it is, and of what is not that it is not' (EPM, §42).

I want to connect this with a comment on deVries's remark that I am 'notably mute' on 'the major problem facing every modern Kantian: what to do about the thing-in-itself'.

It can seem that that the thing-in-itself is something that is a certain way, though it is beyond our powers to know what way that is. I think this version of the idea should be rejected out of hand. But Kant also points towards a much better conception. At Bxxvii in the first Critique, for instance, he implies that the idea of the thing-in-itself is what we are left with if we start with the idea of things as they figure in our knowledge, and think away the conditions on us that are required for it to be possible that things figure in our knowledge at all. On this interpretation things-in-themselves just are the things that figure in our knowledge, but conceived in a way that abstracts from what we know about them, since it abstracts from anything whose presence in our conception of things depends on our capacities to acquire knowledge.

In Sellars's Kantianism, things-in-themselves are things as they would figure in an ideal scientific world view. This avoids the unknowability in principle, by us, that is the core of the first of those two readings of Kant's idea. So far as it goes, that is a good thing. But by my lights this take on Kant misses the point of the Kantian idea on its best construal, which is the second of those two interpretations. On Sellars's interpretation the idea of the thing-in-itself does not involve abstracting from our capacities to acquire knowledge, in particular our capacities to do science. This reflects Sellars's attempt to force Kantian thinking into a frame fixed by his scientism.

Of course I cannot try to establish here that Sellars's scientistic gloss on the Kantian idea misses its point. But it seems obvious to me that Kant would not be willing to say, as Sellars does at EPM §42, in a remark for which he offers the *'scientia mensura'* thesis as a less paradoxical replacement: *'Speaking as a philosopher*, I am quite prepared to say that the common-sense world of physical objects in Space and Time is unreal'. That is not Kant's attitude to the common-sense world of physical objects in Space and Time. Transcendental ideality is not a kind of unreality.

However that may be, the situation is not, as deVries implies, that Sellars offers modern Kantians a way to deal with the problem of the thing-in-itself while I am mute about it. It is part of my Strawsonian partial appropriation of Kant in *Mind and World* that the idea of the thing-in-itself on the interpretation that involves the idea of something beyond our cognitive powers is misguided. And I take issue with Sellars's scientistic conception of the thing-in-itself, and sketch the second interpretation, in a long footnote (p. 469, n. 23) in 'Having the World in View'.

2. DeVries says my critique of Quine is sound philosophy. But he misdescribes my treatment of Quine and its relation to my treatment of Sellars.

He says I accept Quine's criticism of the thesis—one of the 'dogmas of empiricism'—that statements have 'empirical significance' one by one. This is at best misleading. Given how Quine interprets the phrase 'empirical significance', he is right to deny that individual statements have empirical significance of their own. But that is not much of a concession to Quine. I urge that what Quine calls 'empirical significance' is not recognizable as any kind of significance. And if we reclaim the phrase 'empirical significance' for something recognizable as *empirical significance*, it becomes simply wrong to deny that empirical significance can be attributed to statements one by one. (See *Mind and World*, pp. 156–61.)

Quine undercuts his image of 'the tribunal of experience', and thereby any possibility that 'empirical significance' as he interprets it could genuinely be a kind of significance, by conceiving experience in terms of irritations of sensory nerve endings. After rehearsing my argument to that effect, deVries says I think Sellars is ultimately no better off than Quine. This too is at best misleading. It is true that, though Sellars's impressions (at least as he uses that language in EPM) are not irritations of sensory nerve endings (except perhaps in some prospective integration into a unified science), they are no more capable of serving as a tribunal, standing in judgment over beliefs, than irritations of sensory nerve endings would be. But that would leave Sellars in a position that simply matches Quine's, in respect of entitlement to conceive experience as a tribunal, only if Sellars's resources for spelling out the tribunal image were restricted to impressions. And that is not at all how Sellars thinks, and not at all how I understand him.

DeVries misunderstands a passage from *Mind and World* (p. 144) whose point is to concede that Sellars is not stuck with holding that impressions, conceived as nonconceptual, cannot have *any* relevance to epistemological warrant. In that passage, I acknowledge that on Sellars's principles, *beliefs about* impressions can figure in the justification of beliefs about the environmental objects and states of affairs that cause them. DeVries reads this as an objection to Sellars's argument that impressions, being nonconceptual, have no epistemological role to play. But I think Sellars is right that if impressions are nonconceptual, as the bearers of that label he envisages in EPM are, then undergoing an impression cannot *itself* constitute being entitled to a belief. And he is right that that exemplifies an important constraint on the epistemology of perception. It is not an objection to that Sellarsian thesis to note that on Sellars's principles a belief about an impression might justify one in a belief about its environmental cause, if one knew enough about how environmental objects and states of affairs bring about impressions.

So far as I know, Sellars does not work with an analogue to Quine's image of experience as a tribunal. But if he wanted to exploit such imagery, he would not be in a position that matches Quine's, and the point that can be put like that has always been part of my reading of Sellars. DeVries says that in my Woodbridge Lectures I realize that I was too quick in assimilating Sellars's conception of experience to Quine's, but there was never any such assimilation for me to take back.

Given Quine's conception of experience as irritations of sensory nerve endings, and therefore not conceptual states of perceivers, he is not entitled to think of experience as rationally related to belief. Experience as Quine conceives it could not be a tribunal. That is (*mutatis mutandis*) a way of putting *Sellars's* correct point that impressions, as he conceives them, cannot themselves play an epistemological role. (For these purposes it is not important that beliefs about impressions can.)

But of course there is more to experiences, in Sellars's conception, than impressions. There is the feature of experiences Sellars begins to put in place (in EPM §16) by saying, at first in a promissory spirit, that experiences contain propositional claims. The point of this can be put by saying that experiences purport to reveal something about how things are in the environment. How an experience purports to reveal things to be is its propositional content. If the experience does what it purports to do, then enjoying it is perceiving that things are the way the experience purports to reveal them to be, and that is certainly rationally relevant to believing that they are that way. (I have come to think this Sellarsian conception of experiences as having propositional content is not quite right; see 'Avoiding the Myth of the Given'. But it is certainly Sellarsian doctrine, and it blocks any assimilation of Sellars to Quine.)

I bring Sellars's conception of experiences as having propositional content into play by saying (among other things) that Sellars can conceive the course of experience as the succession of appearings. That is meant to capture the gist of Sellars's discussion, in EPM, of what he calls 'the logic of "looks"'. If one enjoys a visual experience, it at least looks to one as if things are a certain way, the way one would be saying things are if one made the propositional claim the experience contains. In the best kind of case, enjoying the experience is seeing that things are that way. In other cases enjoying the experience is having it merely look to one as if things are that way. And 'looks' expresses a particularization, to visual experience, of a concept expressible by 'appears'. So experiences, conceived as having propositional content in the way Sellars explains, can be conceived as appearings: occurrences or states in which it appears to a subject that things are a certain way.

DeVries thinks conceiving the course of experience as a succession of appearings 'seems to imply that knowledge gained from experience must either be direct knowledge of appearances or knowledge inferred therefrom'. But what my formulation implies is just that knowledge gained from visual experience (to stay with that sensory modality) is knowledge of how things are that one has because one sees how things are. There is no question of such knowledge being *inferred* from appearances. 'Direct knowledge of appearances', deVries's other alternative, might be all right, but only if 'appearances' is understood to include facts making themselves apparent to subjects.

DeVries says that to him 'the ideas that facts can just impress themselves on subjects and that experience is a succession of appearings smack of the given . . .'. (He means Sellars's mythical Given, not the innocuous given that appears in EPM §1.) But that is absurd. It is Sellars's own conception of experience that makes room for talking in terms of facts impressing themselves (we should probably not say 'just' impressing themselves) on subjects. To say that something's being the case impresses itself visually on one is just to say that one sees it to be the case. The Myth of the Given is the supposed idea of an availability for knowledge (in a demanding sense involving the idea of a standing in the space of reasons) that presupposes nothing about the knower except, perhaps, natural endowments, for instance sensory capacities—an availability for knowledge that presupposes no learning or acculturation. No such thing is implied by my talk of facts impressing themselves on a subject. When something's being the case impresses itself visually on a subject—that is, when the subject sees it to be the case—its being the case is the content of the claim that is as it were contained in the subject's visual experience, and we can cash that out in terms of the idea that the experience is an actualization of acquired conceptual capacities on the part of the subject. It is wildly wrong to find a whiff of the Myth of the Given here.

It is true that in *Mind and World* I argued that Sellars's conception of experience ultimately fails to provide for the rational openness to the world that is required for a proper understanding of empirical significance. This was because Sellars kept impressions separate from appearings, whereas I urged that a proper understanding of empirical significance requires perceptual appearings to be themselves impressions, shapings of sensory receptivity. In my Woodbridge Lectures I thought Sellars, after all, had a conception of perceptual appearings as themselves shapings of sensory receptivity. (See §6 below for more on this.) But this is not at all to say, as deVries does, that I began by putting Sellars in a box with Quine and then repudiated that. Appearings—perceptual episodes with conceptual content—are obviously part, at least, of Sellars's conception of perceptual experience. In that respect he differs radically from Quine, to his advantage. And nothing in my earlier reading of Sellars was inconsistent with that.

3. In SM Sellars says that the manifold of sensory impressions is postulated on transcendental grounds. I understood this use of 'transcendental' to imply that the postulation of impressions belongs in a project of showing how it is possible for thought to have its objective purport.

DeVries says my interpretation of Sellars's remark 'cannot be made consistent with Sellars's own conception of the transcendental'. I am baffled by this. DeVries cites a passage in which Sellars describes 'epistemology', conceived as a transcendental enterprise, as 'the theory of what it is to be a language that is about a world in which it is used'. On Sellars's behalf, deVries writes: 'Transcendental concepts and principles are those meta-level concepts and principles that are essential to understanding how a conceptual framework can be about the world in which it occurs'. My talk of objective purport, to encapsulate the transcendental question as I understand it, is an obvious gloss on those two uses of 'about'. As far as I can see, my understanding of Sellars's conception of the transcendental is exactly the one deVries, purporting to be correcting me, extracts from Sellars.

I spoke of visual impressions playing a transcendental role for Sellars. DeVries thinks this is a confusion, because transcendental reflection should be at a meta-level. But this is just nitpicking. I can easily reformulate the thought I was attributing to Sellars, and up to a point applauding him for, as follows. In transcendental reflection, according to Sellars, we have occasion to speak of impressions. So (if you insist) what figures in Sellarsian transcendental philosophy is *talk* of impressions, not impressions themselves. In those terms (that is, taking care to restrict the transcendental to a meta-level), my point was this: the talk of impressions that, in Sellars's view, has this transcendental significance is talk of them in their role as enabling openness to environmental objects and states of affairs, not talk of them as themselves objects of attention, which, in different circumstances, they can be. The shift to the meta-level makes no substantive difference here.

The 'sense-impression inference' in SM focuses on what Sellars calls 'minimal conceptual representations'. DeVries writes, as if to set me straight: 'This is a very different matter from justifying the conceptuality of our representations generally'. Well, of course! But why should that seem to imply I was wrong to think Sellars intends the sense-impression inference to be a contribution to the general transcendental project: in deVries's words, 'understanding how a conceptual framework can be about the world in which it occurs'? On Sellarsian principles, one could not fully vindicate our entitlement to conceive even 'minimal conceptual representations' as conceptual, let alone make the 'aboutness' of our representations in general unmysterious, by considering nothing but 'minimal conceptual representations'. One would need to situate those representations in relation to non-minimal representations acquired in perception, and to situate perceptual representations in general, minimal and non-minimal, in relation to representations whose claim to be knowledgeable would depend, in a broadly inferential way, on perceptual representations. (Here I have in mind the image of knowledge as a structure whose elements are related to one another along two different dimensions of dependence: EPM §38.) It does not follow that Sellars cannot have conceived the thesis that those minimal conceptual representations are 'guided' by sense impressions in just the way I thought he did: as an essential element in the general transcendental project of vindicating the objective purport of our conceptual activity, an element that—of course—does its work only as one piece in a complex picture.

4. Early in his paper, deVries says I think it is compatible with Sellars's philosophy that sense impressions are causally dispensable, though he says I acknowledge that this thesis was not seen by Sellars to be compatible with the Kantian structure of his thought. Later on, the thesis that sense impressions are causally dispensable becomes one that deVries simply says I attribute to Sellars. One might be forgiven for finding this hard to follow. In fact I do not think that thesis is compatible with Sellars's philosophy, let alone attribute it to him.

I think this strand in deVries's paper reflects a confusion about my claim that Sellars moves from a scientific sense-impression inference in EPM to a transcendental sense-impression inference in SM (which is where he uses the label 'sense-impression inference' for an argument that we need to postulate sense impressions as an element in perceptual experience). As I read it, the sense-impression inference in EPM postulates impressions, 'in scientific style', as common causes for veridical and non-veridical perceptual representations with the same conceptual content. DeVries has apparently concluded that when I take Sellars to replace that inference with a transcendental sense-impression inference, I must take him to be abandoning the idea that sense impressions stand in causal relations to conceptual representations. But there is no reason why the transcendentally grounded acceptance of sense impressions that Sellars recommends in SM cannot include the thought that sense impressions stand in causal relations to conceptual representations. The point is that as Sellars now sees things, the thought that sense impressions stand in causal relations to conceptual representations is not just a bit of empirical science, which is how he seemed to conceive it in EPM. His idea now is that the relation between sense impressions and conceptual representations, which can still be a causal relation as far as this goes, is something we are transcendentally required to acknowledge, if we are to be able to understand how it can be that the minimal conceptual representations that figure in perceptual experience are the conceptual representations they are, and ultimately—given the place of that thought about minimal conceptual representations in the complex transcendental project—if we are to be able to understand how it can be that our conceptual framework is about the world we use it in.

In a note, deVries goes so far as to say I construe §42 in the first chapter of SM as a license to discard sensations altogether. I cannot fathom this. 'Sensations' is just another word for what the sense-impression inference is supposed to warrant us in postulating. Of course nothing in a work in which Sellars endorses the sense-impression inference could be a license to discard sensations altogether. I do not see why deVries thinks I find such a thing in Sellars.

I meant to applaud Sellars for the move to conceiving the sense-impression inference as transcendental. DeVries will have none of this praise for Sellars; he thinks my objection to the scientific sense-impression inference in EPM fails. Sellars speaks of 'the proximate cause' of a kind of visual sensation as something that 'is *only for the most part* brought about by the presence in the neighborhood' of an object with the associated perceptible property. I asked: why would this proximate cause not itself suffice for the explanatory work for which Sellars argues that we need to invoke sensations? Incautiously, I suggested that the proximate cause of visual sensations of, say, red might be a specific kind of retinal image. DeVries points out that retinal images are not necessary for sensations of red. Fair enough; my hasty attempt at an identification of a proximate cause does not work. But the fact remains that Sellars himself clearly envisages a kind of thing, characterizable as the proximate cause of sensations of a specific kind, and only for the most part brought about by the presence in the environment of an instance of the associated perceptible property. I accept deVries's correction: to identify something that might stand in that relation to sensations of red we would need a more complex exploitation of the machinery that underlies perceptual consciousness than my hasty offering envisaged. But the argument of EPM §7 still raises this question: whatever can be meant by this talk of the proximate cause of sensations of a given kind (which is something Sellars himself goes in for, not some importation on my part), why does that, whatever it is, not suffice for the explanatory work that the EPM argument calls for? If what we need is an explanation 'in scientific style' of the fact that the concepts of *red* and *triangular* are activated not only when one is visually confronted with something red and triangular, but also sometimes when one is not, why does the explanation need to posit a common cause *in consciousness* at all? In the SM version of the argument, what we are looking for is no longer a common explanation, 'in scientific style', for veridical and non-veridical conceptual representations with the same minimal content. And this means that the question that is pressing about the EPM version is no longer pressing. A common cause that was not in consciousness at all could not play the transcendental role Sellars envisages.

As I have just said, what Sellars looks for in the EPM version of the sense-impression inference is an explanation of the fact that the concepts of *red* and *triangular* are activated not only when one is visually confronted with something red and triangular, but also sometimes when one is not. DeVries thinks reading Sellars like that is open to objection on the score that it omits the element in Sellars's conception of experiences constituted by impressions. But as I read it, the point of the argument in EPM §7 is precisely to force that element into the picture. The argument explicitly addresses the question how the idea of a nonconceptual element in perceptual experience arises in the first place. Sellars asks: 'How does it happen that people can have the experience which they describe by saying "It is as though I were seeing a red and triangular physical object" when either there is no physical object there at all, or, if there is, it is neither red nor triangular?' And he answers by saying that such experiences include visual impressions corresponding to those characteristic of seeing red and triangular physical objects.

In §45, after repeating that experiences of seeing something to be the case and experiences in which it merely looks to one as if that is the case are alike in propositional content, Sellars goes on, in a passage deVries cites: 'But over and above this there is, of course, the aspect which many philosophers have attempted to clarify by the notion of *impressions* or *immediate experience*'. The argument in §7, as I read it, constitutes a purported justification for that 'of course'. It is not a good justification, in my view. But deVries's objection to my reading would leave the claim to which Sellars attaches that 'of course' no better than a bald assertion.

5. I said Sellars 'undertakes to vindicate the objective purport of conceptual occurrences from outside the conceptual order'. DeVries thinks he can dismiss this, on the ground that for Sellars semantic concepts are not concepts of *relations* between the conceptual order and the real (that is, extra-conceptual) order. That is certainly true. But deVries fails to mention this fact: Sellars thinks a complete account of how semantic concepts work must include not just the talk of functional roles of elements in the conceptual order, as opposed to relations between the conceptual order and the real order, that exhausts his conception of the semantical, strictly so called, but also relations of *picturing*, which hold between, for instance, linguistic acts considered in abstraction from their role in norm-governed linguistic practices ('natural-linguistic' items), on the one hand, and extra-linguistic items, on the other. It would be quite wrong to say that Sellars's conception of semantics precludes invoking relations to the extra-conceptual in transcendental reflection. Sellarsian picturing is precisely a matter of relations to the extra-conceptual, and its position in Sellars's account of linguistic meaningfulness and intentionality is itself a case of the Sellarsian approach to transcendental questions as I described it.

6. In SM Sellars allows a different use of 'impression', in which impressions are conceptual representations (as in 'a visual impression that there is a man in the corner of the room'). In my Woodbridge Lectures I understood this as making explicit an idea of conceptual representations that are themselves shapings of sensory consciousness, and so do not need to be accompanied by sensations for there to be a sensuous or qualitative aspect to enjoying them. That made it puzzling for me why Sellars thinks a complete account of perceptual experience needs to include sensations, which are nonconceptual, as well as those conceptual representations. It was in that context that I attributed to Sellars that

conception of the transcendental project as undertaken from outside the conceptual order, with sensations playing a role in the part of the project that relates specifically to the conceptual goings-on involved in perception.

Here (at last) is a substantive point of Sellars interpretation on which I think deVries is right to object to me. I think deVries is right that Sellars does not envisage conceptual representations that are themselves shapings of sensory consciousness.

The interesting question that remains is whether he should. I thought crediting Sellars with that conception of perceptual experience, as I had not done in *Mind and World*, improved the philosophy I was finding in him. And I still think the conception is better than the one that, as deVries argues, Sellars holds. So, granting, as I do, that deVries is right that the conception is not in Sellars, I think that is a pity. This is a complex matter, and I shall here say only a couple of things about it.

First, Sellars's wish to acknowledge an intimate connection between the sensuous or qualitative aspects of experience and some conceptual goings-on is not restricted to the remark deVries cites about painters and musicians. In the same context (SK, p. 305), Sellars says, about visual perception itself, that it 'is not just a conceptualizing of colored objects within visual range—a "thinking about" colored objects in a certain context—but, in a sense most difficult to analyze, a *thinking in color* about colored objects'. This is phenomenologically insightful on Sellars's part. And it would have been easier for him to accommodate the insight if he had seen his way to the idea that the conceptual goings-on in perception are conceptual shapings of sensory consciousness itself, rather than standing in an intimate and mysterious relation to distinct goings-on in sensory consciousness.

Second, why does Sellars think it is compulsory to credit the sensuous or qualitative aspect of perceptual experience to a separate nonconceptual element in the story, distinct from the conceptual element? The short answer is that he thinks that is the only way to respect a Kantian insight: the insight that—to put it in Kantian terms—sensibility by itself does not yield cognition. But this is wrong. In my paper 'Sensory Consciousness in Kant and Sellars' (forthcoming in *Philosophical Topics*), I show how the insight can be accommodated by a different reading of Kant, in which intuitions are occurrences in sensory consciousness itself, informed by capacities that belong to the understanding.

I attributed a transcendental exploitation of sensations to Sellars to answer the question why, given that he already had conceptual shapings of sensory consciousness in his picture, he thought he needed nonconceptual sensations as well. What I am conceding to deVries is that my question had a false presupposition; Sellars does not have conceptual shapings of sensory consciousness in his picture. But the thought that invoking nonconceptual sensations can contribute to the transcendental project, in connection with the conceptual goings-on in perception, can now serve for me as an explanation (one among others) of why Sellars is blind to the fact that there is an alternative—a better alternative, in my view—to his reading of Kant on sensibility.

7. DeVries ends with two problems he says I face if I am to fill in my position.

The first challenge is to specify the difference between a content's being the content of a visual experience and its being the content of an auditory experience. But why not say the difference is already specified in the formulation of the supposed challenge? And if more is needed, I am no worse off than Sellars. For these purposes, what is important about Sellars's account of the difference between visual and auditory sensations is not the 'vague and arm-wavy' character deVries notes, but the fact that it is based on a differentiation Sellars simply presupposes, between visual and auditory *proper sensibles*. What characterizes visual sensations, say, is supposed to be that they display similarities and differences that line up with the similarities and differences among perceptible colours and among visually discriminable shapes. If Sellars can simply assume that the proper sensibles of vision are colours and visually discriminable shapes, so can I. So I can say that an experience that discloses to one that a locomotive is approaching is visual if its content includes colours and visually discriminable shapes. Analogously with what it is for an experience to be auditory. If Sellars has more to say about the principles on which the proper sensibles of the different senses are to be distinguished, I can take it over from him.

DeVries poses the second challenge by remarking that 'an ostensible object's ostensibly impressing itself on a subject is not and cannot be a case of causation'. This is at best overstated. An ostensible object's ostensibly impressing itself on a subject can be an actual object's actually impressing itself on a subject. And an object's impressing itself on a subject *is* a case of causation. It is true that if the object and the impressing are *merely* ostensible, the ostensible impressing cannot be the causation it seems to be. But there is no problem about the idea of an experience in which it seems—merely seems—to a subject as if an object is impressing itself on her; that is, as if there is an instance of that kind of causation. This is simply an application of Sellars's treatment of 'the logic of "looks"'. How things knowably are, in a case of perception, can be the same as how, in a case of merely seeming to perceive, things merely seem to be.

DeVries seems to think the passage in SK that he cites as a 'wonderfully prescient discussion' of the way I use 'ostensible' *shows* that this sameness at the level of conceptual content needs to be underpinned by a sameness at the level of nonconceptual sensations. That is certainly something Sellars thinks. But whether he is right to think so is just what is in question. It is merely presupposed, not argued for, in that passage in SK. Sellars thinks it is established by the 'sense-impression inference', but I have put that in dispute. By calling it a 'wonderfully prescient discussion', deVries implies that in that passage Sellars anticipates and responds to my contrasting proposal, but that is simply not so.

Hans Fink

1. Philippa Foot's ethical naturalism, as I understand it, takes ethics to be concerned with facts about 'what animals of a particular species [the human

species] need in order to do well in the sort of life they naturally live'. (That is wording Fink quotes from me.) But it makes a great difference how we understand the idea that ethics is—as I have, with studied vagueness, formulated the thought—*concerned* with such facts.

There is a temptation to interpret the idea on the following lines. (Fink speaks of a sort of ethical naturalism that, as he says, Foot's naturalism 'comes quite close to exemplifying', and he is talking about a position that conforms to this interpretation of the idea.) Facts about what human animals need in order to do well in the sort of life that is characteristic of our species serve as a *grounding* for ethical reflection. The picture is that those facts—the facts about 'the animal side of human nature', as Fink puts it—are available for investigation independently of our employment of what we take to be rationality in addressing ethical questions. If the grounding facts are the facts about the animal side of human nature, it would be hard to preclude those putative exercises of rationality from being understood to engage a side of our nature other than the animal side. But the facts about the animal side of our nature, on this view, would *validate* those putative exercises of our practical intelligence, at least the ones that deserve to be validated, thereby—if it turns out that we get enough right by such standards—reassuring us that the propensities in question really deserve the honorific titles of rationality and intelligence.

In the paragraph Fink quotes from the beginning of my 'Two Sorts of Naturalism', I was introducing a paper in which my aim was to draw attention to a risk that Foot's naturalism might be interpreted—misinterpreted, I think—on those lines. On a different reading, which I meant to be exhorting Foot to espouse explicitly, there is no question of finding a validation of ethical reflection, from outside itself, in facts about a separated side of our human nature, the animal side. There is no question of human nature's having an animal *side*, with the implication that it also has a side that is not animal. On this view, our lives are animal lives through and through; it is just that we are animals of a rather special kind. The capacity to engage in rational reflection about how we should live belongs to our nature, as the kind of animals we are, no less than, say, the capacity to walk on two legs. And to speak of trying to achieve correct views about what human animals need in order to do well in the sort of life we naturally live is not to describe a kind of investigation that would be distinct from putatively rational reflection about ethical questions. It is not to describe an investigation of human nature whose results might show—from outside an attempt to gauge the strength of putative arguments, not framed in terms of human nature, for answers to ethical questions—the correctness of some conclusions rather than others, reached by trying to bring reason to bear on ethical questions. On the contrary, this talk of what animals of our species need in order to live well is just another way of describing the topic of ethical reflection itself—a mode of reflection whose aim is to have our thinking about what is ethically admirable, obligatory, and so forth shaped, so far as is within our powers, by responsiveness to rational considerations that bear on such questions. We do our best to line up our ethical thinking with reasons for thinking one thing rather than another. The invocation of nature is not supposed to point to a reassurance, external to our best efforts to be responsive to those reasons, that the results of our ethical reflection are as they should be.

The interpretation of Foot's naturalism is not Fink's topic. But his remark about how close her naturalism is to something I attack might encourage the thought that I conceive the attack as an attack on her naturalism. So I want to stress that I meant that paper of mine to separate a reading of her naturalism that is vulnerable to the attack from one that is not. I did not mean to saddle her with the reading according to which nature supplies an external validation for ethical reflection.

2. Fink urges that I need to say more about the content of a naturalism that would be acceptable according to me. He thinks what would serve my purposes is a completely unrestricted conception of the natural, according to which it includes absolutely everything. If I resist that, he suggests that '[I owe] an account of exactly where and how [I draw my] line between nature and something else, and in particular what the something else is supposed to be'.

As Fink notes, I indicate that I approve of a way of thinking for which I use a variety of labels, including 'Aristotelian naturalism', 'Greek naturalism', 'naturalism of second nature', 'relaxed naturalism', and 'liberal naturalism'. I suppose all those '-ism' phrases can easily look like descriptions of some positive doctrine, whose content I can then reasonably be asked to be more specific about. But I want to resist Fink's pressure to place myself in the landscape he so elegantly describes. Perhaps I should not have used such labels at all. In any case, I want to insist that they do the work I want them to do only in a certain sort of dialectical context, and one falsifies what I wanted to do with them if one lifts them out of the context and presses for a formulation of a positive doctrine they might be names for.

The point of the labels is inextricably connected with a perfectly intelligible temptation towards a scientistic naturalism. That phrase does label a positive thesis, or—better—a family of theses. In its crudest form, a scientistic naturalism is purportedly universal in scope or coverage. The claim is that absolutely all the things we can talk about—all objects, all properties and relations, all facts—are capturable by means of the conceptual apparatus that is characteristic of the natural sciences. But, as that formulation indicates, the thesis, though ontologically universal, is ideologically restrictive; any conceptual apparatus that cannot be represented as bringing things within the reach of the kind of comprehension that the natural sciences achieve is, according to such a thesis, disqualified from capturing aspects of reality.

All kinds of options open up if we try to make such a thesis more precise. Does the conceptual apparatus that is characteristic of the natural sciences include the conceptual apparatus of pure mathematics? One could say 'Yes'. Or one could say 'No', but achieve the same effect, entitling oneself to a realism about the mathematical, by relaxing the claim that the vocabulary of the natural sciences covers everything there is. In the end the claim of universal coverage is not particularly important for me; I shall come back to this.

Here is another question: what does it take to represent some conceptual apparatus as bringing things within the scope of the kind of comprehension that is characteristic of the natural sciences? One could insist on conceptual reduction, but it is possible to preserve the spirit of this sort of naturalism while being less demanding about what counts as naturalizing a conceptual apparatus or vocabulary in the relevant sense.

Here is yet another question: if a vocabulary is disqualified, by a naturalism of this sort, from capturing aspects of reality, what status is still possible for it? Here options range from dismissing vocabulary that resists naturalization, in the relevant sense, as good for nothing, through conceiving some such vocabulary as available for expressing useful illusions (as in error theories of ethical discourse), to the more complex possibilities Sellars makes room for in limiting his '*scientia mensura*' claim to 'the dimension of describing and explaining the world'. (See the passage quoted in my comment on Willem deVries's paper.)

But none of this range of varying interpretations really matters for me. The point is the intelligible *spirit* of some thesis in the general area I have gestured towards. We can appreciate the temptation towards some version of a scientistic naturalism without needing to be precise about the details. For this purpose, it helps to invoke a simple answer to the question why the rise of modern science was, intellectually speaking, a good thing. I say 'intellectually speaking' to indicate that the question is meant to ask for something other than the fact that with the rise of science came the possibility of labour-saving machines and so forth. The answer I have in mind—putting it very crudely—is that the more science extended its reach, the less room was left for superstition. Where scientific understanding is available, we know there is no need to posit explanatory factors that are occult or magical: factors that are, in a word that is very helpful in this context, supernatural.

Now my use of those labels, 'relaxed naturalism' and the rest, comes in contexts in which I am considering the plausibility of theses to the effect that some region of human life exemplifies free responsiveness to reasons, with such theses understood to imply that the characteristic phenomena of those parts of human life are beyond the reach of natural-scientific understanding. And the point of the labels is captured by this thought: by dint of exploiting, in an utterly intuitive way, ideas like that of the patterns characteristic of the life of animals of a certain kind, we can insist that such phenomena, even though they are beyond the reach of natural-scientific understanding, are perfectly real, without thereby relegating them to the sphere of the occult or the supernatural. We can accept that a distinctively human life is characterized by a freedom that exempts its distinctive phenomena from natural-scientific intelligibility, without thereby being required to push it back into the region of darkness, the region supposedly occupied by phenomena that resist the light cast by natural science because they are occult or supernatural—a region whose extent has shrunk for us with the advent of a modern scientific outlook, in the most extreme version of the outlook to nothing at all.

Of course it is tendentious to use the word 'superstition' for continued belief that that region is not empty, and to use imagery of darkness for what would supposedly occupy that region. But someone who continues to believe the region is not empty, rejecting that tendentious description of it, might nevertheless acknowledge how unattractive it is to suppose that the supernatural includes human responsiveness to reasons. In its most extreme form, the restrictive naturalism that gives its point to my call for a relaxation says that *nothing* is supernatural. But for my purposes it is enough to consider a position that, without necessarily ruling out supernatural phenomena altogether, holds that at any rate they had better not be taken to include phenomena that are biological, in the sense that they are characteristic of the lives of animals of our species. The point of my call for a relaxation is this: the thought that such phenomena are natural, in the sense of not being supernatural, provides no ground for supposing that the conceptual apparatus that captures free responsiveness as such must be naturalizable, in any sense congenial to scientistic naturalism. It provides no ground for resisting a separation between the realm of freedom and the realm of phenomena completely explicable in terms of explanatory factors whose operations can be handled by the natural sciences. As I noted, there are various interpretations for the idea of a naturalization congenial to scientistic naturalism. I need not choose one: the point relates to the spirit common to any position in the area I gestured towards.

We can hold that free responsiveness to reasons is *extra*-natural, in a sense of 'natural' that suits scientistic naturalism, without thereby implying that it is *super*natural. So we can accept the thought that underlies the attractiveness of scientistic naturalism—the thought that it is a good thing to eliminate belief in the supernatural, or at least to confine it to a region that does not include human responsiveness to reasons—without taking ourselves to be obliged to engage in a project of naturalizing, in a scientistic-naturalistic sense, the distinctive features of human life. What 'natural' means, as the root of 'naturalism' in, say, 'relaxed naturalism' as I use that phrase, is: not supernatural (not occult, not magical, . . .). And there is no need for me to take a stand on whether *everything* is natural in that sense (thereby, among other things, giving needless offence to people who think respect for modern science is compatible with a kind of religious belief that preserves room for the supernatural).

Fink suggests that Wittgenstein's remark about our natural history, at *Philosophical Investigations* §25, expresses the unrestricted naturalism Fink thinks I should embrace. But I think the remark is better understood as expressing something like the different thought I have been trying to explain. That commanding and so forth belong to our natural history conveys that they are no more mysterious than walking and so forth. Wittgenstein's point is that we should not be tempted to find something *magical* in, say, a word's being a word for a thing. To make this point, he has no need to pronounce on whether or not it might be all right to find something magical in some other place. His thought need have no wider scope than what is explicit in his formulation of it.

3. When I wrote of 'Greek naturalism', I meant the naturalism I was finding in Aristotle's ethics. There was not meant to be an implication that any Greek thinker whatever would use the idea of the natural in the way I was considering. If my use of that phrase is taken in its context, there is no threat of an inconsistency with the presence in Greek thought of the materialistic and idealistic naturalisms that Fink finds in Plato's *Laws*.

Perhaps I should not have spoken of 'Aristotelian naturalism', given that, as Fink points out, Aristotle says that the virtues of character are not engendered in us by nature. Aristotle seems not to have a use for the word '*physis*' and its cognates that would allow him to say, for instance, that acting as virtue requires is as much a part of the natural history of a virtuous human being as walking, eating, drinking, playing. But I am inclined to say this is more a verbal than a conceptual point. In a passage Fink quotes, Aristotle conceives the virtues of character as realizations, brought about by habit, of capacities that belong to nature. That is just how the virtues are conceived in what I call 'naturalism of second nature'. It does not seem to me to matter if Aristotle does not explicitly conceive properties of persons of the kind he takes the virtues of character to belong to as natural properties of persons. There is an intelligible way of using the concept of the natural on which we can say that Aristotle conceives the virtues as natural to their possessors, even if he does not have a family of terms that would enable him to put it like that.

Christoph Halbig

1. Halbig thinks the weight carried by the concept of second nature in my approach to philosophical anxieties about empirical content requires me to have a constructive philosophy of nature. He does not want to let me get away with saying, as I do, that I need no more than a reminder of something one can easily forget in the throes of philosophy. Much of what I say in my comment on Hans Fink's paper is to the point here too, but I shall say a little more here, with specific attention to Halbig's way of putting the claim that I need to say more about nature.

2. The philosophical peace my reminder is supposed to bring is piecemeal and local, not a promised termination to philosophy *überhaupt*. I trace certain supposed problems about empirical content to a difficulty there can seem to be in combining the idea that conceptual capacities, conceived as aspects of our free responsiveness to reasons, are operative in perceptual experience itself, on the one hand, with the obvious thought that perceptual sensibility is a natural endowment, on the other. The supposed problems disappear—they are unmasked as illusions of problems, not real problems to which there is a solution—once we realize that the sense in which conceptual capacities are non-natural does not rule out the possibility that such capacities might shape our sensibility, natural as it is. Consistently with being non-natural in a sense that

connects with their belonging to freedom, conceptual capacities can be seen to belong to our second nature. And though sensibility is natural in a sense that belongs with its being something we share with non-rational animals, the operations of our sensibility can be informed by capacities that are distinctive to our second nature.

Halbig cites my response to a paper by Mischa Gubeljic, Simone Link, Patrick Müller, and Gunther Osburg, but oddly fails to mention that I there express *regret* for having aligned the distinction between first and second nature with the distinction between the realm of law and the space of reasons. Halbig cites a sentence in which I confess to having done that (from which I go on to renounce the alignment) as if it justified an unqualified attribution of the alignment to me.

There are two points to the renunciation.

First, 'the realm of law' was a bad attempt to capture the idea of a logical space that contrasts with what Sellars describes as 'the logical space of reasons'. What I wanted to bring into view was the realm of natural-scientific intelligibility, and it was wrong to suggest that all natural-scientific explanation is a matter of subsuming phenomena under law. In particular, that imposes a distorted understanding of biological intelligibility.

Second, the idea of second nature does not line up straightforwardly with the idea of the logical space of reasons. Our human second nature makes us inhabitants of the logical space of reasons. But the idea of second nature fits any propensities of animals that are not already possessed at birth, and not acquired in merely biological maturation (like, for instance, the propensity to grow facial hair on the part of male human beings), but imparted by education, habituation, or training. Trained dogs have a second nature in that sense. And the manifestations of the second nature of a trained dog, for instance obedience to commands, have an intelligibility that does not differ interestingly from the intelligibility of manifestations of its first nature. This kind of intelligibility, even though it attaches to phenomena of second nature, is not a matter of placement in the logical space of reasons.

Halbig thinks I face two questions about the distinction between first and second nature. First, what unifies them as two aspects of one thing, nature, and how are they connected? Second, what is the ontological status of the distinction?

In a remark Halbig quotes from my response to Gubeljic et al., I claim that the only unity I need, to answer the question why the first-natural and the second-natural are both modes of the natural, is captured by the contrast with the supernatural, the spooky, the occult. Halbig brushes that aside, on two grounds.

First, he thinks it ignores a possible position for the supernatural in ordinary unphilosophical thinking. But this seems wrong. Any thinking that traffics in the supernatural explicitly excludes the supernatural items it envisages from the realm of the natural. How could it be a problem, for a conception according to which what holds the idea of the natural together, in such unity as it has, is the contrast with the supernatural, that such a conception does not accommodate anything supernatural? It would be a problem if it did.

Second, Halbig suggests that there is a risk of triviality. This seems wrong too, for related reasons. If it is possible to suppose our free responsiveness to reasons belongs to a supernatural element in our makeup, perhaps one in virtue of which—to pick up on Halbig's suggestion of how the supernatural figures in a certain style of unphilosophical thinking—we are immortal, it cannot be *trivial* to affirm that the freedom that comes with rationality requires nothing super-natural. That is to affirm something denied by people who have the sort of belief Halbig alludes to.

That dispenses with the supposed risk of triviality. However, this should not be taken to imply that the addressees for my reminder of second nature are people who positively believe rationality is not natural. My reminder is addressed to people who get into philosophical difficulties because of not being able to see how, if rationality figures in explanations of a kind that cannot be lined up with the sort of explanation that displays natural-scientific intelligibility, phenomena that manifest rationality *can* be natural. It is for such people that the remark that phenomena that manifest rationality are second-natural can serve as a helpful reminder, a liberation from a philosophical anxiety. The other kind of person would not find the idea that free responsiveness to reasons is non-natural a source of philosophical anxiety in the first place.

The 'how connected?' limb of Halbig's first question seems urgent, I think, only against the background of an attempt to make something more contentious and theoretical out of my play with the idea of second nature than it is meant to be. In my response to Gubeljic et al. I express regret for my 'foothold' remark. I note that 'it seems to promise more, in the way of a continuity between the naturalness of human responsiveness to reasons and the naturalness of phenomena subsumable under natural law, than my purposes require' (and I might have replaced 'phenomena subsumable under natural law' with 'phenomena explicable in a natural-scientific way'). But Halbig insists on taking my 'foothold' remark as a gesture towards a structure in which the differentiation of first from second nature does substantial theoretical work. I acknowledge no obligation to elaborate such a structure. I should have restricted myself to the obvious claim that the second-natural is no less natural than the first-natural. There was no need to offer to make a connection between them beyond their both being natural.

Halbig's second question is about the ontological status of the distinction between first and second nature. I am doubtful whether it is helpful to see second nature, as such, as an ontologically distinct compartment of reality. The distinction between the first nature and the second nature of a dog is interesting, though perhaps not under that specification, to dog trainers, but it does not have the kind of interest—which might perhaps be called 'ontological'—that I attach to the distinction between the first nature and the second nature of a human being. It is not even the case that second nature as such is sharply divided from first nature, if the distinction is drawn as I have drawn it, in terms of whether a propensity is or is not acquired by education, habituation, or training. It comes naturally to domestic cats to bury their faeces. They are not born with the propensity to do this. I do not know if a kitten deprived of the companionship of adult cats, in particular its mother, starts burying its faeces when it reaches a certain age. Suppose the mother's example is essential. On that supposition, is acquiring this behavioural propensity a case of ordinary biological maturation—because learning to bury its faeces is just as much part of the normal maturation of a kitten as coming to be able to walk—or a kind of education? Is the propensity first-natural or second-natural? Nothing would turn on answering one way rather than another; if someone pressed the question, it would be perfectly reasonable just to shrug one's shoulders.

Halbig correlates values, conceived as there to be discovered in reality, with second nature. He concludes that on my picture 'our initiation into second nature opens our eyes to a different level of reality than that with which we were familiar before'. So as he understands it 'the distinction between first and second nature cannot be just the result of a useful methodological distinction but refers to a two-level structure within reality itself'. But I resist this. We need conceptual capacities, and so a second nature of the special human kind, in order to be familiar, in the distinctively human way, with reality at all—not just with values. Various interesting differentiations of level can be drawn within reality itself, including a separation of values from a level of reality that does not include instantiation of evaluative concepts. But that distinction of levels, which is no doubt ontological, is not to be aligned, in the way Halbig suggests, with the distinction between first and second nature.

3. Halbig says that what Hegel discusses under the heading of second nature is not equivalent to the issues at stake in my discussion of second nature. I do not believe that poses a problem for the suggestion that there my thinking has a Hegelian character. As I noted, I appeal to second nature in the context of a particular philosophical anxiety, focused on this question: if free responsiveness to reasons is beyond the reach of natural-scientific understanding, how can it not be unnatural? The point of the appeal to second nature is that being beyond the reach of natural-scientific understanding is not the same as being unnatural. The remarks Halbig considers from Hegel about habit, and about the internalization of the ethical life of one's community, are not offered in such a context. Indeed, so far as I know, Hegel does not address the philosophical anxiety that I try to unmask as based on a mistake. But there can still be an affinity between where I end up, in the interest of showing that anxiety to be one that we need not feel, and where Hegel ends up, not having arrived there in that way.

Those remarks from Hegel about second nature are, as far as I can see, consistent with the way I use the notion of second nature. Halbig says that legal or ethical norms that an individual does not identify with but nevertheless feels normatively subject to would be part of second nature in my sense, but not Hegel's. This seems wrong to me. The feeling of subjection would no doubt have to be second nature in my view, but I see no reason not to suppose it would be second nature in Hegel's view too. (There can be no guarantee that a second nature is as it should be.) Why does Halbig think those alien but still supposedly authoritative norms, which perhaps do not deserve to be recognized as norms at all, would themselves have to belong to second nature in my sense? Whose second nature would they belong to? If there are people who identify with them, their identification with the norms would be part of the second nature of those people, for me and Hegel alike. The norms, or apparent norms, themselves are another matter. Halbig's thought here seems to belong with his idea, which I resisted, that for me second nature includes an evaluative and normative level in the reality that human beings confront, as opposed to constituting a region of the nature of human beings (and, less interestingly, other animals) themselves.

Halbig focuses on §381 of the *Encyclopedia*, where Hegel says spirit is the truth of nature, which vanishes in this its truth. As Halbig rightly says, the point cannot be that nature disappears from the scene with the advent of spirit: 'What vanishes . . . is not Nature itself, but only Nature's claim to be the adequate form of the Idea'. On the strength of this passage, Robert Pippin credits Hegel with 'leaving nature behind', but the truth is that Hegel's progressions leave nothing behind. Rather, their earlier stages are reconceived, as 'moments' in a larger totality. In so far as nature is something we belong to, the idea of seeing it as a 'moment' in a totality that includes spirit is quite a good fit for the general shape of the way of thinking we are left with by my response to the philosophical anxiety I try to deal with.

It is true that my piecemeal move does not involve anything analogous to the Hegelian thought that nature in general is an incomplete realization of the Idea. But it is not clear that that thought is beyond my reach. A domesticating gloss on it might start like this: nature is intelligibly what it is only as part of a package whose unifying principle is—to pick up on that passage from the *Encyclopedia*—an understanding of the unity of thinking subject and object of thought.

Halbig is confident that such Hegelian conceptions cannot be domesticated. That is why he is so sure that my 'therapeutic' approach, in which illusions of problems are unmasked by reminders of the obvious, is alien to Hegel's approach. He thinks Hegel's conception of reality as the realm of 'objective thoughts' is an idealism that implies a rejection of ontological realism. I think this is a mistake. The identity of subject and object in thought *can* be domesticated. What it comes to, formulated in terms other than Hegel's own, is that reality is everything that is the case, and what is the case is what can be truly thought to be the case. Correctly understood, I think that is truistic.

Obviously this raises issues too large to deal with here. But I think there is plenty of scope for resisting Halbig's reading of Hegel, according to which he puts forward 'a hyperbolic system', something difficult or impossible for us to accept. There is plenty of scope for taking Hegel's project to be, rather, on these lines: to make clear a way of thinking composed of elements that are—when properly understood, which can take a lot of work—innocuous, like Wittgenstein's reminders, put together in such a way as to ensure that certain sorts of philosophical difficulties cannot arise if one holds fast to framing one's thinking in that way.

4. I shall end with some points of detail.

First, Halbig credits me with the idea that 'in experience our conceptual capacities are exercised in a *passive* way'. I am not happy with this formulation, for two reasons. First, just because of the passivity, this actualization of conceptual capacities is not felicitously described as an *exercise* of them. (See also my comment on Michael Williams's paper.) And second, though it is not wrong to say that the actualization of conceptual capacities I envisage in experience is passive, that is not by itself enough to capture the character of the conception of experience I recommend. Conceptual capacities are passively actualized when, for instance, one is involuntarily struck by a thought—perhaps a sudden realization that one has forgotten to do something one intended to do. What is special about perceptual experience is not yet in view if we speak of conceptual capacities being actualized passively. The actualization of conceptual capacities in perceptual experience is not just passive, but *receptive*. That is why experience, on this conception, can be seen as enabling the world itself to be present to a subject's rationality.

Second, Halbig attributes to me a 'critique of competing theories of the foundations of ethics like that of Aristotle in Bernard Williams' interpretation . . . or that of Philippa Foot'. This is the misreading of my discussion of Foot that I consider at the beginning of my comment on Hans Fink's paper. I do not think Foot's naturalism should be seen as a theory of the foundations of ethics. My point in discussing such theories in connection with her was that some of her formulations risked being taken that way, and I wanted to urge her to distance herself from any such interpretation. I do not myself espouse anything appropriately describable as a theory of the foundations of ethics, with which other such theories might be seen as competing. Particular ethical judgments are justified by whatever arguments one can muster in favour of them; as I see things, there is no ground for supposing the practice of justification in ethics can be organized into a foundational structure.

Third, Halbig follows Michael Quante in urging that 'our point of view', in *Encyclopedia* §381, must be the point of view of common sense. Quante and Halbig evidently think it cannot be the philosopher's point of view because from that point of view it is clear that spirit is the truth of nature, and Hegel says that from our point of view nature is the presupposition of spirit. But this depends on assuming that the claim that nature is the presupposition of spirit is inconsistent with the claim that spirit is the truth of nature. (Halbig says the former claim cannot be identical to the latter, but it is obscure why mere non-identity should seem to show that the two claims cannot be made from the same point of view.) It does not seem compulsory to suppose that the two claims are inconsistent. On a different reading, those wordings are two ways of saying the same thing—two ways of expressing the thought I put, above, by saying nature is intelligibly what it is only as a 'moment' in the unity of subject and object in the concept. On this reading, the point of view for the whole sentence is the point of view of philosophy. This makes for a smoother reading of the sentence.

Finally, Halbig reads a remark of mine, in which I suggest that second nature can drop out of the picture once my reminder has done its work, in terms of Wittgenstein's image of a ladder that is to be thrown away after one has used it to climb up to a vantage point from which one can see things aright. But that Wittgensteinian echo is wrong for the thought I meant to be expressing. Wittgenstein's ladder is a series of what look like meaningful propositions, concerning which one comes to realize, at the end of working through them, that they were not meaningful after all. So they must be discarded as the nonsense they were all along, though working through them, under the false impression that they were not nonsense, has led one to see things aright. And of course my remark was not meant to imply that it is *nonsense*—though perhaps useful—to say that responsiveness to reasons is second nature to human beings. On the contrary, I think it is correct, and indeed obvious; that is why it has the status of a reminder.

The context for my remark was Robert Pippin's suggestion, in connection with the passage in the *Encyclopedia* Halbig focuses on, that Hegel's approach to spirit 'leaves nature behind'. What is right about this is that nature does not have a positive thematic role in Hegel's approach to spirit. My point was simply that it does not have a positive thematic role in mine either. And that is so independently of the differences I considered in the previous section of this comment.

Stephen Houlgate

1. With some hesitation, in view of my amateur status, I want to suggest that Houlgate's reading of the material he considers from Hegel's philosophy of subjective spirit is questionable on some points. Partly for that reason, I think the contrast he draws between me and Hegel is exaggerated. (Though of course I would not want to represent myself as a faithful disciple of Hegel in every respect.)

2. In *Mind and World*, I said—using Kantian terminology—that receptive sensibility does not make an even notionally separable contribution to its cooperation with the spontaneous understanding.

I may have seemed to be denying that one can draw even a notional distinction between sensibility and understanding. But that would be absurd. What else is one doing when one talks of a cooperation between them? Sensibility is responsiveness, mediated by sense organs, to features of the environment; understanding is the capacity for conceptual thought. Sensory responsiveness on its own does not enable its possessors to think; the capacity for thought on its own does not provide for sensory responsiveness to features of the environment. That is a sketch of a distinction—notional, if you like—between the two capacities that cooperate in experience on the Kantian picture.

What I denied was not that sensibility and understanding are, at least notionally, distinguishable, but that sensibility makes an isolable contribution *to experience*. The point was that experience is not to be understood in terms of the idea that sensibility provides something without the form characteristic of thought, on which understanding proceeds to impose that form.

I think that is a Kantian insight (though I would not claim that Kant's grip on it is firm). And sometimes Houlgate's Hegel seems to have a version of the insight. For Houlgate's Hegel, like Kant, the availability of objects to us in perceptual experience cannot be understood just in terms of their causal impact on our sense organs. On the contrary, the capacity of experience to make objects available for cognition is intelligible only on the basis that experience draws on our powers of thought. And Houlgate tells us, on Hegel's behalf, how *not* to understand this: 'It is not the case . . . that we *first* have bare sensations or intuitions and only afterwards bring thought to bear on what we see. As mature human beings, we have sensations only in so far as we intuit things, and we intuit things only in so far as we employ empirical concepts and general logical categories and so exercise both our imaginative and conceptual capacities'. I think that is almost exactly right. (I have a reservation about 'exercise', which I shall come to. But for now I can leave that aside.) I would put the point like this: the sensational character of our (mature human) perceptual experience—unlike occurrences in the sensibility of human infants and non-human animals—can be properly understood only as an aspect of our sensory consciousness of objects, which, to be the consciousness *of objects* that it is, must be informed by our powers of thought. The sensational aspect of our experience comes into view only as a result of prescinding from the involvement of our powers of thought in our experience.

For my present purposes it does not matter that Hegel does not formulate this idea exclusively in terms of understanding, which would make his version of the insight a detailed match for Kant's. As Houlgate notes, Hegel reserves the concept of understanding for just one of the three modes of consciousness he distinguishes, in a classification that corresponds to the stages of the progress of consciousness in the *Phenomenology*. (Houlgate does not remark on this correspondence, perhaps because it might seem to recommend qualifying his suggestion that the *Phenomenology* is not germane to the Hegelian thinking he wants to consider.) But we can register a convergence between Hegel's thinking about experience and Kant's by a generic appeal to our powers of thought, as I did above, without needing to go into the detail Houlgate rehearses about the faculties that are operative, according to Hegel, when our powers of thought are in play.

However, Houlgate's Hegel's grip on the insight seems shaky. Elsewhere Houlgate formulates the thought he attributes to Hegel like this: 'Human beings do not have—or, rather, are never aware of—any raw, unconceptualised sensations'. The implication of the afterthought is that we do have raw, unconceptualized sensations, though we are not aware of them. And that is a version of what I meant to be rejecting, and what I took it we are required to reject by a Kantian insight, which I would be surprised if Hegel does not share. On this picture sensibility does after all yield items without the form characteristic of thought, and our intellectual capacities proceed to work up those deliverances of sensibility into something that has that form.

In the version of this picture Houlgate finds in Hegel, this happens without our being conscious of it. Sensibility yields its raw, unconceptualized input in a way that does not impinge on our consciousness, and the intellectual activity by which we impose on it a form suitable for thought goes unnoticed by us. (Houlgate speaks repeatedly, on Hegel's behalf, of unnoticed intellectual activity operative in the generation of experience.) But it is not clear why this move—relegating the supposedly isolable contribution from sensibility, and the intellectual activity that supposedly works it into a different form, to a position below the threshold of consciousness—should seem to open any relevant distance between this position and the one that Houlgate, rightly in my view, says is not Hegel's: the position according to which we first have bare sensations and then bring our powers of thought to bear on them.

The idea that we have raw, unconceptualized sensations, though we are not aware of them, seems unHegelian to me. Houlgate quotes Hegel saying, in the *Science of Logic*: 'Logic permeates every relationship of man to nature, his sensation, intuition, desire, need, instinct'. *Qua* unconceptualized, raw sensations would be untouched by logic, and so would fall outside the scope of Hegel's affirmation that logic is pervasive in a distinctively human relation to nature. But the affirmation is surely not meant to leave room for exceptions.

Of course logic can have that pervasiveness only in the lives of thinking beings. In that remark from the *Logic*, 'man' must be meant to apply to mature human beings, not members of the human species in general. Human infants, like non-human animals, have sensibility. They have sensations that logic does not permeate, since they cannot yet engage in thinking, the activity governed by logic. This can make it tempting to suppose we can discern a sensational element in, or prior to, our perceptual experience, corresponding to the sensations of infants (and non-human animals) in being unaffected by our powers of thought. And Houlgate's Hegel does not fully resist this temptation. Houlgate writes:

> Hegel believes that we can isolate the distinctive contributions to experience made by our passive, receptive sensibility and the unnoticed activity of thought. Yet he also insists that in concrete human experience these two contributions are inseparable. As very young children, we can be aware of sensations without any understanding of objectivity. In more mature human beings, however, the (unnoticed) activity of thought confers objectivity on sensory content *as* the latter is being received into the mind.

I have a reservation, which I shall come to later, about the talk of unnoticed activity of thought. But I can put that on one side for now and still find something right in the last part of this. As soon as sensory content is received into a mature human mind, it is already equipped with objective purport, already conceptually informed. But then what is left of the idea Houlgate attributes to Hegel at the beginning of the passage I have quoted, the idea that we can isolate a distinctive contribution to experience made by our passive, receptive sensibility? In a picture in which sensory content is already conceptually informed as soon as it is in the mind of a mature human being, what place is there for an isolable contribution to our mature human experience from our passive, receptive sensibility?

If objectivity is conferred on sensory content as it is being received into the mind, the picture must be that the supposedly isolable contribution from our passive, receptive sensibility is to be found only in an antechamber of the mind. A successor to that separable contribution gains admittance to the mind only through having been worked on by the unnoticed activity of thought. Once through the door, sensory content is no longer the separable contribution from sensibility it previously was. But now we confront, again, the question why this should seem importantly different from the picture Houlgate, rightly in my view, says Hegel rejects: the picture according to which we first have raw sensations and then work them into shape. Why should it make a difference to suppose this happens before sensory content gets to figure in our consciousness?

3. Talk of intellectual activity, which would have to be unnoticed, is central in what Hegel says about the position of powers of thought in a proper understanding of our experience. As Houlgate notes, that is a continuation of something already to be found in Kant.

I think Houlgate misformulates the Kantian ancestor of this Hegelian talk, and he carries the misformulation over into how he reads the Hegelian descendant. Kant says that the function that gives unity to an intuition is the same function that gives unity to a judgment. That is not to say that experiencing *is* judging, as Houlgate implies. Kant does not say that. Nor, so far as I can see, does Hegel. Houlgate cites Hegel connecting the idea of experience with the idea of knowing-that. An implication of that could be put by saying that the content of experience is content that could be the content of a judgment. (That might be the beginning of a gloss on Kant's remark that the same function gives unity both to judgments and to intuitions. Interpreting this needs some care; see 'Avoiding the Myth of the Given'. There must be articulation if the content of an experience is to become the content of a judgment.) But this connection between the content of experience and the content of judgment does not imply that experiencing itself *is* 'a judging-that', as Houlgate suggests. In the view shared by Kant and Hegel, perceptual experience is inseparable from the making of judgments, as Houlgate says. But that is because the ability to enjoy intuitions is inseparable from the *ability* to make judgments (the same function of unity is in play in both cases), not because to enjoy an intuition is itself to make a judgment.

On the strength of this misstatement, as I believe it is, of the connection between the capacity for experience and the capacity to judge, Houlgate attributes to Hegel this thought: 'Strictly speaking ... we do not *see that* things are thus and so; rather, in seeing we *judge* that things are thus and so'. I do not believe Houlgate justifies this attribution. (I shall come back to this.)

It is true, however, that Kant talks of intellectual activity operative in the generation of intuitions. What I have been objecting to is just the claim that he identifies that intellectual activity with the activity of judging. In the opening section of the B Deduction (§15) he says that all combining is an act of the understanding, and he implies that we engage in some acts of combining without being aware of doing so. This opens into a discussion of a notion of intuitions as exemplifying categorial unity. It is natural to suppose he leaves room, in the opening section, for unifying acts we engage in without being conscious of them in order to accommodate acts of the understanding responsible for the unity of intuitions. And Houlgate is surely right that the 'unnoticed activity' strand in the Hegelian material he considers is a continuation of this strand in Kant.

Now if we take the talk of unnoticed intellectual activity conferring objectivity on sensory content (as Houlgate puts it) at face value, it imports, irresistibly I think, the idea of sensory content as it was before objectivity was conferred on it. One might put that by saying Houlgate was right, given his assumptions, to back off from the claim that we do not have raw, unconceptualized sensations, and replace it with the claim that we are not aware of them. But as I have urged, the result is a position that will not cohere with the insight Houlgate also wants to attribute to Hegel, the insight that we do not first have bare sensations and then bring thought to bear on them. It does not help to say we are not aware of sensations on which thought has not yet been brought to bear. The idea that we have them is enough to make trouble.

Something has to give. We could change our minds about its being an insight that we do not first have bare sensations and then bring thought to bear on them. But everything falls into place if we read the talk of unnoticed intellectual activity as no more than a *façon de parler*.

Staying, for simplicity, with Kant's version of the picture, what he wants to say is this: experience makes objects available for cognition only because our powers of thought are operative in the constitution of experience. Our powers of thought belong to a faculty whose essential character is revealed in its active employment in judging. That is why it is right to describe the faculty in terms of spontaneity. And that gives a kind of appropriateness to bringing intellectual activity into the picture—to put the point with studied indeterminateness—whenever we want to say the faculty is in play.

But there is a difference between the following two claims: first, that the constitution of experience involves a faculty to whose identity it is essential that it is the faculty we exercise in intellectual activity; and second, that experience results from our actually engaging, without being aware of it, in intellectual activity. I acknowledge, of course, that Kant says the second kind of thing, and so does Hegel in the context of his more complex picture of the 'mental operations' involved in experience. But I have been urging that if we take such talk at face value, we lose the insight that, to echo the remark Houlgate quotes from the *Logic*, logic permeates even the sensational aspect of our distinctively human relation to the world. We commit ourselves to countenancing a sensational precursor to full-fledged experience, a sensational element in our relation to the world to which logic does not penetrate: sensory content on which objectivity has not yet been conferred. To preserve the insight expressed in Hegel's claim that logic is pervasive in the human relation to the world, we need to understand the talk of unnoticed intellectual activity as no more than a vivid expression for something that would be more soberly put in the first of those two ways. Capacities whose characteristic expression is intellectual activity are operative in the constitution of experience. That is not to say, unless we are saying it only as a *façon de parler*, that experience acquires its objective purport through intellectual activity on our part.

For Hegel as Houlgate reads him, mere consciousness is unaware of the intellectual activity by which it differentiates its objects from itself, whereas intelligence 'is aware that it is active and that the world it experiences is opened up by its own intelligent activity'. What this comes to, if we read the talk of unnoticed activity as a *façon de parler*, is this: for consciousness, it is as if objects are immediately given to it, without any involvement on the part of powers of thought; whereas intelligence realizes that objects are not immediately given to it, in a sense of 'immediately' that excludes a role for powers of thought. We can put the point by saying intelligence sees what is wrong with the Myth of the Given. Nothing is lost here by not taking the talk of unnoticed intellectual activity at face value.

I would not dream of claiming that Kant is nowhere confused by the *façon de parler*, misled into taking it at face value and thereby putting his own insight at risk. And perhaps that is true of Hegel too. But if so, it is not something we should hold Hegel to. In our reading of him, we should not insist on the mode of expression that, if taken literally, threatens the insight he shares with Kant: to repeat, that we do not first have bare sensations and then work them into conceptual shape.

I am urging that we should take Hegel's talk of unnoticed intellectual activity to be no more than a vivid expression for the claim that powers of thought enter into the constitution of our experience. At one point Houlgate shows, I think, that he feels the attractions of such a proposal. Houlgate writes, on Hegel's behalf:

> Experience in the ordinary, everyday sense is ... the product of the cooperation of sensibility and various forms of understanding. Such understanding, though freely active, is not conscious and deliberate. Rather, our conceptual capacities are drawn into operation automatically on encountering things.

This last sentence is exactly right. But it is hard to see how Houlgate thinks it could be consistent with saying, as he does in the previous sentence, that in its involvement in experience, understanding is *freely active*. I suppose Houlgate says that because he thinks he needs to, in order to respect Hegel's talk of unnoticed intellectual activity. But I have urged that to preserve Hegel's hold on a central insight that he shares with Kant, we should do him the favour of not taking that talk at face value.

4. The pervasive role of 'positing' in Hegel's characterization of sensory experience of the world makes it seem a pressing question how it can be that he is not recommending a merely subjective idealism. Understanding Hegel's talk of 'positing' literally, as he does, Houlgate thinks Hegel is debarred from the idea that experience takes in objects and facts. Rather, objective and factual form is 'posited' by the mind, in unnoticed intellectual activity in response to bare sensations of which we have to suppose the mind is not aware. And that makes it seem that what we wanted to conceive as facts that we perceive to be the case are, according to Hegel, actually products of an intellectual construction on our part, only partly constrained by our sensory intake. How is that not a subjective idealism?

Houlgate's Hegel responds to the charge of subjective idealism by arguing that thought 'cannot but disclose the true character of being, because it is nothing but *being's own understanding of itself'*. Of course I do not want to dispute the Hegelian character of that claim. But, offered in this context, it leaves the temptation to find a subjective idealism *implied by Hegel's conception of sensory experience* pretty much untouched. The response Houlgate equips Hegel with seems to change the subject rather than answer the charge. Houlgate's Hegel holds that we do not take in facts or objects in sensory experience. He says we 'posit' them, in intellectual activity in response to deliverances of sensibility that do not amount to access to the facts or objects that, in ordinary thinking, we take ourselves to be enabled to know, or know about, in experience. Since thought is being's own understanding of itself, we are in a position to know *'a priori that there is . . . a world of spatio-temporal, causally connected objects out there'*. So we can be confident that if we take things to be as we seem to perceive them to be, our beliefs are not out of line with the a priori knowable character of reality. But if our seeming to perceive things to be a certain way is a result of 'positing' on our part, then our experiencing, even in the best sort of case, is not something that itself puts us in a position to know things to be a certain way. At best we can reassure ourselves that the result of the 'positing' has the sort of structure we know a priori a fact must have. Someone who was inclined to accuse Hegel of subjective idealism in connection with his conception of sensory experience might reasonably say: 'That is just what I was complaining about'.

Things look different if we understand the talk of 'positing' as no more than a way to give vivid expression to the insistence that conceptual capacities are operative in experience. Now we make it possible for Hegel to exploit a distinction unavailable to Houlgate's Hegel: the distinction, implicit in Sellars, between the mythical Given and the innocuous given. (See EPM, §1.) In a passage Houlgate cites, Hegel attacks the idea 'that the content or object is *given* to knowledge, something coming to it *from outside'*. As I read this, his point is that nothing is Given, that is, available for knowledge independently of the operation of conceptual capacities. And the idea that we can take in objects and facts in experience, as I spell it out, is only the innocuous idea of the given. It is exactly not an idea of an availability for knowledge that is independent of the operation of conceptual capacities. It is not in Hegel's target area.

Understood like this, Hegel's conception of experience allows him to rebut the accusation of subjective idealism directly. He does not need the change of subject that figures in Houlgate's reading. He does not need to deny that sensory experience has the cognitive character attributed to it by ordinary thought, the character of being, in the best kind of case, a taking in of facts and an awareness of objects.

Such denials figure at various points in Houlgate's reading. I drew attention earlier to a denial that depends on identifying the unnoticed intellectual activity that experience involves, on a face-value construal of Hegel's talk of 'positing', with judging. I urged that the identification is wrong anyway. But we do not require that identification to see that, if we take the talk of 'positing' at face value, Hegel cannot countenance the idea that experience is openness to facts and objects. And it is in this context that Houlgate credits Hegel with thinking that 'when we see a car going by . . . we do not actually *see* a car', and that when we take ourselves to see a tree, 'we do not actually *see* the tree, if "seeing" is taken in its precise sense'. However, if we take the talk of 'positing' as I have proposed, it does not require that divergence from common sense.

If Hegel does want to modify common sense in that way, that need not be connected with the role of 'positing' in his account of experience. There is a quite different line of thought that would motivate the claim that we do not actually *see* cars and trees.

Houlgate attributes to Hegel the idea that 'our visual and tactile sensations take in directly the look and shape of things'. But that cannot be right. It is inconsistent with the basic insight Hegel shares with Kant. Anything we take in in experience is available to us to be taken in only because our conceptual capacities are operative in the constitution of experience. The sensational aspect of experience is an abstractable element in experience's possession of objective purport, not something that already has objective purport on its own. So it is wrong to say that sensations themselves take in something—something we need to go beyond, in constructive intellectual activity, in order to equip ourselves with sensory content that is objective. In the only sense in which sensory experience takes in anything, what it takes in is that things are as they are represented to be by the sensory content of experience, which, as Houlgate's Hegel acknowledges, is conceptually informed as soon as it is received into the mind.

But this does not eliminate the possibility of a position according to which we do not strictly see cars and trees. Sellars distinguishes what we see, as common ways of talking would have it, from what we see *of* what we see, the proper and common sensibles that what we see instantiates. For instance, when in ordinary speech we would say we see a car, what we see *of* the car is something other than the car itself, perhaps its colour, shape, and motion or lack of it. It would be possible to introduce a notion of what we see, strictly speaking, that coincides with this notion of what we see *of* what we, speaking ordinarily, see. And for some purposes it would be a useful notion. Houlgate cites Hegel saying one can bring something's qualities before the eyes, but not the something itself. I think that belongs in this kind of context, not the kind of context determined by

Houlgate's exploitation of Hegel's talk of 'positing'. What we see *of* what we see is not something taken in by our visual sensations, from which we would need to go on, in an act of 'positing', in order to arrive at something with the form of thought. In seeing what we see *of* what we see, our seeing is already informed by our conceptual capacities. What is in question here is a restriction, well motivated for some purposes, on what conceptually informed content can count as strictly speaking *sensory* content—not a gesture in the direction of content that is not yet conceptually informed at all.

5. The departure I have urged from Houlgate's reading of Hegel dissolves, to a large extent, the contrast Houlgate wants to draw between my thinking and Hegel's. In the course of elaborating his suggestion that my analogue to the Hegelian idea that reason is in the world is 'more pared down' than Hegel's idea, Houlgate says Hegel holds both of two views that I think are incompatible: 'Hegel ... holds *both* that conceptual capacities are operative in receptivity *and* that our understanding works on the non-conceptual deliverances of sensibility'. But I have argued that Houlgate does not justify attributing the second of those views to Hegel. I have urged that that view is inconsistent with an insight Houlgate credits to Hegel, I think rightly: that our experience is not a matter of receiving bare sensations and working them up into conceptual form.

Houlgate suggests that my motivation for the claim that conceptual capacities are operative in experience diverges from Hegel's. My motivation turns on the requirement that experience should be something in the light of which judgments can be rationally warranted; Hegel's thought is that 'experience must involve understanding because without it no experience of "things" with "properties" and "causal" connections would be possible in the first place'. But I think this is only a difference of emphasis. I can easily bring my thinking into alignment with that characterization of Hegel's thinking. It is only if experience is intelligible as a *rational* openness to the world that it is intelligible as experience of the world at all.

It is true, and surely important, that nothing I have said about experience lines up with what Hegel does in the *Logic*. I have recommended a conception according to which experience instantiates forms that belong to thought. But I have not addressed the question what the forms of thought are. Hegel accuses Kant of dogmatically accepting his list of forms of thought from current logic. He offers to establish what the forms of thought must be, in a line of argument that avoids exploiting anything given from outside, but simply traces out a necessity inherent in thought itself. And as Houlgate puts it, thought, for Hegel, is nothing but being's own understanding of itself. So tracing out that inherent necessity is uncovering the a priori knowable character of being itself. I have not discussed this Hegelian project.

It would be absurd to say that *this* is only a difference of emphasis between me and Hegel. A central region of Hegelian thinking has been at most generically in my picture, in the shape of the unspecific invocation of the forms of thought.

(Whatever they are, I might say to play up this divergence.) But there is no problem in principle about the idea of a route to that region of Hegel from what I have urged about experience. Hegel gives determinacy to the invocation of the forms of thought, which figures without further specification in the account of experience I recommend. And there is a benefit to be had from arriving at the *Logic* by that route.

As I said, Houlgate's Hegel appeals to the a priori knowable character of reality *instead of* directly responding to the accusation that his conception of sensory experience implies a subjective idealism about the phenomenal world. If we take Hegel's talk of 'positing' literally, the accusation is no less pressing after Houlgate has brought in the *Logic*. For Houlgate's Hegel, the facts we thought we were taking in in perception are after all results of our 'positing'. A priori knowledge of the general character of reality serves as a sort of consolation for the loss of a conception according to which experience itself yields knowledge of how things are.

My Hegel, in contrast, has a direct response to the charge of subjective idealism. If experience is informed by conceptual capacities, it can open us to the layout of phenomenal reality. What, as common sense has it, we take in in experience is not a result of constructive intellectual activity on our part. In the only sense in which anything is taken in in experience, it is phenomenal facts themselves, not some supposed proto-objective correlates of raw, unconceptualized sensations, that are taken in. The *Logic* connects with this picture of experience in that it elaborates the idea of content that instantiates the forms of thought. The *Logic* is not, as in Houlgate's reading, a *substitute* for holding that experience takes in facts.

Insisting on this difference between my Hegel and Houlgate's is compatible with acknowledging that for Hegel, the knowledge that can be had by enjoying perceptual experience, conceptually structured as it is, is a second-class kind of knowledge, perhaps not even really deserving that honorific title, in comparison with the kind of knowledge that ranks as philosophical, knowledge of the a priori character of the world.

Sabina Lovibond

1. There is no conflict between insisting, for one purpose, on a discontinuity between rational animals and others, and acknowledging, for another purpose, a continuity that extends across that boundary. I welcome Lovibond's clarity about that.

As she notes, the language one chooses to express the continuity is optional. I have been explicit about that in the case of talk of conceptual capacities. It is not that everyone agrees about what conceptual capacities are, but there is a dispute about whether animals without language have them. If someone wants to stress the continuity across the traditional boundary between rational and non-rational animals by saying, for instance, that an animal that is capable of fleeing from danger is thereby shown to have the concept of danger, I need not object. That is just using the concept of a conceptual capacity in a different way from the way in which I find it helpful to use it in order to stress the discontinuity, and stressing the continuity is, in some contexts, a fine and necessary thing to do.

Lovibond is right that the same would hold for the concept of agency, which, for purposes of stressing the discontinuity, I reserved for behaviour informed by conceptual capacities in my narrow sense. If someone wants to talk of agency in connection with the self-moving behaviour of some non-rational animals, I have no substantive objection. My exclusion of non-rational animals from agency, in the demanding sense my remark involved, does not imply what MacIntyre rejects as, in Lovibond's words, a 'reductive picture of non-human animals as being set in quasi-mechanical motion by their environment'.

2. Lovibond connects the discontinuity I want to focus on with 'the traditional view of human beings as the uniquely *ethical* species'. At one point she describes the boundary between ethical animals—animals that can act in the light of a conception of living well in general—and other animals as 'a boundary which seems to be the one we have to cross in order to achieve the Gadamerian "free, distanced orientation" to our world'. I am sure it is right to connect the discontinuity that concerns me with the boundary between ethical animals and other animals, but I not sure about that definite description ('the one we have to cross . . .').

The discontinuity that interests me is on view already in connection with behaviour that, even though it manifests rationality in the sense that places us above the line between rational animals and the rest, cannot be understood as undertaken in the light of a conception of living well in general.

Consider, for instance, the difference between a person who understands schematic signposts pointing to the right and a non-rational animal that has been trained to go to the right in response to objects with that configuration. When the person goes to the right in response to a signpost, she does what she does for a reason, consisting in the fact that the signpost points to the right, as she understands. (This does not require her to advert to the fact that the signpost points to the right in the course of some procedure of thinking out what to do. Her response can be unthinking, but still manifest her understanding of the signpost and her rationality, in the shape of her ability to act as she understands the signpost to be telling her to act.) In the case of the matching (up to a point) response of the non-rational animal, there is nothing but its habituation-induced propensity to appeal to in making sense of the behaviour—nothing corresponding to the person's understanding of what the signpost means. Not that the idea of a habituated propensity is absent from our resources for thinking about the person who understands the signpost. But it is not the whole story. (Compare Wittgenstein's remarks at *Philosophical Investigations* §198.)

Only a creature capable of acting on an understanding, in the sense in which that idea fits the human signpost-follower and not the non-rational animal with a trained propensity to behave in a way that would externally match that of the human signpost-follower, could act in the light of a conception of living well in general. That is to say: only rational animals could be ethical animals, in the sense Lovibond works with. But her suggestion that the boundary between ethical animals and the rest just is the boundary I am interested in would require something different: that all rational animals are ethical animals. It would require that a rational animal—one with the 'free, distanced orientation' that comes with the ability to 'step back' from inclinations and determine whether there is really reason to act as they incline one to act—is just as such an ethical animal. And I am not sure how one might establish such a thesis.

3. Rehearsing MacIntyre's position, Lovibond writes:

> Only under the influence of a somewhat intrusive bit of *theory*, of the kind represented by the Gadamerian opposition of human 'world' to animal 'environment', might we be led to forget that much of the conceptual apparatus we use in interpreting human behaviour—the attribution of purposes, of action with one intention rather than another, of the ability to see a situation in one way or another and to correct mistakes, of the perception of a reason as sufficient, or again as insufficient, to deflect one from one's present course—that much of this, to repeat, is carried over into our interpretation of the behaviour of other intelligent animal species.

Her overall thesis, as I said, is that my stress on discontinuity will cohere with MacIntyre's stress on continuity, so that I can accept much of what MacIntyre urges. But I am not sure how much of the passage I have quoted she means to represent as, contrary to MacIntyre's sense of an opposition, congenial to me.

One point of possible contention is that by my lights the Gadamerian opposition of world to environment is not a bit of theory—any more than my restrictive use of the notion of conceptual capacities is a bit of theory, standing in opposition to a competing theory put forward by people who want to attribute conceptual capacities to non-linguistic animals. In both cases, what is in question is a terminological proposal aimed at providing a way of talking that plays up the discontinuity, without prejudice to the continuity.

But what I want to single out is the suggestion that there is no problem about crediting animals that are placed, in the way of thinking MacIntyre wants to discourage, on the other side of a divide from human beings with the capacity to perceive reasons as sufficient or insufficient to deflect them from courses of action.

In a part of his work that Lovibond discusses, MacIntyre inveighs against the Heideggerian idea that non-human perception lacks the 'as-structure'. MacIntyre insists that a dolphin or a gorilla 'recognizes individuals, notices their absences, greets their returns, and responds to them *as* food or *as* source of food, *as* partner or material for play, *as* to be accorded obedience or looked to for protection and so on'. And that is fine by my lights. Responding to something as food, on a perfectly intelligible interpretation of that idea, does not imply having the concept of food, on the demanding interpretation of what it is to have a concept that belongs with the idea of animals that are distinctive in being rational. So my restrictive use of the idea of conceptual capacities is perfectly consistent with allowing the 'as-structure' in contexts in which what follows 'as' is specifications of the sorts of things to which non-linguistic animals intelligently respond: food, partners, fellow members of the group, dominant members of the group, and so on.

But it is quite another matter to suggest that the 'as-structure' that comes with the intelligence of non-linguistic animals can extend to perceiving *reasons* as sufficient or not. There is no problem about taking a non-rational animal to have something in view as food or a partner. But being able to have something in view as a reason (sufficient or not: having something in view, we might say, as a candidate for being enough to act on) is exactly what, as I see things, distinguishes those animals that can respond to reasons as the reasons they are—rational animals—from those animals that can respond to reasons only in the sense that belongs with saying, for instance, that fleeing (something non-rational animals can perfectly well be capable of) is as such a response to danger, and danger is a reason for fleeing. Responding to danger by fleeing is responding to it *as* the reason it is only on the part of a subject who can raise the question whether here and now it is indeed a reason to flee. And that requires more than animal intelligence.

Guard dogs can be trained to be fierce in response to intruders but to recognize certain individuals and allow them to pass. I have it from James Conant that a dog's response to an individual it has been trained to allow to pass may show what it is natural to describe as signs of conflict. It may growl and bare its teeth, as if inclined to attack, but not attack. It would be merely fanciful to describe this by saying that the dog is partially swayed by a reason to attack—a person moving along the prohibited path—but perceives that reason as insufficient to deflect it from the course of allowing the recognized individual to pass. That would be to credit the dog with a capacity that I think it does not make sense to attribute to it: a capacity for genuine deliberation, for weighing the rational cogency of candidate reasons to act. Deliberation so conceived needs to be contrasted with what Hobbes says deliberation is, which there is no problem about supposing we have in the case of the guard dog torn between motivations: a competition of strength between inclinations, each no doubt rational in the way in which the inclination to flee is a rational response to danger, in which the last inclination left standing thereby constitutes itself as the animal's will, in the sense of the motivation it ends by following.

4. A couple of minor points.

First, at one place Lovibond credits me with a project of 'incorporating into a naturalized epistemology the Kantian notion of the mind's "spontaneity". Since

Quine's famous article with that title, the phrase 'naturalized epistemology' has, I think, belonged to a project of bringing epistemology within the purview of a kind of naturalism that I deplore. It would be better not to use it in connection with my project.

Second, Lovibond says, of the 'environment/world' contrast: 'It expresses a kind of dualism, but a dualism in the "non-rampant" style'. I would prefer not to describe it as any kind of dualism. I think it is worth keeping that label for divisions into two that are philosophically problematic, and it is Lovibond's own point in that remark that there is nothing philosophically problematic about the 'environment/world' duality.

Kenneth R. Westphal

1. Westphal begins by saying he and I agree that it is 'the fundamental task of contemporary epistemology' to establish a set of theses. This starts things off on the wrong foot. It ensures that he will fail to take the measure of the fact that my 'transcendental project' aims to vindicate the objective purport of thought not out of the blue, for its own sake, but in the face of a specific apparent difficulty—which I aim to unmask as merely apparent—about how our thought can have its objective purport. The apparent difficulty turns on how plausible it is to suppose that our thought could not have its objective purport if it were not possible for us to be rationally open to the world in perceptual experience. It can be difficult to see how that condition can be met, given that sensibility has an essential place in the constitution of anything recognizable as perceptual experience, and given that sensibility is a natural endowment, something we share with non-rational animals.

So described, my project is undeniably 'therapeutic', not aimed at establishing theses. Conceiving it that way is not some dispensable quirk on my part, as Westphal sometimes seems to suggest.

At the end of his paper he makes explicit a thought that, with hindsight, one can see to have shaped much of what he has said: that my 'therapeutic' aim debars me from being entitled to employ the Kantian conceptual apparatus of sensibility and understanding, receptivity and spontaneity. As a blanket prohibition, this seems bizarre. It would be a strange restriction on 'therapeutic' philosophy if it were not allowed to use philosophers' terms. They can be very helpful in displaying how supposed problems seem to arise. And it would be wrong to suppose such terms have no possible use except to put forward substantive philosophical theses. Once one has learned how terms like 'sensibility' and 'understanding' function, they can perfectly well figure in saying things with the obviousness that is requisite in Wittgensteinian reminders. It is an interesting question how much of what Kant and Hegel say can be understood in that spirit. Westphal does not address that question, though he would need to if he were to entitle himself to the sharp distinction he presupposes between their philosophical activity and mine.

Westphal says I do not use the Kantian terms either in Kant's sense or in some determinate sense of my own, which he suggests would have to be theoretically based. But even if everything he says in his paper were correct, he would be entitled to deny that I use the terms in Kant's sense only if that required accepting everything Kant wanted to say with them (interpreted as Westphal, sometimes contentiously, does). Westphal's idea is that, given that I do not accept everything in Kant, I would need to provide a set of definitions or axioms or some such thing to explain the terms, as opposed to letting what they mean emerge partly from the echoes of Kant and partly from the use I make of them. But I believe readers of reasonable good will have had no trouble in understanding what I do with, for instance, the ideas of receptivity and spontaneity, or in seeing that my exploitation of those ideas lines up quite well with Kant's, though of course I do not accept everything he says.

2. Westphal has blankly failed to understand my reading of Kant's B Deduction. He takes me to have implied that the footnote at B160 'solves the problem of the Transcendental Deduction'. He concludes from this that in my view the footnote could have replaced 'at least the second half of the B Deduction'. (It is not clear why, if he thinks I think the footnote solves the Deduction's problem, he does not take me to have implied that it could have replaced the whole of the Deduction.) In a note, he says that at the Warwick conference I recognized that this cannot be Kant's view. What I tried to get across to him at the Warwick conference was that I never said, or implied, that it is Kant's view; his reading of me is a travesty. Let me try once more to explain this.

The problem that according to me Kant addresses, in an argument whose thrust can be summarized in terms of that footnote, is not *the* problem of the Deduction, *tout court*: the problem, that is, of showing that the pure concepts of the understanding have objective validity. The B Deduction follows a complex strategy in attempting to show that. A specific sub-problem arises within the execution of that strategy. This sub-problem is the problem Kant faces in the second half of the B Deduction, in a line of argument whose essentials, I continue to insist, can be brought into focus by citing that footnote.

A logician might see that if she could establish a lemma, Q, it could play a role in a complex argument for a conclusion, P. So the problem of establishing Q might be the problem she faces at a certain juncture in her attempt to establish P by the complex argument in which Q is a lemma. What Westphal says about my reading of the B Deduction is as if someone took that to imply that establishing Q solves the problem of establishing P. Whereas of course establishing P would require the whole argument in which Q is a lemma.

Obviously I cannot give a full reading of the B Deduction here. But I shall try to say enough about its organization to explain that analogy. Westphal says nothing in his paper about the well-known issues relating to the two-part structure of the B Deduction. He would need to address those issues if he were to engage seriously with my reading.

In the Deduction's first half, Kant elaborates a conception of intuitions as instantiations in sensory receptivity of forms required by the pure understanding. This is potentially a move towards showing that those forms provide for objective purport. If he can entitle himself to suppose that it is thanks to their categorial form that intuitions make objects immediately present to subjects, that will display those forms as essential to what can be conceived as the ground-level case of objective purport.

But that abstract conception of intuitions does not suffice to show that the categorial form of intuitions is what accounts for their making objects immediately present to subjects. That is because the Transcendental Aesthetic can seem to have provided sensibility-related conditions, on *our* experience in particular, satisfiable independently of the understanding-related conditions that are Kant's concern in the Deduction. (The specific forms of our sensibility have not been in view in the Deduction's first half, as Kant emphasizes.) If those sensibility-related conditions are indeed independent, then the Aesthetic has yielded a self-standing account of a possibility for objects to be present to our senses. But if that is so, the requirement of categorial unity in intuitions is extra to something that suffices for sensory states enjoyed by us to be such that when we enjoy them objects are present to our senses. And in that case the categorial unity of intuitions pulls no weight in explaining how objects are present to our senses in sensory experience. The categorial unity of intuitions secures only that the objects that are present to our senses when we enjoy the sensory states that our intuitions are—instantiations of forms required by the pure understanding not just in sensory receptivity in general, but in our sensory receptivity in particular—are thinkable.

It is true that, since we cannot know objects except through our powers of thought, sensory states in which objects were present to our senses without being thinkable would be nothing to us (see B132). But even so, if there could be such states, the requirement of thinkability would be additional to the satisfaction of a condition that suffices for objects to be present to the senses in our sensory states. And that would include the sensory states that are not nothing to us, intuitions. Only states in which objects are given to us in thinkable form can provide us with subject matter for exercises of our powers of thought. But that is a mere tautology. It cannot help towards showing that conformity to the requirement of thinkability— conformity to the pure concepts of the understanding—has anything to do with the capacity of states of our sensory consciousness to relate to objects at all.

This is why, at the start of the second half of the B Deduction, Kant undertakes to show, 'from the mode in which … empirical intuition is given in sensibility, that its unity is no other than that which the category … prescribes to the manifold of a given intuition in general' (B145). Here Kant is setting out to ward off the threat that the presence of objects to our senses is provided for by conformity to the requirements of our sensibility, independently of any condition involving thinkability.

In the second half of the Deduction, Kant does just that. He argues that the unity of the mode in which empirical intuition is given in our sensibility, the unity involved in the requirement of ordering in space and time, is not other than the categorial unity that is central to the conception of intuitions elaborated in the first half. This is the argument whose drift can be encapsulated in terms of the footnote at B160. The conclusion of this argument—a lemma in the argument of the Deduction, not something that by itself does the Deduction's work—is that the requirements of our sensibility are not satisfiable independently of the requirement of categorial structure. And now Kant can claim, in effect, that the idea of an object's presenting itself to our senses coincides with the idea of our enjoying an intuition, something with categorial structure. He can say, of 'whatever objects may *present themselves to our senses*' (B159: I shall comment on this citation below), that it is in intuitions, with their categorial unity, that they are given to us. There is, after all, no possibility of objects being present to our senses otherwise than in intuitions. It was that seeming possibility that threatened to leave the categorial structure of intuitions an idle wheel in an account of how it is that our intuitions are of objects.

As Westphal says, the formal intuitions Kant considers in the note at B160 are not to be identified with the forms of our sensibility, and neither of these is to be identified with the spatial or temporal form of any actual object of intuition. I cannot see why he thinks this matters. The third item is irrelevant. As for the first two, it is clear that Kant thinks they are closely connected. Otherwise it would be mysterious why he should suppose that the argument of the Deduction's second half—which turns on the unity of the formal intuitions—discharges the undertaking at the beginning of the second half (B145, quoted above), to show that the unity of the mode in which empirical intuition is given in (our) sensibility is no other than the unity prescribed by the category to the manifold of a given intuition in general (the unity he has just given a summary account of, in §20). And it is quite reasonable for Kant to think there is a close connection between the formal intuitions and the forms of our sensibility. There is a unity implicit in the idea of space, say, as a form of our sensibility, and it is that unity that is made explicit in an account of the unity of the formal intuition, space. It seems right to say, contrary to one of Westphal's uncomprehending rebukes to me, that the note at B160 concerns, broadly speaking, the way our sensibility is formed. It is indirectly concerned with that topic, by way of its direct concern with the unity of the formal intuitions.

3. In the sketch of a reading of the B Deduction that I have just given, I repeated a citation of B159 that draws Westphal's fire. He triumphantly insists that B159 comes before the footnote at B160. Of course it does. But that is beside the point. I do not cite B159 as a place where Kant claims to have executed the Deduction's task. I cite a phrase from a passage in which Kant is saying what still needs to be done in order to complete the task. When, further on, Kant takes himself to have done what was to be done, he must be taking himself to have done what he— earlier, of course!—said it still remained for him to do. It is obviously proper to take the forward-looking specification of a task still remaining, in B159, as a proleptic formulation of what will have been done when the task has been executed, and hence of what has been done, in Kant's view, when he claims to

have finished the task. He finishes the task by making a specific argumentative move that, as Westphal irrelevantly insists, he is not yet making in B159. All I need is that he is there describing what the move he has yet to make is going to achieve.

The italics in the phrase I cite from B159 are not mine, as Westphal says. My citation is from Kemp Smith's translation, and Kemp Smith's italics correspond to an emphasis in the German text.

Westphal further muddies the waters about B159 by saying, as if it was a problem for me, that Kant there refers back to §§20 and 21 of the Deduction. True enough, but that is in the first sentence of §26. In the second sentence, which is what I quote from, Kant turns to what he is going to do next, as opposed to what he has already done.

In the context of this confused response to my quotation from B159, Westphal says this: 'omit his account of B160 note, and McDowell has not charted any route forward from Kant to Hegel. This is a key example of how the general level of McDowell's discussion fails to grasp Kant's views, Hegel's views, and the important debates between them'. The idea that we can omit my account of the note at B160 reflects Westphal's not understanding how I read the B Deduction. If that, and the way he mangles my use of B159, are the best he can produce ('a key example') to show my supposed failure of grasp, I see no reason to feel particularly threatened.

4. It is part of Westphal's not understanding my reading of the B Deduction that he thinks the role I credit to the B160 footnote restricts Kant's argument for objective validity, as I read it, to the quantitative categories, because they are the only ones that need to be employed in order to 'generate' the formal unities, space and time.

As I said, the first half of the Deduction puts in place a conception of intuitions as instantiations of categorial form in sensory receptivity. Kant's project is to entitle himself to suppose that their having categorial form accounts for their being of objects, and thereby to show that the pure concepts of the understanding, whose content is constituted by the forms of thought, have objective validity. As I have explained, the first half by itself does not finish the entitling, but the second half does, to Kant's satisfaction. It finishes a job begun in the first half. The conception of intuitions that does argumentative work in the completed argument is still the one that is in play in the first half. The conception is one according to which intuitions are configurations in sensory receptivity informed by *categories in general*. The second half removes the abstraction that omits the specific forms of *our* sensibility from the conception as the first half elaborates it. But otherwise things stay the same. Any category is as relevant as any other. There is no question of a restriction to just some of Kant's list.

For the Deduction's purposes, there is no need to fuss about what exactly the categories are, let alone make a restriction to the quantitative categories. The argument works at a general level, in terms of the idea of the pure concepts of the understanding, whatever they may be. In the Deduction, Kant mostly talks quite generally about categories or even 'the category'.

Perhaps this false step on Westphal's part is connected with his mysterious suggestion, in a note, that attention to questions about the completeness of Kant's list of categories would have saved me from misreading Kant's 'Clue'. He does not say what the supposed misreading is. He alludes to my Woodbridge Lectures, but I cannot see why he thinks anything I say there has any connection with the question whether Kant's list is complete.

5. In his response to my quotation from B159, Westphal criticizes me on the basis of a supposed superior grasp of Kantian texts. But as I have explained, the criticism collapses when one looks at the texts.

Here is another example of this kind of procedure on Westphal's part. I object to Kant's representing intuitions as the result of activity on the part of the spontaneous understanding. Westphal says the complaint is misplaced: it should be 'the transcendental power of imagination (not "understanding", *pace* McDowell . . .)'. But the sharp contrast between transcendental imagination and understanding that this presupposes is not in Kant. Westphal overlooks the fact that in the B Deduction Kant explains the transcendental synthesis of the imagination as an effect of the *understanding* on sensibility (B152). And at the beginning of the B Deduction Kant formulates a principle that frames what is to follow, by saying that all combination is an act of the *understanding* (*Verstandeshandlung*, B130). That must apply, in particular, to the kind of unity that characterizes intuitions, which is what he goes on to elaborate in the first half of the Deduction, culminating in §20. Westphal's supposed correction to the way I formulate the Kantian thesis I object to is groundless.

Westphal says: 'McDowell claims that Kant claims that empirical "intuitions" are "cases of sensory consciousness of objects" . . .. Kant says this, but does not mean by it what McDowell presumes it to mean'. He does not make it clear what he thinks I presume it to mean. Perhaps what follows is a clue: 'Sensations and sensory intuitions are states of consciousness, according to Kant, though they are not (as such) states or components of *self*-conscious awareness . . ..' This unwarrantably lumps together sensations and intuitions. I have no idea how Westphal thinks his denial, on Kant's behalf, that intuitions are states of self-conscious awareness could possibly cohere with the first half of the B Deduction, where Kant explicitly connects the unity that characterizes intuitions with the transcendental unity of *apperception*. (See B143 for a summary statement.)

I object to Kant's conceiving intuitions as generated by spontaneous intellectual activity. In response to this, Westphal makes much of the fact that Kant does not use the language of freedom in connection with the *Verstandeshandlung* that is supposed to result in the unity of intuitions. (My formulation, not Westphal's; as I have noted, he has to blind himself to the fact that it is, for Kant, a *Verstandeshandlung*, in order to rebuke me for not crediting it to the transcendental power of imagination.) I cannot see why it should matter that Kant does not use the language of freedom in connection with the 'generation' of intuitions. He does not use the language of freedom in connection with the spontaneous activity of the understanding in judgment either, where I have no objection to the talk of spontaneous activity. That he does not gloss the spontaneity of the understanding in terms of freedom reflects complex issues about how he sees the relation between the topics of the first and second critiques. But this is irrelevant to the issue I meant to raise. My complaint does not turn on the *word* 'freedom'. (Though it seems innocuous to use that word in a context in which the special role of the concept of freedom, for Kant, in connection with pure *practical* reason is not to the point.) It is already bad enough, from my point of view, to say that intuitions result from the *spontaneous activity* of the understanding—as Kant does; Westphal's denial of this involves ignoring those key passages in the B Deduction.

Westphal thinks my resistance to Kant's conception of intuitions as generated by spontaneous intellectual activity reflects an unjustified refusal to give credence to a certain kind of epistemological externalism, a position that posits 'sub-conscious proto-cognitive activities' entering into the constitution of cognitive states. He is right that I give no credence to a reading of Kant in such terms. Whether this is unjustified is another question. I know some people want to read Kant as an armchair cognitive scientist. But reading him like this seems to me to ensure that we miss the point and interest of his thinking. When Kant seeks to see the spontaneity of the understanding as involved in the constitution of intuitions, what he wants is not an involvement on the part of something only *proto*-cognitive, of which we can cheerfully suppose it is submerged below the surface of consciousness. It needs to be a *cognitive* faculty that Kant is invoking. His insight is that objects are present to us in experience only thanks to our powers of thought, in a sense in which thought is essentially apperceptive. And he can have that insight—I show how—without needing to suppose that in experience we spontaneously *exercise* those powers, though we are not aware that we are doing so. (See also my response to Stephen Houlgate's paper.)

The insight is not that objects are present to us only thanks to the operations of 'proto-cognitive' machinery. No doubt that could truly be said also, but it would be irrelevant to the epistemological issues—in Sellars's 'transcendental' sense of 'epistemological'—that Kant is concerned with. And, since I have mentioned Sellars, let me note that Westphal is wrong to enrol Sellars as a protagonist of the externalist approach he wants to read into Kant. The sensations that Sellars thinks must 'guide' conscious perceptual awareness of objects are exactly not sub-conscious, as Westphal says. Sellars's thought about the 'guiding' role of sensations is not a contribution to speculative cognitive science. In fact Sellars's epistemology is staunchly internalist.

I cannot here argue for epistemological internalism, or for attributing views in that spirit to Kant. But the most this would enable Westphal to claim is a standoff, not the emphatic rejection of my stance that he writes as if he is entitled to.

He makes a number of proposals for a diagnosis of my sympathy for internalism. The most bizarre involves crediting Davidson, of all people, with an 'exclusive contrast between reasons and causes', on which I am supposedly fixated. The fact is that Davidson argues, in a famous and influential paper, against any such exclusive contrast, and I follow him in that.

Offering diagnoses presupposes that something has gone wrong, but I cannot find anything in Westphal's text, or his long note about this topic, that constitutes an argument for that. In connection with my 'Knowledge and the Internal', where I defend a kind of epistemological internalism, Westphal suggests that I neglect the role of infallibilism in my recounting and rejection of the argument from illusion. One of his diagnostic speculations is that I may have inherited a lingering Cartesian infallibilism. Can he have failed to understand that infallibilism figures in my treatment of the argument from illusion as a way in which, if epistemology is structured by that argument's assumptions, it is led astray, not as something I am trying to preserve? I can find no sign that he has understood my defence of internalism, let alone produced any reason to reject it.

6. Westphal tries to make trouble for me by exploiting wordings of mine against the grain of what I say. For instance, in one place I allowed myself to speak of 'answerability to impressions'. In the context of everything else I say, it should be obvious that this can only be a variant on 'answerability to the tribunal of experience'; that is, expressed in a less shorthand way, answerability to the world as made available to us in experience, answerability enabled by impressions. But Westphal reads into my shorthand a conception on which impressions are themselves objects of awareness, in a way that would turn them into a veil of perception intervening between us and the world. In the spirit of correcting me, he recommends instead a conception of impressions as conduits for our self-conscious awareness of worldly objects. But that is just my picture. It has nothing to do with dabbling in cognitive psychology, as Westphal suggests.

Again, in connection with the Transcendental Deduction I say that the objective purport of intuitions can be understood on the basis that they have categorial unity. Westphal reads into this the crazy idea that 'the objective purport of experience is *solely* a function of the categorial structuredness of sensory intuitions' (my emphasis). The overall aim of the Deduction, as I read it, is to show that the categories have objective validity by revealing the categorial form of intuitions as what enables intuitions to have objective purport. *Of course* a particular intuition needs more than its categorial structure to have its specific objective purport (otherwise if two intuitions have the same categorial structure it would follow that they have the same objective purport). Obviously the specific objective purport of an intuition depends also on what it is that is unified in it by the forms prescribed by the pure concepts of the understanding—its matter as well as its form. In the context of the Deduction, however, there is no reason to mention this obvious point. It is bizarre to take its going unmentioned to imply that the need for it in the complete picture is being explicitly denied.

How the idea that intuitions have matter as well as form is to be understood is of course a serious question in the interpretation of Kant. Westphal does not engage with the question. He takes it to be simply obvious that Kant thinks intuitions are constituted as it were from the bottom up, by a 'categorial structuring that converts sensations, which lack objective purport, into empirical intuitions, which have objective purport'. This conversion 'involves exploiting the primitive information embodied in sensations in order to incorporate sensations into *acts* . . . of referential and (ultimately also) ascriptive awareness of surrounding objects'. This picture of the constitution of intuitions fits congenially into Westphal's conception of Kant as doing speculative cognitive science. But it is not obvious at all that this is how Kant thinks. Here is an alternative: the role of sensation in perceptual experience, as Kant views it, is to be understood by way of an abstraction from a complete picture of experience itself, equipped with its objective purport. On this reading, the sensational aspect of cognition-yielding experience is not such as to embody anyway, independently of its being an element in experience, 'primitive information', as Westphal assumes Kant thinks. On the contrary, the connection of the sensational aspect with the idea of information is only that the sensational aspect of experience is an abstractable element in a picture in which experience is displayed as a way of acquiring full-fledged knowledge of surrounding objects, information that is not primitive at all. Westphal evidently does not even understand that his interpretation of how Kant conceives the role of sensibility in experience confronts such an alternative. He certainly does not argue against the alternative. Nevertheless he confidently pronounces that without going further into the psychology of perception I cannot deliver on my suggestion that we should understand the objective purport of intuitions and the objective purport of judgments together.

7. I cannot comment on everything in this paper. Much of it deals with material I do not consider, and I think Westphal does not justify his suggestion that it would have improved my handling of material I do consider if I had taken account of these other areas of Kant and Hegel (and in particular of the way he reads them). I shall end with a remark about one more of his criticisms.

Westphal evidently thinks that by rejecting the conception I attribute to Sellars, according to which transcendental reflection on the objectivity of thought is to be engaged in from a sideways-on point of view, from outside thought, I commit myself to denying Kant's claim that no purely analytic argument could succeed in the critical endeavour. But the approach I sketch as preferable to the Sellarsian one, though it is, in my sense, from inside the conceptual, is not 'purely "conceptual"' in the sense Westphal envisages. It is not an attempt to do transcendental philosophy by exploiting truths that are in any relevant sense analytic. I think this is just one more case of Westphal's failure to understand my work, though unfortunately, here as elsewhere in his paper, that has not deterred him from confidently pronouncing it unsatisfactory.

Michael Williams

1. Williams thinks I understand 'empirical justification' in terms of 'constraint by items involving the exercise of conceptual capacities'. He thinks I hold that 'in

experience our conceptual capacities are exercised passively'. This is a common misdescription of my view. (See also my comment on Christoph Halbig's paper.) In experience, on my view, our conceptual capacities are drawn into play. But they are not *exercised*. Not all goings-on in which conceptual capacities are operative are goings-on in which subjects exercise conceptual capacities, and in particular that is not true of experiences. (For why this matters, see my comment on Stephen Houlgate's paper.) It does not meet the point to talk, with only dubious intelligibility, of passive exercises of capacities.

This may seem only a verbal fastidiousness on my part. But Williams's carelessness on the point is connected with the fact that, following Crispin Wright, he thinks my 'epistemological outlook' pivots on a 'quasi-inferential conception of empirical justification'. In crediting me with holding that experiencing is exercising conceptual capacities, Williams implies that for me a judgment's being justified by experience is like a judgment's being justified by another judgment, except that in 'empirical justification' the exercise of conceptual capacities in the justifying item is passive. Justification of one judgment by another is inferential. So this assimilation might seem to warrant the label 'quasi-inferential' for my conception of how judgments are justified by experience. Later in his paper, echoing Wright again, Williams attributes to me 'an evidentialist (quasi-inferentialist) conception of justification'.

But 'evidentialist' is wildly wrong for how I conceive the warrant for perceptual beliefs. In the central case of visual 'empirical justification', seeing that things are a certain way justifies one in believing that things are that way. And it would be idiotic to cast how one sees things to be as *evidence* for a belief as to how things are. It *is* how things are. There is nothing even remotely like inference here.

Visual experiences—to stay with that sensory modality—are experiences in which one sees how things are, or at least seems to. In an experience in which one only seems to see that things are a certain way, one only seems to have the sort of justification for believing things to be that way that one would have if one were seeing things to be that way. The wrongness of invoking an evidential conception of justification carries over to this case. If one believes that things are a certain way, falsely taking oneself to have a justification consisting in one's seeing that things are that way, one's belief is not evidentially based, any more than it would be if one's justification were of the sort one falsely supposes it to be.

It is true that the justification for believing things to be a certain way that one has by virtue of seeing that things are that way is, to use a term Williams cites from Wright, 'content-sensitive'. What one is entitled to believe in that way depends on how it is that one sees things to be. But that is truistic. It cannot be distinctive of an idiosyncratic 'epistemological outlook'. There is no warrant for Williams's idea that my view is 'evidentialist'.

This misconception starts to matter a good deal, later in Williams's paper, and I shall come back to it.

2. Williams frames his paper by first making it seem that there is a structural convergence between me and Sellars, and then moving to divergences. I suppose

that is all right as an expository device. But I am uncomfortable at his letting it seem, even temporarily, that there is anything in Sellars that corresponds to my 'diagnosis', as he does when he says that 'the parallel between McDowell and Sellars looks to be complete'. The most obvious thing to say in this connection is that for me the idea that 'in the dimension of describing and explaining the world, science is the measure of all things' (EPM §42) is the villain of the piece, the source of illusions that we are beset by philosophical problems; whereas for Sellars it is correct, and sets the philosophical task of reconciling its correctness with the character of the manifest image. So there is no parallel at all, let alone a complete one.

This is a divergence from Sellars that I would not dream of playing down. I think I am more Sellarsian about experience than Williams allows, and I shall say more about this in a moment. But I have no sympathy with Sellars's scientism. I shall come back to this at the end.

3. I urge that experiences are, as Williams puts it, 'nonjudgmental justifiers'. And I find such a conception in Sellars too. Williams objects, on the ground that for Sellars experiences have an 'assertional character'.

That is true, but not in the sense it would need to bear if it were to undermine the idea that experiences are nonjudgmental justifiers for Sellars too. What Williams systematically ignores is that Sellars attributes assertional character *to experiences themselves*, not (instead, as it were) to assertoric performances on the part of subjects of experience. Of course associated performances by subjects of experience who take their experiences to be veridical—performances in which they say how they think they perceive things to be—have an assertional character. But that assertional character is not to be identified with the assertional character of experiences themselves. The sense in which experiences have an assertional character, on Sellars's conception, is not that their content is asserted, or judged, to be so by their subjects.

Sellars introduces the idea that experiences have intentional content by saying that experiences so to speak make claims. When one credits someone with perceiving that things are a certain way, one attributes to the person an experience that so to speak claims that things are that way, and one endorses that claim (EPM §16). It is *the experience* that one describes as making the claim, not the person. To describe experiences as making claims is of course metaphorical (as Sellars signals with 'so to speak'); it attributes to experiences something that literally makes sense only as attributed to persons. And Sellars works to entitle himself to the metaphor. But Williams writes as if what Sellars does is not to entitle himself to the metaphor but to abandon it, in favour of conceiving the intentional content of an experience as asserted (or judged) by the subject of the experience rather than, as in the metaphor, asserted by the experience itself.

Williams says 'Sellars takes the assertional character of experiences very seriously'. Indeed he does. His metaphor is that experiences make claims. And the point of the metaphor would be spoiled if we described experiences as, say, broaching suppositions. An experience in which one seems to see that there is a red cube in front of one does not just present for one's consideration the idea that there is a red cube in front of one. It *claims* that there is a red cube in front of one (to speak in Sellars's metaphorical way). So the content of an experience is not present in it as a mere claimable, as Williams implies I must suppose when I represent experiences as nonjudgmental justifiers. The content of an experience is the content of a claim the experience makes (to stay with the metaphor).

An experience makes its claim in such a way as to represent endorsing it as incumbent on the subject of the experience. That is a way of saying the experience purports to reveal to its subject that things are the way she would be saying they are if she made that claim. ('Purports to reveal' is still metaphorical there, but the metaphor is different.)

I think that is all I needed to say about Sellars's remark, in EPM §16 bis, that the claim an experience makes 'is, so to speak, evoked or wrung from the perceiver by the object perceived'. That is an elaboration of the original metaphor (signalled, here again, by 'so to speak'). Sellars is not withdrawing from the essential element in the metaphor, that the claim is made *by the experience.* He is adding that the experience makes the claim in such a way as to represent endorsing that claim as rationally obligatory for the subject of the experience.

I was wrong to think I needed to discount this remark, in a bit of supposed charity that Williams objects to. The remark does not point in the direction Williams takes Sellars in, in which the original metaphor is abandoned in favour of taking the intentional content of an experience to be asserted (or judged) by the subject of the experience, as opposed to the experience itself. The remark leaves Sellars free to acknowledge that one can resist an experience's attempt to evoke or wring a judgment from one. One can withhold the endorsement that the experience demands. One does that if one reports one's experience not by claiming to see that things are thus and so but by saying it looks to one as if things are thus and so. Even if one thus withholds one's endorsement, the experience still makes its claim, vainly—in this case—representing one's endorsement of it as compulsory.

Williams does not pay proper attention to Sellars's metaphor. The material he cites against me is what Sellars appeals to in order to entitle himself to the metaphor, not something to say instead. The metaphor has a point, and I think Williams roundly misses it. This comes to a head when he says: 'Like Travis, Sellars finds no place for the problematic idea that "experience" itself represents things as being this way or that.' When Sellars introduces the intentional content of experience, it is experience itself of which he says that it, so speak, claims that things are this way or that. That is precisely to say (of course using a metaphor) that experience itself represents things as being this way or that. It is astonishing that Williams denies Sellars this thought, in the teeth of what Sellars plainly says.

4. Williams says: 'Carefully put, Sellars's point is that experiencings are mental episodes with assertional force. They are like claimings, but they are not produced on purpose'.

The first of these sentences is fine. As I have explained, the point about assertional force, properly understood, does not tell against finding in Sellars a conception on which experiencings are not to be identified with judgings. In Sellars's metaphor it is experiences that make claims, not subjects of experience. An experience as it were demands an assertion, or judgment, from its subject. If she conforms to the demand, her doing so is her response to her experience, not what her experiencing is.

But the second sentence is strange. It implies that experiencings are *produced*, though not on purpose. But experiencings are not produced at all. They happen.

Williams is here working into his accusation that I ignore or mishandle Sellars's distinction between acts and actions. I think this is what he has in mind when, at the beginning of his paper, he says that I do not 'take heed of one of Sellars's most important epistemological insights, an insight that any account of perceptual knowledge ought to take on board'. But there is nothing here to threaten me.

Sellars's distinction, which I agree is an excellent one, is between performances produced on purpose, for which he reserves the label 'actions', and performances not produced on purpose, which he counts as acts but not actions. The most fundamental way of giving expression to how one sees things to be is in performances of the kind Sellars describes as noticing-out-loud. Noticings-out-loud are acts, not actions. They are governed by 'ought-to-be' normativity, not 'ought-to-do' normativity. Here is a way people ought to be: not prone to engage in noticings-out-loud to the effect that certain things are green unless the things in question are indeed green. Such performances are not governed by 'ought-to-do' rules, for instance a rule that one should say that things are green only if they are indeed green. Whatever the status of such a rule may be, to suppose it governs noticings-out-loud would imply that they are actions, which they are not.

Now it is true that I do not invoke this distinction of kinds of normativity when I try to follow Sellars in rejecting the Myth of the Given. And Williams is right that Sellars argues for the following thesis: the idea that observation reports are governed by 'ought-to-do' normativity brings us 'face to face with givenness in its most straightforward form' (EPM §34). But it is absurd to suggest, as Williams does, that this casts doubt on whether my putatively Sellarsian argument against the Given—that mere causes cannot justify—is Sellarsian.

The Myth of the Given is the idea of an availability for cognition—in the demanding sense in which a case of cognition is a standing in the space of reasons—that requires nothing of the knower except naturally possessed capacities. Against that, Sellars sets the conviction that coming to inhabit the space of reasons, and hence coming to be capable of cognition in that demanding sense, requires initiation into a shared norm-governed practice.

His point in EPM §34 is that if we conceive observation reports as governed by 'ought-to-do' normativity, we fall into an egregious form of the Myth. In this form of the Myth, the reports owe their correctness to their using the right words for expressing what is anyway knowledge. The knowledge expressed by the reports does not depend on one's having the conceptual capacities exercised in making the reports. Those conceptual capacities are operative only in finding the right words, not in having the knowledge that the words are used to express.

But that is just one particularly egregious form of the Myth. Sellars's target in attacking the Myth is quite general, as he makes clear at the beginning of EPM. The target is also exemplified in the idea I attack: the idea that merely being impinged on by a causal force originating in an object can constitute a cognitive status. Williams implies that an argument against the Given cannot be Sellarsian unless, like the argument of EPM §34, it turns on the distinction between 'ought-to-do' and 'ought-to-be' normativity. But that is absurd.

Williams suggests that for Sellars 'there is no reason why mere causal connections to objects cannot be epistemically significant'. Of course a connection's having a causal character does not disqualify it from being epistemically significant. A perceiver is causally connected to the objects she perceives, and that is obviously relevant to her epistemic standing. But epistemically significant causal connections are not *mere* causal connections. The causation that is operative, by all means, in the acquisition of perceptual knowledge results in actualizations of the subject's conceptual capacities. In contrast, the bare idea of being impinged on by a causal force that can be traced back to an object presupposes at most a natural sensibility. It is an application of Sellars's attack on the Given to say that such a causal connection cannot be epistemically significant. So the thought expressed in the slogan 'Mere causes cannot justify' is Sellarsian. Nothing Williams says casts any doubt on this.

Noticings-out-loud are overt linguistic acts, not actions. They are produced, but not on purpose. Sellars thinks experiencings that are perceivings should be modelled on noticings-out-loud. But of course experiencings need not be perceivings. And in general when one thing is modelled on another not all the features of the model carry over to what is modelled on it. There is no ground for taking experiencings to share with noticings-out-loud, the model for some of them, the feature of being produced, though not on purpose. Williams's implication to the contrary belongs with his idea that the assertional character Sellars undoubtedly attributes to experiences is a matter of assertion or judgment on the part of their subjects. But as I have urged, that falsifies Sellars's metaphor, and there is nothing in the distinction between acts and actions to indicate otherwise.

5. I said that Sellars 'expands the topic from seeings to a wider class of experiences, which he initially introduces as ostensible seeings'. Williams says 'Sellars does no such thing'. He is wrong here, and this initiates a seriously point-missing stretch of his paper.

It is true, as Williams says, that the phrase 'ostensible seeing' occurs in a passage in which Sellars is spelling out what he calls an 'unfortunate, but familiar, line of thought' (EPM §7). The line of thought is one according to which we make empirical knowledge look unsatisfactorily shaky if we suppose its foundations 'consist of the veridical members of a class not all the members of which are veridical, and from which the non-veridical members cannot be weeded out by "inspection"'. In the case of visual acquisition of empirical knowledge, the class is the class of ostensible seeings. Some ostensible seeings are seeings, but some are *merely* ostensible seeings, and there is nothing internal to the experiencings in question that enables one to sort them into those two sub-classes. If one takes that to show that none of the members of the class can provide foundations, and if one is impressed by the fact that it does not make sense to speak of unveridical sensations, one can be tempted to cast sensations as foundations of empirical knowledge instead. (Though, as Sellars points out, this temptation should be undermined by the reflection that it does not make sense to speak of veridical sensations either.)

Williams implies that the conceptual apparatus Sellars exploits in setting out the 'unfortunate line of thought', including the idea of ostensible seeings, is shown by its presence there to be alien to Sellars. But that would merely deprive us of language for making a point Sellars clearly wants to make. Before Sellars goes on to describe how the line of thought 'gets tangled up' with the idea, in itself (he thinks) legitimate, 'that there are such things as sensations of [for instance] red triangles', he pauses to consider its credentials. He suggests that just about anyone, if not distracted by the temptation to cast sensations as foundations, would respond like this: we should 'take the contrapositive of the argument, and reason that *since* the foundation of empirical knowledge *is* the non-inferential knowledge of such facts [for instance, that the facing surface of a physical object is red and triangular], it *does* consist of members of a class which contains non-veridical members'. The thought Sellars is driving at here can be put as follows: contrary to what the 'unfortunate line of thought' aims to make plausible, it is perfectly all right to suppose that the foundations of (visually acquired) empirical knowledge are supplied by those ostensible seeings that are seeings, even though the ostensible seeings that are merely ostensible seeings cannot be distinguished by inspection from those that are seeings. Here I have used the terminology with which Sellars sets out the 'unfortunate line of thought', in order to give the thrust of a response to it that he represents as common sense.

Sellars's discussion of the 'unfortunate line of thought' leads (after a digression on the conception of sense-datum language as a code) into his treatment of 'the logic of "looks"'. The 'taking the contrapositive' response to the 'unfortunate line of thought' amounts to this. Continuing with the restriction to visually acquired knowledge, the foundations of empirical knowledge are things one sees to be the case. Experiences of seeing things to be thus and so are the veridical members of a class of experiences, having it look to one as if things are thus and so, which also contains non-veridical members (experiences in which it merely looks to one as if things are thus and so), and from which the non-veridical members cannot be weeded out by inspection. That is just what Sellars urges when he offers his own account of 'the logic of "looks"'. This confirms that the response to the 'unfortunate line of thought' that, in §7, Sellars says just about everyone would make, if it were not for the distracting effect of the idea that sensations might be a firmer foundation for empirical knowledge, is the response he himself endorses.

Specifying the class in question as the class of ostensible seeings is simply a way to capture a good thought of Sellars's own. Williams says the phrase 'ostensible seeings' is not used by Sellars in EPM except in the passage in which he spells out the 'unfortunate line of thought'. But if that is true, it is irrelevant. (Sellars does use the phrase in his own voice elsewhere, for instance in SK.)

6. I do not believe Sellars gets his good thought quite under control, and this is another point Williams makes a mess of.

Sellars puts his thought in terms of a difference in commitments undertaken in crediting a subject with seeing that things are thus and so, on the one hand, and in attributing to a subject an experience in which it looks to the subject as if things are thus and so, on the other. In each case one attributes an experience that so to speak claims that things are thus and so. (That is the metaphorical way of talking that I have discussed.) In the former case one endorses the claim the experience makes; in the latter case one withholds that endorsement.

That is all right so far as it goes. The trouble is that Sellars falls into supposing that to say that much is to give a complete account of the difference between visual experiences that are seeings that things are thus and so and visual experiences that are cases of having it merely look to one as if things are thus and so. Thus he formulates his account of 'looks' statements like this (EPM §17): 'to say that "X looks green to S at t" is, in effect, to say that S has that kind of experience which, if one were prepared to endorse the propositional claim that it involves, one would characterize as *seeing x to be green at t'*. That implies that, given that a subject has a visual experience that so to speak claims that X is green, it will be correct for one to characterize the experience as an experience of seeing X to be green if one thinks the claim that X is green is worthy of endorsement. That amounts to what Williams thinks I was wrong to find Sellars implying, 'that veridicality is all it takes for an ostensible seeing to be a seeing'. And the implication is wrong in just the way I argued. Being prepared to endorse a visual experience's claim is not enough to make it correct for one to characterize the experience as an experience of seeing things to be the way the claim represents them as being. One can seem to see that things are a certain way when they indeed are that way (so that the experience's claim is endorsement-worthy), but without one's experience being an experience of seeing things to be that way.

This misstep on Sellars's part, in EPM §17, fits with the fact that the 'unfortunate line of thought', as he spells it out, works with a differentiation of ostensible seeings into those that are veridical and those that are not—rather than into those that are seeings and those that are merely ostensible seeings. The 'taking the contrapositive' response works with the same differentiation. The response is that, contrary to what the line of thought urges, the veridical members of the class can acceptably supply foundations for empirical knowledge. But an experience of seeming to see that things are a certain way, if it is not an experience of seeing that things are that way, does not yield something fit to be a foundation for empirical knowledge, even if things are the way one seems to see them to be; that is, even if the experience happens to be veridical. Foundations for knowledge would have to be bits of knowledge, not things one just happens to be right about.

The thought Sellars really needs is that foundations for empirical knowledge can be supplied by those ostensible seeings that are *seeings*. He was wrong to imply that the sub-class of ostensible seeings that can supply foundations can be singled out as comprising the ostensible seeings that are veridical.

It is beyond question that in the text of EPM Sellars implies that a visual experience is one of seeing how things are if the claim it contains is worthy of endorsement. There is no other way to read the passage I cited from EPM §17. This is not, as Williams suggests, a distorting reading that, with my own epistemological agenda, I impose on the text.

Williams thinks I foist this implication on Sellars because I am fixated on an idea of 'appearings that are, as it were, sworn to veracity'. This idea is a complete importation on his part. Sellars tries to capture the thought he is driving at in terms of appearings whose content is endorsement-worthy: that is, merely veracious, not sworn to veracity. And when I urge that the attempt fails to capture what Sellars is driving at, my point is that what Sellars wants is the idea of experiencings that are seeings, experiencings in which how things are is visually revealed to one. The claim made by an experience that is a seeing is endorsement-worthy in a special way: it is not just that things are as the claim represents them as being, but that in the experience the fact that things are that way is directly available, visually, to the subject of the experience. This is not an idea of something that is sworn to veracity.

Why does Williams import this irrelevant idea? This belongs with his placing my approach to the epistemology of perceptual knowledge in 'the dialectic surrounding ... "the Agrippan problem"'. In that dialectic, it is made to seem that the only options for understanding epistemic warrant are an infinite regress and a circle. Trying to avoid the conclusion that knowledge is impossible, we land in an uncomfortable dilemma: one horn is a foundationalism that pretends to halt the regress, and the other is a coherentism that pretends to make the circle palatable. The idea of appearances that can be sworn to veracity would be a way of pretending to halt the regress. And that is where Williams locates me in the epistemological scene. But here his misconception of my approach as 'evidentialist (quasi-inferentialist)' is doing real damage.

What I find in Sellars, and applaud, is a grope in the direction of a conception of a sub-class of ostensible seeings, seeings, that makes possible a satisfactory *avoidance* of the Agrippan dialectic. There is no regress, because there are foundations for empirical knowledge in the nuanced sense Sellars envisages at EPM §38.

In the text of EPM, Sellars tries to single out this sub-class as the veridical members of the class of ostensible seeings. Later he sees that that was wrong. In footnotes added for the reprinting in SPR, he adds a condition over and above veridicality: that the subject knows that the viewing conditions are suitable. For instance, if one is to be able to see what colour something has, one must know that the light is such that the colours things look to have are the colours they have. I objected that one can see what colour something has but suppose one does not, because one falsely supposes the light is not suitable. What matters is that the light is suitable, not that one knows that it is. My point here is not, as Williams thinks, that requiring that the subject should know that the conditions are suitable fails to ensure satisfaction of a supposed need to get the appearings in question sworn to veracity. My point is just that the added condition does not correctly draw the distinction Sellars wants, between the ostensible seeings that are seeings and the rest.

To avoid the Agrippan dilemma in the way he begins to put in place in his response to the 'unfortunate line of thought', Sellars needs to do two connected things. First, he needs to show how, contrary to the 'unfortunate line of thought', it can be acceptable to hold that foundations for empirical knowledge are provided by those members of the class of ostensible seeings that are seeings (to stay with the focus on visual acquisition of empirical knowledge). He needs to show that this is not a version of the kind of foundationalism that gives only the illusion of a satisfactory halt to the regress. And, second, he needs to specify how seeings—the members of the class of ostensible seeings that can provide foundations, contrary to the 'unfortunate line of thought'—differ from merely ostensible seeings.

He discharges the first of those tasks by explaining that the foundations yielded by seeings are foundations only in the nuanced sense of EPM §38. The non-inferential acquisition of knowledge that seeings enable is not a case of getting bits of the mythical Given. This non-inferential knowledge is acquired in actualizations of conceptual capacities, the very possession of which requires substantial worldly knowledge. So there is no go in the picture that is characteristic of a standard foundationalism: a picture in which empirical knowledge can be rationally reconstructed in terms of an atomistic getting of bits of the Given, on which one erects a superstructure of knowledge inferentially grounded on those foundations. Acquiring the knowledge that is foundational in the nuanced sense requires a superstructure to be already in place.

On the second task, Sellars is less successful. His first shot is the idea that seeings differ from merely ostensible seeings in being veridical. When he realizes that that is inadequate, since veridicality does not exclude an ostensible seeing's being a merely ostensible seeing, he adds those footnotes. But his further condition, over and above veridicality, is a condition for *knowing* that, say, one sees what colour something has, not a condition for seeing what colour something has. An experience in which one sees what colour something has brings its having that colour within the reach of one's knowledge, whether or not one knows that one's experience is doing that.

What Sellars does not seem to realize, either in the original text of EPM or in those added footnotes, or perhaps anywhere, is that he has made available a simple and satisfactory execution of the second task. What is needed, and within his grasp, is the idea of a kind of experience in which the fact that things are a certain way is visually revealed to a subject. In the context of his fine execution of the first task, we can see that this idea is completely untainted by the Myth of the Given.

Williams concludes this phase of his discussion by saying: 'At bottom, McDowell and Sellars are very different'. In part this reflects his thinking my approach is stuck in the Agrippan framework. As I have explained, that is completely misguided. But Williams's verdict also reflects his failure to appreciate the shape of the escape from the Agrippan framework that Sellars brings within our grasp. I put it like that to leave room for the possibility that Sellars himself never gets the good thought he makes available, about how seeings can innocuously provide foundations, under control. Williams clearly does not understand the anti-Agrippan direction in which I read Sellars's thinking as tending. His remark about how far I am from Sellars betrays his not understanding the reading of Sellars, no doubt partly cooperative, that I offer.

7. Sellars thinks experiencings involve not just the conceptual goings-on I have been discussing so far, but also sensations, which are nonconceptual. Here I acknowledge a substantive divergence from him. I urge that those conceptual goings-on should be understood as actualizations of conceptual capacities *in sensory consciousness*. So understood, they themselves provide for the sensuous or qualitative aspect of experiencings. There is no need for an extra nonconceptual element in the full account of what experiencing is. (In my Woodbridge Lectures, I thought Sellars actually had the idea of actualizations of conceptual capacities in sensory consciousness, but I now think that was wrong. See my comment on Willem deVries's paper.)

Williams tries to motivate a defence of Sellars, on the score of the supposed need for nonconceptual sensations in a full account of experiencings, by sounding a note of doubt, on Sellars's behalf, about my talk of 'glimpses of reality'. This is bizarre. As Williams says, the topics of observation reports include properties that are 'iffy'; 'objects can look solid, heavy, hard to reach, etc.'. But so what? There is a condition on our being able to make sense of glimpses in which a subject takes in that objects have such properties. Such glimpses are intelligible only as enjoyed by a subject who knows more about the world than she takes in in any such glimpse. That is a Sellarsian point that I myself insist on. It does not tell against supposing that one can take in, in a single glance, that an object is, say, solid (in an exercise of a capacity to tell by looking whether things are solid that is, of course, fallible). Glimpses of reality can be enormously rich in content, but only because they occur against a background of worldly knowledge. There is no ground here for supposing we need an idea of 'strictly momentary' perceptual consciousness, restricted to arrays of sensations.

Williams also says the existence of nonconceptual cues is implied by the possibility of training children into, for instance, 'the colour-shape language game'. But what exactly does the possibility of training imply? It would be mysterious how a child could be initiated into the colour language game, say, if the child did not have a propensity, in advance of the initiation, to have different things happen in its sensory consciousness when it confronts things with different colours. And at that stage, before the child has acquired colour concepts, those differential shapings of sensory consciousness must be nonconceptual. So the possibility of training implies the existence *at some time*, in the subjects of training, of nonconceptual sensations. But it implies nothing about the visual consciousness of colours enjoyed by subjects who have acquired colour concepts. It provides no basis for denying that with the acquisition of colour concepts, visual sensory consciousness itself comes to have a conceptual form. We do not need to suppose that acquiring colour concepts merely adds a layer of conceptual goings-on on top of a nonconceptual layer that remains as it would have been if the training had not taken place.

8. Williams ends by considering the divergence between Sellars's project of a synoptic vision combining the scientific and the manifest images, on the one hand, and my approach to the transcendental question, on the other. My approach to the transcendental question aims to show that an element in the manifest image—our conception of ourselves as engaging in thought about the world we live in—is not problematic in a way it can seem to be. Williams says that this deconstruction of an apparent problem for the manifest image 'is no part of Sellars's project'.

Of course I agree that it does not belong with the project of a synoptic vision. I think that project is misconceived. In EPM Sellars offers only embarrassingly bad grounds for the '*scientia mensura*' remark. And in order to represent reconciling the images as a pressing task for philosophy (in PSIM and elsewhere), he has to distort the manifest image's conception of colour, for instance saddling the manifest image with the idea that there would still be colour in parts of coloured things however minutely they were divided.

Williams says, rightly: 'Sellars does not think we can rest content with philosophies that recall us to common sense. Sellars does not think that common sense is discomfort-free, at least for those with naturalistic proclivities'. But putting it like this opens neatly into my approach. According to me, things go wrong precisely with the naturalistic proclivities, which I diagnose as a scientistic skewing of a well-placed resistance to the supernatural. By my lights Sellars is simply wrong to suppose there is an inescapable *philosophical* problem about how certain animals evolved into being language-users.

It would not be right to say Sellars has no interest in the transcendental project: vindicating our entitlement to conceive ourselves as engaging in thought about the world we live in. I think his execution of such a project is at some points led astray by his scientism. But it is remarkable how much of his philosophy retains its interest even after being removed from the context of his scientism. For me he is a great philosopher in spite of the fact that his ground project is misguided.

Williams ends by saying Sellars would see me as just one more proponent of 'the *philosophia perennis*, making explicit the complex contours of the Manifest Image'. In this context, the label '*philosophia perennis*' is lame. I diagnose the supposed problem about the manifest image that I aim to deconstruct as stemming from our tendency to be dazzled by science. Philosophy could not have faced the task of deconstructing such supposed problems before there was a risk of that dazzlement. The task is not perennial; it is essentially modern. I suppose Williams thinks my philosophy is less time-bound than that because he thinks it belongs in the Agrippan framework. But as I have said, he is quite wrong about that.

For Sellars, science is the measure of all things, in the dimension of describing and explaining the world, and that gives philosophy an obligation to reconcile the scientific image with the manifest image. In the work in which I find some of Sellars's thinking helpful, I aim to display a certain apparent problem about the manifest image as resulting from the temptation to hold that science as the measure of all things. I have put things like that with a view to emphasizing a symmetry in this divergence between me and Sellars, which, as I said earlier, I would not dream of playing down. The divergence is between different views of what has become incumbent on philosophy with the rise of modern science. Whether it is appropriate to frame the divergence as between a complacent defence of the status quo, on my side, and an exciting new project, on Sellars's side, depends entirely on the credentials of the Sellarsian attitude that I have been describing, disparagingly, as his scientism. That is an issue Williams explicitly refrains from addressing. But without endorsing Sellars's scientism, he is not in a position to deprecate my non-Sellarsian view of the tasks that the rise of modern science has posed for philosophy.

Charles Travis

1. In *Mind and World*, I consider a line of thought that seems to undermine our right to suppose experience enables our surroundings to bear rationally on what we should think. I argue that we need to find something wrong with that line of thought. Otherwise we make a mystery of our capacity to direct our thinking at objective reality.

As Travis sets things up, the threatening line of thought exploits what he calls 'the Condition', which restricts the sorts of thing that can bear rationally on what we should think. And he thinks he and I diverge in that I accept the Condition, whereas in his view it must be rejected.

The Condition Travis thinks I accept excludes 'what I experience, notably perceive' from bearing rationally on what I should think. Accepting that exclusion can seem inconsistent with supposing experience enables our surroundings to bear rationally on what we should think. As Travis reads me, I try to show that that is not so by trying to make out that the Condition does not exclude '(some of) experiential intake' from having a rational bearing on thought. In such a project 'experiential intake' would clearly have to mean something different from 'what I experience, notably perceive'.

By 'what I experience, notably perceive' in his specification of what the Condition disqualifies from bearing rationally on what I should think, Travis means items on the left-hand side of what he calls 'Frege's line'. Frege's line separates non-conceptual items, on the left, from conceptual items, on the right. I have a reservation about some of what Travis says in exploiting the Fregean distinction, and I shall come to that. But I can put in place the way Travis connects Frege's line with the Condition while leaving my reservation on one side. In a situation like one Travis envisages, in which I see a piece of meat on a rug, the piece of meat—which belongs on the left-hand side of Frege's line—is an instance of 'what I experience, notably perceive' as Travis is using that phrase when he says what the Condition excludes. When Travis says the Condition is failed by 'what I experience, notably perceive', he means it is failed by things I perceive in the sense in which I perceive, for instance, pieces of meat: things that belong on the left-hand side of Frege's line. Travis thinks I accept a condition on rational bearing—the Condition—that will not allow us to say, when I see a piece of meat, that the piece of meat bears rationally on what I should think about it.

But this reading gets me wrong.

There is a condition I do accept, which can be formulated like this: reason's reach extends no further than conceptual capacities can take it. It is understandable that Travis should take this to be his Condition. My condition can be put (perhaps dangerously) by saying reason's reach extends no further than the conceptual. And it may seem obvious that if that were so, items on the left-hand side of Frege's line, for instance pieces of meat, could not bear rationally on what one is to think.

But any such reading of my condition would be mistaken.

In *Mind and World* I offer an image of the conceptual as unbounded. There is nothing outside the conceptual. That is as much as to say: there is nothing beyond the reach of reason. In this context, to say reason's reach coincides with the conceptual cannot be to draw a boundary around reason's reach, leaving some things outside it. The image precisely rejects any boundary, any line beyond which reason's reach would not extend. Certainly pieces of meat, say, are not conceptual; they belong on the left-hand side of Frege's line. But they are not *outside* the conceptual, in a sense that could possibly cohere with my image of unboundedness. When I say reason's reach extends no further than the conceptual, I am not separating things into two sorts, those that can bear rationally on what a subject should think and those that cannot, with the second category including pieces of meat. That would contradict the claim of unboundedness.

Certainly my condition sets a *limit* to reason's reach. If it did not, there would be no point in affirming it. But a limit need not be a boundary, and this limit had better not be one. What my condition disallows is the idea that something, for instance a piece of meat, can impinge on a subject's rationality without conceptual capacities, capacities that belong to reason, being drawn on in the subject's being thus related to it. The idea of such impingement is a myth, a version of the Myth of the Given. (I shall come back to this.) But that leaves it open that a piece of meat can impinge on a subject's rationality, provided that capacities that belong to reason are drawn on in the subject's being thus related to it.

My condition could be expressed by saying reason's reach coincides with the realm of thought, in something like the sense Frege attaches to '*Gedanke*': the realm of the thinkable. Travis thinks my condition leaves a piece of meat I see, a left-hand side item, outside reason's reach: unable to bear rationally on what I should think. But that is as if one supposed Frege's conception of thinkables as *Sinne* leaves left-hand side items—which belong in the realm of *Bedeutung*, not in the realm of *Sinn*—outside the reach of thinking. Certainly pieces of meat are not thinkables: not *Gedanken* or constituents of *Gedanken*. They belong on the left-hand side of Frege's line. But that does not put them beyond the reach of thinking. Just so, my condition does not put them beyond the reach of reason.

So Travis's account of how he and I diverge is wrong from the start. He is wrong to think I accept a condition that precludes a piece of meat I see from bearing rationally on what I should think about it. My condition says how the experience that is my seeing the piece of meat must be conceived if it is to be intelligible that it enables the piece of meat to bear rationally on what I should think about it, as I agree with Travis that it can.

2. My condition allows a piece of meat I see to bear rationally on what I should think, because according to me the experiencing that is my seeing the piece of meat draws on conceptual capacities, capacities that belong to reason. And if experiences are actualizations of conceptual capacities, they must surely have conceptual content.

Travis says I have assured him that I do not need to conceive experiences as being such that in them things are represented as so. He thinks this is all to the good, because he thinks any such conception of experiences is misguided.

There is a complication about responding to this. As it happens, I have come to think it is a mistake to think of experiences as having propositional content. (See 'Avoiding the Myth of the Given'.) But this change of view postdates the assurance Travis reports. What I meant to be indicating to him was just that I had no particular need for the *word* 'represent' or its cognates. I did not mean to be renouncing the idea that experiences have the sort of content judgments have. The word 'represent' and its cognates can trigger irrelevant worries about experiences as intermediaries, needing perhaps to be sworn to veracity (see my response to Michael Williams); all I meant to assure Travis of was that my conception of experience was not vulnerable to problems in that area.

And though I have stopped thinking experiences have the kind of content that judgments have, I hold on to this idea: perceptual experience, on the part of rational subjects, is an actualization of conceptual capacities, unified in a way that needs to be understood as part of a package with the kind of unity with which conceptual capacities are exercised in judgments. The content of an experience is, as it were, all but propositional. All it takes to bring the kind of content expressible in 'that' clauses into the picture is for a subject of experience to articulate elements in the already conceptual content possessed by her experience. So Sellars's idea that experiences as it were make claims, though wrong in the letter, is right in spirit. (Again, see 'Avoiding the Myth of the Given'.)

In renouncing the conception of experiences as having propositional content, I have arrived at a verbal *rapprochement* with Travis's insistence that experience does not represent things as so. But my continuing to hold that experiences are actualizations of conceptual capacities marks a continuing divergence from him. It seems beyond dispute that in experience, we stand in cognitively significant relations (expressible by words like 'see') to things that belong on the left-hand side of Frege's line, for instance pieces of meat. But in my picture we stand in those cognitively significant relations to left-hand side items by having experiences in which conceptual capacities of ours are actualized. In Travis's picture, by contrast, conceptual capacities are in play, in connection with experience, only in rational responses on our part to left-hand side items that experience anyway makes available to us for such responses: for instance in recognizing something we see as a piece of meat. In Travis's picture, the presence to us of left-hand side items in experience, available to be recognized, or not, as what they are, does not itself draw on capacities that belong to our reason.

I shall come to why this divergence matters at the end of this comment.

3. As I said, I have a reservation about some of what Travis says about the Fregean division.

Travis thinks phrases like 'things being as they are', or, more specifically, 'the meat's being as it is', can apply to items on the left-hand side of Frege's line. He considers cases in which one can say something on these lines: 'Things being as they are counts as things being as Sid said they were'. (Sid has said that he has been driving.) And he thinks such a remark relates a left-hand side item, things being as they are, to a right-hand side item, things being as Sid said they were. Similarly with a remark like 'The meat's being as it is counts as the meat's being on the rug'.

I think this rides roughshod over the grammatical distinction marked by Frege's line. I do not believe there is any way to understand a phrase like 'the meat's being as it is' except as giving expression to a form common to, say, the meat's being (truly sayable to be) on the rug, the meat's being (truly sayable to be) underdone, …. Such a phrase alludes compendiously to anything that exemplifies that form. If the meat is underdone, then the meat's being as it is is, among other things, the meat's being underdone. Similarly, 'things being as they are' gives expression to a form common to any case of things being (truly sayable to be) some specific way or other, and so alludes compendiously to anything that exemplifies that form. If Sid has been driving, then things being as they are is, among other things, Sid's having been driving. These forms characterize right-hand side items, and the phrases that make compendious allusion to instances of these forms also belong on the right-hand side.

I am not suggesting that 'counts as' cannot link left-hand side items and right-hand side items. Non-conceptual items, say pieces of meat, instantiate conceptual items, say being underdone. We can say, if we like, that a piece of meat counts as underdone. ('Counts as' functions here as a version of the copula, framed so as to emphasize the connection between the idea of something's being a certain way and the idea of its being correct to judge it to be that way.) But if we say, not that the meat counts as underdone, but that the meat's being as it is counts as its being underdone, we are moving entirely on the right-hand side of Frege's line. What counts as the meat's being a certain way, for instance underdone, is the meat's being a certain way, for instance red in the middle. (It need not always be possible to find two different expressions to go after counterparts to those two occurrences of 'for instance'.) Contrast what counts as, say, underdone, which in our example is the meat.

Travis says that the meat's being as it is is not 'in the business of being instanced'. That is a respect in which the meat's being as it is is like the meat, which is certainly a left-hand side item, and Travis thinks that licenses supposing that the meat's being as it is is also a left-hand side item. But this is mistaken. It is true that the meat's being as it is does not admit of a range of possibilities all of which would still instantiate that very thing, the meat's being as it is. But that merely reflects the fact that the meat's being as it is includes any way the meat is, where a way the meat is is a way the meat can be truly said to be and so a right-hand side item. For any way the meat is, the meat's being as it is is, among other things, its being that way, so if it had not been that way, it would not have been as it is. I think Travis has allowed his gloss on the generality of the conceptual to confuse him about the grammar of these phrases.

As far as I can see, this grammatical confusion spells failure for Travis's objection to Davidson on the dualism of scheme and content. There is no left-hand side item that can play the role supposedly played by content, in the conception Davidson exposes as unacceptably dualistic. Things being as they are, as Travis understands that, might have seemed to be such a thing, but, as I have urged, counting such a thing as a left-hand side item violates the grammatical distinction marked by Frege's line. Genuinely left-hand side items do not relate to conceptual items as content is supposed to in the conception Davidson attacks. As Davidson himself remarks, rejecting the dualism leaves thought's bearing on the objects that figure in our world view—for instance, we can say, pieces of meat—unquestioned. This corresponds to the point I have insisted on, that my condition does not put those objects beyond reason's reach.

4. There can be different understandings of what one is saying if one uses certain words to say something. Suppose I say 'The meat is on the rug'. Even assuming it is clear which meat and which rug I am talking about, there are different ways I might be saying things are. Suppose the meat is on a plate, which is on the rug. That might count as the meat's being on the rug. ('Where is the meat?'—'In the dining room'.—'I don't see it'.—'It's on the rug'.—'Thanks, now I see it'). Or it might not. ('How dare you put the meat on my new rug'?—'It's all right; it's not on the rug, it's on a plate'). Something about the occasion of utterance (including, as in my examples, surrounding utterances) might determine one rather than another understanding as correct for a particular saying made by uttering those words. Understandings, that is, are occasion-sensitive.

Travis thinks my condition would prevent us from acknowledging this phenomenon. He writes: 'If the non-conceptual lies without the reach of reason, we are not entitled to the idea of occasion-sensitivity'.

As I have insisted, Travis is wrong to think my condition puts the non-conceptual beyond the reach of reason. And I can add now: properly understood, my condition is perfectly hospitable to the occasion-sensitivity of understandings.

If I use words to specify something someone sees to be so, and the words I use admit of different understandings, and the occasion on which I speak determines my words to one of the understandings they might admit, then what I am saying the person sees to be so is that things are as my words would say they are *on that understanding*. If the occasion does not determine a particular understanding, I may need to say something more to make clear what understanding I intend my words to bear. I can specify what someone sees to be so only by using words in such a way that they bear an understanding on which what they say to be so is indeed what I want to say she sees to be so. On other understandings of those words, they may not express what I want to say she sees to be so.

Imagine an occasion in which someone could speak truly by saying 'There is a red cube in front of me'. A visual experience in which someone directly sees to be so what she would say to be so if she used those words in that context to say something is, at least, an actualization in her visual consciousness of conceptual capacities whose content can be expressed, *on that occasion*, by 'red' and 'cube'. If one articulates the experience, in respect of its content, like that, it may be a question *which* conceptual capacity one means when one speaks of a conceptual capacity whose content is expressible by 'red'. If I use 'red' in such an articulation of the experience into conceptual capacities actualized in it, my specification of a conceptual capacity admits of different understandings in just the same way as when I use 'red' in specifying what it is that the subject of the experience, in enjoying the experience, sees to be so. That is, in just the same way as when I use 'red' in saying that there is a red cube in front of the subject. It is simply wrong to suppose occasion-sensitivity goes missing.

In a comment he makes on this kind of articulation of the content of experience in terms of conceptual capacities that are actualized together in it, Travis muddies the waters by implying that there is a clash, or at least a risk of a clash, with the point Frege makes when he denies that a given *Gedanke* can be understood as structured in just one way. It is true that Frege denies that. But if the structure of a *Gedanke* can be understood in terms of, say, thinking that a certain object falls under a certain first-level concept, it is, for Frege, essential to that *Gedanke* that it *can* be credited with that structure, and as Frege sees things, that structure determines what has to be so for the *Gedanke* to be true. Frege's point is this: that articulation of the *Gedanke* does not compete with the possibility of articulating it differently, for instance in terms of thinking that a first-level concept (the same one that figures in the other articulation) falls within a second-level concept. There is nothing in Frege that tells against supposing it may be essential to an experience that it *can* be articulated, in part, as an actualization, with a suitable togetherness, of conceptual capacities expressible—on the occasion, by all means, on which one describes the experience like this—by 'red' and 'cube'.

5. In connection with my talk of experience as openness to the layout of reality, Travis suggests there is a risk of conflating a conception of layouts as left-hand side items with a conception of layouts as ways things are, right-hand side items. Left-hand side layouts would be objects of perception in the way in which other sorts of left-hand side items, for instance pieces of meat, are. Ways things are could not be. If one fell into this conflation and tried to exploit the result in a conception of seeing that . . ., one would arrive at the absurd idea that someone might visually take in the meat's being on the rug but mistake that object of her awareness for a different kind of thing—as one might see a piece of meat but mistake it for a different kind of thing.

Travis speculates, in passing, that when Wittgenstein proposed, in the *Tractatus*, that a proposition represents reality as a picture does, he may have been inspired by the first of those two conceptions of layouts. That seems implausible. Certainly the *Tractatus* distances itself from Frege in some respects. But the distinction it insists on between facts and complex objects is in the spirit of the distinction Travis dramatizes as Frege's line, with complex objects on a counterpart to the left-hand side and facts on a counterpart to the right-hand side. The so-called layouts that are left-hand side items would be complex objects, not facts. And the *Tractatus* conception of propositions as picturing is a conception of facts representing facts, not a conception of complex objects representing complex objects.

When he discusses seeing that . . ., Travis suggests that my condition, which as I have explained he conflates with the Condition, commits me to something akin to that conflation of two conceptions of layouts. That the meat is on the rug is a right-hand side item. It could not be there to be seen (visible) in just the same sense in which, say, the meat, a left-hand side item, is there to be seen (visible). But, Travis suggests, in the context of the Condition those words, 'that the meat is on the rug', would have to be conceived as introducing an item whose being there to be seen (visible) would be like the meat's being there to be seen (visible) in that its being visible would not depend on which recognitional and judging capacities a subject has. No doubt it would require particular recognitional and judging capacities for a subject to be able to *respond* to that supposed *visibile* by taking it to be so that the meat is on the rug. But in the conception Travis thinks the Condition commits me to, it is the *visibile* it is anyway, independently of anyone's ability to recognize it for what it is and thus respond to it by taking it to be so that the meat is on the rug. This conception resembles that conflation of two conceptions of layouts in that it involves conceiving things one can judge to be so, which are right-hand side items, in a way that could fit only left-hand side items. So the conception does not respect Frege's line.

Travis connects this conception, which he is of course right to find unacceptable, with the obliteration of occasion-sensitivity that he thinks I am committed to. As I have urged, he is wrong to suppose that my condition prevents me from acknowledging occasion-sensitivity. And he is equally wrong to suppose my thinking tends in the direction of this unacceptable conception of seeing that . . . .

Here, as when occasion-sensitivity was directly in question, the fundamental problem with Travis's treatment of my thinking lies in his not letting me have the idea that conceptual content is possessed by perceptual experiences themselves, not just by rational responses to what is experienced anyway, independently of any actualization of conceptual capacities. I suppose this reflects the assurance he thinks I have given him, along with his conviction that he has elsewhere put paid to the idea that experiences have content.

If someone sees that there is a red cube in front of her, that there is a red cube in front of her is, as I understand things, a direct articulation of (some of) the *content* of her visual experience, not, as in the conception Travis foists on me, an *object* of her experiential awareness. That there is a red cube in front of her is not something she sees in *anything like* the sense in which she sees the red cube. It is not enough differentiation between these to say only, in a kind of lip service to Frege's line, that there are different notions of seeing in play. That is insufficient so long as the two notions are assimilated to this extent: the grammatical complementation of 'see', in 'see that there is red cube in front of her', is construed—as in the picture Travis thinks I am committed to—as introducing a *visibile* that is what it is anyway, independently of anyone's ability to respond to it by taking it that there is a red cube in front of her. (I have shifted away from the example of seeing that there is meat on the rug to avoid complications stemming from how plausible it is that that would involve a recognitional capacity, extra to any conceptual capacities actualized in the experience itself. See 'Avoiding the Myth of the Given'.)

My picture involves no such item. In my picture, the conceptual capacities that would be exercised in judging that there is a red cube in front of one are already actualized in having an experience whose content can be in part articulated by saying there is a red cube in front of one. The idea of a *visibile*, called 'that there is a red cube in front of the subject', that is what it is independently of the subject's capacities to recognize red cubes as such makes no sense.

If there *is* a red cube in front of one (as usual, we have to envisage an occasion that determines an understanding for those words), there is a sense in which it is there to be seen that there is a red cube in front of one. But that just means that, since it is so that there is a red cube in front of some subject, it is possible for the subject to see it to be so—that is, if she has the requisite conceptual capacities. What one can see to be so depends on one's conceptual capacities. There is no question of the implication Travis draws from my condition, that an item nameable by 'that there is a red cube in front of the subject' is there to be seen by any subject with working eyes and a suitably illuminated red cube in front of her, though with any such subject it is a further question what she is able to make of that item.

6. In writing this paper, Travis hoped he could leave aside the idea that perceptual experiences have content, on the strength of the assurance he reports receiving from me. But it should by now be clear that his hope was vain.

Of course I cannot here engage in a full discussion of the work, offstage in this paper, in which Travis attacks the idea that perceptual experiences have content. I think his hostility to the idea is, at least to a large extent, driven by the thought that if we attribute content to experiences, we cannot accommodate the common-sense conviction that perceptual experience directly presents us with objects in our surroundings. But that thought is simply wrong. (See my response to Bill Brewer's paper.) In thinking on these lines, Travis misconceives the resources of the conception of perceptual experience I have recommended. This misconception is the same one that is operative in his idea that my condition puts left-hand side items, for instance pieces of meat, beyond the reach of our reason.

My conception of perceptual experience does not, as Travis supposes, conflict with the common-sense conviction he, rightly, wants to preserve. But to say that much is not yet to adduce a reason for preferring my picture to Travis's. One might suppose that his picture accommodates that piece of common sense more straightforwardly. In fact I think it does not accommodate that piece of common sense at all.

In Travis's picture, as I said, the availability to us in experience of left-hand side items is not itself a matter of actualization of conceptual capacities. Actualization of conceptual capacities comes into play only in rational responses to things we anyway experience.

This is a form of the Myth of the Given. The Myth of the Given is the idea, or supposed idea, that things can be available to a subject's rationality without capacities that belong distinctively to the subject's rationality being operative in her being thus related to them. And that is just how it is in Travis's picture of experience.

This is obviously not the place for a full-scale defence of the claim that the Given is mythical. But I want to stress that Travis's paper embodies, not a case against that claim, but a failure to understand what kind of claim it is.

The claim that the Given is mythical does not imply that left-hand side items cannot impinge on a subject's rationality. That is another way of expressing the point I have insisted on in distinguishing my condition from the Condition Travis thinks I am committed to. As I said, my condition does not separate things that can impinge on a subject's rationality, right-hand side items, from things that cannot, left-hand side items. When I invoke the Myth of the Given, what I claim is mythical is not, as Travis supposes, the idea that pieces of meat can impinge on a subject's rationality, thanks to being seen. Properly understood, that is just the idea that pieces of meat can be given, which is innocuous—not the idea that pieces of meat can be Given. What lands Travis in the Myth is the idea that the impingement of pieces of meat on a subject's rationality need not itself draw on capacities that belong to the subject's rationality.

Of course a cat, say, is no less capable of seeing a piece of meat than I am. And, since cats are not rational animals, a cat's seeing a piece of meat cannot be its having an experience in which conceptual capacities in my sense—capacities that belong distinctively to their subject's rationality—are actualized. But that is irrelevant. What it is for a rational subject to see a piece of meat is, or anyway can be, different in that respect from what it is for a cat to see a piece of meat. For a cat to see a piece of meat is not for the piece of meat to be available to the cat's rational faculties; the cat has no rational faculties. When I see a piece of meat, the piece of meat is available to my rational faculties. Let me emphasize again that my picture accommodates insisting that when I see a piece of meat, the piece of meat is directly present to my view.

The kind of thing that is knowable in perceptual experience—its being so that there is meat on the rug and the like—belongs on the right-hand side of Frege's line. Travis suggests that to secure conformity to the Condition, it would have been enough for me simply to register that fact about what is knowably so; there was no need to attribute representational content to experience. (That is the point of his play with what he calls 'the Clue'.) But this just shows that he has not understood the point of my condition. What motivates my condition is the need to avoid the Myth of the Given. Certainly what is knowably so, in experience or any other way, is conceptual. But registering that does nothing to avert the risk of falling into the Myth of the Given—as Travis cheerfully does—when we go into detail about how exactly experience figures in our coming to know things to be so.

Index